WEYERHAEUSER ENVIRONMENTAL BOOKS

Paul S. Sutter, Editor

WEYERHAEUSER ENVIRONMENTAL BOOKS explore human relationships with natural environments in all their variety and complexity. They seek to cast new light on the ways that natural systems affect human communities, the ways that people affect the environments of which they are a part, and the ways that different cultural conceptions of nature profoundly shape our sense of the world around us. A complete list of the books in the series appears at the end of this book.

DEFENDING GIANTS

The Redwood Wars and the Transformation
of American Environmental Politics

DARREN FREDERICK SPEECE

UNIVERSITY OF WASHINGTON PRESS
Seattle and London

Defending Giants is published with the assistance of a grant from the Weyerhaeuser Environmental Books Endowment, established by the Weyerhaeuser Company Foundation, members of the Weyerhaeuser family, and Janet and Jack Creighton.

UNIVERSITY OF WASHINGTON PRESS
www.washington.edu/uwpress

Cataloging information is on file with the Library of Congress
ISBN 978-0-295-99951-7

The paper used in this publication is acid-free and meets the minimum requirements of American National Standard for Information Sciences—Permanence of Paper for Printed Library Materials, ANSI Z39.48–1984. ∞

CONTENTS

Illustrations follow page 100

FOREWORD

Old Growth and a New History

of Environmental Activism

PAUL S. SUTTER

Tree hugger is a curious epithet. The phrase has its origins in India's Chipko movement of the 1970s, when rural villagers—many of them women—in the Himalayan region of Uttar Pradesh launched a series of nonviolent protests against commercial timber harvesting. Some of them did so by hugging trees to prevent their destruction, acts that gave the movement its name (*chipko* means "embrace" in Hindi). Forests were critical to these villagers as sources of food, fuel, and fodder, and so they opposed commercial forest destruction as a major threat to their livelihoods. From Uttar Pradesh, the Chipko movement spread across India over the following decades, achieving important political successes and capturing the imagination of the global environmental community. In the context of Chipko, tree huggers were rural peoples working to protect their local economies of forest use from the increasingly globalized forces of commercial timber exploitation.

In the North American context, however, *tree hugger* has taken on a different set of meanings. Over the last several decades, those who opposed limits on timber harvesting, or environmental regulations of any sort, have deployed the moniker to suggest that environmental protesters care more about trees than about people or the vitality of their local economies. While there are certainly some who embrace the identity, *tree hugger* largely has become a term of derision used to portray environmentalists as privileged and misguided nature lovers, sentimental preservationists who are out of touch with the economic struggles of those who work in rural extractive economies. Whereas tree huggers in India were rural people protecting local economies against outside forces threatening their destruction, in North America the term has come to mean almost exactly the opposite. To be a tree hugger here is to embrace nature, not people; it is to love the wild at the expense of the human.

One might be tempted to conclude that this fundamental contrast is a product of two different environmental traditions. It is certainly true that the majority of Americans who have engaged in direct action protests to defend ancient forests in places like the Pacific Northwest, where the timber wars have been heated in recent decades, are not local peasants whose livelihoods are at stake in the commercial cutting of these forests. Rather, they have usually been principled opponents of ecological destruction. The divergent meanings and uses of the term *tree hugger*, then, may well reflect the very real differences between the environmentalisms of the rich and the poor. But to rest one's analysis there, to not ask deeper questions about the rhetorical power of the term's use in the North American context, is to miss some of the most important aspects of the history of modern environmental protest and activism in the United States.

Several weighty historiographical assumptions have influenced our understanding—or, perhaps, our misunderstanding—of the activists central to the postwar American environmental movement. The first, simply put, is the apparent incommensurability between utilitarian conservation and aesthetic or ecological preservation. We cannot quite shake the conviction that John Muir and Gifford Pinchot, the avatars of these two traditions, embodied competing rather than complementary environmental ideologies. The second is that modern environmental politics emerged as a broad cultural impulse in the postwar years as urban and suburban Americans came to value a clean, healthy, and beautiful environment as a kind of consumer amenity, and as increasingly powerful environmental organizations lobbied Congress to pass landmark environmental laws—from the Wilderness Act to the Endangered Species Act—that reflected the environmental values of these middle- and upper-class consumers. While environmental historians have traditionally referred to postwar environmentalism as a movement, we have treated it more like a zeitgeist or a values revolution, and we have assumed that, after a quick flurry of protest in the late

1960s and early 1970s, environmental politics settled into an institutional groove with big national membership organizations functioning as an environmental lobby. Because of these foundational assumptions, environmental historians have paid surprisingly scant attention to American environmentalism *as a social movement*, and to the ways in which environmental politics have evolved since the 1970s as a result of continued movement activism. In our neglect, we have largely let stand the logic that dismisses environmental activists as mere "tree huggers."

In *Defending Giants*, his compelling new history of California's Redwood Wars, Darren Speece insists that this neglect has been a mistake. The Redwood Wars—battles over the last remaining stands of old-growth redwood forest—roiled California's North Coast during the last several decades of the twentieth century. They were, as Speece convincingly argues, "one of the longest, most violent, and most intractable environmental conflicts in American history." These battles—and particularly efforts to save a grove known as the Headwaters Forest—were marked by dramatic direct action protests by activists who opposed the multinational Maxxam Corporation's efforts to clear-cut some of the few remaining ancient redwood groves. And, yes, activists employed tree-hugging, tree-sitting, and other confrontational tactics to protect these trees and to raise national awareness and support for redwoods preservation—though these were only the most visible features of a sophisticated political strategy that also included lawsuits, legislative lobbying, the full use of public comment provisions, and public relations. One of Speece's signal achievements in *Defending Giants* is to provide us with a truly three-dimensional portrait of this movement and the activists who sustained it, a portrait that is far more nuanced than our caricatures and reigning historiographical assumptions have allowed. In the process, Speece shows how fierce battles in a remote region of the American West transformed American environmental politics.

The environmental activists at the center of Speece's story, men and women, came from varied backgrounds, but few fit the mold of middle- and upper-class metropolitan consumers. Many were "locals" to one degree or another, rural people by birth or choice who valued the North Coast as a place to live and work, a retreat from the very consumer culture that had engulfed postwar America. Rather than embodying a consumer ethos, their environmentalism rejected consumer culture. Perhaps more surprisingly, most of these activists believed that logging and working in the woods ought to have a central place in the North Coast's economy, and they built a movement that respected timber workers and accepted that the forests of the North Coast would continue to be central to the local economy. They tried to embrace trees and people, even if that embrace was not always returned. What they objected to was not logging per se, but a dramatic change in corporate control over some of the last remaining ancient redwood groves, a change that presented new threats to the region in the late 1980s. Speece not only gives us a fuller sense of who those activists were but also provides us with an empathetic portrait of the local timber industry that preceded Maxxam's corporate takeover, particularly the Pacific Lumber Company, which had been a presence on the North Coast for more than a century. The best way to see the Redwood Wars, Speece suggests, is not as a battle between stereotypical loggers and tree huggers, but as one theater in the larger conflict we now call globalization. While environmental activists fought doggedly to protect the few remaining tracts of ancient redwoods from the maw of industrial timber cutting, they knew, accepted, and even embraced the idea that much of the rest of the North Coast landscape would still be managed for its timber resources. These were not pure preservationists out of touch with rural work. Rather, they believed that preservation and wise use (another term appropriated from one environmental tradition to serve another) were of a piece, and they hoped to preserve local economies and resources from distant corporate control and the forces of global capital. While they may have hugged trees, then, they were not the tree huggers of common American caricature. If anything, their advocacy shows some surprising parallels with India's Chipko activists.

One of those parallels was a deep history of local activism that the Redwood Wars would build upon. As Speece shows, there was a long regional tradition of fighting to preserve the most spectacular groves of ancient redwoods, often through direct action protest. Speece devotes the early chapters of *Defending Giants* to tracing this deeper history of redwoods activism. In doing so, he lays out a critical dimension of this story that differentiated it from other battles over old-growth forests: almost all of the redwood forests on the North Coast were privately owned rather than public domain or federal conservation lands. As a result, redwoods activism had long focused on two goals: the purchase and public protection of the most spectacular groves of privately owned redwoods and the effective regulation, in this case by the State of California, of logging and other land management practices on redwood lands that remained in private ownership. As Speece shows, early campaigns to "save the redwoods" produced a substantial patchwork of state and national parks, efforts that culminated in the creation of Redwood National Park in 1968. But logging practices on those lands outside state and federal protection continued to concern activists, particularly because of a corporatist tradition of forest regulation in California that gave timber interests disproportionate power in shaping the state regulations under which they themselves worked. This corporatist system would be one of the major targets of North Coast activists.

Despite this venerable tradition of redwoods advocacy, several new developments distinguished the Redwood Wars of the 1980s and 1990s from earlier activism. The first was Maxxam's hostile takeover of the Pacific Lumber Company and its valuable old-growth redwood lands—most importantly, the Headwaters Forest. Maxxam's sudden appearance and its avowed intent to liquidate its redwood holdings expanded a new industrial logging regime that had already set activists in motion, and it upset traditional channels of redwoods politics, which had often relied on negotiations between activists and local timber companies. The second development was the rise of a brand of activism that rejected the increasingly institutionalized and ossified environmental politics in the nation's capital, a brand of activism embodied by groups like Earth First!—and particularly its North Coast chapter, led by Judi Bari and Darryl Cherney. But perhaps the most important change came with a series of new environmental laws at the state and federal levels—the Endangered Species Act of 1973 most importantly—that both opened up new avenues for citizen participation in environmental decision making and gave activists powerful new tools to challenge land use practices on private lands. Here Speece makes one of his most important interventions in how we have understood the history of American environmental politics, for he argues that the Redwood Wars fundamentally changed the course of environmental decision making in the United States. The "modern environmental protection regime" that had emerged in the 1970s simply could not handle the intractable legal and local conflicts that emerged on the North Coast, conflicts marked not only by direct action protest but also by lawsuits and injunctions. As a result, environmental politics as usual on the North Coast had resulted in a logjam by the 1990s.

From this clogged regulatory channel there emerged a new course for American environmental politics in which the executive branch gained expanded authority to broker compromise solutions among stakeholders. Speece aptly refers to this as an "administrative turn" in environmental politics, and it was pioneered in the Headwaters Forest deal that finally emerged in the 1990s. That deal preserved a significant portion of the Headwaters Forest from timber cutting, though much less than activists had wanted. As importantly, it also included the first multispecies Habitat Conservation Plan (HCP) in the nation's history for the entirety of the forest, a plan brokered by the executive branch to break the stalemate in the courts, and in the woods, that had resulted from the strict provisions of the Endangered Species Act. While neither side was entirely happy with the result, the HCP did represent a victory of sorts for North Coast activists. It not only preserved and put under public ownership a portion of an ancient redwood forest threatened with industrial clear-cutting, but also undid California's corporatist forestry regime and held the timber industry accountable for how it treated its working lands. While the particulars of the Headwaters deal left many activists feeling deflated, the deal nonetheless embodied their desire to balance the preservation of old-growth redwoods with a sustainable timber economy for the North Coast. More than that, though, it spoke to the power these activists had to provoke a presidential intervention and a new model for mediating environmental disputes. Ultimately, Speece suggests, a small group of determined people working in a remote corner of the country effected a sea change in national environmental politics.

Defending Giants is a complicated story elegantly told, one full of fascinating characters with nuanced political positions that sometimes got lost in the heat of battle. More than that, it is a book that demonstrates how our easy resort to caricature has obscured the substance of what happened behind the North Coast's Redwood Curtain in the late twentieth century. Darren Speece has given us a history of environmental activism that simultaneously demonstrates the power of direct action protest to bring stakeholders to the table and ponders the importance of mediated compromise. At a moment when our environmental politics are deeply polarized, that might be the most useful contribution of all.

ACKNOWLEDGMENTS

This book exists because groups of Americans have, over the past 150 years, worked and fought to ensure that forests of ancient redwoods continue to inhabit this planet. I fell in love with these trees and forests more than twenty years ago, and they might not still exist were it not for the efforts of fellow travelers in California and across the nation. Citizens, timber executives, and government officials of all stripes were critical in the development of Redwood Country—sometimes collaboratively, many times confrontationally. This book traverses the contours of those relationships, and the various relationships between human communities and the redwood forest. Much of this book revolves around the stories of small groups of rural Americans grappling with the forces of industrialization. My hope is that they, and others, find inspiration in the example offered by the residents of the North Coast as they, against great odds, exerted incredible influence over the future of the land, the economy, and the culture. Activists, timber workers, and local officials pushed on the impersonal forces of globalization and made them budge. It was a feat worthy of notice.

The stories in this book would not have been possible without the cooperation and assistance of the North Coast. I was awestruck by the generosity of many of the individuals I was fortunate enough to write about in this book. Kathy Bailey, in particular, deserves special recognition. She opened her home, memory, and office to me on countless occasions. Her unprocessed personal papers documenting her work related to North Coast forestry and redwoods issues were invaluable, the most organized files I've encountered off a dirt road back in the mountains. Scott Greacen and the staff at the Environmental Protection Information Center literally handed me the keys to their storage unit, and my work would not have been possible without their unprocessed archives, and their repeated and numerous follow-ups to my various questions and requests. Dan and Carrie Hamburg also opened their memories, home, and office to me, and Carrie, during her fight with cancer, even sorted through the congressman's boxes in the attic to find the ones related to his Headwaters bill. Many others on the North Coast were vital resources as well: Robert Sutherland, Richard Gienger, Darryl Cherney, Alicia Littletree, Paul Mason, Kevin Bundy, Sharon Duggan, and Kate Anderton each provided me with marvelous oral histories and follow-up e-mails. Photographer Evan Johnson came to my rescue on deadline day, giving me permission to reproduce his incredible black and white photographs from Redwood Summer. Debbie Untermann graciously allowed me to once again use a photograph of hers that we found in the EPIC hard drive archives. Greg King quite generously contributed some of his excellent photography to the gallery in this book as well. The Humboldt Historical Society mailed me copies of documents from their files at no charge when I was back on the East Coast. Finally, I owe a deep debt to the late John Campbell and his family for generously allowing me to interview John when he was nearing the end of his battle with cancer.

On the East Coast, I am thankful for the assistance of Cheryl Oakes at the Forest History Society. The History Department at the University of Maryland, along with the Graduate School and the College of Arts and Humanities, provided crucial funding throughout my graduate career. I am additionally grateful to my colleagues at Sidwell Friends School for their encouragement, support, and collaboration over the past six years.

I owe a heartfelt thanks to the many people and institutions that made this project possible. In particular, David Sicilia guided, supported, and challenged me from the first day I stepped into his office in August 2004 as a new advisee and teaching assistant. This project bears the indelible marks of his years of patience and mentoring, and I am deeply indebted to him. David forced me to challenge my interpretations, writing style, and research more times than he probably cares to recall, and this manuscript is orders of magnitude better than it would have been without his persistent presence in my life and work. Thomas Zeller read and reread multiple drafts of research papers, article manuscripts, and dissertation chapters, and his insights and questions helped improve my analysis at every step, especially at those times when I didn't want to take a step back to rework ideas. Joe Oppenheimer, Robert Nelson, David Freund, and Whit Ridgway provided crucial feedback and support throughout my graduate education and dissertation work. I also owe a hearty thanks to Saverio Giovacchini, who not only served on my comprehensive exam committee but I suspect also played a critical role in my acceptance to the PhD program at Maryland.

I am forever indebted to all the people who shared their time, energy, feedback, commentary, and advice as I sorted out this book. I am grateful to editors and reviewers at *Environmental History* for publishing an early version of my analysis of the legal history of the Redwood Wars. I am grateful to Paul Hirt for revealing himself as a reviewer of that article so I can publicly thank him for pushing me to clarify my arguments and to better situate them within the historical literature. There are numerous others who helped shape this book through comments on presentations at American Society for Environmental History conferences or the manuscript itself, especially Emily Brock, Jared Farmer, John Flower, Robbie Gross, Marcus Hall, Erik Loomis, Kathleen McDermott, Paul Milazzo, Shields Sundberg, and Emily Wakild. Each offered excellent feedback over the past six years. Erik Christiansen, Claire Goldstene, Kate Keane, and Jeremy Sullivan helped me formulate and sharpen my ideas during our dissertation writing group sessions. I owe Jay Turner a special thanks. He has provided sage wisdom over the years regarding my research and the process of turning the dissertation into this book. His feedback was always characteristically thoughtful, thorough, encouraging, and incisive. I truly appreciate the hours he has put into this project since we first met in 2009. Many, many thanks to you all. Finally, thanks to Paul Sutter and Regan Huff at Weyerhaeuser Environmental Books. I was, and am, inspired by how much energy Paul put into this project. Working with Paul has truly been a collaborative process. His candor, brilliant feedback and suggestions, and his copy editing helped me transform the manuscript, always for the better. I am forever in his debt. I am grateful that Paul and Regan agreed to take on this project, shepherding a first-time author seemingly effortlessly and quickly through this process.

This project, of course, would not have been possible without the unending support of my family. In particular, my parents, Fred and

Linda Speece, supported and helped fund my venture into the history of conflicts over logging the redwoods. By moving to a wooded lot on Minnehaha Creek in 1980, they afforded me the opportunity to tramp about in the woods and along the creek for hours every day. From that wellspring grew my passion for forests and natural history. Those early memories exploring the woods reemerge every time my wife, Tiernan, and I take our young boys, Porter and Alexander, to hike along the creeks in Rock Creek Park in Washington, DC. We took Porter to the North Coast when he was not quite a year old, and I am grateful to have been able to share some of my fieldwork with him. Alexander will visit the redwoods during the summer of 2016 thanks to a generous Faculty Travel Grant from Sidwell Friends School! I hope Porter and Alexander develop the same affection for imbibing the smells, sights, and sounds of the forest that has motivated me since those early years as a boy in Minnesota. Finally, I cannot appropriately express my gratitude to Tiernan, who sacrificed a great deal to support my fascination with understanding the Headwaters Forest conflict. She has endured my distraction, late nights, research trips to California, and boxes upon boxes of documents arriving at our house. She also read countless versions of this book over the years, and I appreciate her deft eye for clunky language. I dedicate this book to Tiernan. Thank you!

ABBREVIATIONS

CDF   California Department of Forestry
CEQA California Environmental Quality Act
CESA California Endangered Species Act
EPA   Environmental Protection Agency
EPIC   Environmental Protection Information Center
ESA   Endangered Species Act
FPA   California Forest Practices Act
HFCC Headwaters Forest Coordinating Committee
HLAP Headwaters Legislative Action Plan
HCP   Habitat Conservation Plan
NEPA National Environmental Policy Act
NMFS National Marine Fisheries Service
SYP   Sustained Yield Plan
THP   Timber Harvest Plan

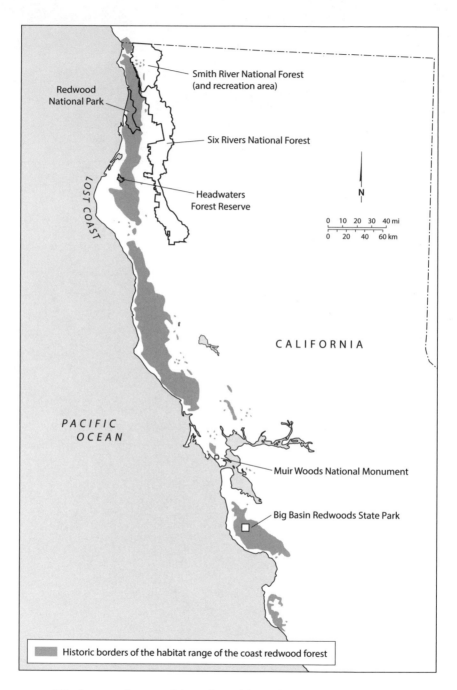

Smith River National Forest
(and recreation area)

Redwood
National Park

Six Rivers National Forest

Headwaters
Forest Reserve

LOST COAST

N

| 0 | 10 | 20 | 30 | 40 mi |
| 0 | 20 | 40 | 60 km |

CALIFORNIA

PACIFIC
OCEAN

Muir Woods National Monument

Big Basin Redwoods State Park

Historic borders of the habitat range of the coast redwood forest

MAP 1. The historical range of the redwood forest hugged the Pacific Coast from south of San Francisco to just north of the Oregon border. Big Basin Redwoods State Park was the first redwood park, Redwood National Park is the largest, and the Headwaters Forest Reserve is the most recent. Map by Bill Nelson, 2016.

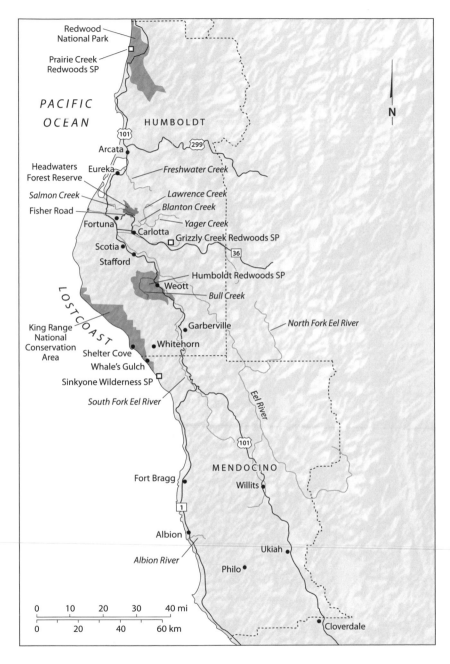

PACIFIC OCEAN

HUMBOLDT

Redwood National Park

Prairie Creek Redwoods SP

Arcata

Freshwater Creek

Headwaters Forest Reserve

Eureka

Lawrence Creek

Salmon Creek

Blanton Creek

Fisher Road

Yager Creek

Fortuna

Carlotta

Grizzly Creek Redwoods SP

Scotia

Stafford

Humboldt Redwoods SP

Weott

Bull Creek

King Range National Conservation Area

LOST COAST

Garberville

North Fork Eel River

Whitehorn

Shelter Cove

Whale's Gulch

Sinkyone Wilderness SP

South Fork Eel River

Eel River

Fort Bragg

MENDOCINO

Willits

Albion

Albion River

Ukiah

Philo

Cloverdale

| 0 | 10 | 20 | 30 | 40 mi |
| 0 | 20 | 40 | 60 km |

MAP 2. The North Coast is traversed by numerous fault lines and mountains. The only north-south highway through Mendocino and Humboldt counties is Highway 101. Most of the Redwood Wars were fought in these two counties. Map by Bill Nelson, 2016.

DEFENDING GIANTS

INTRODUCTION

IN THE SPRING OF 1990, A BOMB EXPLODED UNDER THE DRIVER'S
seat of Earth First! activist Judi Bari's car, nearly killing her. It was
late morning on a weekday in Oakland. Bari and her activist partner
and former lover, Darryl Cherney, were headed to Santa Cruz when
the pipe bomb, fashioned with a timer and motion detector, abruptly
ended their road trip. "I knew it was a bomb the second it exploded.
I felt it rip through me with a force more powerful and terrible than
anything I could imagine. . . . [The bomb] shattered my pelvis," Bari
recalled. The car ricocheted off a few cars parked on the street, stopping near a school. Bari was screaming when officers from the Federal
Bureau of Investigation and the Oakland Police Department arrived at
the scene. The Oakland police detained both Bari and Cherney at the
hospital on suspicion of domestic terrorism because they thought the
bomb belonged to the activists and was intended for use in some sort
of Earth First! sabotage plan. Cherney was treated and released from
the hospital. Bari, however, remained in the hospital due to the serious
and extensive nature of her injuries.[1]

Earth First! was a decade old in 1990, founded by disgruntled wilderness activists to bring a sense of urgency to the threats posed by
development to the country's wild landscapes. By 1990, this loosely
affiliated group of activists had used direct action regularly to disrupt
logging activities, primarily via roadblocks and tree-sits. However,
some members had adopted a strategy they referred to as "ecotage,"

which often involved destroying machinery used in logging. Earth First! was initially created to stop the development of public lands, but in the farthest reaches of northern California, where Bari and Cherney had been active, those who affiliated themselves with Earth First! were most concerned about the logging of giant redwoods on private property.

The two activists were East Coast transplants who had found a place for themselves in the expanding radical environmental movement of the North Coast of California. In fact, Bari and Cherney had traveled to the Bay Area to recruit students to participate in Redwood Summer that year. The project was modeled after the 1964 Freedom Summer campaign in Mississippi, undertaken to empower African Americans to exercise their voting rights. The idea for Redwood Summer was to create a similar mobilization to halt industrial logging on the North Coast and to prevent logging inside an area known as Headwaters Forest and in other groves of ancient redwoods. The activists wanted to create a mass movement focused on defending the giant trees. Their strategy was to occupy the far northern California coastal counties via marches, direct actions against private property, and mass rallies, thus bringing attention to their grievances and demands.

Before the bombing, North Coast activists were on the verge of dismantling a relatively new industrial logging regime—liquidation logging—that was highly mechanized, focused on clear-cutting, and heavily reliant both on dense networks of logging roads that penetrated the forests and on pesticides to clear logged-over areas. Since World War II, liquidation logging had been used to denude landscapes across northern coastal California, plaguing the region with mudslides and unstable hills. Through their work, the activists had parted the "Redwood Curtain"—the colloquial phrase used by North Coast residents to describe the physical and cultural isolation the redwood forest offers and imposes upon Mendocino, Humboldt, and Del Norte counties—and successfully shined a spotlight on these destructive practices. They had won injunctions stopping several old-growth logging projects and begun a colorful, pesky direct action campaign to disrupt logging activities in ancient forests. Some of them had also crafted Forests Forever—a popular 1990 ballot initiative to overhaul logging practices in California.

The injuries to Bari and Cherney, along with the criminal investigation and bad press that followed, could have sunk the Redwood Summer campaign, but instead the bombing contributed to the protraction of the Redwood Wars. Environmentalists around the nation were stunned by the violence, and some larger national organizations began to assist the North Coast activists in their efforts to protect Headwaters Forest. Emboldened, activists expanded their campaign to reform logging practices, locking into a decade-long cycle of litigation and protest with timber companies, the State of California, and the federal government. By the end of the first decade of the twenty-first century, North Coast activists had secured the protection of nearly all the remaining privately owned redwood groves containing ancient trees, transformed California's forestry regulations, and forced the federal government to seriously grapple with its responsibility to protect endangered species located on private property. Additionally, a federal jury in 2002 awarded Cherney and the estate of Judi Bari, who had died of cancer in 1997, a multimillion-dollar settlement after evidence emerged linking the FBI and North Coast timber companies to the bombing and subsequent framing of the activists.[2]

The bombing was one of the better-known events of the Redwood Wars, among the longest, most violent, most intractable environmental conflicts in American history, lasting from the 1970s until the first decade of the twenty-first century. The drama of the bombing underscored the uncertainties produced by the Redwood Wars—uncertainties about the future of the local logging industry, giant redwood trees, the redwood ecosystem, and the culture of the North Coast. In the midst of those uncertainties, tempers flared. Corporate executives, law enforcement officers, loggers, and environmental activists each had a major stake in this contest. Some of these hostilities have been documented in detail elsewhere, but the bombing raises serious questions about how and why peaceful environmental protest, so widespread and popular during the 1970s, became the locus of widespread physical and political violence by the 1990s.[3] Scholars have yet to fully grapple with the causes of the Redwood Wars, their complex dynamics, and their legacy for American environmental politics in the twenty-first century.

The Redwood Wars had several important impacts. First, they severely eroded corporate power in California and across the nation.

Litigation was the activists' most effective weapon in the fight to limit the prerogatives of private landowners. Beginning in the late 1960s, a series of citizen lawsuits in California ended the state's official policy of allowing the timber industry to self-regulate and to promote development as its top priority. The resulting environmental protection laws included provisions for public participation in agency decisions about land management, and activists on the North Coast took advantage of those provisions to develop an aggressive legal strategy to reform logging practices across the state. By the 1990s, lawsuits had eroded the traditional alliance between the California Board of Forestry and the timber industry, forcing the agency to enact rules protecting giant redwoods and associated endangered species. The activists' litigation strategy then landed them in federal court, and as had happened in the state courts, federal justices, using the provisions of the Endangered Species Act, placed wide-ranging restrictions on private landowners. The activists' victories in court prompted the Pacific Lumber Company to file lawsuits against the State of California and the United States, alleging that the court rulings had deprived them of their property without just compensation, a violation of the Fifth Amendment. To avoid a lengthy and risky court case, President Bill Clinton intervened and authorized an unprecedented land deal: the public purchased some of the redwood forest from Pacific Lumber, and in return, the company agreed to an extensive set of long-term land management plans approved by state and federal agencies. Thus the company received millions of dollars in cash but also agreed to further restrictions on its private property prerogatives. So began a growing national regulatory trend marked by the expansion of executive branch authority into environmental policy.

The activists' legal strategy was part of a broader political strategy that employed legislative reform efforts and direct action in addition to citizen lawsuits. The roadblocks and tree-sits temporarily prevented the logging of particular groves of ancient redwoods, while the court cases permanently prevented logging in many of those selected stands of trees. The activists used rallies and demonstrations to draw attention to their efforts, and they used the public support garnered by such activism to support legislation that would apply the court rulings more broadly to logging practices across the state. The legislative proposals would have banned clear-cuts, prevented the logging of ancient redwoods, and mitigated erosion and mudslides. In the legislature and at the polls, however, the activists confronted a powerful and well-funded opposition in the timber industry and its corporate allies. Activists lost in the California Assembly and in Congress, and uncertainty prevailed on the North Coast. The campaign to eliminate liquidation logging therefore continued, especially the battles in the forests and in local courtrooms. The overall strategy of the activists successfully frustrated the timber companies' efforts to log their last ancient redwoods and frustrated political leaders who wished the fighting would end. When the Clinton administration intervened in the Redwood Wars in 1996, it crafted a deal that could be replicated with other landowners across the country. Additionally, the collaborative negotiations between landowners and federal agencies could proceed without the need to build support in gridlocked legislatures or to litigate in court. The result was an executive branch more firmly in control of environmental policy than in earlier administrations.

The activists' successes in the Redwood Wars also highlight the diversity of the environmental movement and the strength that diversity afforded the North Coast environmental movement. North Coast activism was not monolithic, and the region's activists defied easy caricature. Many were native-born northern Californians, others had migrated during the late 1960s and 1970s, and some were more recent transplants. Some were homesteaders, some were shop owners, some were lawyers, some were teachers, some were loggers. Some were strict preservationists who viewed logging the redwoods as inherently immoral. Most, however, believed logging had a place on the North Coast and in the local economy and culture. Some were reformers and others radicals. Some were willing to compromise; others were not. Many of the leaders were women. Nearly all were against concentrated corporate power. As a movement they did not always agree nor did they always cooperate or act in concert. They were sophisticated strategists and tacticians, and yet they struggled to accommodate each other. Nonetheless, they cultivated a broad base of support locally and nationally because people of varied interests and passions could find a place in the movement or empathized with some part of the movement. Their history thus demonstrates the necessity of studying environmentalism as a movement with multiple priorities, goals, strategies, and origins.

Media and scholarly fascination with the violence in the Redwood Wars has made uncovering the movement's origins and appreciating its larger significance more challenging. The popular coverage of the bombing of Judi Bari's car and the many controversial direct actions of the Redwood Wars—such as the two-year tree-sit of Julia Butterfly Hill—has oversimplified the conflict, defining the Redwood Wars more as an ahistorical battle among a handful of archetypal tree-huggers rather than as the product of a large and diverse set of characters and decades of economic and cultural transformations. For too many of us, the battle over Headwaters Forest has become the story of radical environmentalists who valued trees and birds more than humans, and publicity more than meaningful land management reform. The Redwood Wars were more complicated than that, however. Indeed, like so many other conflicts over natural resources during this period, they were the product of the contested terrains of industrialization, the rise of the modern corporation, globalization, and the future of rural America during the twentieth century.

The fight over logging the redwoods is much larger than the events immediately surrounding the 1990 bombing of Judi Bari and Darryl Cherney, and that deeper and broader history has much to teach us. This book uncovers the long, winding roads leading to the Redwood Wars, of which the battle over Headwaters Forest was but a part. This is the story of the actions of some of the people who lived on the North Coast, recounting how they fought for more than a century to define their places among the redwoods. Those battles not only helped define which redwoods would be logged but also determined how government would regulate the development of private property across the nation. Before 1964, decisions about logging the redwoods were largely made privately, in discussions among the timber companies and in negotiations with land trusts. The public had little say in such decisions. After 1964, the conflicts grew more tense and more frequent as logging increased and the number of old-growth trees declined. Those battles were a part of efforts across the globe to place limits on the behavior of increasingly large multinational corporations, as a new brand of citizen environmentalism, defined against increasing corporate power, succeeded in giving the public increased power in environmental decision making. Thus, at its core, this book is about the efforts of small groups of Americans and how they were able to exercise power, influencing much larger and wealthier institutions.

When I began work on this project, I thought I would be telling a narrower story of how a group of radical environmentalists stood up to a multinational corporation during the 1990s to prevent Headwaters Forest from falling prey to the chainsaw. I was interested in the people who defended ancient giants. It was going to be the story of how citizens tried to fight for the public interest in a political system dominated by special interest campaign contributions and a seemingly single-minded focus on economic growth. That was the narrative I had read in the newspapers, in books, and in magazines, and it was compelling. I envisaged a story about Headwaters Forest, the Pacific Lumber Company, radical environmentalists, the ecology of redwood forests, and political power in America. Headwaters Forest, located approximately 250 miles north of San Francisco, became the center of the Redwood Wars in 1986 because the exigencies of Wall Street financing drew attention to the land. Historically, Pacific Lumber had a reputation as a timber company that did not clear-cut its redwoods but rather cooperated with conservationists and workers alike. In 1985, Texas-based Maxxam Corporation acquired the Pacific Lumber Company, using more than $700 million worth of Michael Milken–issued junk bonds. Michael Milken became the central figure in the insider trading scandals of the late 1980s, and the Pacific Lumber transaction was the first such acquisition underwritten by Milken. To pay off the debt it incurred by purchasing Pacific Lumber, Maxxam, led by financier Charles Hurwitz of Houston, developed a plan to liquidate the company's remaining inventory of old-growth redwoods—those more than two hundred years old. The liquidation plan alarmed North Coast environmentalists, who then investigated Pacific Lumber's landholdings to figure out what was at stake. Their discoveries sparked the battle for Headwaters Forest.

In the heart of the property, trespassing activists found a vast forest filled with old-growth redwoods, an ancient forest as they saw it, because it had not been logged by timber firms during the redwood lumber boom of the nineteenth and twentieth centuries. By the 1980s, nearly 90 percent of the redwoods from before the California gold rush had been harvested, leaving only a tiny fraction of a once-expansive temperate rain forest. The activists named Pacific Lumber's most important remnant of ancient redwoods Headwaters Forest and developed a campaign to prevent Pacific Lumber from logging the area. After a decade of court battles and direct actions, President Clinton signed the 1996 agreement with Pacific Lumber for federal acquisition of approximately seven thousand acres of Headwaters Forest. The activists were both relieved and disappointed: they had wanted to protect nearly sixty thousand acres to ensure the integrity of the ancient forest ecosystem, but seven thousand acres was better than nothing. As I learned more about the Redwood Wars, I was particularly interested in how and why the battle for Headwaters Forest ended the way it had.[4]

My interest in unraveling the Headwaters Forest conflict grew out of my own experiences on the North Coast. From 1995 to 1997, I attended Humboldt State University as a geology student, witnessing the Redwood Wars during their most prominent years in the national spotlight. I attended the two largest anti-logging rallies in American history, passed through the gauntlet of logging families lining the road to the rally, and became immersed in the life of a small rural college town behind the Redwood Curtain, where, as journalist David Harris described it to me, there seemed to be only two types of residents: "Those who looked like they just got out of the Marines, and those who looked like they just got out of a Grateful Dead concert."[5] I worked at a bar in Arcata called the Alibi, a place frequented by both "locals" and college students. I observed the vast cultural differences between the two groups. Because I worked at the Alibi, I was able to straddle both worlds to a degree, but my sympathies were clearly with the radical environmentalists and my fellow college students. Environmental issues had motivated me to transfer from Southern Methodist University to Humboldt State. I was not interested in becoming a Texas oil company geologist: I wanted to do US Geological Survey research, I thought. I wanted to understand the history of the earth and humanity. I wanted to protect ancient forests from logging. I wanted to protect the Amazon rain forest from development. After graduation, I worked with nonprofit environmental groups on campaigns to prevent pollution, clean up toxic waste sites, and stop logging and development in roadless areas on public land. Later, as a graduate student, when I had the opportunity to study the conflict that had haunted me for nearly a decade, I dove headfirst into that research. In the process, I realized that some of my initial impressions were all wrong.

Defending Giants is about those radical environmentalists, that multinational corporation, and Headwaters Forest. Thankfully, it also developed into much more than that—something richer, more complex, and more deeply historical. The sources drove me further into the past than I had ever imagined I would go, and they, along with the hours of oral history I conducted, shattered many of my preconceptions about the people involved in the battle over Headwaters Forest and even the nature of the conflict. This battle had deep roots and was only one front in the war that erupted in the late twentieth century over the character of the North Coast. The people I studied defied easy categorization, and the environmental movement on the North Coast did not match the caricature I had of it. It became clear, though, that the larger Redwood Wars were more important in American history than I had imagined, and they had far more to teach about environmentalism and environmental politics than I had expected.

The Redwood Wars were conflicts over massive, magnificent trees. That was their primary importance. Indeed, the trees initially drew me to the North Coast and interested me in the fights over logging, as they had compelled people in the past to try to protect them. Americans have tended to most value the oldest and largest redwoods, and stands of those trees garnered the most attention and sparked the critical conflicts during the Redwood Wars. But the actors in this drama had invested the trees with conflicting meanings. Timber companies prized the oldest trees because they were worth the most in the timber market. Earlier scientists revered them as specimens of evolutionary magnificence. Hikers, picnickers, and sojourners sought out the stands of the oldest trees as refuges and sanctuaries where they could escape industrial society and breathe the forest air. Modern environmentalists and ecologists valued the larger ecosystems inhabited, and in some senses constituted, by the oldest redwoods because they were rich with biodiversity and housed rare species. The various values placed on the redwoods and differing conceptions of how to best utilize the forest were central to the conflicts among North Coast residents during the twentieth century.

Naming those forests was critical to the activists' efforts, yet it was also problematic. During the late twentieth century, American environmentalists came to refer to forests dominated by old trees as "virgin" or "pristine" because they had not been molested by the machinery of white loggers of European descent during the preceding two centuries. The image of a pristine or virgin forest could create a sentimental attachment for the public and was thus useful for generating public concern about the fate of forests. The terms *virgin* and *pristine*, however, are problematic because they imply that these forests had been untouched by humans. But Native Americans had manipulated forests in North America for thousands of years, transforming their appearances and inhabitants, and the redwoods of the North Coast were no exception. People also adopted the term *ancient* to describe those unlogged forests, and though it substituted a deep temporal integrity for a mythical and racially dismissive ideal of untouched nature, that term also misrepresented the long history of human manipulation of these ecosystems. Nonetheless, *ancient* did capture a critical feature of redwood forests—that the redwoods themselves could live for thousands of years and that individual specimens had been alive since ancient times.

More recently, foresters and environmentalists have preferred to use the term *old growth* to refer to the forests along the West Coast that had not been logged since the European conquest of the Americas. An old-growth forest anywhere is one where trees are allowed to grow old and the forest is allowed to develop a complex canopy and a rich biodiversity. Accordingly, forests that have regrown after being logged are referred to as second-growth or new-growth forests—though they could become old growth with time. The term *old growth* thus seems to avoid the cultural, racial, and historical errors inherent in the other terms, but it doesn't really capture the particular kind of violence involved in cutting down an old-growth redwood forest. Because coast redwoods can grow for thousands of years, those forests are vastly different from forests dominated by Douglas fir, lodgepole pine, or white oak, where it is rare for an individual tree to live beyond five hundred years. Old-growth habitat thus takes much longer to develop in redwood forests, where it takes a thousand or more years to replace fallen giants. More than that, two-thousand-year-old redwood trees stand as monuments to the deep history of the earth, and they provide a direct connection to an ancient past for modern humans. And the individual trees are irreplaceable. Their roots and trunks are living artifacts of an ancient world; once gone, they are gone forever, along with the connections to that ancient past. Because of the complexities involved with describing the redwood forest, I prefer to use the term *old growth* to describe the habitat characteristics of a forest and *ancient* to describe the age of the giant trees.[6]

In Redwood Country, the image of the ancient forest was an incredibly powerful tool for environmentalists, but so too were the material and ecological benefits derived from those forests. The activists involved in redwood preservation understood the oldest redwoods as nonrenewable because they took more than a thousand years to grow, and they argued that the trees were most valuable to society when left in the ground. Those forests would provide the North Coast and the planet with rich biodiversity, a refuge from the pressures of an industrial society, and a laboratory for understanding forest ecology. The timber companies, however, considered the trees renewable, arguing that the present market value of the oldest trees was high enough to offset the prospect of growing less-valuable younger trees on the logged landscape. Harvesting the oldest trees would provide valuable employment and create second-growth forests more quickly, sustaining employment in the region. Thus some people on the North Coast were defending a different kind of giant: the timber companies, their profits, and their ranks of employees. The battle lines were drawn, but they were not always clear. Workers feared the effects of both liquidation logging and forest preservation on future employment. Activists wanted to make the North Coast hospitable to both giant trees and timber workers. And some timber executives were acutely aware of the desirability of managing their land to maintain long-term harvest levels rather than facilitating short-term liquidation.

Fights to save the redwoods were sparked by fears that timber companies would eliminate the oldest and largest redwoods, turning them into shingles and decks and hot tubs, leaving the North Coast with a damaged economy, society, and set of ecosystems. The first such battles emerged in the early twentieth century in the San Francisco Bay Area when activists worked to preserve public redwood preserves near urban centers, such as Big Basin Redwoods State Park near Santa Cruz, just south of San Francisco, which was set aside in 1902 as California's first state park. But logging and clear-cutting increased during and after World War I, and as a result, wealthy patrons and local activists worked hard during the interwar years to establish more such parks, including Humboldt Redwoods State Park. After World War II, logging and clear-cutting increased yet again, further reducing the size and number of stands of massive trees. In response, the patrons and activists continued to create more redwood state parks. But the politics of redwood preservation was also changing. Large multinational corporations were displacing smaller local timber companies and imposing industrial logging practices. At the same time, ecologists had begun to argue that biodiversity was integral to healthy ecosystems and to sustaining life on earth. Influenced by those new ecological commitments, national environmental groups sought to protect entire watersheds in Redwood Country. One major result was the creation of Redwood National Park in 1968, a demonstration of the power of combining the differing approaches of older and newer redwood activist organizations. This recurring conflict escalated into the Redwood Wars in the 1970s, as the oldest and largest redwoods became scarcer and their value to all members of North Coast society increased exponentially. Activists continued to work to create and expand redwood parks, but they also began to demand wholesale changes to logging practices to protect redwood forests on private property. The Redwood Wars would determine the fate of the last stands of ancient redwoods: whether they would be turned into quick profits for multinational corporations and short-term wages for workers or remain for humans to enjoy for the long run, for fauna to occupy, and for future ancient redwoods to sprout beneath.

The battle over Headwaters Forest has garnered a lot of attention, but it was not a singular event. On the contrary, it was a part of a half-century-long effort by California environmental activists to break down the corporatist regime created in the nineteenth century. I had not initially appreciated the larger battle, which was obscured by the fireworks of the Redwood Wars. The corporatist theory of industrial economics posits that those individuals who best know an industry can manage and regulate it most efficiently. In practice, that meant placing the timber industry in charge of regulating timber operations in an attempt to ensure smooth and ever-increasing production levels into the future. The State of California facilitated industry participation by forming official regulatory boards on which industry held a majority of seats. By contrast, corporatist boards never dominated the US Forest Service, the Bureau of Land Management, or the Fish and Wildlife Service, which oversaw land owned by the federal government. Ownership entailed a different set of responsibilities and priorities, and the federal agencies developed a hands-on approach to determine where, when, and how development occurred on its lands. During the late nineteenth century, the second wave of industrialization caused cities to expand exponentially, increasing the demand for lumber. With the chaotic growth of urban populations and infrastructure, public health deteriorated and many experts predicted that the nation would be stricken by a timber famine. In response, the federal government decided to take measures to protect urban water supplies and the nation's timber inventory. Toward that end, near the turn of the twentieth century, Congress authorized the creation of national forest reserves on federal property so it could prevent private interests from clearing the land in an effort to maximize short-term profits. California did not own the land in Redwood Country, which had nearly all been sold to private parties and companies during the nineteenth century. As a result, for most of its history, the state acted as a facilitator among competing business interests rather than a regulator. Timber companies got to decide how and where to log the redwoods. Activists could not appeal directly to the state for reforms as easily as they did regarding federal lands.[7]

The Redwood Wars, which began with challenges to industrial prerogatives, were important because they changed environmental politics in California and across the United States. North Coast residents had grown increasingly concerned in the twentieth century, not only about the future of the ancient forest but also about the future of timber jobs and their rural culture as the rate of clear-cutting increased and corporate giants swallowed up land, especially after 1950. Eventually, the North Coast was awash in direct actions, litigation, and media scrutiny. In 1983, a group of back-to-the-landers in Mendocino and Humboldt counties surrounded and occupied the last grove of ancient redwoods on a northern Mendocino part of the Lost Coast, delaying logging until they obtained a court order to stop it. The courts then halted dozens of logging plans because the activists convinced judges that the plans violated state environmental protection laws, which mandated that logging not harm watersheds, endangered species habitat, or the health of forest ecosystems more broadly. Those actions were dramatic but not unique; the activists were repeating a drama from 1924 in the same region. That pattern of direct action and litigation escalated for the twenty years following 1983 as the battle over the last unprotected ancient redwoods proceeded at breakneck pace. As a result of their organizing, the activists elevated logging practices and redwood preservation as major issues for voters across the state by 1990, and they helped make direct action a viable tactic to implement activists' policy strategies.

The passage of the new environmental protection laws of the 1970s in California was vital to the escalation of the Redwood Wars, for they gave activists legal grounds on which to challenge logging practices. The laws, including the California Environmental Quality Act (CEQA), the California Endangered Species Act (CESA), and the 1973 Forest Practices Act (FPA), made California's private property owners responsible for protecting habitat and water quality. CEQA supplemented the federal 1969 National Environmental Policy Act, mandating that state agencies review and approve all development projects to prevent substantial harm to the environment. CESA mandated that the agencies actively work to prevent the extinction of California flora and fauna on public and private property. And the Forest Practices Act officially ended corporatist management of the timber industry and required the industry to prevent ecological degradation. The laws represented the legislature's responses to citizen lawsuits and mounting public enthusiasm for preventing ecological damage. More critically, each of the laws afforded citizens the right to intervene in the management of private property in California.

Although the Redwood Wars were largely fought over state issues, they had a profound effect on national policy, and their history highlights the bottom-up forces that drove the development of modern environmental policy. First of all, the Redwood Wars forced the federal courts to use the Endangered Species Act to prohibit logging on private property for the first time since the law's enactment in 1973. Secondly, they contributed to the critical administrative turn in federal environmental policy making. When President Clinton took office in 1993, he faced a Congress gridlocked by partisan rancor and a near rebellion in the Pacific Northwest. Because of citizen efforts to protect the habitat of the spotted owl, federal judges had halted nearly all logging in national forests in the Northwest, and Congress was proving incapable of resolving the crisis. Thus the president looked for policy tools that could circumvent Congress and the courts. The Redwood Wars had created a similar political crisis, and the president intervened to negotiate a compromise with the various stakeholders, as he would in the Northwest. In California, the resulting Headwaters Deal was the nation's first multispecies Habitat Conservation Plan (HCP), and the agreement opened the gates for hundreds more HCP negotiations as well as the use of other innovative administrative tools in negotiated settlements. In a context of increased partisan hostilities and growing opposition to environmental regulation, the Redwood Wars were critical to defining the pathways open to businesses, activists, and the executive branch to achieve meaningful compromise.[8]

The stories of the people of the Redwood Wars and their actions can help us better understand twentieth-century American environmentalism and environmental politics as well. Traditional scholarly interpretations of American conservation and environmental protection focused overwhelmingly on the federal government and national actors. More recently, however, scholars have turned to the stories of local people, analyzing a history of environmental politics closer to the ground so as to unearth the complexities of how environmental policy was enacted and implemented in relation to local activism. A close reading of the history of the Redwood Wars highlights the grassroots diversity of the environmental movement. Most importantly, study of the Redwood Wars suggests some of the ways local communities have exercised power at the state and federal levels in the era of globalization. During the last half century, multinational corporations have been able to move capital and production across the globe to take advantage of weaker environmental and labor laws. As a result, governments in the twentieth century increasingly accommodated those companies to preserve jobs and revenue, neglecting local citizen demands. In response, North Coast activists developed strategies to improve their leverage. Thus the Redwood Wars illustrate the important role played by rural, marginalized communities in the formation of national environmental policy and politics.[9]

The more I studied North Coast activism during the Redwood Wars, the more I noticed the way it contradicted a scholarly literature that has privileged the actions and values of middle-class urbanites and suburbanites in the making of modern environmentalism. This once-dominant narrative of postwar environmental politics emphasized the nationalization and professionalization of "modern" environmentalism and the development of command-and-control federal environmental regulation. At its core, this was a story of how an expanding and largely white middle class, animated by its understanding of popular ecology and the destructive forces of modern industry, rose up in the 1960s to demand a cleaner, more beautiful environment filled with greater recreation opportunities. Those opportunities had been threatened by the frenzied pace and scale of logging, grazing, suburbanization, and dam building, all enthusiastically supported by federal agencies. In this narrative, federal agencies, once seen as allies of the conservation movement, became an enemy to many activists during the postwar decades. Their activism helped spur passage of the Wilderness Act of 1964 to protect public wild lands from agency-assisted development.

Earth Day 1970 represented the culmination of that popular insurgency. From there, professional "environmentalists," politicians, and bureaucrats supposedly took the reins and built the modern environmental protection regime: the laws, agencies, and regulations that now protect public health and the nation's myriad ecosystems. That regime resulted from the National Environmental Policy Act, Endangered Species Act, Clean Air Act, Clean Water Act, and National Forest Management Act, among others, as well as the creation of the Environmental Protection Agency. It was a regime largely built on legislative action. The new laws created rules that directly regulated the behavior of governments, businesses, and individuals in what became known as command-and-control regulation. Once the laws were passed, environmental politics was integrated into the everyday horse-trading on Capitol Hill. There, DC-based environmental groups, business interests, and state actors lobbied and debated the scope, intent, implementation, and enforcement of these new environmental laws, and the courts rendered judgments about their competing interpretations. Many of the debates were over science—specifically, whose science contained the best prescription for protecting the environment from the destructive habits of industrial America. That narrative of postwar environmentalism was based on the development of middle-class affluence and resulting environmental values based on consumption—of recreation and leisure, and clean air and water. Just as the New Deal made the government responsible for protecting Americans from the worst economic effects of industrial capitalism, the modern environmental protection regime made the government responsible for protecting Americans from the deleterious environmental effects of industrial capitalism.[10]

This historical literature, with its focus on how postwar metropolitan Americans valued the environment, has overestimated the shift away from resource conservation and toward modern ecological and broadly consumerist environmental values. On the North Coast at least, Pinchotian conservation was a powerful source of ideas throughout the twentieth century, and it was easily integrated with modern ecological theories and Muirian preservation. Gifford Pinchot, the nation's first national forester and leader of the early twentieth-century conservation movement, believed in efficient resource use based on scientific forestry as a necessary path to the improvement of human society by preventing resource scarcity and resulting social conflict. Additionally, Pinchot believed the government, as promoter of the public good, needed to safeguard the nation's resources from profit-focused corporations. John Muir, founder of the Sierra Club, was also skeptical of business's ability to protect natural resources, but Muir was interested less in protecting the economic value of resources and more in protecting the sublime qualities of the grandest landscapes in America. He viewed wild places as sources of spiritual renewal that enabled individuals to fight off the ills of industrial society. Those two worldviews were never as mutually exclusive as was once described. Muir and Pinchot both viewed landscapes in terms of their benefits to humanity, but they simply prioritized different sets of benefits. Likewise, the North Coast activists believed they could create a landscape that utilized conservation methodology to protect economic, spiritual, aesthetic, and ecological resources and traditions. While North Coast activists were avid preservationists when it came to protecting the few remaining ancient forests, they also thought deeply about the region's need for a sustainable and equitable timber economy. To see them merely as tree huggers, then, is to miss an important part of the story.[11]

The nationalization and professionalization narrative looks at American environmentalism from the center outward. Those stories are largely about the efforts of white, middle-class professionals to reform government and society. They center on Washington, DC, and how it developed into the center of environmental policy and politics. From that vantage, late twentieth-century environmentalists developed a disdain for the working class because workers were complicit in activities like cutting down trees, building dams, and running paper mills. In the aggregate, environmentalists prioritized recreation over work, scientific knowledge over knowledge of nature gained through work, and consumer rights over worker rights. A growing divide opened between rural workers on the one hand and professional environmentalists and urban consumers on the other. White-collar workers were blind to the environmental destruction caused by their own white-collar work and consumer habits, and they blamed environmental destruction on the workers who carried out the demands of their corporate bosses—in the fields, in the woods, and on the water.[12]

The story of the Redwood Wars challenges that narrative. Radical environmentalism emerged at the end of the 1970s in reaction to the nationalization, professionalization, and moderation of the large environmental groups and of environmental politics. Dissidents left mainstream politics as the pace of wilderness designation via the Wilderness Act slowed because of congressional politics, industry contested the implementation of pollution control laws, and the largest environmental groups seemed to be losing their ability to force change. Groups like Earth First! and the Sea Shepherds were founded in the syndicalist tradition: to prevent industry and businesses from operating by physically placing human bodies between machines and nature; to deny companies profit in order to force changes to business models; to hug trees to prevent logging; to block logging roads so crews could not enter forests; to prevent whalers from firing harpoons at their targets; to rewild the American West and defend wilderness from humanity. Such activism has been easy to caricature. Dave Foreman, cofounder of the national Earth First! movement, has been the poster child for a modern wilderness ideal that removes humanity from the wild. But probably the best-known local affiliate of his group, the North Coast Earth First! group led by Bari and Cherney, doggedly pursued goals that integrated wildlands preservation and human land use. While the style and tactics of the new insurgents were used on the North Coast and many people affiliated themselves with Earth First!, the Redwood Wars were fought over how to best integrate human society with nonhuman communities, not how to separate humanity from the wild. Nearly every local participant wanted humans to actively manage the landscape so that giant redwoods, Douglas firs, timber workers, farmers, marbled murrelets, northern spotted owls, Pacific giant salamanders, and the other inhabitants of the North Coast could cohabitate in perpetuity. Additionally, while the North Coast activists leaned heavily on direct action and civil disobedience, they also utilized many mainstream political tools, including lawsuits, lobbying, and public relations.[13]

The people on the North Coast whom I encountered, both during my time living there and in my subsequent research, were certainly committed to clean air and water, healthy and diverse forests, and opportunities to commune with nature in wild places. But they were also highly critical of American consumer culture, the culture that had supposedly done so much to shape modern environmental sensibilities, and of the global corporate capitalism that fed such consumerism. They were skeptical of the federal government but sympathetic to timber workers, millers, and farmers. The activists on the North Coast during the Redwood Wars were more anti-corporate than they were strictly preservationist. Yes, they were back-to-the-landers, counterculture refugees, and homesteaders, and as such, they believed that if corporate, industrial logging operations could be forced out of the North Coast, the locals—farmers, loggers, homesteaders, shopkeepers, activists—would make decisions promoting the economic, ecological, and social sustainability of the region. They decided they needed to stop logging projects on what they determined were the most sensitive landscapes while they worked to reform timber harvesting practices that would apply to all California lands. The former efforts, designed to ensure that ample old-growth habitat would remain to be integrated into the landscape-wide management plans of the future, have garnered the most attention from the media and subsequent historians. But the traditional narrative that views American environmental politics from thirty thousand feet above Washington, DC, does not always hold when events are viewed closer to the ground.[14]

The late twentieth-century campaign that produced the Redwood Wars was largely the product of a small group of activists. There was a cohort of Mendocino residents that included Kathy Bailey, the volunteer chair of Sierra Club California's state forestry program; Sharon Duggan, a native North Coast attorney working in the San Francisco Bay Area; Gary and Betty Ball of the Mendocino Environmental Center; and Judi Bari, cofounder of North Coast Earth First!. In Humboldt County, the effort was guided by the activists who created the Environmental Protection Information Center (EPIC) and Humboldt members of North Coast Earth First!, including Robert Sutherland, Darryl Cherney, Alicia Littletree Bales, Richard Gienger, and Cecelia Lanman. Throughout the 1980s and 1990s, those activists combined direct action, litigation, legislative and administrative advocacy, public relations, protests and rallies, and grassroots organizing to defend the giant trees and the ancient forest ecosystem, as well as promote a social and economic vision for the North Coast of California that included timber harvesting as a major part of the economy. In every land management proposal they created, they included worker provisions and logging plans, though they also insisted on limits to corporate prerogatives. They attempted, and often failed, to mobilize workers to support their efforts. Those efforts failed because the activists' direct actions often led to physical confrontations between loggers and activists in the woods, and because timber companies drove wedges between the two communities. Timber companies closed mills in retaliation, arguing the layoffs were necessary due to litigation and activism. Workers decided that their current job security was valuable enough to risk more dramatic job losses in the future due to timber shortages. It grew difficult for the workers, and some of the activists, to see how their interests aligned. But local environmental leaders tried. Those activists were simultaneously preservationists, conservationists, unionists, mainstream activists, radicals, hippies, and sophisticated strategists. And many of the most important leaders were women, a fact omitted from many studies of environmentalism.

The two major protagonists in the Redwood Wars differed dramatically in their approaches to management of the land and the local economy, however. The activists wanted to rid the county of distant corporate landlords, place local people in charge of county development, create a landscape composed of a variety of protected habitats and work environments, and block harvesting of the last old-growth redwoods. The leaders of the timber industry wanted to maximize new wood growth and efficiently harvest trees, based on an eighteenth- and nineteenth-century European model of forestry that emphasized sustained yields and rotational harvests to maximize annual timber yields and growth, an approach that treated forests as crops. The companies believed that enough ancient redwoods were already protected by 1980 to provide adequate old-growth habitat, and that species previously found in old-growth forests would adapt to second-growth habitat. Lumber workers and the State of California were caught in the middle, with both groups recruited as allies by the two protagonists with uneven results. The Redwood Wars thus resemble other historical battles pitting industrialists against local residents and workers over the trajectory and consequences of industrial capitalism.[15]

Our understanding of the broad, deep forces behind the challenges to industrial resource extraction is incomplete because the spotted owl conflicts of the 1980s and 1990s have come to dominate analysis of forest and endangered species politics. Those conflicts, along with the fights over dams and wilderness, largely centered on national institutions and public lands. Such studies have shed light on the postwar politicization of "science" and the importance of having "science" on one's side. The result was not policy clarity but confusion, with politics determining final decisions. Less well known are the battles and debates over private land management, including those involved in the Redwood Wars. Indeed, one of the most important features of the Redwood Wars was that they were almost entirely fought over the fate of private lands. This book views private property, and the Headwaters Forest conflict in particular, as central to the transformation of modern American environmental politics whereby the executive branch expanded its power to directly regulate private land use, bypassing Congress and the courts. And the people who fought in the wars underscore the diversity and complexity of the modern environmental movement and the ways local communities helped erect a new modern environmental protection regime.[16]

Defending Giants traces the roots of the Redwood Wars back to the development of Redwood Country immediately after the gold rush and follows the three main institutions in the Redwood Wars through the twentieth century. The California Board of Forestry, the Pacific Lumber Company, and the redwood preservation movement all originated in the second half of the nineteenth century, and they all were critical players in the conflicts surrounding the Redwood Wars. In fact, the Redwood Wars enacted a competition among the three entities over whose prerogatives would rule Redwood Country. Before World War II, the timber industry had more or less free rein behind the Redwood Curtain. Groups periodically demanded that some places be protected from logging, and to accomplish their goals they engaged the landowner and the State of California in real estate negotiations to create public parks. That tradition dominated until after World War II, when citizens began not only increasing their demands for park creation but also insisting that the timber industry change its logging practices to protect the landscape and forest ecology more broadly. The public's intrusions on the management of private property, rooted in claims that such private lands held public goods, were met with resistance from the timber companies and the Board of Forestry. But they found a sympathetic ear in the State Assembly. During the late twentieth century, conflicts over logging the redwoods grew more complicated as the California legislature and courts increasingly limited the prerogatives of private property owners at the behest of citizen activists. In turn, the timber companies and their allies on the Board of Forestry stiffly resisted the new regime. The confrontations between activists and companies grew more hostile and more frequent, both in the courtroom and in the forest. Eventually convinced by the courts, the Board of Forestry was forced to abandon its allies in the timber industry, but timber companies persisted in their opposition to the forestry reforms. Activists responded by pressing their case in federal court instead of the California court system. The seemingly intractable battles were resolved at the federal level by the actions of the Clinton administration, but hardly anyone on the North Coast was satisfied with the compromise.

The Redwood Wars were complicated, and so is their legacy. They divided an already combustible North Coast; they helped push endangered species protection out of the legislative arena; they launched a series of legal challenges to private property "takings"; they protected more than three thousand acres of redwood forest populated by ancient trees; they allowed for the harvest of tens of thousands of acres of redwood forest that activists deemed critical to present and future old-growth habitat; and ultimately they led to the removal of Pacific Lumber from the North Coast. The Redwood Wars did not change the social structure of the North Coast, but they did begin to break down California's corporatist regulatory regime. All the parties had believed they were fighting for the best interest of the forest and the community, but their visions grew incompatible. In the end, it was a war that neither side won.

ONE

DEEP ROOTS

A Rare Forest

TO WALK INTO A STAND OF TWO-THOUSAND-YEAR-OLD REDWOODS is to enter deafening silence. It is rare to hear songbirds, or the sound of a squirrel scampering in the canopy, or the condensation of the thick fog dripping off redwood needles like rain. It's not that those noises are entirely absent; it is just that the shade, the moisture, the fog, the deep bed of soft needles on the ground, and the ropy red bark of the trees seem to absorb all sounds before they can radiate outward from their source. A redwood grove is also visually striking. It has no visible horizon, just giant trees situated in a variable field of human-size ferns with periodic skunk cabbage in low-lying areas near creeks and the occasional western hemlock. The odor of the skunk cabbage *is* noticeable. In the creeks Pacific giant salamanders await their prey, while flying squirrels and spotted owls in the trees invisibly watch and wait. Occasionally, a black bear or a herd of Roosevelt elk might wander through the grove, the elk headed for the coast or a nearby pasture.

It is the giant redwoods themselves, though, that pull on the gaze of visitors. Able to live and grow for more than two thousand years, they can reach heights greater than three hundred fifty feet and diameters of twenty-five feet. The root systems are shallow but long, traversing outward just a few feet below the surface for up to one hundred feet. The entangled roots in a grove stabilize all the trees, collectively anchoring the giants to the ground. From their base, the trunks shoot up into the air, almost magically straight. The auburn bark is deeply fluted and grooved, in a perpetual state of apparent splintering, sloughing, and peeling off the sides. That appearance of disintegration, however, is deceiving because the bark can be up to two feet thick, making the trees insect and fire resistant. The first branches, called epicormic branches, often start more than fifty feet up the trunk, and they seem fragile, growing perpendicular to the trunk from small buds or scars, with little fronds of feathery leaves and branches, referred to as epi sprays, bursting out like spread fingers on a similarly horizontal plane. The redwood needles, or leaves, are soft and short compared to many other conifer families, such as the pine family. The leaves are a deep green, extending from the skinny branches in a flaccid V-shaped pattern, like a yew tree. The epicormic branches are easily dislodged from the trunks and litter the surrounding ground, adding to the almost squishy sensation of walking on top of what could be a three-foot-thick bed of leaves and epi sprays covering the soil in the redwood forest. The dense bed of leaves and branches inhibits the growth of understory shrubs, vines, and plants, except the ubiquitous five-finger and sword ferns, along with salmonberry, redwood sorrel, and a few other species.

Redwood is a rather recent name for the species of massive, evergreen coastal trees found on the West Coast of the United States. Native Americans have referred to the giants as *gahsay*, *cholay*, and *loomeen*. When Father Juan Crespí of Spain penned the first known written description of the coastal trees in 1769, he gave them the Spanish name *palo colorado* (red wood). In the nineteenth century, botanists first named them *Taxodium sempervirens*, and in 1874 they reclassified the trees as *Sequoia sempervirens*. The State of California officially designated the California redwood as its state tree in 1937, and by the turn of the twenty-first century the trees had become known as coast redwood, California redwood, or simply redwood.[1]

While redwoods are well known today as one of North America's iconic tree species, redwood ecology remains a frontier of scientific exploration. Until the late twentieth century, no one even knew what existed in the canopy beyond the forest floor and the epi branches. When scientists led by Steve Sillett began to scale the giant redwoods to explore the canopy, they discovered an entire ecosystem in the air. Near the tops of the giants, new trunks sprout from the main trunk, reaching out and curving up, as if snaking their way toward the sunlight. From those trunks grow other trunks, and other redwoods, hundreds of feet above the ground, forming the redwood crown. The branches growing off the airborne trunks reach out to one another, cross, and form a redwood cage where tree meets blue sky. Lichen is abundant in the crown, as are large mats of leather ferns growing as epiphytes—plants that grow on the bark of other trees, or in tree cavities, and ingest nutrients out of the air. When the ferns, lichens, and redwood leaves die and fall, they are held captive in the crown, decomposing to form soil at the base of the secondary trunks of the redwood.[2]

Modern coast redwoods live only along a narrow strip of land beginning south of Monterey Bay and extending just across the Oregon border along the Chetco River. The redwood belt hugs the land just east of the immediate coast, stretching to the Coast Range at its widest point along the North Coast—a mere twenty-five miles across. Redwoods and their relatives, as a group the tallest trees in the world, once dominated the temperate zone of the globe, however. The coast redwoods are the sole surviving species of the *Sequoia* genus, but they have two extant Cupressaceae family relatives: *Metasequoia* (dawn redwood) and *Sequoiadendron* (giant sequoia). Each genus lives on a single continent, *Sequoia* and *Sequoiadendron* in North America, *Metasequoia* in Asia—testimony to their long evolution and adaptation to niche environments. The species colloquially referred to as "Sequoias," like the dinosaurs, retreated after the early Tertiary period (approximately sixty-five to twenty-four million years ago). Unlike the dinosaurs, the coast redwood, the giant sequoia, and the dawn redwood survived, albeit within a shrinking range. Beginning in the late Tertiary, due to cooler and drier conditions, the sequoias that had occupied a wide belt around the globe (from current Alaska to Oregon) migrated south and west toward warmer climates. Three million years ago, redwoods disappeared from Europe, Asia, Greenland, and Japan.[3]

The modern range of the coast redwood is both tranquil and rugged. Near the coast, the land is drenched with thick fog in the summer and heavy rain in the winter. The coastline of the North Coast combines steep, jagged cliffs with undulating bays where Coast Range rivers empty into the Pacific Ocean. The meandering rivers are lined with grasslands and shrub forests between the coastal bays and the foothills of the Coast Range. The relatively low mountains rise abruptly behind the coast, the product of millions of years of squeezing along the Cascadia Megathrust Subduction Zone, where the North American and Gorda Plates collide, just north of where the San Andreas Fault slips out to sea. The slopes of the Coast Range, covered with a variety of redwood forests, is in a state of perpetual mass-wasting due to the rain, the near-daily earthquake activity, and the unstable rock formations lifted up from their beds. The areas hit hardest by mudslides look as if the soil is oozing down toward the valleys. The valleys to the east of the coastline are dry and hot in the summer, prone to regular fires. The redwoods dominate that rugged coastal landscape of diverse geography because their thick bark protects the trees from fire, they reproduce easily, and the nightly draw of the coastal fog up the valleys maintains the moisture of the redwood crowns even when the valley floors are dry. They are not reliant on pollen or seed distribution because they have the ability to sprout new saplings from basal buds and tree stumps. And they can thrive in shade-drenched environments for centuries, their dark red interior heartwood growing slowly, increasing in density and reducing knots and irregularities.

Despite its relatively small acreage—approximately 1.9 million acres of forest at the time of European arrival on the West Coast of North America—the modern redwood belt contains surprisingly diverse landscapes and biological communities. Eighty-eight percent of modern redwoods reside in California's Sonoma, Mendocino, Humboldt, and Del Norte counties, from south to north. Most of them live on the North Coast—the three most northern counties—in three types of forests. The alluvial flats of northern rivers such as the Eel, Smith, and Klamath are dominated by redwoods and contain the tallest trees as a result of the well-drained soil and abundant sunlight along the riverbanks. As slope and elevation increases, tree size decreases and species diversity increases. On the slopes rising above the river bottoms, one finds a mixed forest of redwood and Douglas fir (*Pseudotsuga menziesii*). Mixed in with the conifers are more drought-resistant trees, such as tanbark oak and madrone. Above one thousand feet, the redwoods and Douglas firs are accompanied by an understory of western hemlock, Sitka spruce, huckleberry, and California rhododendron, along with tanbark oak and madrone.[4]

Along with diverse plant communities, an array of wildlife species inhabits the modern redwood forest, especially those that contain abundant ancient trees—often labeled old-growth forests by foresters and ancient forests by environmental activists. Scientists consider a redwood forest old growth, or ancient, if it is "relatively old and relatively undisturbed by humans," to use the words of famed conservation biologist and occasional redwood ecologist Reed Noss. The grove must contain eight trees per acre over three hundred years old and have developed a complexly layered canopy. Additionally, an ancient forest contains considerable numbers of snags (standing dead trees) and downed trees and branches. Colloquially, most define an ancient forest as one that has not been logged by people of European descent since their migration to North America in the sixteenth century. Many insect and animal species of the redwood belt are endemic to the region, including the banana slug and redwood bark beetle. Additionally, eleven of the twenty-nine amphibians found in the belt are found only in the redwood forest, including the red-bellied newt, lungless salamander, Pacific giant salamander, and the world's most primitive frog: the tailed frog. The forest is home to rare mammals such as the Roosevelt elk, the northern flying squirrel, ring-tailed cats, and the Humboldt marten, as well as more common western conifer residents such as shrews, beaver, chipmunks, squirrels, bats, and mice. It was, however, the bird and fish species of the forest that, aside from the redwoods themselves, received the most popular attention from activists, scientists, and the media during the Redwood Wars—especially the various salmonids, the northern spotted owl, and the marbled murrelet.[5]

The rare species of fauna, the giant trees, the ecological complexity, the forest's limited range, and the unique aesthetics of the forest, as well as its deafening silence, captivated Europeans and Americans from the nineteenth century on, but so did the forest's commercial potential. The myriad economic, cultural, and scientific opportunities offered by the forest inspired diverse Americans to compete throughout the twentieth century over the fate of the giants. Humans have occupied the West Coast of North America for at least 8,600 years, yet conflict over the redwoods is a modern phenomenon. Early residents, such as the Yurok tribe, resided on the "balds"—hilltops devoid of trees—and used fire to clear the redwood understory just as Native Americans did across North America. There is no evidence those West Coast inhabitants logged the giant trees, and because of their sparse populations, conflict over the vast expanse of trees was unlikely. Conflict over the trees required population pressures and industrial demand, which led some Americans to grow concerned over the fate of the giant trees even as others grew rich because of them. By the late nineteenth century, citizen activists began to propose land management regimes based on the noncommercial value of the forest; timber companies in California steadfastly resisted.[6]

The communities that inhabited the North Coast after 1850 were products of those migratory, industrial, and political developments. Like the redwood belt, the North Coast is longer than it is wide. Three features dominate the region's two major counties, Mendocino and Humboldt, which define the terrain of North Coast culture and economics: the Coast Range, which runs along the western portions of the counties; US Highway 101, dotted with the small towns that make up Redwood Country's commercial and residential centers, defining the central axis of the North Coast; and the numerous rivers that flow out of the Coast Range, connecting the mountains to the ocean and transecting the counties along east–west and north–south axes. As the terrain is quite variable due to the subduction zone forces, the most prominent ridgelines tend to run from northwest to southeast. The most prominent rivers flowing northwest are, from north to south, the Eel River (which divides in southern Humboldt into the South Fork and the North Fork), the Mattole, the Elk, and the Mad. Into each flow dozens of creeks, which run downslope off the Coast Range.

Eureka, in central Humboldt on the south side of Humboldt Bay, has historically been the largest city on the North Coast. On the north side of the bay sits Arcata, a small college town with a traditional town square sitting at the base of the foothills within sight of the Pacific Ocean at the mouth of Mad River. South of Arcata and Eureka lie Ferndale, Fortuna, Carlotta, and Scotia/Rio Dell, small farming and logging towns. Scotia originated as a lumber camp during the late nineteenth century and was developed as a company town by the Pacific Lumber Company. The small counterculture town of Garberville, which sits along Highway 101 at the Mendocino border, had become, by the end of the twentieth century, the supply outpost for a prolific illegal marijuana trade, as farmers found ideal growing conditions among the drier, hotter hills behind the Kings Range, which provides shelter from the fog bank of the Pacific Ocean.

Mendocino is similar to Humboldt, with a few more county highways traversing the valleys. Ukiah has long been the largest city in Mendocino, and Highway 101 runs through the town, which sits in the middle of the county. Like Garberville, Ukiah also developed into an outpost for marijuana farmers. The coast in Mendocino is more developed than that of Humboldt, dotted with small towns including Fort Bragg and Albion, with Philo and Booneville sitting in the Anderson Valley, which runs between Highway 101 and the coast. Farmers, loggers, fishermen, and mill workers were long the most prominent residents of the North Coast, and the history of Redwood Country is thus intimately connected to the history of resource extraction, predominately the harvesting of redwoods.

"LOGGING THE REDWOODS"

The late nineteenth- and twentieth-century history of the North Coast was inextricably tied to the development of the redwood logging industry, and to understand the conflicts that erupted after 1970, we need to understand that history.[7] The development of the logging industry can be divided into three eras: American invasion and industrialization (1850–1914), stabilization (1914–55), and transformation (after 1955). During the invasion and industrialization period, Americans from the East permanently settled the North Coast and began to aggressively log the redwoods from south of San Francisco up to the Oregon border, increasingly incorporating industrial practices and institutions in the logging campaigns. The State of California was largely the partner of the timber firms during that era, promoting stable and efficient growth. Periodically, protests erupted in response to industrialization. The result was a powerful, independent timber industry with the power to self-regulate, as well as growing citizen concern over the fate of the oldest and largest redwoods. During the era of stabilization, the state, citizen activists, and timber companies largely worked together to develop a system for determining which stands to log and which to preserve through private real estate negotiations involving wealthy benefactors and timber executives. After purchasing a grove of ancient redwoods, the benefactors donated the land to the state to create a public park. Even in that era, local North Coast residents protested, forcing larger institutions to accommodate their demands. Finally, during the era of transformation, the partnership between the state and the timber industry was undermined, citizens began to exert more control over the fate of the redwoods, and protests grew more frequent and more hostile, leading to the Redwood Wars. The transformation was incomplete, however, and the earlier patterns and traditions continued to exert their influence.

Those shifting historical patterns in redwood politics are neatly viewed along Bull Creek, near the town of Weott. Bull Creek features giant stands of redwoods along alluvial flats, many of them sitting at the base of the Coast Range, where rivers begin to carve large meanders and oxbow lakes into the soft soil of the flatlands. The stands of giant redwoods along Bull Creek were central to the early development of redwood logging and to the expanded logging regime during the early twentieth century, as well as a major piece of the interwar stabilization. Those stands were also critical to the onset of the era of transformation. During the winter of 1954–55, heavy rains pounded the North Coast of California, producing massive flooding along river ways and in low-lying areas. The raging floodwaters produced mass-wasting along the steep slopes above Bull Creek and destroyed part of Highway 101 along the perimeter of Humboldt Redwoods State Park. All along the Bull Creek Flats, inside the park, preserved giant redwoods collapsed in the waterlogged soil under the weight of the mudslides. With their fall, a new era of redwood conservation was born.

Those giant redwoods had remained in the ground until 1954 because more than two decades earlier, John D. Rockefeller Jr. had donated much of the money needed to acquire the groves of ancient trees. Rockefeller was the only son and namesake of the founder of Standard Oil. The younger Rockefeller dedicated his life to spending his inheritance on philanthropy, and conservation was a major emphasis of his efforts. He had donated land for Acadia National Park in 1916 and played a major role in the creation of Shenandoah, Great Smoky Mountains, and Grand Teton National Parks. After World War I, North

Coast logging companies had expanded their operations and the use of clear-cutting to harvest redwoods. Save the Redwoods League, a citizen activist group founded in 1918 to acquire stands of giant redwoods and preserve them from logging, along with many local supporters, had convinced Rockefeller to help them acquire the land along Bull Creek from the Pacific Lumber Company so the state of California could protect the trees inside a state redwood park. Yet there they were in 1955, enormous toothpicks scattered about the creek bottom. Park rangers Henry Saddler and Carl Anderson asserted that "poor logging practices" and related wildfires had triggered the mudslides that toppled these trees. And in fact, above Humboldt Redwoods State Park, Pacific Lumber had been clear-cutting redwoods high up the steep slopes of the river valley, and the slides had originated from those logged areas. Thus, despite the efforts of Rockefeller and Save the Redwood League, they could not protect the groves from the larger landscape-level ecological damage inflicted by the timber industry. The disaster at Bull Creek proved to be a turning point in redwood politics, as environmental groups decided giant redwoods could be protected from destruction only if the state regulated logging practices in combination with creating public redwood parks.[8]

The five years beginning in early 1955 mark the beginning of the erosion of what had been a more or less stable relationship among redwood preservationists, the State of California, and the North Coast timber industry. The Sierra Club, long a bit player in Redwood Country, grew increasingly interested in redwood preservation, vilifying the North Coast timber industry for its aggressive clear-cutting practices. In 1957, the Sierra Club urged the California Board of Forestry to more closely regulate private timberland so as to prevent tragedies like the one at Bull Creek. It also began to actively track threats to Rockefeller Forest. By 1960, even the California Division of Beaches and Parks was criticizing the Board of Forestry's logging regime, and the Sierra Club suggested the state should buy the denuded land on the slopes above Bull Creek Flats to rehabilitate the area and add it to the park acreage. That same year, the Sierra Club published *The Last Redwoods and the Parkland of Redwood Creek*, which promoted creation of a large park in northern Humboldt County to protect the health of an entire ecosystem rather than simply set aside isolated stands of grand trees.

The conflict between environmental activists and California timber companies over how best to manage the redwood forest may have entered a new phase in the mid-1950s, but it had been percolating beneath the seemingly stable surface of genteel park negotiations since the late nineteenth century.[9] In 1850, when the first Americans of European background laid eyes on the vast redwood forest of the North Coast, nobody could have imagined that people would one day fear for the future of the giant trees. It was even less likely that the giant trees would spark the development of powerful institutions devoted to protecting redwoods from the saw blade, or that competition over the fate of the giants would generate the Redwood Wars. Nonetheless, conflicts over the most beneficial use of the redwood forest arose soon after 1850, and they bubbled up periodically before exploding in the late 1980s.

The redwood forest has generated intense conflict because of its beauty, scientific properties, and economic value. To understand the late twentieth-century Redwood Wars, we need to understand the roots of the conflicts as they developed in the second half of the nineteenth century. From 1850 to 1960, the institutions, governance traditions, conflicting values, and North Coast radicalism that fueled the Headwaters Forest conflict developed. The 1955 uproar over the Bull Creek floods may have engaged the Sierra Club in Redwood Country logging, but it wasn't until 1968 that the state, the courts, and the newly radicalized redwood preservation movement dramatically transformed redwood politics. Despite the transformation of the conflicts in Redwood Country, deep ties to the first era remained. Women activists provided leadership and initiative from the earliest redwood preservation campaigns through the Redwood Wars, and national and state institutions had to accommodate local Humboldt activists because the locals were often more forceful, confrontational, and independent than the larger institutions. Investigating the deep roots of conflict pulls the Redwood Wars into the historical stream of a more than century-long struggle among industrial timber firms, the state, and residents on the North Coast over their relationships with, and valuations of, the redwood forest.[10]

Redwood Country was relatively undeveloped by Europeans until after the California gold rush, when American and European immigrants built the redwood logging industry and introduced Americans to the giants. The North Coast was far from the population centers of California, and there were no roads or rail lines up the coast, so the northern logging outfits operated without state oversight for nearly seventy years. Like most business in the nineteenth century, North Coast logging was a boom-and-bust industry dominated by larger companies.

Although the United States acquired California from Mexico in 1848, Europeans did not invade the North Coast in earnest until gold was discovered along the Trinity River in 1850. The Spanish had visited Humboldt Bay in 1775, and Americans employed by the Russian American Company visited in 1806, but they did not remain. The bay was rediscovered by people of European decent only accidentally, as an American expedition looked for a shorter route to the Trinity County gold country in 1849. That expedition led to a permanent American settlement on the North Coast. Eureka rapidly sprang up on the bay, and after the gold rush died down, the town quickly transitioned into a timber mill town. As immigrants streamed into California after 1848, timber demand and prices rose. San Francisco expanded and mining camps appeared throughout the Sierra Nevadas, driving industrialists toward the North Coast. Chinese immigrants moved to the region to mine the rivers and eventually work for the railroad companies, and mill owners recruited Canadian "Blue Noses"—the nickname of Nova Scotian loggers—to work the woods and mills.[11]

Existing tools were inadequate for the giant redwoods, and loggers struggled to invent and adopt new technologies to make mass production possible. At midcentury, it could take a team of two men an entire week to chop down an ancient redwood with axes. Then the axmen needed to chop the tree into smaller, more manageable pieces, which were then moved by teams of oxen along skid roads—sand roads with logs placed crosswise to help the giant logs to slide along. By 1854, even with such primitive techniques, nine mills operated along the shore of Humboldt Bay near Eureka, with approximately twenty miles of roads routing logs from the forest to the shore. In Mendocino

County, which had no adequate bay, loggers built enormous wooden chutes from the rocky cliffs to carry the logs to awaiting schooners. The boats would tie onto one of several moorings offshore, and the chute was lowered to meet the deck of the schooner. From the cliff, workers slid logs down the chute while sailors used a rope and hinged gate as a braking system, depositing the logs directly onto the ship.[12] The redwoods' location along the Pacific Coast, so critical to their unique ecology, also made them easy to exploit even under primitive technological conditions.

The development of North Coast timber operations followed a trajectory similar to other American industries of the period. First, managers reorganized workers into specialized teams to increase efficiency and speed up production. Then companies mechanized the work sites— transportation, logging, and milling operations. Soon railroad and timber industries were nearly inseparable, with timber firms owning railroads and vice versa. From the Civil War until the early twentieth century, the number of lines increased annually. Major technological inventions included the steam donkey in 1882 and the bull donkey in 1883, both by John Dolbeer, who became a large mill owner in Humboldt. The steam and bull donkeys, steam engines that could transport logs through the woods, eventually replaced the teams of oxen and skid roads. At the end of the nineteenth century, timber mills, logging operations, and railroads dotted the North Coast. The region still had a logging camp atmosphere, but it was becoming more settled and increasingly industrial. Several firms important to the Redwood Wars were developed during this founding era: Union Lumber Company, Dolbeer and Carson Lumber Company, the Albion Railroad, Simpson Lumber Company, and most importantly, the Pacific Lumber Company. Pacific Lumber, propelled by the firm's long history, was more intricately enmeshed in the Redwood Wars than any other company.[13]

The Pacific Lumber Company: Industrial Force

The Pacific Lumber Company played no role in early contests over the fate of ancient redwoods, but its development as a diversified business with a small-town image was central to the later Redwood Wars. The company straddled the worlds of national corporations and small-town proprietors, a strategy that eventually produced a near-monopoly position in the old-growth redwood lumber industry while securing the loyalty of workers and the local community. It was not an easy balancing act, but it was successful. Timber companies like Louisiana-Pacific, which never established deep roots on the North Coast, were able to retreat when profit margins dwindled and the heat of the Redwood Wars escalated. However, Pacific Lumber could not, or would not, retreat because of its business model and its corporate culture. The company thought it had steeled itself against attacks from corporate raiders and environmental activists, but its strategy of trying to satisfy diverse stakeholder groups made it an ideal target for both.

The logging operation that would become the Pacific Lumber Company was founded in 1863 when A. W. McPherson and Henry Wetherbee bought six thousand acres of land in northern California, near the coast approximately two hundred fifty miles north of San Francisco, for $7,500. In 1882, "various interests," according to a newspaper article of the day, merged to establish the company town of Forestville, a large lumber operation on the Eel River, south of Eureka and Humboldt Bay. The deal included a railroad running to the bay. By 1888, the company had three hundred employees and was the largest lumber producer in Humboldt County, producing twenty million board feet of lumber annually. Three developments worked in concert to fuel growth of the Pacific Lumber Company in the late nineteenth and early twentieth centuries. First, the eastern and midwestern forests were depleted of their timber. Subsequently, Pacific Lumber was sold to eastern timber investors who folded the company into their diverse holdings. And finally, a destructive earthquake near San Francisco in 1906 increased demand for redwood lumber and shingles.[14]

Simon Jones Murphy and his family—the eastern purchasers—transformed Pacific Lumber with their aggressively expansionist and innovative business outlook. Murphy was a second-generation American born in Maine on April 22, 1815. He developed into an atypical industrialist for the late nineteenth century, focusing on diverse holdings rather than horizontal or vertical integration. Murphy bought his first lumber mill in Maine in 1840, and after the Maine forest stock was largely harvested, he moved his family to Wisconsin to take advantage of the Midwest lumber boom. From there, Murphy acquired an iron ore mine in Michigan, moved his family to Detroit, and expanded his business empire. From Detroit, Murphy acquired a copper mine in Arizona, railroad interests in New Mexico, a citrus ranch in Southern California, oil interests, and real estate. Back in Detroit, Simon Jones founded the Murphy Power Company, which eventually became part of Detroit Edison Company. He also created the Detroit Automobile Company in 1899 to build "fordmobiles." Henry Ford was the chief engineer for Murphy Power, and he convinced Simon his automobile model was suitable for production. Ford, however, eventually left the company, and in 1902 the Murphys changed the name of the automobile company to Cadillac. Simon Jones Murphy's expanding empire led him to Humboldt County when the Midwest timber boom faded and the railroads grew interested in connecting San Francisco with Seattle.[15]

The same year the Murphys formed Cadillac, Simon Jones Murphy and Hiram Smith of San Francisco purchased Pacific Lumber for an unknown sum and relocated company headquarters to Detroit, adding the small timber firm to its corporate empire. In 1905, the year of Simon Jones Murphy's death, the Pacific Lumber Company incorporated in Maine, setting into motion its thrust toward growth and modernity. A Murphy would either run the company or sit on the board of directors from 1905 until 1986. By 1913, the company had acquired sixty-five thousand additional redwood timber acres, producing 106 million board feet of lumber annually. The company changed the name of Forestville to Scotia and began running the updated mills "'round the clock," according to Pacific Lumber's annual reports. By 1920, Pacific Lumber employed 1,500 workers and operated two mills and one railroad line. Company reports claimed that inspectors called it the largest and most modern redwood mill complex in the world.[16]

All the while, the firm rapidly clear-cut old-growth groves for the benefit of eastern shareholders, denuding miles of forests behind the carefully manicured town of Scotia, with its tree-lined streets enveloped in a pocket of forest. Although the company behaved much like any other industrial firm of the early twentieth century, people on the North Coast viewed Pacific Lumber differently. Its size and industrial character were not initially a liability, but after World War I, Pacific Lumber's industrial might would come under attack just as other big businesses had in the late nineteenth century. Pacific Lumber responded with a strategy to create strong bonds between itself and the community, and for the remainder of the century, the company's attempt to straddle the worlds of big business and small-town America would prove to be its greatest strength and its greatest vulnerability.[17]

The State of California: Industrial Corporatism

During the late nineteenth century, the California state government facilitated the growth of industrial logging on the North Coast through corporatist regulation, a form of industrial self-regulation that would become popular in the Progressive Era. Corporatism was designed to generate stable growth in production and employment. Under corporatist governance, the state allows industries to improve industrial operations via self-regulation, facilitating industry participation by forming official regulatory boards on which industry holds a majority of the seats. California officials created the corporatist Board of Forestry in 1885 because they feared a timber famine would soon hit the nation, as did officials in other states and in the federal government. Across the nation—and across the Atlantic Ocean—experts and government officials searched for mechanisms to bring order and stability to the rapidly growing western industrial order. Industrial leaders, too, looked for an economic and development trajectory that was knowable and predictable. Citizens focused on social justice wanted to protect consumers, workers, and future generations. As a consequence, states began to more actively regulate businesses. The federal government timidly entered the regulatory waters as well, creating institutions such as the Interstate Commerce Commission and reserving public forest land as timber reserves. Unlike the federal government, California implemented a corporatist system to allow the timber industry to protect its long-term interests and stability.[18]

The corporatist development of the California Board of Forestry contributed to the onset of the Redwood Wars by granting timber companies extraordinary power in the state, especially on the North Coast. The California Board of Forestry was a model of corporatism long before Herbert Hoover popularized the concept, and it remained an official corporatist body until 1970. In 1885, California became one of the first states to regulate private timberland, and the Board of Forestry appears to be one of the first corporatist regulatory bodies in the United States. California logging companies with intimate knowledge of the industry were permitted to guide timber operations through the Board of Forestry. Its mission was not to wrest control of the timber industry from large companies and landholders for the benefit of the public, but rather to efficiently manage the industry by safeguarding its interest in long-term timber harvests. However, and perhaps not surprisingly, the Board of Forestry was more committed to economic development goals than it was to a conservation mission.[19]

To protect their perceived long-term interests, the first board mostly concerned itself with recommendations to the Assembly to protect the inventories of the state's private timber operators rather than addressing harvest methods or forest regeneration to head off the projected timber crisis. Indeed, from 1885 until its dissolution in 1893, only one law was passed that dealt with a forestry issue other than prevention of fires and trespassing. Timber harvesting methods were thus left to the judgment of individual timber operators, a structure that became problematic as the interests of some citizens diverged from those of the timber companies.[20]

Citizens: Placing Boundaries on Industrialization

By the end of the nineteenth century, the North Coast was largely ruled by timber companies. White Americans, Canadians, and Europeans had migrated up the coast and across the nation to take advantage of profit and employment opportunities in the redwood forest. Those new migrants displaced Native Americans and discriminated against Chinese migrants with the blessing of the powerful timber companies who owned the land, owned the railroads, owned some of the towns and camps, and virtually operated as the state on their property. Meanwhile, the giant redwoods fell at breakneck pace. Toward the end of the nineteenth century, citizens of various interests began to challenge to industrial order of the North Coast. As the twentieth century wore on, conflict expanded to include issues of ecology and corporate power. The boundaries of industrial capitalism sat at the heart of each battle.[21]

The early redwood preservation movement initially grew out of the American romantic movement, encompassing nascent conflicts over the limits of capitalism and industrial society. By 1874, the mystique of the giant trees was powerful enough to inspire Walt Whitman to memorialize them in "Song of the Redwood-Tree," which put forward a vision of an American society that might replace the redwoods as nature's highest form of life. Whitman valued the trees as a reminder of what he saw as humanity's best aspiration. It was that combination of reverence for the trees and hopes for America that animated the early activists who sought to protect giant trees from the axmen. Whitman and others saw spirituality, purity, and regality in the redwoods.

> Not wan from Asia's fetiches,
> Nor red from Europe's old dynastic slaughter-house,
> (Area of murder-plots of thrones, with scent left yet of wars
>   and scaffolds every where,)
> But come from Nature's long and harmless throes—
>   peacefully builded thence,
> These virgin lands—Lands of the Western Shore,
> To the new Culminating Man—to you, the Empire New,
> You, promis'd long, we pledge, we dedicate.

In the redwoods, Whitman saw an image of American exceptionalism and the rightful place of white Americans in the natural order. Five years after Whitman published his poem, and well before Congress first authorized the creation of public forest reserves, the secretary of the interior, Carl Schurz, recommended forty-six thousand acres of Redwood Country be withdrawn from sale and held in public trust, but Schurz's effort failed to gain traction because legislators in California and Washington, DC, deemed the redwood forest too vast to exhaust and too valuable to place limits on redwood logging.[22]

During the closing decades of the nineteenth century, however, scientists and progressives pushed back on the scale and pace of logging because they perceived the forest as a source of knowledge and human salvation. The youthful regime of industrial logging in California had already dramatically reduced the size of the forest, and San Francisco Bay Area professionals feared the forest would be lost before they personally, and society more broadly, could benefit from the forest as respite from civilization and as repository of ancient biological systems yet to be explored. During the 1860s, the redwood forests around Berkeley, Marin, and Santa Cruz were heavily logged, and during the 1880s, newspaper editors sounded the alarm about the decimation of the giant trees. For example, Ralph Sidney Smith of the *Redwood City Times and Gazette*, from a town just south of San Francisco, suggested the state establish a park and resort either on Butano Creek or at Big Basin, near Santa Cruz. The Board of Forestry sent some staff members to Big Basin but took no action at that time. But other Bay Area residents continued the push to make Big Basin a public park.[23]

During the 1890s, progressive Bay Area residents worked to enlist the Sierra Club in the redwood park preservation effort. The Sierra Club, founded in 1892 by John Muir, was an organization of elite and professional Californians who wanted to protect the Sierra Nevadas for outdoor recreation. The group was not originally focused on the fog-shrouded coast redwoods. It was largely an outing club of hikers and mountaineers who used their positions and connections to protect spectacular hiking areas in the Sierras. William R. Dudley, a Stanford botanist, founding member of the Sierra Club, and close friend to John Muir and Gifford Pinchot, the nation's first national forester, studied the redwoods and developed into a major force in redwood politics. On November 23, 1895, Dudley urged the Sierra Club to address the fate of the redwoods and to work to establish "several federal redwood parks," including one at Big Basin. Dudley believed the coast redwoods also needed the Sierra Club's "immediate attention" because redwood was the highest valued timber, it was the "loftiest species of conifer," and like its Sierra relatives, it needed protection from the "rapacity of men and scourge of fire."[24]

Dudley and the Sierra Club represented a strain of progressivism that believed the government needed to protect the public interest by acting as a countervailing power to the rapidly expanding corporations of the day. For some reformers, the public interest meant higher wages and better working conditions. For others, it meant eliminating corruption from politics. And for some, like Dudley, Muir, and Pinchot, the public interest was heavily invested in preventing the disappearance of the nation's natural resources. Dudley believed the forest needed active management to provide timber, fish and game habitat, and opportunities for scientific study and recreation. In many respects, Dudley differed from Muir and other Sierra Club members, who focused on outdoor recreation and scenic preservation as a means to uplift themselves and humanity in the rapidly industrializing modern world. Dudley was seemingly as interested in sustainable forestry as he was in more typical Sierra Club endeavors.[25]

At Dudley's behest, the Sierra Club moved into Redwood Country and the field of forestry. In fact, Dudley's ideas and proposals laid the foundation for all twentieth-century redwood preservation efforts. In 1898, he foresaw the greatest challenges facing park advocates, as well as the advocates' greatest asset. The first challenge was acquiring the requisite parkland. Since the failure to prevent the sale of some tracts of federal redwood land in the decades after 1860, virtually all of Redwood Country had been purchased by private interests from the public domain. Dudley proposed creating a citizen fund to purchase the Big Basin grove and giving the grove to the state for use as a park. He argued that the public's interest in creating such parks was "almost wholly one of sentiment," and all that was required was a vigorous appeal. In essence, Dudley believed people loved the redwoods and wanted to preserve the opportunity to see and experience the groves of giant trees. The plan reflected the emerging progressive model of reform, which relied on publicizing problems, developing solutions, building institutions, organizing the public, and advocating policy changes.[26]

The effort to protect the giant trees at Big Basin set the pattern for redwood activists for the next one hundred years. Photographer Andrew P. Hill was shooting redwoods inside the private Welch's Big Trees Grove Park, near Felton in the Santa Cruz Mountains, when the owner approached him. Mr. Welch tried to confiscate the photograph plates because the trees were on private property and he had not authorized the photo shoot. Outraged, Hill took his story to newspapers and prominent citizens. Op-eds appeared in the *Santa Cruz Sentinel* and the *San Jose Herald* calling for public acquisition of Welch's park. On May 1, Hill, John F. Coope, a Santa Cruz winemaker, Dudley, Carrie Stevens Walker of the San Jose Women's Club, and Dr. C. L. Anderson met to discuss the Welch's Park incident. They decided to focus on Big Basin, no doubt at Dudley's urging. The group surveyed Big Basin and created the Sempervirens Club of California to advocate for a public redwood park for future generations of hikers and scientists.[27]

Soon after the surveying trip, the Sempervirens Club launched its first campaign to protect the redwoods. In July 1900, the group created a citizens' fund, as Dudley had urged two years prior. Simultaneously, the activists developed a media presentation consisting of photographs and text that conveyed an imminent threat. Andrew Hill lobbied the Assembly in Sacramento with photographs, and they enlisted the support of the American Association for the Advancement of Science, the American Forestry Association, and other scientific groups. Additionally, the group recruited sympathetic business leaders, including H. L. Middleton, the largest stockholder of the Big Basin Lumber Company. Middleton used his position to forestall logging in the basin while the activists rallied support for a bill.[28]

The publicity and lobbying campaigns followed Dudley's prescription of appealing to sentiment by describing the "solemn grandeur" of the redwoods and their "silent majesty." The advocates argued that the groves were important to the "nation and world," providing a place where people could "seek health and restoration" in "God's own temple." The ancient trees, in essence, were important to the public interest. Like Walt Whitman decades earlier, the new redwood advocates described the trees as "the last of their race." In November, the California Assembly considered a bill appropriating funds for public purchase of a park. By March 16, 1901, Governor Henry Gage had signed a bill appropriating $250,000 to purchase 2,500 acres of old-growth redwood forest. On September 6, 1902, the state completed the purchase of 3,800 acres in Big Basin containing marvelous canyon-bottom groves of ancient redwoods. It was California's first state park, inaugurating a tradition of using the state park designation to protect redwoods. The nation's first successful redwood preservation campaign was completed with minimal conflict, and it established a blueprint for future environmental campaigns, especially those in Redwood Country. The combination of urgency, sentimentality, scientific credibility, graphic imagery, accommodation with private interests, elite citizen support, lobbying power, and news coverage became the persistent tools of redwood activists as well as many other environmentalists. After World War I, the attention of activists moved north, and what they discovered on the North Coast compelled them to use those tools to limit industrial logging.[29]

ACCOMMODATION AND STABILIZATION ON THE NORTH COAST

Acquiring Redwoods

While conflict was averted in the San Francisco Bay Area, the timber industry on the North Coast continued to develop and expand out of sight of the government and the vast majority of the state's residents. The most violent and contentious conflicts on the North Coast pitted labor against industrialists as they fought over the prerogatives of capital. All across the western United States during the first third of the twentieth century, loggers and miners fought their employers over pay and safety issues, often violently. The forests of the West and the mines of the Rockies were remote and largely unsupervised, except by industrial leaders. The work was hard in the male-dominated work camps in the West, and workers repeatedly struck, shutting down operations and engaging in fights with corporate security forces. After World War I and through the Great Depression, worker strikes on the North Coast were broken by local police and their timber company allies, especially in Eureka, the hub of the North Coast timber industry. However, conflict over redwood preservation appeared briefly after World War I, when preservationists realized that the only remaining old-growth redwood forests of significant size were located at the northern end of the newly completed Highway 101. As late as 1925, an estimated two-thirds of the ancient redwoods were still standing in Redwood Country, with the vast majority located in Humboldt and Del Norte counties. The highway permitted travelers to glimpse the vast forest up north, as well as to see the impact of clear-cutting.[30]

The Bohemian Club retreat in the summer of 1917 provided the forum that led to a permanent institution devoted to redwood preservation. The Sempervirens Club had disappeared after the creation of Big Basin Redwoods State Park, and no active group was working to protect ancient redwoods. The Bohemians were a fraternal group of writers, artists, academics, and successful businessmen who gathered annually to enjoy fellowship and the arts. After the 1917 retreat, members Madison Grant, Dr. John Merriam, and Henry Fairfield Osborn drove north to see the giant redwoods of the North Coast. The three men were primarily interested in the cultural and scientific value of the redwoods. Grant was a New York attorney and author best known for his eugenics manifesto, *The Passing of the Great Race* (1916). Merriam was a paleontology professor at the University of California in Berkeley. Osborn was a professor of paleontology at Columbia University, president of the American Museum of Natural History in New York, and like his friend Grant, a firm believer in eugenics. For those men, the ancient redwood forest represented evolution's highest achievement. Understanding the redwoods, they believed, could help humans better understand evolution and how to direct it to promote the proliferation of the Teutonic race.[31]

Eugenics was a pervasive force in early twentieth-century American society, and the redwoods had been pulled into its orbit. President Roosevelt's foreign policy was influenced by eugenics, as were public school testing and immigration policy, with the latter culminating in the 1924 National Origins Act, an explicit, and successful, effort to increase the percentage of the American population descended from northern and western European stock. It was a time of perceived crisis for Caucasians and masculinity, and the three Bohemian Club members hoped the redwoods could offer white America some guidance. To celebrate the redwoods was thus to celebrate American and Nordic superiority. When they finally arrived on the North Coast, however, the three travelers saw clear-cuts and destruction all along the highway. For the three eugenicist friends, the destruction of the giant trees seemed to mirror the ways they believed industrialization was destroying the masculinity of Teutonic peoples.[32]

Appalled at the seemingly wanton destruction, Grant, Osborn, and Merriam decided to create an organization to protect groves of ancient redwoods. The Save the Redwoods League was thus born in 1918, its mission and strategy reflecting the progressive, scientific, and eugenicist beliefs of its founders. The group dedicated itself to preserving representative groves of ancient redwoods by enlisting private support from the wealthy and professional classes. Alongside Grant, Osborn, and Merriam, the league recruited secretary of the interior Franklin K. Lane to be its first president, and secured its first donations from William Kent, the wealthy Bay Area congressman who donated the Muir Woods National Monument grove; Stephen Mather, director of the National Park Service; and E. C. Bradley, assistant secretary of the interior. Like the first donors and officers, the early members were nearly all doctors, lawyers, professors, scientists, writers, and men and women of independent wealth—typical California progressives wary of big business but committed to private property and competitive capitalism. The league was thus formed out of the same mold as the Sierra Club and other organizations devoted to expert civil management of the nation's interests. They believed that those who wanted redwoods protected ought to raise private money and negotiate with private landholders to purchase specific groves. The groves could then be donated to the state or federal government to be managed as public parks or as laboratories to benefit the public interest. The original strategy, with occasional help from the state, stayed in place for nearly fifty years.[33]

Humboldt County residents had already created their own redwood preservation movement, and as the league set its sights north, its members were forced to ally with, and accommodate, those locals. The Humboldt movement to protect groves of ancient trees was largely driven by women who seized political opportunities that fit into their family caretaker roles. However, when they deemed it necessary, women's organizations utilized more aggressive and radical tactics. Residents of the North Coast had been promoting a redwood park since at least 1905, when George Kellogg, secretary of the Humboldt Chamber of Commerce, petitioned the State Assembly to promote tourism to the North Coast by creating a redwood park. In 1908, local women's groups and the chamber of commerce continued to press their park proposal using their roles as social housekeepers to provide leverage. For example, they delivered to the US Forest Service a two-thousand-signature petition circulated by Eureka schoolchildren. Theodore Roosevelt responded to the petition, voicing his support for their cause. In 1909, the Humboldt County Federation of Women's Clubs officially joined the movement. The chamber was primarily interested in the park idea as a way to extract state funding for a railroad connecting Eureka to San Francisco. The women, like their counterparts in the East, such as the Cambridge Plant and Garden Club, wanted a park where people could study and enjoy nature. They also wanted a place where they could take their families to escape the onslaught of commercialism, such as it was on the remote and rural North Coast. The women were concerned about the health of their families and believed nature recreation could heal body and soul. Their activism followed in the tradition of "social housekeepers" such as Florence Kelley and Jane Addams of the National Consumers League. In an era when men disapproved of women engaging in public political activity, many women used the so-called cult of domesticity to their advantage: if women were supposed to focus on raising the next generation of morally upstanding citizens, they had every right to engage in public debates about issues related to health and education. For some women on the North Coast, the preservation of redwood parks was one such issue. Thus, in Redwood Country and around the nation, women cracked open the world of politics, forcing men to accommodate their demands. In 1912, the Humboldt Federation convinced their congressman to introduce a bill to look at the feasibility of a national park in Humboldt County. The legislation stalled until 1913, when then congressman William Kent pledged to donate $25,000 to acquire land for a national redwood park. The Humboldt County Federation of Women's Clubs, led by Laura Perrott Mahan, a local artist, organized a petition drive to support Kent in Washington, DC, developed a set of site recommendations for a park, and even hired a Washington lobbyist. The bill to create the park, known as the Raker-Kent bill, died in 1915, however, and the federation set aside its park fund for a better day.[34]

Despite the defeat of the federal park bill, Save the Redwoods League and the Humboldt activists reorganized and continued their work. One of the league's first actions on the North Coast was to publicize the giant redwoods to a national audience. The officers of the league, using their personal connections, recruited the *Saturday Evening Post* and *National Geographic Magazine* to write articles about the redwoods and the increased harvest levels that accompanied the highway, the railroads, and the war. In 1919, Stephen Mather, National Park Service director and league officer and donor, visited Humboldt County to tour the redwoods and explore the possibility of a national redwood park. His visit further encouraged local redwood activists and the league. The Humboldt County Federation of Women's Clubs created the Women's Save the Redwoods League in Humboldt County to work on behalf of a local redwood park. Save the Redwoods League hired Newton B. Drury, a California public relations professional and later the fourth director of the National Park Service, to manage the organization's campaign to create a redwood park. The local Women's League created a park committee, headed by Laura Mahan, to survey Humboldt lands and recommend site locations. However, redwood activists did not always agree on substance or tactics. Compelled by the immense size of the trees and the site's potential for scientific study, the league wanted to protect the groves along Bull Creek—the tributary of the Eel River in southern Humboldt subsequently damaged in the 1954–55 floods. The Women's League wanted a park located at Dyerville Flats, in the same vicinity but closer to the highway and more suitable for a family park and picnic area. During the frenzied pace of redwood politics in the 1920s, both groups would get what they wanted, though they utilized different tools.[35]

Patterns of conflict and negotiation took root in the 1920s that would drive redwood politics until the 1960s. Save the Redwoods League's local women's branch and the national leadership cooperated with great success, convincing the California legislature to jump-start the park acquisition process in 1921. The assembly appropriated $300,000 to acquire acreage along the Redwood Highway in order to stop local timber companies from logging right up to the edge of the road. The assembly's move was designed to encourage use of the highway by tourists and to prevent public outcry about unsightly clear-cuts lining the road. Notably, Save the Redwoods worked with Pacific Lumber to make sure the appropriation authorized purchases only in southern Humboldt, a restriction that kept Pacific Lumber land safe from condemnation. Although we cannot be certain, given the league's subsequent acquisition strategy, early cooperation with the company was likely intended to generate goodwill among timber leaders and thus pave the way for more ambitious purchases. Regardless, their work on the highway appropriations bill was the first step in developing a long-standing working relationship.[36]

After the state's land appropriation, Save the Redwoods aggressively worked to acquire ancient groves on the North Coast and create an expansive state park system. In August 1921, the organization made its first purchase, the Bolling Memorial Grove near Bull Creek Flats in what would later be designated as Humboldt Redwoods State Park. In 1923, the league secured a donation of 166 acres of ancient redwoods in northern Humboldt to create the Prairie Creek Redwoods State Park.

In 1924, the first acquisition of redwoods in Del Norte County was completed, a 288-acre grove that would become part of the Del Norte Coast Redwoods State Park. True to the interwar pattern of voluntarism and philanthropy, the first groves for the redwood park plan were acquired in private negotiations between timber companies and the league.[37]

While the league acted quickly and quietly, Humboldt County locals pushed more aggressively for state action, establishing a tradition of local independence and confrontation. The league, on the other hand, wanted to bypass state involvement in real estate negotiations and to avoid on-the-ground conflicts. While working to secure the Dyerville Flats park, local Humboldt women aggressively used state and national public support to gain leverage with Pacific Lumber. In 1924, after the company rejected the activists' purchase offers, the Women's League convinced the board of supervisors to condemn Pacific Lumber land for the park. To prevent that action, the company offered the county a purchase agreement that failed to include Dyerville Flats. Laura Mahan and the Humboldt County Board of Supervisors then obtained a court order halting the harvest of Dyersville Flats until the condemnation could be finalized.

In what would develop into a pattern much later in the century, Pacific Lumber did not honor the court order, and the activists retaliated. On November 10, 1924, Mahan and her husband received word that Pacific Lumber had begun logging the flat. Mahan and her husband alerted the press and recruited a group of activist women to occupy the grove. Pacific Lumber subsequently agreed to halt the logging operation near Dyerville Flats and to negotiate a purchase agreement. However, as much as it appeared locals had snatched victory from the jaws of Pacific Lumber, the involvement of national groups was crucial to the locals' success. First, Save the Redwoods League informed Pacific Lumber that an anonymous donor was ready to contribute $1 million for the acquisition of Dyerville Flats. The Women's League enlisted the support of the national garden clubs. Both actions increased the pressure on Pacific Lumber to return to the negotiating table, though it took seven years to finalize the deal. The combination of depressed land prices and reduced demand for timber at the onset of the Great Depression certainly made the deal more attractive to Pacific Lumber, and in 1931, the Dyerville Flats purchase and other groves acquired from Pacific Lumber were put together to form Rockefeller Forest in Humboldt Redwoods State Park—the largest contiguous ancient redwood forest remaining in the world, named after the league's 1924 anonymous donor, John D. Rockefeller Jr. The league paid more than $3 million for the 13,629-acre Rockefeller Forest: $2 million from Rockefeller, $1 million from the state, and smaller donations from the Humboldt Women's League. That land contained the groves at the Bull Creek alluvial flat that were destroyed during the winter storms of 1954–55.[38]

The conflict over the Humboldt park highlights the vital role local women played in the fights over the redwoods. From Carrie Stevens Walker in the nineteenth century to Laura Mahan in the early twentieth century, women in leadership roles in the redwood conflict have roots as deep as the conflicts themselves. During those early periods, women used their position as social housekeepers to open opportunities for political involvement, just as women around the nation were doing in myriad fields. On the North Coast, the giant redwoods and opportunities to retreat from commercialism and industrial society persuaded women to advocate and agitate on behalf of redwood preservation. The conflict over Dyerville Flats also highlights the persistent tools and forces at play in Redwood Country land conflicts: local radicalism, the quest for national support, public relations, direct action, litigation, and private negotiation.[39]

Despite the tense moments, those early negotiations enabled the league, the state, and the timber companies to develop a stable system of park creation to protect stands of giant redwoods while logging continued around them. League activists identified places they deemed particularly beautiful, scientifically valuable, or recreationally important. The organization then approached the landowner privately, and if there was a potential seller, the league raised private money to purchase the groves of giant redwoods. When the real estate deal was complete, the league handed the land over to the state to manage as a public park. The system created an expansive state redwood park system from the Oregon border to south of Monterrey, and it generated goodwill for the timber companies. Pacific Lumber, in particular, cultivated and promoted its image as a good corporate neighbor in an effort to forestall future tensions and possible financial losses.

Pacific Lumber Accommodation

Workers, like conservationists, resisted corporate prerogatives during the interwar period. Pacific Lumber and the other "Big Five" timber companies of the North Coast had to contend with unionizing efforts and labor strikes primarily at the conclusion of World War I. In 1919, strikes plagued industries across the nation after wartime industrial controls were lifted but wages failed to catch up with inflation. North Coast timber workers were no different from their fellow workers in the forests of the Pacific Northwest, on the docks in San Francisco, in the police department in Boston, or throughout the city of Seattle. In the Pacific Northwest, workers in the timber, fishing, and railroad industries all struck for better wages and shorter hours. As a result, American businesses worked to dampen unionizing efforts in the 1920s to prevent production losses and wage increases. Often, strikes were forcefully broken, but businesses also developed programs to reduce worker unrest, including paid vacation, sick days, and pensions.[40]

For timber workers, the early Great Depression was even more difficult than the immediate aftermath of World War I, as construction ground to a halt, leading timber companies to close mills and cut wages. By 1935 the timber industry was recovering and workers wanted to share in the recovery. The repeal of the National Industrial Recovery Act that spring, which had granted workers the right to collectively bargain, made the workers' efforts more difficult. Thus, on June 21, 1935, workers from myriad timber companies gathered at the Holmes-Eureka redwood mill to stop scab workers and disrupt operations. In the confusion of the day, police fired warning shots and tear gas, resulting in retaliatory stones from the workers and more gunshots from the police. The violence was the Humboldt climax of the summer's national labor troubles. Pacific Lumber kept its workers safe, sending its security team to escort them out of the melee. The violence shocked the community, and the local papers and timber leaders chastised nonresident "communist leaders" responsible for the "terrorist campaign" that led to the riot. Eureka police arrested more than one hundred suspects, and the strikes slowly died. The interwar strikes demonstrate that workers, along with preservationists, had begun to actively challenge the prerogatives of the timber companies on the North Coast, and both would continue the challenges.[41]

Faced with regionwide labor discontent, a surprisingly aggressive redwood preservation movement, and a dynamic competitive environment, Pacific Lumber changed its business model during the interwar period to improve its position in both the industry and the community. In its 1917 annual report, the company stated it expected "continuous agitation" on the part of labor, but it was not concerned because its employees were "paid well and cared for." The company was generous to its employees by industry standards, and it enthusiastically embraced the 1920s welfare capitalism movement, offering benefits, bonuses, education, and cultural opportunities. The company was clearly trying to co-opt labor, but management also seemed genuinely interested in creating a stable work environment to maximize production. Regardless, Pacific Lumber's image as a beneficent employer endured until the 1980s. The company's early support of conservation measures also differentiated Pacific Lumber from the larger timber industry. During the 1920s and 1930s, the company, unlike most of its competitors, experimentally replaced clear-cuts with selective harvesting. During the Great Depression, the North Coast timber industry had adopted those techniques, but most companies had abandoned them by the end of the 1950s to capitalize on the demand for lumber during the post–World War II housing boom. Pacific Lumber did not. In 1923, the company hired some of the state's first private foresters and developed a tree nursery to aid second-growth regeneration. More directly related to redwood preservation, Pacific Lumber chief Albert Stanwood Murphy met with Newton Drury of the Save the Redwoods League in 1928, while the group was raising money to purchase the Dyerville and Bull Creek Flats. At the meeting, Murphy committed to protect those ancient trees until fund-raising was complete, a gesture of cooperation and goodwill.[42]

Conservation values certainly played a role in Pacific Lumber's decisions to refrain from logging along the Eel and to eschew clear-cutting, but so too did a change in the California tax code that provided incentives to leave some trees standing. So long as a landowner cut at least 70 percent of a harvest area, taxes did not have to be paid on that land for forty years, which contemporary foresters deemed to be the maturation time for second-growth trees—those trees seeded or planted after an area has been logged. On the one hand, the tax code encouraged some landowners to clear-cut their holdings to avoid taxes. Pacific Lumber saw the new tax code as an opportunity to conserve its inventory of giant redwoods while also lowering its tax bill. It could leave 30 percent of its ancient trees standing and still not pay taxes on the land. Thus, while other firms were furiously cutting all their ancient stock, Pacific Lumber retained some trees to sell at higher prices in the future. Combined with a desire to appease conservationists, the tax code and its monopoly strategy thus kept the company committed to selective harvesting through the 1970s. The sale of Rockefeller Forest and other groves to create Humboldt Redwoods State Park further reduced the global supply of old-growth timber while improving Pacific Lumber's relationship with the league. Thus the conservation, preservation, and modernization programs improved the company's business model. Its development patterns suggest that Pacific Lumber was trying to insulate itself from both industrial competition and activist agitation.[43]

Pacific Lumber's strategy and patterns were based on market share concerns and community loyalty; they formed part of the broader set of stable relationships constructed on the North Coast between World War I and 1960. Timber companies and the State of California worked with Save the Redwoods to preserve some groves of giant redwoods. Once the public had acquired the land, a park was created and managed by the California state parks agency, of which Newton Drury, the first director of the league, was in charge by the 1950s. Between 1920 and 1960, the league acquired more than one hundred thousand acres for the parks system. But that system was rooted in the belief that private landowners could and should manage their lands as they thought best suited their interests. If the public wanted to set aside particular places for public use, they needed to raise the money to acquire the land. There was not yet any strong momentum behind the idea of regulating timber cutting on private lands.[44]

As a result of these dynamics, the politics of logging the redwoods differed from timber politics in much of the rest of the American West after World War II, and those differences were critical to the shape the Redwood Wars would take. Despite the postwar push by Weyerhaeuser and other timber firms to create private tree farms across the West, logging in publicly owned national forests and on Bureau of Land Management lands became a dominant trend. Throughout the West, the federal government could decide when and where to log on its property, and the agencies largely decided to cut often and everywhere. But the federal government was still an active and important party to decisions about the scope and scale of logging in the United States. In Redwood Country, by contrast, most of the remaining timberland of value was privately held, and the state had delegated its regulatory responsibilities to the timber companies through the corporatist Board of Forestry system. The timber companies and private citizens on the North Coast accommodated each other through market relationships. Pacific Lumber developed additional strategies to insulate itself from workers and conservationists, developing a powerful system of alliances and loyalties through its corporate welfare and conservation work. The firm's strategy worked well for more than six decades, and when activists after World War II challenged the firm's land management, it was well positioned to absorb their assault.[45]

THE ERA OF TRANSFORMATION

"If you've seen one redwood, you've seen them all." Regardless of whether California governor Ronald Reagan actually uttered the infamous words often attributed to him, they sum up nicely the State of California's official attitude toward redwoods during the West's post–World War II economic boom. Like the US Forest Service on western public land—of which very little existed on the North Coast—the Board of Forestry was invested in "getting out the cut." Nonetheless, the basal buds that sprouted the Redwood Wars emerged from the established roots of bilateral negotiations and state cooperation. The redwood preservation movement, the Board of Forestry, and the Pacific Lumber Company all faced challenges during the postwar era that changed the relationships among them, as well as altering the tenor of the conflict over the redwoods. Official corporatist timber regulation continued to direct the Board of Forestry's activities, but the California State Assembly, other state agencies, and groups of citizens grew increasingly frustrated with the system and its consequences for the forest.[46]

After World War II, Pacific Lumber continued to solidify its economic position and to head off challenges to its regime. The company's previous investments in mill technology, its selective harvesting of ancient trees, and its retention of a permanent workforce in the company town meant that its profits and stability were sufficient that Pacific Lumber did not need to capitalize on the postwar housing boom. Because it was not a publicly traded firm, the Murphys and their partners were the only ones who needed to be content with the company's financials. The timber industry at large, however, did scramble to expand their harvests by modernizing and mechanizing, and they did it with great success. Across the industry, annual increases in worker output went from 0.8 percent in the period 1896–1947 to 2.1 percent in 1958–80. And like Pacific Lumber earlier in the century, timber companies diversified their businesses after 1950, though most companies diversified into related industries, such as paper.[47]

Like its peers, Pacific Lumber expanded its property holdings to improve its position in the old-growth redwood market. In 1940, the company bought twenty-two thousand acres of timberland in the Lawrence Creek and Yager Creek watersheds of Humboldt County. In 1950, Pacific Lumber acquired Dolbeer and Carson Lumber Company of Eureka and its property along the Elk River, which adjoined Pacific Lumber's land in central Humboldt along the western hills of the Coast Range. The company acquired Hampton Plywood Corporation that same year to capitalize on the new plywood market and to aid its efforts to more fully utilize redwood logs of both old-growth and second-growth harvests. In 1958, Pacific Lumber acquired Holmes Eureka Lumber Company and its land along the Van Duzen River. Altogether, Pacific Lumber doubled its assets from 1931 to 1961, remained the world's largest redwood lumber producer, and diversified its product line. It also acquired what eventually became known as Headwaters Forest.[48]

Meanwhile, Pacific Lumber continued to cultivate its image as a small-town company with small-town values as a part of its labor and conservation strategy. In 1951, Pacific Lumber cooperated with the *Saturday Evening Post* to produce an article about Scotia. The article referred to the town as a "workers' paradise," where 950 employees lived and worked on the 131,000-acre "tree farm." The company had a reforestation program and actively planted saplings across its harvests, but to call Pacific Lumber property a tree farm was a stretch. The company was still mainly harvesting giant trees out of the surrounding forestland, and it certainly did not own a conventional tree plantation. The author described Scotia as a place where the resident manager of Pacific Lumber was the "mayor," and his office repainted houses, fixed leaky pipes, and repaired windows. Pacific Lumber was portrayed as a giant family; resident employees resented the term "company town" and competed over the quality of the gardens they planted on their rented land. The *Post* and the *Christian Science Monitor* marveled at how welcoming the company was and the way it openly encouraged tourists to visit the Scotia complex using a printed tour guide. In 1961, Pacific Lumber began offering college scholarships to all employee children, and in 1964 it touted its generosity by pointing out to a *New York Times* reporter that the company promised to hold on to the Pepperwood Groves near the Avenue of the Giants—despite the taxes it paid for not logging the land—because it hoped Save the Redwoods League would be able to buy the ancient trees. Thus the company displayed a continuing commitment to the interwar strategies developed by the Murphys with respect to labor and conservation—all hard-nosed business decisions designed to protect Pacific Lumber and its future profits and position in the redwood industry.[49]

Those initiatives were generous to workers, environmentalists, and tourists, and the company benefited as well. The Pacific Lumber workforce was not unionized, and the company likely hoped that its paternalism would insulate it from postwar union drives and the excitement generated by the United Auto Workers' "treaties" with Ford and others. Furthermore, the timber industry was under attack in California after World War II for what many residents and visitors considered destructive practices, ever more apparent from the Redwood Highway. Under those conditions, Pacific Lumber decided to invest in worker and conservationist loyalty. Those investments were at least partially based on a long-standing desire to reduce resistance from those communities to Pacific Lumber operations, as evidenced by the repeated references to mitigating labor agitation in annual reports from the interwar period.

The Board of Forestry faced the most serious challenges to its operations during the postwar era, despite its independence from the public and the State Assembly. After World War II, the legislature made some cosmetic changes to the regulatory regime but maintained its corporatist orientation. For example, a 1943 law prohibiting the harvest of trees less than eighteen inches in diameter may appear to mark a move away from corporatism and toward greater legislative oversight, but that law was in fact another in the long history of regulations devised by businesses to protect their markets. The minimum-diameter law protected big timber companies from competition from small, independent "gyppo" contractors best suited to harvest small trees. Like the minimum diameter law, the 1945 Forest Practice Act governing timber operations on private land also appeared to undercut corporatism while promoting conservation. The law required the Board of Forestry to create forest practice rules to ensure that the state's private timber operators used the best conservation practices. However, it also perpetuated industry self-regulation because the board still included a majority of members from the timber industry, and when the board created rules, it predictably declined to include penalties for violations. Though timber companies were still able to craft rules to best suit their financial interests, the new laws opened a wedge for activists in that the state was assuming some responsibility for timber practices in California.

As with the minimum-diameter rule, the board was able to move away from pure corporatism without eroding the practical operation of the corporatist model. In 1960 the board began approving large clear-cuts, contrary to the recommendations of the US Department of Agriculture, because the timber industry wanted to capitalize on the housing boom and timber production was slowing in the Pacific Northwest. None of those postwar logging developments are surprising; the Board of Forestry had never operated as a conservation or forest practices regulator. Its postwar priorities were to prevent fire from destroying timber and to protect the timber industry from unfair competition from within—priorities that reveal the influence of the postwar housing boom on the timber industry as well as the board's commitment to helping the timber companies operate profitably and maintain stability.[50]

The resilience of California's corporatist Board of Forestry stands in stark contrast to the rising tide of "modern environmentalism" and the resulting changes in environmental politics after World War II. The popularity of outdoor recreation increased dramatically, as did concern about suburban development and humankind's impact on the planet. As a result, national environmental groups like the Sierra Club and the Wilderness Society grew in size and stature during the immediate postwar years. While the nation's environmental attention swung from nuclear fallout, to Dinosaur National Monument, to the Wilderness Act, the California Board of Forestry remained largely beyond reproach. No groups organized sustained, active political opposition to the board's operations, apart from loud complaints, until the late 1960s. And why would there have been such opposition? Most of the state's residents did not live near enough to timberlands to witness the increased logging and clear-cutting. The Redwoods League purchased grand redwood groves and created parks for recreationists and scientists. And the timber industry was a major contributor to California's postwar prosperity. Residents of the North Coast were unwilling to bite the hand that fed them, and other Californians were not concerned with North Coast logging.[51]

Nascent opposition to the board's power first emerged in the 1950s, when citizen groups such as the Sierra Club began to complain about the rate of timber harvesting and the prolific use of clear-cutting in Redwood Country. This was especially true after the Bull Creek floods in 1954–55. As a result, the legislature authorized a series of commissions to study logging on the North Coast, even though a US Department of Agriculture report in 1932 had already strongly recommended dramatic changes in Redwood Country logging methods. The report had recommended that the timber industry adopt selective harvesting to mitigate watershed damage and mass-wasting on North Coast slopes. Nonetheless, by the 1950s, clear-cutting and industrial logging had become even more prominent on the North Coast. But opposition was mounting. In 1962, a report commissioned by the legislature concluded that forest practice rules "failed to provide adequate enforcement to protect public values in water, fishing, and recreation." In 1967, another legislative report concluded that the rules needed to be broadened if California was to avoid major damage to its most important watersheds. A final legislative study of forest practice rules concluded in 1971 that logging was one of the primary causes of the 80 percent decline in salmon and steelhead runs in northern California. Agitation by the Sierra Club and others thus helped undercut confidence in the corporatist regulatory regime by pressuring the legislature to study the industry in more detail. But in spite of these findings, there was no sustained effort to reform the laws or regulations.[52]

Despite transformations emerging within the preservation community, Save the Redwoods remained committed to private negotiation. From the 1940s until the mid-1960s, Save the Redwoods continued to negotiate with landholders to expand California's redwood parks. Thanks to these efforts, groves along the Smith River and a National Tribute Grove recognizing the service of men and women during World War II were established in Jedediah Smith Redwoods State Park in Del Norte County. The Montgomery Woods State Natural Reserve in Mendocino County was also donated to the league. The Avenue of the Giants was completed forty years after its conception, then expanded during the late 1960s. And the league expanded Prairie Creek Redwoods State Park by acquiring Gold Bluffs Beach and Fern Canyon from Pacific Lumber in 1965.[53]

While Save the Redwoods negotiated with landholders, the Sierra Club was by the 1950s engaged in more public and political disputes, which eventually ushered in a new era of militantism and conflict in Redwood Country. Three events drove the Sierra Club in its new direction, of which the third event is the least known and most important for the Redwood Wars. The first event was the conflict over a proposed dam near Dinosaur National Monument, which galvanized opposition to the prerogatives of conservation agencies; the second was David Brower's appointment as executive director, which introduced an adversarial combativeness into preservationist politics. But the third event—the winter floods on the North Coast in 1954–55, which decimated the giant trees at Bull Creek Flats in Rockefeller Forest—was just as important. Historians have long understood the importance of the first two events in American environmental politics, but not the third. A growing recognition that the giant redwoods were nearly all gone, as well as increased understanding and appreciation of ecology, helped forge a national constituency for the redwood parks movement. That movement drove a wedge between the Sierra Club and Save the Redwoods League. The Sierra Club grew more concerned with ecological health, while the league remained committed to preserving exquisite redwood specimens. The Sierra Club crafted provocative advertisements and books, adopted anti–big business rhetoric, worked to organize grassroots activity, and demanded federal action to protect ecosystems. The league, meanwhile, retained its faith in private negotiation, industrial cooperation, and voluntarism.

In 1952, David Brower, a military veteran and longtime Sierra Club activist, was hired as the club's first executive director, a move that cemented a change in the leadership culture of the organization from genteel advocate to public organizer. From Muir's death until 1950, the organization acted as a literary and educational club concerned with national parks and adventure stories. In May 1950, however, a feistier element reared its head. Joe R. Momyer organized a letter-writing drive resulting in the delivery of three hundred letters to the US Forest Service opposing a tramway project in the San Jacinto Valley. In March 1951, the club held its second biennial wilderness conference in Berkeley, with panels devoted to "Wilderness and Mobilization" and "Conflicts in Land-Use Demands." Late in 1951, the club republished an op-ed by paleontologist and Izaak Walton League officer Joseph W. Penfold roundly criticizing the assistant secretary of the interior for proposing a dam near Dinosaur National Monument. The club's drive toward national constituencies and public organizing was in full motion.[54]

The 1950s conflict over the dam in Dinosaur National Monument and Echo National Park has received the most attention as the campaign that transformed both the Sierra Club and postwar environmental politics, but the winter floods of 1954–55 trained the Sierra Club's sights on the redwoods, forestry, and private property issues. The tactics used during the Dinosaur controversy energized the expanding postwar environmental community and constituency; the Sierra Club's focus on the redwoods and logging practices on private land transformed redwood politics. The dam campaigns of the 1950s, rather than marking a wholesale change in tactics, instead revived many strategies used in the Big Basin campaign and the unsuccessful effort to stop the dam at Hetch Hetchy Valley near Yosemite. In the 1950s, the Sierra Club published *This Is Dinosaur*, began conducting river trips to get people into the canyons, and launched a public relations and citizen organizing campaign to pressure Congress to defeat the proposed dam, which would have flooded portions of Dinosaur National Monument. Muir had similarly penned national articles, taken President Theodore Roosevelt camping in the Sierras, and organized petition drives to Congress. The Sempervirens Club had developed a public relations, media, and lobbying campaign to protect the giant redwoods at Big Basin. In addition, Brower and the Sierra Club used film for the first time to promote protecting the canyons. The Dinosaur conflict of the 1950s and the Wilderness Act campaign that followed provided Sierra Club leaders with national campaign experience and increased the popularity of the organization.[55]

Despite the high profile of the Dinosaur conflict, it was the damage to the giant redwoods at Bull Creek Flats that demonstrated the transformation in the Sierra Club's philosophy regarding the natural world and environmental politics. The 1954–55 floods knocked down thousand-year-old redwoods just off Highway 101, leaving them strewn about the alluvial flats like toothpicks. Afterward, mud continued to flow into the creek, filling it with sediment. A state park ranger described the damaged alluvial flats as "a lunar landscape, with the raw edges of the mountains exposed." The parks agency focused on stabilizing the creek bed rather than addressing the logging practices that had led to the mass-wasting on the slopes above Bull Creek. Sierra Club blamed Board of Forestry practices for the disaster. In 1957, the Sierra Club urged changes in the law to prevent what they deemed an abuse of private and public land alike. In doing so, the Sierra Club vilified the timber industry and worked to raise a public outcry over the logging practices allowed by the Board of Forestry. In 1958, a new Redwood Chapter marked the Sierra Club's increased presence on the North Coast.[56]

By the end of 1960, the Sierra Club was fully engaged in redwood politics, albeit with a different tenor, a different set of goals, and a different strategy from those of Save the Redwoods League. In early 1960, the club newsletter published a two-part series, "The Tragedy of Bull Creek," written by Peggy Wayburn of the Sierra Club and Newton Drury of Save the Redwoods League. The article traced the damage at Bull Creek Flats to clear-cuts performed in 1947 above the basin. Because the official corporatist forestry regime in California prevented direct citizen engagement in logging regulations, the Sierra Club proposed that the state purchase the cutover land above the basin, add it to the state park, and rehabilitate the slopes. The club also advocated for expanded state responsibility for logging activities on private land to prevent future damage. Despite Drury's cooperation on the project, the league did not immediately embrace the principles promoted by the Sierra Club. Thus, in the 1950s, the solution to problems like those at Bull Creek remained the purchase of private land for a park. Later in the century, activists would look to regulation to limit the destructive effects of logging on ancient redwoods.[57]

In the 1960s a new era in redwood politics thus emerged, an era in which conflict escalated, relationships frayed, and the nation's eyes turned to the world's last privately owned redwood forests dominated by ancient trees. Though the late twentieth-century Redwood Wars would be fought in a greater number of arenas and would prove more public, more hotly contested, and more violent than the earlier eras of redwood politics, they were not separate from those earlier contests. The later conflicts were extensions of those earlier conflicts, part of the long struggle to limit and define the power of industrial corporations, Western capitalism, and federal governance. The more recent activists would draw from the pool of tactics developed by Robert Dudley, Laura Mahan, Newton B. Drury, John C. Merriam, the timber workers of the region, and David Brower. The late twentieth-century activists repeated the public relations campaigns suggested by Dudley and implemented by John Muir, then perfected by David Brower. They continued to look to private donors, as had Drury, Kent, and Merriam. And they would take to the woods like Mahan.

For its part, the Pacific Lumber Company continued to rely on its past philanthropy, paternalism, and small-town image to protect it from environmental activists and regulators. The Board of Forestry remained committed to development-focused corporatism. However, the fight for a national redwood park in the 1960s shone a bright light on North Coast forests and North Coast timber companies, and citizens redoubled their efforts and attacked the corporatist regime governing logging on private land. When most of the remaining ancient redwood forests were protected inside state and national parks, the activists set their sights on the condition of the remaining unprotected old-growth groves and of the second-growth forests of the North Coast that had matured since the initial logging bonanzas in the era of industrialization. By doing so, they transformed redwood politics and put themselves on a collision course with two formidable adversaries: big business and private property rights.

TWO

THE WAR BEGINS

THE FIRST TIME THAT CHARLES HURWITZ, CEO OF MAXXAM GROUP
Holding, addressed his new employees at the Pacific Lumber Company
in 1986, he explained his intentions with a pithy remark: "There's a
little story about the golden rule. Those who have the gold, rule." Hurwitz's cynical twist on the proverbial Golden Rule, which dictates
that one should treat others as one would like to be treated, became
shorthand for an oft-told morality tale in the popular press about the
conflict between Wall Street and local environmentalists over the fate
of Headwaters Forest. Hurwitz's words also encapsulated the history of
California forestry regulation to that point. Until 1971, state law officially granted the timber industry the authority to regulate itself to
maximize timber production. Those with the gold did indeed rule. Even
after the courts destroyed official corporatism, a de facto regime of self-
regulation endured. By the time Hurwitz orchestrated the takeover of
the Pacific Lumber Company and uttered his infamous phrase, the long
struggle over the limits of industrial logging and corporate prerogative
had finally begun to favor local environmentalists. The two-decade-
long citizen assault on the state's commitment to production-oriented
logging practices and its deference to timber companies was critical to
loosening Wall Street's grip on California forests.[1]

The Redwood Wars and the modern environmental movement
were products of the myriad social and economic transformations
in postwar America. The housing boom and the dramatic growth of

American economic power, the growing awareness of ecology and environmental degradation, and the unfolding rights revolution all exacerbated existing tensions in Redwood Country. Nationally, the liberal federal government largely assisted citizen activists in their efforts to expand voting rights, political rights, and the right to a healthy environment. Congress passed the Wilderness Act in 1964, which created a statutory system of protected wilderness areas on the nation's public lands. It followed with the National Environmental Policy Act in 1969, which required federal agencies to methodically review projects and to make plans reducing environmental degradation. Those successes, combined with disasters such as the 1969 Santa Barbara oil spill and the combustion of the Cuyahoga River in Ohio, inspired activists to demand further governmental action to protect ecosystems and public health. Business interests had a different agenda. They wanted to be able to capitalize on global economic trends to maximize near-term profits. Environmentally, that meant businesses wanted unfettered access to the trees and other resources of the West. In response, environmentalists worked to set aside land for new national parks, monuments, and wilderness areas, and to pass the Endangered Species Act, the Clean Air Act, and the Clean Water Act, among a host of new laws in the 1970s. The activists wanted to erect a bulwark protecting the nation's landscapes, resources, air, and water from destruction at the hands of industrial and increasingly extralocal, multinational firms. Company leaders responded in kind, fighting new regulations, moving operations, and waging public relations campaigns. A political tug-of-war thus developed over the modern environmental regime, and Redwood Country was pulled in.[2]

In 1960, Gilded Age and Progressive Era traditions still dominated industrial politics and conflict, but those traditions would not hold for much longer. Workers in discrete factories and industries still wanted to negotiate with, and sometimes fight, corporate executives and owners over pay, benefits, and hours. The government still acted as an arbiter and as a regulator determining best practices. However, the corporate world, spurred by a new phase of conglomeration, was changing dramatically in ways that undermined the old order. By 1986, the United States was in the early stages of globalization, when resources and industries flow more easily toward the highest rates of immediate return, diffusing the geographic centers of power and unmooring traditional industrial conflict. The Redwood Wars straddled those two eras: one dominated by Fordist production and site-specific struggle, the other by geographically decentralized industry and battles over corporate power more generally. Battles in Redwood Country retained characteristics of both eras due to the geographic immobility of the timber industry's primary inventory—redwoods—as well as some of the firms' deep roots on the North Coast. Thus, while labor unions and rain forest activists struggled to gain their footing in the era of globalization, North Coast activists held fast to the traditions of confrontation and negotiation that had originated in the Progressive Era in California, and they added new tools to their toolboxes as they became available. The Redwood Wars thus emerged because the North Coast timber industry entered the world of global capitalism, and activists, animated by a deep concern for ecological health, repeatedly attempted to circumscribe the timber industry's private property prerogatives.[3]

THE RUPTURE

The postwar reemergence of national park proposals for the North Coast helped blow apart the stable, patrician politics of redwood preservationists and timber operators. The Redwood National Park campaign was but one reaction to increased logging in the West, yet the campaign cultivated a new culture of mistrust and hostility between activists and the timber industry on the North Coast. As a result of that mind-set, whenever activists subsequently pressed for further restrictions or regulations, the timber industry pushed back with great force. Elsewhere in the West, conflict emerged over the management of public lands. The proposal for a redwood park was particularly vexing, however, because it required condemnation of private land, challenging nearly three centuries of expansive private property rights. Thus, before the command-and-control pollution regulations of the 1970s drew the ire of manufacturing industries, conflict over land management galvanized extractive industries, establishing the patterns and precedents utilized by later opponents of environmental regulation. The battles over Dinosaur Monument, Echo Park, the expansion of Olympic National Park, and the creation of wilderness areas in the Pacific Northwest forced timber and development companies to devise strategies and tactics to resist environmental protection well before the passage of the National Environmental Policy Act and the other environmental protection laws of the 1970s. Industry warned of economic catastrophes, massive job losses, and the destruction of small rural towns if resources were "locked up." Those were the same arguments and strategies employed by manufacturing interests during the 1970s in response to the erection of the modern environmental protection regime laws.[4]

The 1960s campaign to create Redwood National Park exemplified the evolution of the national park system as well as the increasing hostility between environmentalists and resource extraction companies. As best articulated by historian Alfred Runte, the national park system developed in three overlapping stages: the protection of grand scenery, the development of public recreational parks, and the preservation of ecosystems. The earliest parks, including Yosemite, Yellowstone, Mount Rainier, Glacier, and Sequoia, were designed to protect majestic landscapes from the encroachment of industry and development, and to avoid the degradation and national humiliation that had occurred at Niagara Falls after it was overrun by the tourism industry. The park boundaries encompassed only those areas deemed economically unviable for natural resource extraction. After World War I, partly as a result of losing Hetch Hetchy Valley, activists promoted parks as economically beneficial tourist and recreational sites. By the 1930s, some activists began to look to parks as places to protect ecosystems, watersheds, and wildlife. The Everglades was the first attempt at such a system; Redwood National Park and Olympic National Park followed. Ecological and wilderness preservation concerns combined to open up more landscapes to possible protection than in the past, threatening industrial access to the nation's natural resources. Redwood preservation nicely fit into the first, "majestic" stage of national park priorities, and the additional ecological priorities enhanced the potential value of a redwood park.[5]

The actions of the timber industry during the fight over Redwood National Park galvanized a frayed environmental community in California. During the 1960s, the Sierra Club, led by Dr. Edgar Wayburn, resuscitated the idea of a redwood national park, and Wayburn doggedly pressed his case for eight years. At the 1961 Sierra Club Wilderness

Conference, Wayburn and his wife, Peggy, who had written the seminal article about the Bull Creek devastation in the 1950s, requested that secretary of the interior Stewart Udall and President John F. Kennedy purchase enough private redwood forest to create a Redwood National Park. In 1962, the Sierra Club decreed that any new park should encompass the greatest number of acres possible and not simply focus on protecting the tallest trees, because it was the old-growth redwood ecosystem that needed protection.[6]

The California Highway Commission unintentionally boosted the Sierra Club's efforts in 1963 when it announced plans to expand Highway 101 through Prairie Creek Redwoods State Park, turning the road into a freeway. The park hugs the coast through the northern part of Humboldt County, abutting what is now Redwood National Park to its east. Prairie Creek contains the famous Fern Canyon, which connects an ancient redwood and Sitka spruce forest with the Pacific Ocean. In 1963, the Highway Commission proposed two alternative freeway designs. The first option ran along the coast, separating Prairie Creek from the beach. The second option expanded the existing scenic byway that cut through the park, further fragmenting the meadows and main redwood groves of the park, both used daily by a massive herd of Roosevelt elk as it grazed from meadow to beach. Both options were problematic for the Sierra Club and its allies, especially the Ford Foundation, which had donated money to Save the Redwoods League to purchase Gold Bluffs Beach—the section of beach that the first alternative would have covered in pavement. The foundation subsequently pressured President Lyndon Johnson to convince Governor Pat Brown to stop the proposed project. Secretary of the interior Stewart Udall then directed the National Park Service to investigate two potential national park sites: one at Mill Creek and the other at Redwood Creek. The Mill Creek site sat between Prairie Creek and Jedediah Smith Redwoods State Parks, almost due north of Prairie Creek Park. The Mill Creek site, in Del Norte County, was remote and filled with giant alluvial flat redwood trees. Prairie Creek is a tributary of Redwood Creek, and the Redwood Creek site abutted Prairie Creek Park to its south and west. Rather than a grove of exquisite giant redwoods, the Redwood Creek site occupied a more or less unlogged watershed.[7]

Save the Redwoods League bristled at the Sierra Club's reengagement in redwood park issues. It had been negotiating with Pacific Lumber for land along the Eel River near Bull Creek, completing the acquisitions for Humboldt State Redwoods Park and the Avenue of the Giants. Those negotiations were critical to the league's vision for the Humboldt park; they didn't want to make the timber company anxious, and they believed condemning private land for a park would produce great anxiety. Save the Redwoods continued to believe that private citizens should take the initiative to protect redwoods. The Sierra Club, by contrast, insisted that the federal government was obligated to protect the public interest, and they thought a national park would define redwood preservation as a national interest. And the national interest was not just invested in parks. The wilderness movement, critical of what they saw as overdevelopment of the parks, found great public interest in creating wilderness reserves. The Sierra Club found value in both parks and wilderness. Save the Redwoods League, like the Sierra Club, agreed that parks were in the public interest, and when a national redwood park became a legitimate possibility, it engaged in the process to make sure any national park contained the "best" trees while disrupting industrial cooperation as little as possible. However, the league was not as eager as the Sierra Club for a national park.[8]

Initially, the goals of the Sierra Club and Save the Redwoods were incompatible. Save the Redwoods League was still stuck in the old monumental park paradigm. In September 1964, the Park Service proposed a thirty-thousand- to fifty-thousand-acre park located around Redwood Creek, abutting Prairie Creek Park. The league had pushed for the location near Mill Creek because of its wide alluvial flats and grand grove of very tall trees, and because the Mill Creek site was smaller and more removed from the major corporate landholders of the North Coast. Thus a Mill Creek site might cost less and was less likely to raise the hackles of the biggest timber companies. The Sierra Club had pushed for the Redwood Creek location because the area contained a much larger ancient forest covering a diverse biological and geological range. However, the club had proposed a ninety-thousand-acre park, so they were not satisfied with the Park Service proposal either. The disagreement over the location of a national park was only the beginning of tensions between the Sierra Club and the league, however.

The Sierra Club's commitment to watershed and ecosystem protection and Save the Redwoods's preference for quiet diplomacy that would not alienate business and industry leaders created an awkward situation for Congress and the Johnson administration. After the 1964 Park Service report, the club organized students and professors at Humboldt College (now Humboldt State University) to write letters in support of the Redwood Creek site. The Sierra Club also ran advertisements in newspapers across the country and even procured a desk for Sierra Club activist Michael McCloskey in Rep. Jeffery Cohelan's office to work on writing a park bill. Save the Redwoods League, meanwhile, relied on the influence of Laurance Rockefeller and other prominent individuals to shape the park bill. The Sierra Club was using the populist tools it had developed in the wake of the Hetch Hetchy and Dinosaur conflicts, and it called upon the public to bolster the efforts of organizational leaders who lobbied and negotiated in the halls of the legislature. This disturbed the league, which believed genteel discussions, not mass protest, provided the best results for the redwoods and society.

In 1966, after two years of cajoling by President Johnson and study by the National Park Service, the Senate and House separately introduced bills to create a forty-thousand-acre park at the Mill Creek site. The Sierra Club was stunned. President Johnson and the National Park Service had proposed a park containing both the Mill Creek and Redwood Creek sites. The Sierra Club publicly accused Save the Redwoods and the timber industry of colluding to reverse Park Service policy in backroom negotiations. Most major environmental groups, along with the United Auto Workers, supported the Sierra Club's position, and it appeared that an ugly round of redwood infighting might threaten the legislation altogether. To make matters worse for the league and the bill's proponents, the timber industry opposed both park plans because companies believed they could earn a higher financial return by logging the areas and milling the timber. Eventually, it was the Sierra Club that killed the bills through another backroom deal: convincing its allies in Congress to attach an amendment to the Mill Creek bill that substituted the ninety-thousand-acre plan at Redwood Creek for the Mill Creek plan. With no clear legislative path forward and no united constituency, the bill died.[9]

In the aftermath, the North Coast timber industry reacted rashly, however, inadvertently assisting Sierra Club efforts to create a much more expansive Redwood National Park. Miller Redwood Company, which owned the property adjacent to Jedediah Smith Redwoods State Park, including the Mill Creek site, quickly began to log the area to make it less desirable as a park. They clear-cut a swath of their property all the way to the boundary of Jedediah Smith Park, then harvested a strip of trees right through the middle of the proposed Mill Creek site. Miller then logged a circle around the entire Mill Creek site. The clear-cuts dramatically reduced the size of the contiguous forest Save the Redwoods League wanted protected, making it less desirable as a potential park site. More importantly, the aggressive actions convinced the league and officials in the federal government that the North Coast timber industry could not be trusted. To make matters worse for the timber industry, Georgia-Pacific began logging near the Redwood Creek site. It appeared that the North Coast companies were hell-bent on derailing any discussion of creating a national redwood park, and disgusted, the league announced it would no longer oppose the Redwood Creek site.

The vindictive actions of the two timber companies increased President Johnson's leverage in Congress, as it looked like the industry was putting self-interest above the public interest. As a result, President Johnson's plea to "save the redwoods" during his 1968 State of the Union address was met with greater enthusiasm. Congress worked quickly that year, and with the help of the Sierra Club, it passed a Redwood National Park authorization bill before year's end. On October 2, 1968, Johnson signed the law authorizing Congress to condemn the land and then compensate four timber companies for fifty-eight thousand acres of forest at the Redwood Creek site and some of the Del Norte County land originally proposed near Mill Creek. Together with Jedediah Smith, Del Norte, and Prairie Creek Redwoods State Parks, the redwood park complex totaled eighty-five thousand acres of contiguous redwood forest straddling the coastal region along the Humboldt–Del Norte border. The authorization was the beginning of a long collaboration between the state and federal governments regarding redwood parks. By 2004, the redwood park complex covered 133,000 acres, including the original Mill Creek site. The federal and state governments retain separate ownership of their respective parklands, but they jointly manage the parks as one unit. However, as would be the case with many battles in the Redwood Wars, nobody was fully satisfied. Environmentalists bemoaned the clear-cuts around Mill Creek; the timber industry chafed at the federal confiscation and acquisition of so much acreage of private property; and timber workers feared logging and milling jobs would disappear as a result of the reduction in the region's commercial timberland. Most problematic in the long run was Congress's invention of the "legislative taking" of land. Timber companies feared that the days of negotiating land deals as willing sellers were over, and they worried that they wouldn't receive just compensation in future deals. A climate of mistrust was growing on the North Coast.[10]

TORN APART

While the fight over Redwood National Park played out on the national stage, California residents had begun to challenge the very nature of industrial logging and its environmental impacts. The inability or unwillingness of the California Board of Forestry to accommodate the public's growing desire to consider the noneconomic value of the forest would lead directly to citizen actions that repealed the 1945 Forest Practice Act and transform the Board of Forestry itself. The demise of the Forest Practice Act began in 1969, far from the North Coast, when Bayside Timber Company obtained a logging permit from the Board of Forestry for its property in San Mateo County, near a residential neighborhood. Downslope residents in the Skylonda neighborhood objected to the logging plan because of projected erosion and watershed damage, fire hazards, traffic congestion, and the destruction of the neighborhood's scenic beauty. Some residents organized the Skylonda-Skywood Citizens Committee and successfully pressured the County Board of Supervisors to reject Bayside's road-building permit.

Bayside Timber subsequently sued the county to overturn the rejection of its permit, but in 1971 the First District Court of Appeals in California affirmed the county's right to block the proposed logging plan. Bayside Timber had argued that the 1945 Forest Practices Act clearly granted the Board of Forestry the authority to regulate timber operations. Counties, they argued, had no jurisdiction when it came to timber harvests. The First District Court decided the county did have the authority to approve permits within its political boundaries, not because they were imbued with any superior authority but because the court deemed the 1945 Forest Practice Act unconstitutional and thus devoid of any authority. The court ruled that the act violated the state constitution because it delegated legislative authority to "persons pecuniarily interested in the timber industry." In essence, the court ruled that industrial self-regulation was no longer a legitimate form of policy making. Official corporatism thus died at the hands of the justice system; citizens had begun the first serious efforts to curtail the property rights of timber companies.[11]

The court identified two main problems with the 1945 law, despite recent amendments. First, the law mandated timber industry domination of the Board of Forestry; three of the five board members had to come from the timber industry, one from the grazing industry, and one from the general public. Second, all forest practice rules were to be approved by two-thirds of the timber owners in any forest district before being finalized by the Board of Forestry. Those two requirements established a system giving the industry the power to legislate in its own financial interest. While the *Bayside* case was working its way to appeal in 1970, the legislature attempted to head off the court and fix the self-regulation problem by expanding the board to seven members. The additional two members were to come from the general public and have "an interest in and knowledge of the environment." The court noted that the additional board members did not change the fact that two-thirds of a district's private timber owners had to approve all forest practice rules and again declared the 1945 law unconstitutional. The legislature began to work on a new law. North Coast timber operators were "stunned" and prepared themselves for a "bitter legal and legislative fight over who should manage the state's timber resources," in the words of *Times Standard* reporter Dan Walters. That battle did come, and it lasted more than thirty years.[12]

As the first successful attack on the Board of Forestry and the industry's independence—and on the dominance of development-focused corporatism—the *Bayside* decision marks the beginning of citizen activism to overhaul California's forestry regime. Previously, the Sierra Club and Save the Redwoods League had largely focused on removing land from timber production, as had groups working nationally. Park enthusiasts worked to create parks out of wild areas, and wilderness activists worked to designate roadless areas off limits to all development. In California, *Bayside* opened the door for the state to manage timber operations, thus expanding the definition of public interest in the state's forests located on private land. That possibility threatened a century of corporate practice and tradition.[13]

The legislation that resulted from these new legal circumstances, the Forest Practice Act of 1973, ushered in a new era of private land management in California just as the National Environmental Policy Act had on public lands nationally. A bipartisan effort in the California legislature designed the new law to shift the state's policy away from development-first corporatism and toward resource conservation and public oversight. The 1972 and 1973 legislature took up the issue of forestry regulation in what the *Los Angeles Times* called a "basic philosophic tug-of-war." The question, as the paper saw it, was "whether the public interest in California's 8 million acres of privately owned timberland takes precedent over private property rights." In early 1973, the California Senate unanimously approved a bill offered by Republican John A. Nejedly, who claimed that "[we went] as far as we can go in regulation of private property." The California Assembly reviewed a bill offered by Democrat Edwin L. Z'berg requiring timber operators to put up a performance bond before logging, in addition to the increased citizen and agency oversight measures included in the Nejedly bill. Environmental groups, such as the Sierra Club and the powerful state-based citizen group the Planning and Conservation League, negotiated with the legislature and the industry throughout the spring to develop a compromise bill both houses would approve.[14]

The legislature did pass a bill, and it had the support of Governor Reagan, the timber industry, and the Sierra Club. The new law reflected the newfound power of environmental groups and an environmental science opposed to development-oriented land management. The Forest Practice Act was based on a 1972 report to the California Assembly recommending a system of "resource conservation standards to protect watersheds and ecological values." The law charged the California Department of Forestry (CDF) with creating forest practice rules to end the depletion of timber resources, thereby "giving consideration to values relating to recreation, watershed, wildlife, range and forage, fisheries, regional economic vitality, employment and aesthetic enjoyment." The law also required timber companies to submit a Timber Harvest Plan before any new logging, and to allow the Department of Fish and Game and the Regional Water Quality Control Boards to comment on the plans. The new act also reconstituted the Board of Forestry to include five members from the public, three from the forest products industries, and one from the livestock industry, a move meant to break the timber industry's grip on the board. The new law thus imposed greater agency oversight of the state's timber operations and demanded that timberlands be managed with an eye toward sustainable logging practices and the protection of ecological health.[15]

The most important sections of the new law provided greater citizen oversight of the Timber Harvest Plan process. The new legislation mandated public review of Timber Harvest Plans before final approval, and it allowed citizens to challenge agency decisions in court. The model was not new. The Wilderness Act of 1964, the National Environmental Policy Act (NEPA), the federal Clean Air Act and Clean Water Act amendments of 1970 and 1972 also afforded citizens the opportunity to participate in public hearings to review agency decisions. NEPA and the antipollution laws also gave citizens the right to seek redress in court. Indeed, these citizen participation clauses were among the most important legislative developments of the environmental era, and they in turn encouraged increased citizen activism. In California, the citizen suit provision of the Forest Practice Act specifically allowed citizens to sue both the Department of Forestry and the Board of Forestry to obtain judicial review of administrative decisions. Additionally, the state Code of Civil Procedure granted citizens the right to challenge discretionary agency actions.

Because the new law marked a dramatic transformation of California timber regulation, environmental groups, the Board of Forestry, and the industry would battle repeatedly over the implementation of the new regulations. Nationally, environmental groups, industries, and agencies also fought over similar issues with respect to NEPA and its relationship to the Clean Water Act, the Clean Air Act, the National Forest Management Act, and the Endangered Species Act, among a host of new environmental laws. National environmental groups used the new laws to challenge clear-cutting in the Monongahela National Forest and to forestall development on public lands in Alaska in order to force agencies to fulfill their obligations to environmental health. The Redwood Wars also contributed to the ongoing transformation of the relationships among citizens, businesses, and the government, leading to the recognition that private actions on private lands have public impacts and costs that need to be mitigated.[16]

Environmental activists eagerly embraced these new tools of citizen participation and were able to aggressively use the citizen suit provisions because, contrary to federal environmental cases, standing—being recognized as having a legitimate claim for the courts to judge—never became an issue in California. The California courts had long recognized an exception to the specific economic injury/interest test for cases involving a "public right . . . to procure the enforcement of a public duty." That is, the public had the right to seek redress when an official neglected his or her duty under the law whether or not the official's actions had any direct economic impact on the plaintiff. Whereas federal courts typically demanded that plaintiffs demonstrate actual harm to themselves arising from government decisions, there was a tradition in California courts to grant citizens standing if an agency neglected its duties, on the basis that neglecting public duties constituted an injury to the public interest. The new system gave rise to a fierce legal and political battle over control of forestry policies and California's last unprotected ancient redwood forests.[17]

SKIRMISHES

The Board of Forestry, like its federal counterparts at the US Forest Service who were urgently "getting the cut out" on the nation's public lands, largely resisted its new responsibilities during the 1970s, and citizens continued to challenge the state's corporatist tradition. Californians were not unique; citizen groups around the nation were enthusiastically challenging federal agency actions under NEPA. In fact, the federal courts had *completed* 332 NEPA cases by 1975, which accounted for only half of the active NEPA cases at the time. Among those concluded cases was a citizen challenge of the US Atomic Energy Commission's plans to build a nuclear power plant at Calvert Cliffs along Chesapeake Bay and the Wilderness Society's challenge of the Trans-Alaska oil pipeline—both victories for environmentalists. Laws such as NEPA and the California Environmental Quality Act (CEQA) had granted citizens around the nation new power with respect to land management and environmental policy. CEQA, like NEPA, required state agencies to reduce the environmental impacts of development and resource extraction by requiring developers to submit detailed studies of potential projects and an evaluation of all possible mitigations. Both laws required public agencies to consult the public before approving development projects. Behind the Redwood Curtain as well, citizens used the courts to influence timberland management.[18]

National groups kept an eye on Redwood National Park after its creation, placing environmentalists on a collision course with the corporatist tradition in California and the resistance of state agencies and timber companies. In 1973, over the objections of the National Park Service, the Board of Forestry approved a clear-cutting plan in the Redwood Creek watershed above the national park, declaring that Arcata National Corporation's clear-cut would not harm the park. The Natural Resources Defense Council, in line with their federal efforts to clarify and enforce NEPA, sued the state forester and Arcata National, arguing the plan did not adequately consider environmental harm as mandated by CEQA, which required environmental impact studies prior to state agency actions that might cause significant environmental impacts. The law also required that state agencies propose mitigations for environmental impacts. Arcata National argued that CEQA guidelines did not apply to Timber Harvest Plans because plan approval was a ministerial duty of the Board of Forestry, not a discretionary action. In essence, Arcata National argued that approving a Timber Harvest Plan was not a matter of judging the appropriateness of the plan, but rather of ensuring that the proper paperwork was filed. The timber company was essentially asserting that the corporatist tradition of industry self-regulation remained intact despite the contrary approach taken in the new laws passed since the 1969 *Bayside* ruling. Judge Arthur Broaddus of the Superior Court disagreed with the timber company and ruled in 1975 that approving Timber Harvest Plans was a discretionary action and thus governed by CEQA. He further ruled that the content of the contested Arcata National harvest plans failed to fulfill CEQA's Environmental Impact Report requirement. Development-focused corporatism received another major blow when Arcata National's 1976 appeal of Judge Broaddus's ruling failed. However, some damage had already been done, as Arcata National and other landowners had been clear-cutting areas upstream of the park since its creation.[19]

As they had after the Bull Creek floods in the 1950s, park supporters began to pressure Congress to expand Redwood National Park. The Sierra Club had originally argued that a ninety-thousand-acre park surrounding Redwood Creek was necessary to protect the watershed. Part of that assessment was based on an understanding that the giant redwoods of Bull Creek had fallen because of upslope and upstream clear-cuts outside Humboldt Redwoods State Park. The Sierra Club had thus proposed to include most of the Redwood Creek watershed in its park proposal. After 1973, it appeared the Board of Forestry was willing to allow the redwoods along Redwood Creek to suffer the same fate as those on the Bull Creek alluvial flats. Indeed, soil and silt were washing into the park, threatening to choke the roots of the redwoods along the creek bottom. With the *Arcata* case offering a brief reprieve from logging around the park, activists worked to convince Congress to acquire a huge swath of land surrounding the park. In 1978, President Jimmy Carter signed a legislative takings bill for forty-eight thousand acres of the Redwood Creek watershed, reducing the inventory of old-growth redwoods available to harvest by 15 percent. Workers were anxious, and with good reason. President Carter was also concerned, noting that he signed the bill because he believed it ecologically important, but he did not think Congress had included enough provisions for the workers who would lose work as a result. Although redwood preservationists had won the battle, the cost was high in terms of timber industry animosity and mistrust.[20]

By the end of 1978, new patterns were developing on the North Coast that contributed to the escalation of hostility and the emergence of redwood politics that were more adversarial than genteel. Activists had started to use the court system and new environmental protection laws to block logging and development in sensitive habitats. The courts sided with the activists. For the most part, timber companies resisted the laws and court orders. They scrambled to line up traditional allies and economic arguments in their defense, hoping to break their string of losses in court.

New patterns were also emerging nationwide. Across the United States, the timber industry was in combat mode from the *Monongahela* case, when the federal courts had banned clear-cutting in nine Appalachian national forests. The Organic Act of 1897, which defined how national forests would be managed, stated that only mature or dead trees could be cut down, and the trees had to be individually marked. When clear-cutting, logging companies take out all trees in an area regardless of marking, size, or health. The court therefore ruled that clear-cutting violated the provisions of the Organic Act. In response, Congress passed the National Forest Management Act of 1976, which allowed clear-cutting in national forests in exchange for detailed long-range management plans to prevent habitat loss and environmental damage. Despite that legislative victory, timber executives and workers felt under siege. Corporate leaders were concerned that the state was unilaterally transforming the industry's business models. Workers worried that the state, at the behest of environmentalists, was taking away their jobs. To make matters worse, activists convinced President Carter to issue an executive order to protect millions of acres of public land in Alaska from logging and development, further enraging the industry. The timber industry in California did not intend to suffer similar setbacks in Redwood Country, and it prepared for a fight.[21]

It was the Board of Forestry's continued resistance to its duties under CEQA and the nonmarket mandates of the Forest Practice Act, however, that encouraged citizens to continue their legal challenges to corporatism. In 1978, Sonoma County residents Francine Gallegos and Louise Patterson, along with fellow residents of Camp Meeker, sued the Board of Forestry to overturn its approval of a Chenoweth Lumber Company harvest plan. The residents were worried that logging upslope and upstream of their neighborhood would produce erosion and mudslides. In that sense, the court case was similar to the earlier *Bayside* and *Arcata* cases. The California Department of Health had, in fact, previously concluded that the harvest plan would "threat[en] . . . the quantity and quality of water in the Camp Meeker area." Accordingly, the California Department of Forestry, which was supervised by the Board of Forestry and tasked with carrying out Board of Forestry policy, rejected the harvest plan. However, Chenoweth appealed directly to the Board of Forestry to overrule the decision of the Department of Forestry. The Board of Forestry sided with the logging company and approved the plan.

Then the courts stepped in. The district court ruled in favor of the Board of Forestry, but the California Court of Appeals sided with the Sonoma activists in 1978 and overturned the lower court's ruling. During the appeal, Chenoweth argued that CEQA did not apply to harvest plans, just as Arcata National had unsuccessfully argued during the Redwood Creek case in 1973, presumably hoping a new judge would sever CEQA from the Forest Practices Act and the industry would no longer need to concern itself with environmental studies. The appellate judges, however, following the precedent set in the *Arcata* case, ruled again that CEQA requirements applied to Timber Harvest Plans. The ruling additionally reinforced two more CEQA standards on harvest plans that previous courts had not specified. First, the court found that the content of the Board of Forestry approval notice had not adequately responded to citizen comments on the harvest plan. CEQA requires that California agencies respond to public comments, with their analysis backed by "substantial evidence." Second, the court demanded that the Board of Forestry respond *in writing* to public comments regarding significant environmental impacts of a harvest plan. The *Gallegos* case, a victory for redwood activists, nonetheless demonstrated the strength of the Board of Forestry's corporatist tradition. North Coast timber companies would continue to appeal directly to the Board of Forestry on controversial harvest plans, and citizens would continue to challenge de facto corporatism in court.[22]

Together, the *Gallegos* and *Arcata* decisions provided the foundation for nearly all subsequent citizen challenges of Timber Harvest Plans. The two rulings required harvest plans to fully comply with CEQA, including consultation with relevant agencies, implementation of feasible alternatives and mitigation, public notification of harvest plans, and completion of reasoned written responses to public comments. The Department of Forestry, the Board of Forestry, and the timber industry resisted the mandates, but citizen groups sued to force compliance with the laws and court precedents. It was through these new legal channels that local citizens eroded the Board of Forestry's corporatist orientation, forcing the board several times to step away from its traditional alliance with the timber industry in the late 1980s and 1990s, most notably regarding the Pacific Lumber Company and the battle over Headwaters Forest.[23]

THE REDWOOD WARS IN EARNEST

By the early 1980s, North Coast timber operators chafed at the new logging controls and at the increasing activity of citizen watchdogs. Citizen activists grew emboldened and agitated due to industrial logging practices and the intransigence of the Board of Forestry, Department of Forestry staff, and logging companies. Increasingly, groups of activists on the North Coast working on purely local environmental issues became the driving force opposing industrial power in the region, leading to violent eruptions of confrontation and hostility that formed the core of the Redwood Wars. The Board of Forestry remained committed to a mission of facilitating timber production and resisted its new duties as defined by the Forest Practice Act, the California Endangered Species Act, the California Environmental Quality Act, and the court precedents clarifying and enforcing those duties. The timber industry fought to maintain control over land management practices, and it experimented with various legal arguments to hold off the rising tide of regulation. When those legal tactics failed, the industry negotiated with the legislature to minimize regulations; when the legislative efforts failed, the industry leaned on its old ally, the Board of Forestry, to quickly approve Timber Harvest Plans in order to turn timber into lumber before the courts and the legislature could act.

For their part, environmental activists developed a comprehensive strategy that effectively thwarted the industry and the Board of Forestry's efforts to preserve de facto corporatism. Continuing what the Sierra Club had done in the 1950s with respect to timber practices in Redwood Country, the activists expanded and improved their legal campaign. The goal was to protect old-growth trees and to halt the unsustainable practices of the industry. The activists worked with the legislature to create new parks and to reform forestry practices, although the various citizen groups did not always work toward the same end.

Often, the North Coast activists opposed the Sierra Club's positions on forestry and park bills. And when groves were threatened with logging, the activists, picking up where Laura Mahan left off, "occupied" the groves and put their bodies in harm's way to physically prevent logging until a stay could be ordered by a local court.

Soon a predictable pattern emerged: A company would file a Timber Harvest Plan, and North Coast activists would challenge the plan during the Department of Forestry review process. Forestry would approve the plan, and activists would file a lawsuit to overturn the agency's approval. The company and the Board of Forestry would demur, though a local court would issue a temporary restraining order to stop the logging. That restraining order would expire before the trial began, and the timber company would send loggers to the harvest area. After discovering the logging activity, activists would run to the woods to physically prevent loggers from cutting. Law enforcement officers would then arrest the protesters, another restraining order would be granted, and a long trial and subsequent appeals would end in rejection of the harvest plan. However, the company would file another harvest plan, and the cycle would repeat over various harvest plans until either activists purchased the groves from the timber company or the company sold its land and mills, evacuating the North Coast. The pattern was first established in Mendocino County with Georgia-Pacific Lumber Company, after which activists challenged other companies on the North Coast, most notably the Pacific Lumber Company. The Redwood Wars grew out of frequent repetition of that pattern from the late 1970s through the end of the century.

Although the Sierra Club, instrumental in the fights over Redwood National Park, continued to play a major role in California logging politics, the legal campaign to destroy the corporatist traditions of the Board of Forestry was largely driven by a small group of North Coast residents. The activists were committed to sustainable forestry and ecological values, and they were decidedly uninterested in state or national politics or citizen groups. That cadre included Humboldt and Mendocino residents Robert Sutherland, Richard Gienger, Sharon Duggan, Ruthanne Cecil, and other activists, who established the Environmental Protection Information Center (EPIC) in 1977 in southern Humboldt County. One of the earliest environmental groups on the

North Coast, EPIC became the unquestioned leader of the litigation campaign attacking California corporatism.[24]

The founders of EPIC were part of a cohort that had migrated to the North Coast in the late 1960s and early 1970s. Many of the new residents were Bay Area refugees escaping the crumbling counterculture scene and the increasingly volatile politics of the Vietnam War era. Committed to ecological values and social justice, they often adopted back-to-the-land lifestyles, and they forever changed redwood politics. Like local activists of the early century, many of the new residents were willing to challenge tradition, and they brought movement experience and a clearly defined ideology to the North Coast.

Activism seemed to come easily to Richard Gienger, who grew up in New York and was an avid hiker and canoer. He graduated with a master's in architecture from the University of Pennsylvania and moved to the North Coast in 1971 with his wife, Ilona "Noni" Chalfa, whom he met in Philadelphia, to work as an apprentice homebuilder with Whitethorn Construction. The company went bankrupt, and Richard and Noni moved to the Lost Coast to homestead. The Lost Coast is the most isolated coastline in California. It stretches more than twenty-five miles across the Mendocino-Humboldt border and includes the Kings Range. The steep geography makes highways and major roads impractical, so the famous Highway 1 cuts inland when it reaches the southern edge of the Lost Coast, joining Highway 101 inland. The small towns in the area, including Shelter Cove and Whitethorn, are isolated and remote. In 1973, Gienger and Noni moved into an electricity-free cabin off a trail near Whale Gulch on the Pacific Coast.

Gienger's involvement in redwood politics and work with EPIC was a direct result of the location of his cabin. The Wolf Creek Timber Company had owned the land along the Lost Coast until Boise Cascade purchased the property in the early 1970s. Boise Cascade began to log the coast from the Usal Basin up to the Mattole watershed. Before the company finished logging, Georgia-Pacific purchased the land, walking straight into a hornets' nest. In 1975, the state had purchased the Bar Harbor Ranch near Gienger's cabin and held hearings on a potential Sinkyone Wilderness Park, named after a local tribe of Native Americans. Gienger was enthusiastic about the park idea. He conducted stream surveys and used his design skills to repair watersheds with log jams and other architectural structures that mimicked the fallen logs and woody debris that a combination of clear-cutting and winter rains had removed from the Mattole and Eel River watersheds. Concerned about Georgia-Pacific logging plans, local mountain residents, especially Gienger, organized dozens of people to petition California State Park and Recreation Commission to create a park along the Lost Coast. In part the activists looked to landscape preservation as a means to preserve aesthetic and spiritual resources. The homesteaders also wanted to prevent industrial forestry from encroaching on their countercultural refuge and homesteading livelihoods. As the homesteaders organized, conflict with Georgia-Pacific and other timber companies boiled over, pulling in other North Coast residents.[25]

Robert Sutherland, like Gienger, moved to the North Coast in a search for a more rural and peaceful life. Sutherland grew up in Cleveland, Ohio, and Saint Louis, Missouri, the son of Nobel Laureate Earl W. Sutherland. Sutherland went to art school in Cleveland, though he was also interested in science like his father, and those combined interests led him to California and eventually to the North Coast. After art school, Sutherland moved to New York City to work at the Natural History Museum, eventually becoming the conservation chair of the Linnaean Society of New York. He moved to San Francisco in 1966 after a visit during which he "noticed that his friends were looking healthier and happier" than when they had lived in New York. Upon his arrival in San Francisco, Sutherland organized a commune on Oak Street in the Haight-Ashbury district, and subsequently got involved in the music and political scene of the Haight, organizing concerts in Golden Gate Park. As Sutherland told it, he then "got burned out on LSD and trying to keep the scenes together in the Haight" after amphetamine use disrupted ties in the community. Thus, in 1968 Sutherland began exploring new places to live and new opportunities for community organizing.

The North Coast, with its small core of Bay Area refugees and rich biodiversity, suited Sutherland's tastes, and he settled in Humboldt in 1973. One of his first acts on the North Coast was to begin referring to himself as the Man Who Walks in the Woods, an act of defiance against middle-class culture. The name also described what he liked to do with his time. His engagement with local politics grew out of his hikes. While hiking along the Mattole River, Sutherland—now known simply as Woods—spotted Western Timber Services workers rinsing out helicopter tanks used to spray herbicides directly into the river. Woods was already concerned about the effects of aerial herbicide applications on local organic gardens, and the hiking incident introduced a new concern about watersheds. According to Woods, he attempted to negotiate with the timber companies that used the helicopter service; though those negotiations failed, the timber companies eventually did stop spraying to avoid bad press. In 1977 the herbicide issue resurfaced, and this time Woods, Ruthanne Cecil, and others created an ad hoc group to respond to local environmental threats. A logger from Pacific Lumber, Jim DeMulling, proposed the name EPIC for their ad hoc group—an explicit, and positive, reference to socialist author Upton Sinclair's gubernatorial campaign during the Great Depression, which centered on a program called "End Poverty in California." Thus, the environmental group was imbued from the beginning with anti-corporate, countercultural values and an attitude of cooperation between activists and loggers. Richard Gienger, Marylee Bytheriver, and a host of others worked on herbicide and forestry issues from their bases in the EPIC offices. The new group flourished for about six months, during which time they built an herbicide education program for residents, worked with Oregon State University and the State of California to conduct pesticide tests in the area, and put together a lawsuit that ended aerial spraying of 2,4,5-T. The phenoxy hormone 2,4,5-T belongs to a group of chemicals widely used to kill trees and shrubs, and was found to contain dioxin, a known carcinogen and a component of Agent Orange. After the successful pesticide campaign, EPIC lay dormant for two years.[26]

Though his interests were always local, logging issues eventually dragged Woods into state politics and pushed EPIC to become the state's major forestry reform organization. Like New York transplant Richard Gienger, Woods wanted the Sinkyone region of the Lost Coast protected from logging and development to preserve his rural, countercultural life as well as the area's flora and fauna. Because park creation and logging regulations involved state agencies, the local activists were forced to engage state politics to protect their neighborhood. In 1980, Gienger and Gregory O'Brien approached Woods to reorganize EPIC.

Woods agreed, but only if he could incorporate EPIC as a permanent not-for-profit citizens' group with bylaws, tax-exempt status, and a board of directors. Woods envisioned a "workers' cooperative, not a group for hoity-toity middle class people to tell locals what to do" about local environmental issues, as he described it. His vision was something akin to an employee-owned factory that offered work to all the residents. He wanted the people who filed the paperwork and studied the proposed timber harvest plans to run EPIC, and he wanted everyone in the local community to be able to participate in the group's activities and management.[27]

The second incarnation of EPIC would become a powerful tool for local activists, and with the help of Earth First! and the Sierra Club, it would shape redwood forestry practices and endangered species law. In 1981, EPIC was formally incorporated, guided by five organizational goals: to preserve critical old-growth forest habitats, to implement sustainable forestry practices across the North Coast, to create a sustainable local forest economy, to train the public to influence land management agencies, and to act as a clearinghouse on a wide variety of environmental issues as they arose. The local organization, based in the small town of Garberville (with a population of approximately two thousand), quickly developed into a major player in logging regulation by aggressively using the citizen suit provisions of CEQA and the Forest Practice Act to challenge logging practices. In doing so, EPIC paralleled the legal actions of national environmental groups, which increasingly turned to the courts in response to President Reagan's decreased enforcement of environmental laws. Unlike the national efforts, however, EPIC's work was built on a local vision of responsive government and sustainable communities intended to produce timber, jobs, and wildlife habitat in perpetuity. EPIC was not a group of affluent urban/suburban wilderness purists; it was composed of environmentalists who had largely come of age in the social justice movements of the 1960s. Their litigation efforts had state and national implications primarily because of the legal and political avenues available to the activists to pursue local change, not because they set out to change state or national law.[28]

When Lost Coast forest issues led EPIC to challenge the North Coast timber industry's forest practices in the early 1980s, the group's impact was immediately felt across the region. *EPIC v. Johnson*, the group's first lawsuit, was initiated in 1983, and resulted in a landmark appellate decision that further undermined de facto corporatism. The ruling also paved the way for much of the environmental community's forestry reform efforts in California, especially in the state's remaining unprotected and privately owned old-growth forests. The *Johnson* case challenged a seventy-five-acre harvest plan on Georgia-Pacific land in northern Mendocino County, near the Sinkyone Wilderness State Park. The Department of Forestry had approved the clear-cutting of an old-growth redwood grove that also happened to be the last remaining stand of trees on a slope leading down to the ocean. The *Johnson* case was not the Lost Coast community's first attempt to stop Georgia-Pacific from clear-cutting the area; it was the culmination of nearly a decade of tension over the northwest coast of Mendocino and the Sinkyone Wilderness State Park. The development of the conflict illuminates how the new migrants' ideas, strategies, and goals gradually came to dominate redwood politics.[29]

The battle over the Sinkyone and industrial liquidation logging began in the 1970s as a traditional redwoods park issue, but EPIC transformed it into a contest over forestry reform on private land. The decision marked a permanent shift in redwood politics. Locals had grown concerned about the state of North Coast forestry during the early 1970s, when Atlanta-based Georgia-Pacific acquired the Union Lumber Company of Mendocino County as well as surrounding family ranches in what locals referred to as an "unprecedented consolidation of land." During the mid-1970s, Richard Gienger and other activists had failed to convince the state to expand the Sinkyone Wilderness. Simultaneously, Georgia-Pacific was filing Timber Harvest Plans for its Lost Coast property, including a seven-mile stretch along the coast near Sinkyone. In March 1978, Georgia-Pacific began to clear-cut Jackass Creek and Anderson Gulch, small areas on the Lost Coast near the park. On the equinox, at the first Watershed Gathering, held at Needle Rock in the Sinkyone, the Sinkyone Council, headed by Richard Gienger, and EPIC, led by Woods, decided to organize locals to oppose logging in the area.[30]

The activists' first efforts hewed to the redwood political tradition of land acquisition. Since 1979, Richard Gienger had taken elected officials, including Assemblyman Doug Bosco and State Senator Barry Keene, on several field trips into the Sinkyone, where the groups visited the clear-cuts around Little Jackass Creek. In 1983, Gienger and Woods met up with freshman assemblyman Dan Hauser and his Boy Scout troop. The field trips into the forest revived the tradition John Muir had cultivated with President Theodore Roosevelt during the fight to protect Yosemite, when he took the president camping in the Sierras to convince him of the landscape's value. David Brower had resuscitated the field-trip tactic during the fight for Dinosaur Monument, taking political leaders on rafting trips to expose them to the canyon lands. The 1983 group that included Gienger, Woods, and Hauser hiked through the Sinkyone, as the activists pointed out damage to the watershed from recent logging. The field trip seems to have made a significant impact on the hikers: Hauser introduced a bill that legislative session to purchase the Georgia-Pacific Sinkyone property. Gienger spoke at the Assembly hearings for Hauser's bill and worked with the Sierra Club to push a Sinkyone bill onto the floor for a vote. The bill gave the state the right to lease a thousand-acre coastal strip from Georgia-Pacific to provide a hiking trail through the Sinkyone. The bill additionally authorized a land swap with the timber company. The firm would receive three hundred acres of timberland from the state plus $420,000 and a salvage logging permit for the leased coastal corridor. In exchange, the state would receive the company's Duffy Gulch property. The Sierra Club supported the bill as the best deal that could be achieved.[31]

However, Gienger and EPIC both opposed the bill, claiming that Hauser "got woodworked." The salvage logging permit in the bill effectively eliminated environmental protections for the coastal strip. They also believed the price was too high, as part of the purchase area had already been clear-cut during the political battle over park expansion. The activists' positions didn't matter, however. Governor George Deukmejian vetoed the bill because it had been loaded down with pet district projects and the governor had vowed to reduce spending during the recession of the early 1980s. Heading into the summer of 1983, the timber company and the activists remained uncertain about the fate of the Sinkyone region under Georgia-Pacific control.[32]

Despite the uncertainty, or maybe because of the uncertainty, Georgia-Pacific continued to pursue its plans to log Little Jackass Creek, and the Department of Forestry approved a Timber Harvest Plan for the area on September 2, 1983—an act that would eventually transform North Coast and American environmental politics. The North Coast activists, Georgia-Pacific, and the Board of Forestry all appear to have been primed for a showdown in Mendocino County that fall, each frustrated by the legislative process. In particular, EPIC and the Sinkyone Council had had enough of legislative wrangling and uncertainty. They prepared a much more aggressive strategy to challenge Georgia-Pacific's logging plans in Little Jackass Creek. Local environmentalists first wanted to rename the grove to fuel sentimentality for the watershed, judging that "Little Jackass Creek" failed to evoke the grandeur of a park. They decided on Sally Bell Grove. Sally Bell was one of the last living full-blooded Sinkyone Indians and a person familiar in local lore. When she was a small child, she witnessed the murder of her entire family by local whites at Needle Rock. The child herself narrowly escaped. She eventually married a local man named Tom Bell, and they lived on the Lost Coast for the rest of their lives. The grove, like the story, was dramatic. It was situated on a steep slope bound by the Pacific Ocean to the west and clear-cuts on the other three sides. The grove thus acted as the hill's "keystone" by anchoring the slope's soil and preventing it from washing into the ocean. The grove also contained a Native American archeological site that locals wanted to preserve.[33]

The naming of Sally Bell Grove set the North Coast activists apart from earlier practices of federal land agencies and wilderness advocates, who tended to erase Native American legacies. Traditional parks and wilderness areas were supposed to be free of human settlement. On the North Coast, activists embraced the legacy of the Sinkyone tribe, believing it enhanced the value of the stand of ancient trees. Naming the grove set a precedent: when a grove of redwoods was threatened, activists gave it an easily identifiable and relatable name. In the case of Sally Bell Grove, the name pointed to the cultural and natural heritage threatened by what activists saw as violence by Georgia-Pacific. During later battles with Pacific Lumber, activists would name dozens of groves in a similar fashion, evoking local creeks or charismatic fauna, including Headwaters and Murrelet Groves.

The activists then organized on-the-ground resistance to stop loggers from cutting down trees, and they prepared a legal response to any logging plans for the Sally Bell Grove. The on-the-ground resistance plan was developed in consultation with Earth First!, which had been created by Dave Foreman, Mike Roselle, and others to expand wilderness areas across the United States. Their vision included not only designating wilderness via the Wilderness Act but also reclaiming past wilderness areas by removing dams and grazing animals from public lands across the West. The founders of Earth First! were experienced organizers, and most had previously worked for a major national environmental group. Like the North Coast activists, the Earth First! founders were frustrated by the horse-trading in Washington, DC, which delayed wilderness protection and, in particular, reduced the scope of the Wilderness Act. Foreman wanted to create a group that would employ direct action to circumvent conventional political avenues. With its slogan "No compromise in defense of Mother Earth," Earth First! believed that the mainstream environmental groups, including the Wilderness Society and the Sierra Club, had grown too cozy with politicians, too willing to negotiate with big business, and too focused on Capitol Hill.[34]

To shock the political system into action on behalf of wilderness and wild places, Foreman and Earth First! decided to work directly in the wild lands at the points of production. Their strategy included direct action and media stunts à la Greenpeace of the early 1970s, but unlike Greenpeace, Earth First! also advocated "ecotage"—destroying the machines and tools used by workers to cut down trees, and even driving spikes into trees to make the forests immune to logging. For example, at Bald Mountain, Oregon, where activists wanted to stop timber companies from logging old-growth Douglas fir groves in 1983, Earth First! built roadblocks (some inanimate, some human), stood in front of chainsaws or in the path of partially downed trees, sabotaged equipment, and generally harassed loggers to prevent them from logging. The direct action was designed to cost the timber company money, slow logging efforts, attract the media, and allow time for the group's attorney to obtain a temporary restraining order that would prohibit logging until a court could hear the activists' challenge to the legality of the timber sale.[35]

What transpired on the North Coast in September and early October 1983 shows how litigation and direct action worked together. The actions and coordination also reveal the rural, communal, and political visions of the local activists. Woods had read about Earth First! actions in Oregon as well as the tree-hugging of the Chipko women in India—villagers who in the 1970s protested commercial logging of the forests that disrupted their food and fuel gathering. By the early 1980s, in response to expansion of the Chipko movement, the Indian government had imposed bans on the logging of live trees in the Himalayas. Woods became convinced that North Coast activists could combine litigation with direct action to "hit the donkey"—meaning the California Department of Forestry and the timber companies—enough to make it move. Woods invited Dave Foreman and Mike Roselle to visit the Sinkyone, and together with other Lost Coast area activists, they developed a plan to block logging near Sally Bell Grove. On September 2, CDF notified activists that logging was imminent. On September 8, the California Parks and Recreation Commission asked CDF to work with Save the Redwoods League and the Trust for Public Land to "preserve [the] critical area of Sally Bell/Jackass Creek." Meanwhile, EPIC raised $10,000 from the local community in preparation for a lawsuit against the California Department of Forestry, and on September 30 they filed a suit challenging the Sally Bell harvest plan.[36]

The lawsuit would take time, however, so the rest of the plan depended on North Coast activists placing their bodies between chainsaws and trees. On October 6, as Georgia-Pacific began logging in the groves, a sentry in the woods alerted EPIC. The Garberville Theater posted a notice on its marquee: "G-P Cutting Sinkyone. Help Now. EPIC." When the loggers arrived at the grove on the morning of October 7, they were greeted by nearly forty activists accompanied by Eureka television news crews. According to press accounts, the activists "hugged trees and positioned themselves so the giant redwoods could not be toppled without falling on them." The television crews filmed the arrival of the sheriff's office, and two dozen people were arrested for trespassing. The same day, a Santa Rosa judge issued a temporary restraining order preventing Georgia-Pacific from logging Sally Bell. The court ruling was only temporary, however, and the battle continued in the mountains of the Lost Coast. On October 24, thinking the restraining order expired, the company resumed logging in Sally Bell Grove. The logging crew showed up with fifty sheriffs, but their efforts were slowed by protestors. One woman, Mem Hill, was hit by a falling tree but survived. The court order was reinstated on October 25, after twenty-two people had been arrested for trespassing, including several activists who had surrounded a giant tree known as "Medicine Tree," just before the loggers could make their final cut.[37]

The *EPIC v. Johnson* trial challenging CDF's approval of the Sally Bell timber harvest was held in the midst of the action. EPIC faced long odds, but the group had a good litigation team working on its behalf. When Woods decided EPIC should sue CDF, he contacted former Ninth Circuit Court clerk Richard Jay Moller and experienced local attorney Michael Solomon to lead the litigation. Sharon Duggan, another local, advised the group and later joined the litigation team, beginning her long tenure working with EPIC's litigation efforts. Duggan was a North Coast native, and her interest in forestry litigation stemmed from a concern about the rapid changes in the landscape and forest health of the region. Duggan grew up while the local timber companies were selling their land to Georgia-Pacific and Louisiana-Pacific, which led to increased industrial timber operations, including greatly expanded clear-cuts and related watershed damage. Duggan wanted a healthy forest industry to provide stable long-term jobs for the community. Her father owned a tax service that catered to Pacific Lumber workers, so she and her family were committed to the stability of small towns like Scotia and Rio Dell. As a law student, Duggan had accompanied Gienger and Woods on the field trips that engaged Barry Keene, Doug Bosco, and Dan Hauser with the Sinkyone issue. She was thus the type of attorney Woods and Gienger felt they could trust to save Sally Bell Grove.

EPIC was concerned from the outset that it might not find an impartial judge to hear the case, given the power and reach of the timber companies. The group successfully moved the trial from Mendocino to Sonoma County, but it is unclear whether the move made things any better for EPIC. The courts recalled a retired judge to hear the case, who promptly fell asleep during Duggan's opening argument. The state was not taking the case seriously enough for the activists. To make matters worse, Georgia-Pacific hired Jared Carter, a former clerk for US Supreme Court justice William O. Douglas, former Stanford law professor, and former undersecretary of the interior for President Nixon—a man with clout in the courtroom. Probably without surprising anyone, on October 27, the judge ruled against EPIC, but he left the temporary logging ban in place, paving the way for EPIC to acquire a new logging ban from the Court of Appeals on October 31.[38]

While EPIC prepared for its appeal, local activists embarked on a new campaign to pressure Georgia-Pacific to sell Sally Bell Grove and other land to be added to Sinkyone Wilderness State Park. In November, EPIC met with Sierra Club Executive Committee members to patch up their differences and shore up club support for their efforts. The Executive Committee endorsed the EPIC suit and asked the Sierra Club Legal Defense Fund to write an amicus brief supporting the appeal. In January 1984, North Coast activists traveled to Georgia to meet with Georgia-Pacific officials regarding a potential land deal. Richard Gienger, using an innovative tactic that would be adopted by Headwaters activists in the 1980s and 1990s and by national environmental groups in the 1990s, purchased a share of the firm's stock so he could attend a shareholder meeting to plead his case. In July 1984, in response to the litigation, negotiations, and direct action, Georgia-Pacific agreed to postpone logging in the Sinkyone for a year to provide time to negotiate a land swap.[39]

A full year later, the situation on the North Coast had not improved. In early summer of 1985, the California legislature approved a $7 million appropriation for a Sinkyone purchase, and Save the Redwoods League pledged an additional $3 million, but Governor George Deukmejian eliminated the appropriation, arguing the state should focus on park purchases "closer to the state's population centers." In July 1985, EPIC won its appeal of *EPIC v. Johnson*, voiding the 1983 Timber Harvest Plan for Sally Bell Grove. EPIC and its attorneys successfully argued that CDF had violated three CEQA requirements in approving the plan: it had not adequately responded to public comments; it had failed to consider the cumulative impact of the harvests on the hillside, and it had failed to consult with relevant agencies with jurisdiction over the project (in the case of Sally Bell, the Native American Heritage Commission). The agency did not dispute EPIC's claims. Instead, the agency made two separate arguments. First, CDF argued that according to the Forest Practice Rules, it could only consider the Forest Practice Act when approving plans, a claim fundamentally at odds with the legislative history of the Forest Practice Act. Therefore, it claimed CEQA's requirements about consultation, cumulative impact, and public comments were irrelevant to Timber Harvest Plans, making the case moot. It appears that CDF and the timber industry hoped for a judgment that would overturn the previous rulings, because they had made the same arguments in *Arcata* and *Gallegos*. Second, the agency argued that its procedures already indirectly accounted for cumulative impacts: by minimizing the impacts of each individual logging plan, they minimized the cumulative impacts of all logging. Thus, even if the courts ruled CEQA applied to Timber Harvest Plans, CDF argued it was already fulfilling its duties. The agency's assessment of its cumulative impact analysis—coupled with CDF's continued use of the argument that CEQA did not apply to harvest plans—demonstrates the degree of intransigence within the agency. By definition, one cannot analyze cumulative impact without studying past and future plans. The court ruled for EPIC in 1985, striking another blow against the forestry agency's industry-friendly economic development priorities.[40]

At that point, Georgia-Pacific was furious. The company argued that it was being unfairly vilified, especially since it had donated land worth $6 million to the state in 1969. In September 1985, the company refiled the same Sally Bell harvest plan, despite the *Johnson* ruling, highlighting a problem with EPIC's litigation strategy: Under CEQA and the Forest Practices Act, judges could only stop logging plans if the proper procedures were not followed for Timber Harvest Plan permits. They could not stop logging projects permanently, because timber companies and the forestry agency could revise and resubmit the same plan, arguing that they had fulfilled the court's requirements to study the environmental impacts, respond to public comments, and make every effort to mitigate environmental degradation. It wasn't until activists latched on to laws protecting endangered species that they were able to permanently halt logging on particular plots of land.[41]

When it filed the Sally Bell harvest plan for the second time, Georgia-Pacific completed what would become the typical pattern of conflict during much of the Redwood Wars. In December, the Department of Forestry again approved the harvest plan, despite EPIC's announcement that it would again sue the agency if it approved the plan. John Dewitt, executive director of the Save the Redwoods League, commented on the litigation threat by EPIC: "I imagine they will go out and chain themselves to the trees." Richard Gienger cryptically told the press, "The trees are going to be protected." Georgia-Pacific, in what would become a common charge by industry spokesmen during the spotted owl and Headwaters conflicts, accused the activists of trying to stop all logging on the North Coast at the expense of the loggers and mill workers. On January 17, 1986, EPIC, the Sierra Club, Woods, Gienger, and others filed a petition for a writ of mandate—a court order for a government agency to bring its procedures into compliance with the law. Once again, Save the Redwoods League and the Trust for Public Land intervened to negotiate a land purchase with Georgia-Pacific, and the second Sally Bell case was never heard. Instead, the company agreed to sell the land to the land trusts. The Trust for Public Land purchased 7,100 acres from Georgia-Pacific on December 20, 1986, and donated 3,300 of those acres, including Sally Bell Grove, to the Sinkyone Wilderness State Park. The Trust for Public Land held on to the remaining second-growth forest, working with the North Coast tribes to create the InterTribal Sinkyone Wilderness in 1997. Clearly naming the grove after Sally Bell was not simply a sentimental tactic. North Coast activists and local tribes had worked together to restrict industrial logging, sparking the escalation of the Redwood Wars.

The fight over the Sinkyone cooled, but the battles between North Coast activists and timber companies such as Georgia-Pacific and Pacific Lumber had just begun. The basic patterns established during the Sally Bell fight were repeated over and over until, as in the Sally Bell conflict, a land purchase ended the conflict. Timber companies continued to submit clear-cut logging plans for old-growth redwood forests. After the Sally Bell conflict, North Coast activists began to monitor the plans submitted to the Department of Forestry. The activists studied plans, submitted comments on them, and when their requests were rejected, filed suit to stop the logging. They went into the woods to physically disrupt the logging efforts and give EPIC time to obtain court orders. EPIC won repeatedly in court, convincing judges that the timber firms and the forestry agency were failing to follow the environmental protection requirements in CEQA and the Forest Practices Act. The timber companies rarely gave in, appealing rulings as well as refiling rejected Timber Harvest Plans in an attempt to stop the momentum of the activists. Some battles over particular plots of land grew intractable, with the activists and timber companies both working to get the legislature to orchestrate a solution. On the North Coast, frustration set in as activists and companies refused to compromise with each other or with the legislature.[42]

• • •

During the Sally Bell conflict, North Coast activists thus developed both a model for organizing direct action and a strong set of legal arguments for challenging the corporatist timber tradition. Timber companies and the Department of Forestry were required to evaluate the cumulative impacts of logging on the landscape when reviewing Timber Harvest Plans. The agency needed to adequately respond to public comments and those of other agencies. If those requirements were not met, a court could overturn the Timber Harvest Plan and send the company back to revise and resubmit the plan. EPIC and other citizens used the *EPIC v. Johnson* model with increasing frequency and success. Prior to *Johnson*, there were only two published opinions for cases challenging harvest plans. After *Johnson*, environmental groups in California challenged plans every year. But if EPIC members expected that the Board of Forestry and the timber industry would take defeat at the hands of environmental groups as a signal to reform the Forest Practice Rules and Department of Forestry methodology, they were wrong. CDF and the timber industry would continue to argue that they were exempt from CEQA, despite a growing stack of precedents. They were convinced they were correct and just needed a sympathetic judge to overturn the precedents.[43]

Redwood politics had thus changed between World War II and 1985. A more aggressive group of environmental activists was demanding that more be done to protect ecosystems and human health. Increased clear-cutting after World War II had destabilized slopes, increased erosion and siltation, and dramatically reduced the size of the redwood forest dominated by ancient trees. By 1985, approximately 10 percent of the ancient trees standing in 1850 remained. The fight for Redwood National Park and its expansion had been waged to protect those giant trees from negligent private land management. That fight was structured by the genteel tradition of land acquisition created by Save the Redwoods League during the interwar period. The Redwood National Park fight, however, strayed from that model as the Sierra Club and the Save the Redwoods League eventually resorted to federal confiscation of private land. The timber industry had become unwilling sellers during the postwar logging boom, and they especially did not want to lose access to such a large portion of Redwood Country. Thus, a new hostility grew on the North Coast in addition to increased interest in private land management reform.

The assertiveness of the postwar environmental movement led to the dismantling of official corporatism in California, opening the doors for greater citizen oversight of timber operations. On the North Coast, activists believed the new laws could be used to transform the North Coast into a healthier and more sustainable society. For the next twenty years after the Sally Bell case, CDF, EPIC, the Sierra Club, and the timber industry jousted repeatedly over the same basic issues they had fought over during the 1970s and early 1980s. What became known as Headwaters Forest was the focal point of many of these battles because it was the only unprotected old-growth redwood forest of significant size left in the world, and because the forest's owner, Pacific Lumber Company, adopted a new forestry policy in the mid-1980s designed to harvest the company's remaining old-growth groves within twenty years.

FIGURE 1. The Bolling Memorial Grove, established in 1921, was the first major purchase of Save the Redwoods League. The park expanded into what is now Humboldt Redwoods State Park, containing the Avenue of the Giants and the Bull Creek Flats. In 1921, the North Coast was still rather undeveloped and wild. Efforts to protect some redwoods from the saw blade emerged as road development enabled citizens to mingle with the giant trees and see the clear-cutting. Notice the size of the tree to the left of the car. Record Unit 7091: Science Service, Records, circa 1910–1963, Smithsonian Institution Archives, neg. no. SIA 2015–003194.

FIGURE 2. Industrial logging began to shrink the once seemingly endless red-wood forest. At the turn of the twentieth century, industrial logging was still rudimentary, but logging teams could make short work of entire stands of giant redwoods. Here, a man stands by a steam donkey amid a clear-cut grove of enormous trees. Such practices higher up on slopes contributed to winter floods in 1955 and 1964 that decimated alluvial flat redwoods and drew activists' attention to industrial logging on the North Coast. Image 2003.01.2584 from the Palmquist Collection, Humboldt State University Library.

FIGURE 3. After World War II, clear-cutting and industrial-scale logging expanded on the North Coast, and many local timber companies were acquired by multinational corporations, including Georgia-Pacific and Louisiana-Pacific. The logging took place on steep slopes, and the erosion clogged creeks and streams. When homesteaders and locals discovered that Georgia-Pacific was going to clear-cut the remaining old-growth redwood stand on a Lost Coast mountainside (shown here), they mobilized. In what became known as the Sally Bell case, EPIC coordinated a litigation and direct action campaign designed to protect the ancient redwoods and habitat in Sally Bell Grove and to end the development-first priorities of the California Department of Forestry. *EPIC v. Johnson* formed the legal basis of nearly all subsequent challenges to Timber Harvest Plans in California. Photograph courtesy of Richard Gienger and the Environmental Protection Information Center.

FIGURE 4. From left: The Man Who Walks in the Woods, Richard Gienger, and Cecelia Lanman protesting the proposed logging of Sally Bell Grove. The irreverence on display remained a mainstay of the North Coast activist community throughout the Redwood Wars. Photograph by Debbie Untermann. Courtesy of Debbie Untermann and the Environmental Protection Information Center.

FIGURE 5. When North Coast activists began to regularly trespass on Pacific Lumber Company property to survey the remaining forest after the company's takeover by Maxxam Corporation, they discovered what they named Headwaters Forest, as well as active clear-cutting inside the old-growth groves on company land. This clear-cut is at the edge of the main Headwaters Grove. Photograph by Greg King, 1987. Courtesy of Greg King.

FIGURE 6. North Coast activists with various organizational affiliations tres-
passed onto Pacific Lumber property throughout the 1980s and 1990s to gather
information about the forest and logging activities. Their efforts assisted EPIC
in its litigation, informed decisions about where to locate tree-sitters and road
blockades, and provided data for the mapping project of the Trees Foundation.
The trespassers risked arrest each time they entered private property, and hikers
often needed to camp overnight to reach the groves of ancient redwoods. These
hikers in the main Headwaters Grove are concealing their identities. Photograph by Greg King, 1989. Courtesy of Greg King.

FIGURE 7. The North Coast activists wanted to prevent the harvesting of the remaining ancient redwoods, to promote logging reforms to make the industry more sustainable, and to rehabilitate logged-over areas to one day develop into old-growth redwood habitat. In this photo, Darryl Cherney (with hoedad in hand) and other Earth First! activists illegally and secretly plant redwood saplings in All Species Grove inside the Headwaters Forest Complex. Photograph by Greg King, 1988. Courtesy of Greg King.

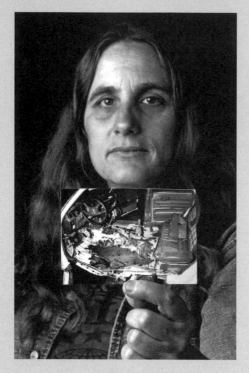

FIGURE 8. Judi Bari was critical to the style and form of the North Coast activist community. As a labor and environmental activist, she was controversial and steadfast. When a bomb exploded under her seat in May 1990, it changed the course and tenor of the Redwood Wars. Photograph by Evan Johnson. Courtesy of Evan Johnson.

FIGURE 9. The activists on the North Coast were deeply influenced by the values of the civil rights movement and antiwar migrants who arrived in the region beginning in the late 1960s. This protest on a logging truck was part of Redwood Summer. Their signs highlight the activists' opposition to corporate and industrial logging. Photograph by Evan Johnson, 1990. Courtesy of Evan Johnson.

FIGURE 10. Relationships on the North Coast were volatile but not always hostile. Here, an Earth First! activist during Redwood Summer talks calmly with a member of the Mendocino County Sheriff's Department. Many people on the North Coast sympathized with the message on this activist's poster. They worried their jobs and landscape might soon be destroyed by multinational corporations who could log the forest, send the raw logs overseas or to mills in Mexico, and then leave the county in the lurch. Photograph by Evan Johnson, 1990. Courtesy of Evan Johnson.

FIGURE 11. By the end of 1990, the North Coast had become an increasingly violent place. The most visible activity involved peaceful public protests organized by North Coast Earth First!, and they drew the ire of the pro-logging Yellow Ribbon Coalition, as well as the timber companies. The protests often brought out environmental activists, protimber counterprotesters, and police. During the summer of 1990, the police assembled near the Georgia-Pacific Lumber Mill in Fort Bragg in anticipation of the planned Earth First! march and rally. Photograph by Evan Johnson, 1990. Courtesy of Evan Johnson.

FIGURE 12. During Redwood Summer, and throughout the Redwood Wars, relationships between environmental activists and the local community were in constant flux. Many timber families resented the environmentalists' persistent actions and opposed their proposals to reform logging practices. This man's T-shirt ("TIMBER FAMILIES: AN ENDANGERED SPECIES") embodied the frustrations of many: the fear of job losses and the perceived threat posed by the Endangered Species Act and the federal government. In 1990, the Redwood Wars were still a local California conflict, however. Photograph by Evan Johnson, 1990. Courtesy of Evan Johnson.

FIGURE 13. One of the appealing facets of Earth First! protests was the often-deployed humor of the group. During Redwood Summer, activists descended upon the house of Louisiana-Pacific CEO Harry Merlo. Some activists decided to get into the hot tub at the house, and some skinny-dipped. The action was humorous and lighthearted but also an incisive display of their irreverence toward private property. Photograph by Evan Johnson, 1990. Courtesy of Evan Johnson.

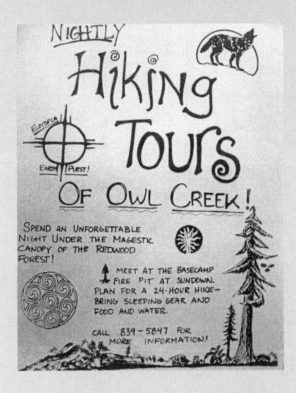

FIGURE 14. By 1992, the Redwood Wars focused almost entirely on Headwaters Forest. The company and the activists were locked in a cycle of litigation, direct actions, and protests. Trespassing remained a critical tactic of the activists to monitor logging activity. After Pacific Lumber twice logged in the Owl Creek Grove in the midst of ongoing litigation, Alicia Littletree organized nightly hikes to keep an eye on the company. Notice how deep into the woods the activists ventured—a full day and night's venture. Ecotopia Earth First! flier, 1992, personal papers of Alicia Littletree.

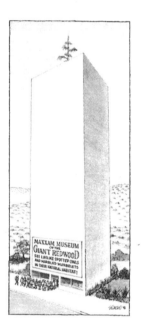

FIGURE 15. When it became clear the Clinton administration was considering acquiring some part of the Headwaters Forest Complex, the North Coast activists raised money to exert influence on the now nationalized conflict. The activists had helped escalate the Redwood Wars to the executive branch, and in 1996 they wanted to make sure the president knew they expected the federal government to take all of Headwaters Forest from Pacific Lumber and Maxxam. The ad makes it clear that the issue was about forests, habitat, ancient redwoods, and sustainable forestry. Voice of the Environment, "President Clinton: We need a forest, not a tree museum!" full-page advertisement, *New York Times*, July 23, 1996. Courtesy of Dan Hamburg.

FIGURE 16. The North Coast activists opposed globalization, industrial logging, and corporate capitalism until the very end. In 1996, when the Clinton administration was negotiating a land deal with Charles Hurwitz and Pacific Lumber Company, activists pressured the president to avoid giving Hurwitz a federal handout. Many activists did not want to reward Hurwitz for holding the ancient redwoods hostage. Voice of the Environment, "Consider it the Charles E. Hurwitz relief fund," full-page advertisement, *New York Times*, August 22, 1996. Courtesy of Dan Hamburg.

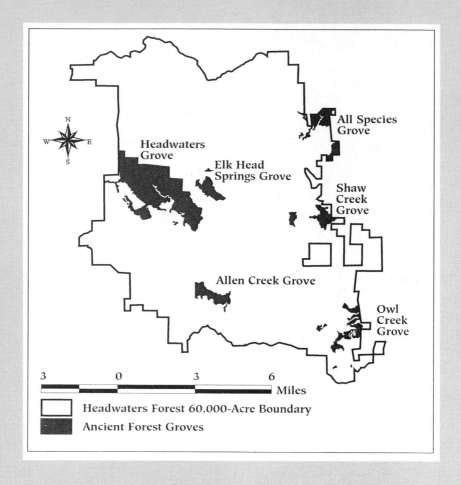

FIGURE 17. In 1997, the Headwaters Forest Coordinating Committee produced their own proposal for the Headwaters acquisition and subsequent management of the land. They prioritized acquiring the six large stands of old-growth redwood forest and the sixty-thousand-acre matrix surrounding them. "Map 2: Headwaters Forest Ancient Groves," in *Headwaters Forest Stewardship Plan*, Trees Foundation, 1997, 5. Courtesy of Trees Foundation.

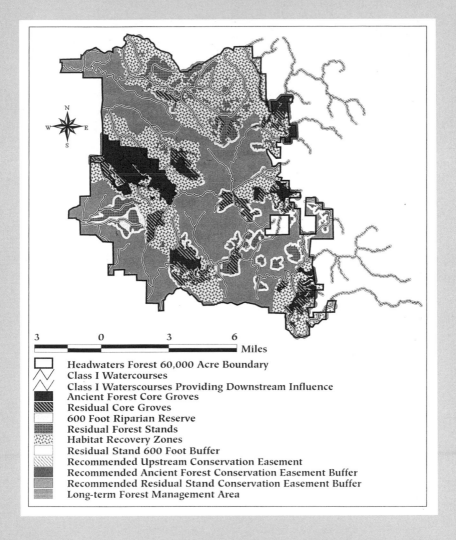

FIGURE 18. The Headwaters Forest Stewardship Plan embodied the decades-long sustainability and restoration priorities of the North Coast activists. This map documents their proposed management plan, which included preservation, restoration, and logging (in the Long-term Forest Management Area). Though there were internal disagreements over the particulars, the North Coast activist community was committed to community-oriented business management. "Map 3: HFSP Management Areas," in *Headwaters Forest Stewardship Plan*, Trees Foundation, 1997, 15. Courtesy of Trees Foundation.

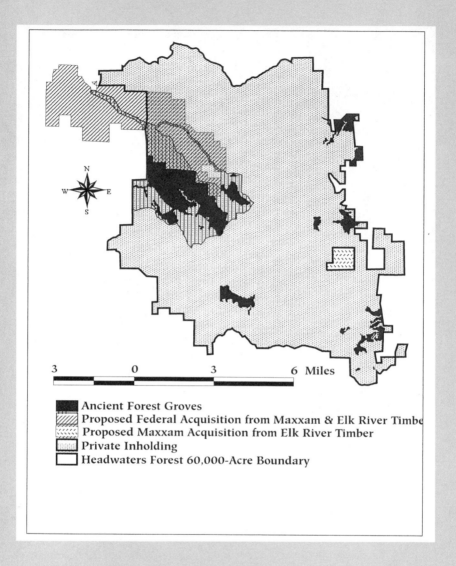

Ancient Forest Groves
Proposed Federal Acquisition from Maxxam & Elk River Timbe
Proposed Maxxam Acquisition from Elk River Timber
Private Inholding
Headwaters Forest 60,000-Acre Boundary

FIGURE 19. In 1996, the federal government and the State of California agreed
to acquire the main Headwaters Grove and the Elk Head Springs Grove from
Pacific Lumber in a complicated series of transactions. The agreement was a
disappointment to many activists who wanted Maxxam relieved of its ownership of the entire Headwaters Forest Complex. Their disappointment fueled
continued opposition to "the Deal" until well after its consummation in 1999.
"Map 9: Comparison of Proposed Headwaters Forest Reserve Boundaries," in
Headwaters Forest Stewardship Plan, Trees Foundation, 1997, 87. Courtesy of Trees
Foundation.

THREE

RADICALIZATION

IN DECEMBER 1988, *OUTSIDE* PUBLISHED "THE PREDATOR'S MAUL," an article about the growing conflict over Headwaters Forest in Humboldt County. The title was a take on the popular book *Predators' Ball*, which described recently concluded insider trading scandals on Wall Street that resulted in the high-profile convictions of Ivan Boesky and Michael Milken. The *Outside* article pitted "Tarzan and Jane" against Texas financier Charles Hurwitz—a central figure in the Wall Street scandals as well as the transformation of the Redwood Wars. Tarzan and Jane referred to Earth First! activists Mary Beth Nearing and Greg King who, a year prior, had perched 150 feet up in two ancient redwoods near the heart of Headwaters Forest in what activists named Elkhead Springs Grove. It took loggers two days to notice the activists and their banner, which read, "Free the Redwoods." Once they were spotted, a Pacific Lumber tree climber scurried up the trees to remove the banner, yelling at the activists for disrupting work, and King unfurled another banner reading, "2000 Years Old/Respect Your Elders!" Anticipating the arrival of law enforcement, King and Nearing escaped in the middle of the night, but weeks later, they went up into the trees again, this time in a different grove of giant redwoods in Headwaters. This time, the two climbed down and were arrested in front of invited media.[1]

Those 1988 confrontations between the North Coast activists on one side and Pacific Lumber and law enforcement on the other were emblematic of the intense battles of the Redwood Wars throughout the late 1980s and the 1990s. From 1985 to 1990, the Redwood Wars expanded and grew more tense and occasionally violent, fueled by the radicalization of the North Coast redwood preservation movement and the takeover of Pacific Lumber by Charles Hurwitz and Maxxam. The radicalism was born of some activists' frustration with the resilience of the corporatist tradition in California forestry, as citizen groups vowed to put an end to industrial logging in California. The timber companies, on the other hand, especially Pacific Lumber, decided after 1985 that they had lost enough harvestable land and authority over logging practices. They were determined to aggressively resist any further encroachments, and even hoped to erase previous legal defeats. Timber workers and forestry officials were caught in the middle of the power play. Timber workers continued to worry about job losses due to both redwood preservation efforts and liquidation logging. The former might result in short-term job losses, the latter in long-term job loss after the forests were gone. The foresters at the California Department of Forestry were likewise conflicted. They needed to enforce the Forest Practices Act and other environmental protection laws, as well as accommodating the corporatist traditions of the governing Board of Forestry. The conflicts in the late 1980s were antagonistic, and they arose from the radicalized activism of the North Coast, which refused compromise with timber companies.

Three interrelated developments made the Redwood Wars intractable during the second half of the 1980s. The most important was the hostile takeover of Pacific Lumber by Maxxam, which posed a new logging threat to a forest previously unknown to the public. After the takeover, Pacific Lumber grew disinterested in compromise. Furthermore, the activists found a charismatic villain in Charles Hurwitz, who would draw the ire of environmentalists, workers, and the media. The activists were intent on dismantling the industrial logging regime on the North Coast, and they decided to force redwood preservation politics out of negotiating rooms and into the public arena. They used disruptive rallies, protests, and direct action to draw media attention and to recruit other activists to their cause. The timber companies resented the negative attention and worked to silence the activists. Alongside those public actions, the North Coast activists also escalated their legal efforts. They repeatedly challenged old-growth logging plans, and the courts almost always sided with them, stopping logging in numerous stands of giant redwoods. By the late 1980s, the activists seemed to have the upper hand, but their success only made Pacific Lumber dig in its heels more firmly. Neither side was willing to compromise.

The two activists sitting in the ancient trees in 1988 were violating the law to draw attention to the logging plans of Pacific Lumber. Greg King had discovered the ancient forest when he and other local activists began to surreptitiously trespass on company property after Maxxam's 1985 takeover of Pacific Lumber. The activists wanted to find out what forests might be threatened by Pacific Lumber's plans to increase logging as the company struggled to pay off the debt incurred in the takeover. They discovered a half dozen large groves of ancient redwoods within an approximately sixty-thousand-acre redwood complex. They named the large grove Headwaters Grove, and the entire complex Headwaters Forest. King described Headwaters Grove as the "epitome" of what was at stake in the Redwood Wars: "It's hard to put into words what I feel except to say that it is life—it is reality." With less than 10 percent of the pre-1850 ancient redwoods still standing, King and the other North Coast activists believed that not enough was being done to protect the "reality" that he found in the few remaining ancient redwood forests. As King said, "We've degraded so much of the planet that reality seems unreal." Indeed, walking into the main Headwaters Grove is an awesome experience. One walks through a second-growth forest filled with remnants of past logging operations such as "goose pens" (burned-out giant redwood stumps loggers used as shelter) and logging roads. At the edge of the Headwaters Grove, one begins a steep incline, and with each step the quiet seems to grow thicker and more deafening. At the top of the ridge lies a large grove inhabited by giant redwoods and human-size ferns. It is easy to understand why King and his peers immediately felt an attachment to the place.[2]

What emerged was a multifront war in the media, the courtroom, and the forests—over the fate not only of Headwaters Forest but of the remaining groves of giant redwoods across Redwood Country. And the battles were explosive. By the end of the decade, violence was on the rise, Timber Harvest Plans (THPs) were regularly held up in court, and radical environmental activists had begun to flock to the North Coast to defend the giant trees and their forest. Pacific Lumber and its peers grew increasingly agitated as well, defending their own giants—the prerogatives of corporations.

The tensions on the North Coast were a part of a broader polarization of American environmental politics. During the 1980s, the modern environmental protection regime erected in the 1970s had withstood a barrage of attacks from conservative politicians and industry, but so had California's corporatist forestry system. The Sagebrush Rebellion of the late 1970s, which argued that federal land in the West should be turned over to the states, had faded quickly because most Americans and politicians were reluctant to give up those public lands. But resistance from businesses and rural westerners to the emerging environmental protection regime had not disappeared. In fact, resistance grew more widespread and sophisticated. Auto companies had fought the timelines for reducing tailpipe emissions imposed on them by the Clean Air Act, and chemical companies were fighting the efforts by residents of Love Canal, New York, to hold past polluters responsible for toxic waste cleanup. Simultaneously, timber and mining companies were forced to confront the Wilderness Act and the National Environmental Policy Act, which required federal land management agencies to survey their holdings and craft environmental impact statements to minimize environmental damage to the nation's landscapes. Public land was being withdrawn from industrial and agricultural use, as environmental groups pushed to protect hundreds of millions of acres across the West and Alaska. And industries had to navigate the new bureaucracy of the Environmental Protection Agency, environmental law in the courtroom, and a public increasingly concerned with pollution and development. The result was massive uncertainty in the business world about the impact of the environmental protection regime on their operations.[3]

President Reagan's administration was an ally to industry, leading the attack on market uncertainty and restricted property rights by arguing that big government and environmental regulations were hurting economic growth. The Wise Use movement, which challenged environmental regulations, emerged from that milieu. Though the movement wouldn't mature until the 1990s, businesses and property owners organized in the 1980s to reduce the impact of environmental protection on their profits and to curtail restrictions on the use of their property. Increasingly, opponents of environmental regulation argued that jobs and profits were at stake, as well as citizens' constitutional property rights, whether private land management or permits and licenses to graze and mine public lands. The arguments were convincing to workers and ranchers across the nation, and the Republican Party championed them. Thus what had once been a bipartisan effort to improve the health of the planet and its inhabitants split into polarized partisan camps.[4]

In response, mainstream national environmental groups established defensive campaigns to prevent rollbacks of the 1970s environmental laws. They too had to develop new technical and bureaucratic expertise. They needed Congress to defend the new laws, and they needed donations to do their work. In Washington, DC, environmental groups hired professional fund-raisers, trained staff and volunteers to lobby, and developed elaborate management structures to supervise the efforts and protect their ability to influence decision makers. Their efforts did prevent Congress from neutering the cornerstone environmental laws, and they additionally worked to improve agency regulations when the collapse of the bipartisan commitment to environmental protection prevented the passage of legislation to strengthen the nation's environmental laws.[5]

While the national environmental groups worked defensively, North Coast activists went on the offensive. Like Dave Foreman and Earth First!, they were less concerned about long-term institutional relationships than with using the tools immediately available to stop what they saw as the destruction of their rural society. The North Coast activists had a weapon that other forestry reformers did not: a set of powerful court rulings supporting their positions and specific state regulations limiting forestry practices on private land in California. Because they focused increasingly on one plot of private land, their actions and strategies were more targeted than those of the Pacific Northwest activists, who were fighting at the same moment to protect old-growth Douglas fir forests and spotted owl habitat across Oregon and Washington. The Northwest activists confronted a large and diffuse group of timber operators using millions of acres governed by federal regulations. The Forest Service was still working on codifying forest practices for public land, which put the spotted owl activists in

Oregon at a disadvantage in some respects. However, because such vast territory was at stake in the spotted owl conflict, the federal government, and especially the president, had greater incentive to intervene than they did in Redwood Country. Besides, North Coast activists did not initially want the federal government to intervene in the region's affairs. Like their libertarian neighbors, they were skeptical of distant power. They preferred local governance—and they likely did not want to draw federal scrutiny to the area given the expanding illegal marijuana farming operations on the North Coast. Confident in the Sally Bell model, North Coast activists escalated their attacks on industrial logging, using the state courts and local direct action as their primary tools. The result was more than a decade of attacks and counterattacks as timber companies and activists vied for leverage in the Redwood Wars.

Maxxam's takeover of Pacific Lumber was central to the changing Redwood Wars. The takeover helped North Coast activists gain the upper hand in the Redwood Wars during the 1980s because the transformation of Pacific Lumber led directly to the discovery of Headwaters Forest and to vilification of the venerable timber company. Almost immediately after the takeover, Pacific Lumber lost its benevolent paternal small-town image with locals and the press. In its place rose the specter of a callous and greedy corporate timber liquidator—much like the image of Louisiana-Pacific and Georgia-Pacific in the region, and a reputation Pacific Lumber had worked hard for decades to avoid. Many workers and environmental activists worried that the "new" Pacific Lumber would cut and run, leaving the forest and the county in poor economic and ecological shape. What had begun as an opportunity to forge a powerful worker-environmentalist alliance in the struggle over the limits of industrial capitalism ended in hostility and violence by decade's end.

THE TAKEOVER

Pacific Lumber: Outlier

Long before Charles Hurwitz set his sights on the Pacific Lumber Company, the firm had already entered the conglomeration and acquisitions world of American corporations. Unfortunately, the history of

Pacific Lumber has almost exclusively been presented as a tale of two companies: the one that existed prior to 1985 and the one created after 1985. The standard pre-1985 history focuses on the company's history of sustainable logging and good corporate citizenship. That narrative is defined by the creation of the company town of Scotia, the land donations and sales made to create state and national parks, the college scholarship fund, and the family-run business. The standard post-1985 narrative describes a company forced into the conglomerate web of a distant financier and the subsequent loss of its benevolent tradition. Looking to sell off assets and make a quick buck from unsuspecting and poorly managed companies, Hurwitz steered Pacific Lumber toward an unsustainable business model sure to doom the workers, the shareholders, the redwoods, and the salmon. While much of that narrative is true, it does not tell the whole story. Pacific Lumber was, almost from the beginning, part family-run business and part diverse business organization, and had already become a multinational conglomerate in the 1970s. So while the company changed dramatically after the takeover, it was not entirely unrecognizable.[6]

Its multifaceted traditions led Pacific Lumber to behave differently than most other major timber companies during the postwar era. Companies like Weyerhaeuser created additional revenue during the postwar era by adding pulp mills to make paper. The strategy of those companies was to ensure that their core business—timber harvesting—generated revenue once the housing boom subsided and timber demand fell. The Pacific Lumber Company, by contrast, behaved like a conglomerate, adding numerous unrelated businesses to its holdings. The company believed its strategy of harvesting ancient redwoods more slowly than its competitors would allow it to maintain stable production while others faltered, thus protecting its core business. Pacific Lumber's strategy to increase revenue, aside from expected increases in old-growth lumber prices, was to add manufacturing facilities that did not place an additional burden on its timber harvesting operations and could generate revenue during slow construction periods. The company's unique strategies eventually made it an appealing target for Wall Street takeover artists because of its solid finances and large inventory.[7]

Because of its diversified revenue strategy, Pacific Lumber dove into the 1960s and 1970s conglomeration wave more aggressively than most timber companies. The plan was initiated with the acquisition of the Victor Equipment Company, the nation's leading manufacturer of metal cutting and welding tools. In 1976, Pacific Lumber purchased tomato, rice, and wheat farmland in the Sacramento Valley. The company explained in its annual reports that the goal of the diversification was to insulate the company from housing market cycles by acquiring what they believed were cycle-free assets. The acquisitions also protected the company from new environmental values and politics that might reduce logging profits. Another major part of the transformation into a conglomerate was the company's change in ownership and management. In 1975, when Pacific Lumber was listed on the New York Stock Exchange, no group, including the Murphy family, held more than a 5 percent interest. For the rest of the twentieth century, men with finance and accounting backgrounds managed the company, and they paid more attention to financial statements and the stock ticker than they did to the operation and management of its production facilities. Pacific Lumber thus entered what is referred to in business school culture as the metric-ruled world of globalization, which is simply another name for a management style driven by the analysis of bulk data.[8]

Those initial forays into conglomeration were only the beginning of the transformation of Pacific Lumber. Between 1977 and 1983, the company acquired a stable of companies in the United States and Europe that manufactured plasma metal-cutting equipment, arc welding equipment, air-fueled gas torches, alloy welding rods, and electric welding tools. The company even purchased a 140-room hotel in San Francisco. Subsequently, Pacific Lumber created Palco Industries to house the cutting and welding operations, and in 1980, it created Palco International Corporation to market the cutting and welding products. By 1981, the company was primarily a manufacturer, with 75 percent of Pacific Lumber's sales revenue coming from nontimber products. Two years later, a Pacific Lumber spokesman underscored the new strategy by describing the firm as a "net investor" to the New York Times. As a net investor, Pacific Lumber focused its energy and resources on purchasing companies that increased the firm's overall return to shareholders. Pacific Lumber was becoming more of a stock-holding company than a logging and lumber company.[9]

Despite that aggressive conglomeration, Pacific Lumber still behaved in ways atypical of postwar timber companies and of other multinational conglomerates. While the lumber production of its peers fluctuated dramatically with demand in the 1970s and early 1980s, Pacific Lumber maintained relatively steady production. From 1974 to 1985, production levels for West Coast redwood and Douglas fir timber operators Louisiana-Pacific, Georgia-Pacific, and Simpson fluctuated on average by 18.68 percent, 20.66 percent, and 10.67 percent per year, respectively. Some years, production for Louisiana-Pacific and Georgia-Pacific fluctuated by as much as 49 percent. During those same years, Pacific Lumber's production fluctuated on average only 8.68 percent, with a maximum change of 16.81 percent. By comparison, Simpson's highest yearly change was 22.27 percent. The stated reason for the relative stability of Pacific Lumber was the company's commitment to harvesting on a "continuous yield" or "perpetual basis," another way of stating it wanted to run a sustainable logging operation. The company's emphasis on continuous yield operations was in part driven by its self-proclaimed "unique" redwood production strategy to improve its position in the market over time by holding on to old-growth trees.[10]

Though Pacific Lumber had become a diversified multinational corporation by 1980, long-held values and oft-told narratives strongly influenced management's decision-making process. The company continued to emphasize traditional strategies for managing production and employee loyalty that prioritized stability and low levels of debt. For example, the company sold some acquisitions during the recession of 1981 to refocus its energies on Scotia timber and the cutting and welding division. To prevent layoffs during that recession, the company put all timber and welding workers on a four-day workweek. This policy, combined with college scholarships and free life insurance, positioned Pacific Lumber to resist union efforts better than most modern companies, which focused on shorter-term margins. The board of directors rejected proposals to increase harvest levels in the early 1980s because of the company's traditional emphasis on restraint and its reluctance to blindly follow industry trends. Without this history of paternal benefits, the workers might not have so strongly defended the company during the Headwaters conflict. Its image allowed Pacific Lumber to ward off union efforts and harvest above its own self-defined sustainable levels without drawing public ire in the era before the Maxxam takeover. The company's 1980 annual report promoted a self-defined sustainable harvest of 120 million board feet per year. However, the data inside the reports reveal that between 1974 and 1985 the company averaged 134 million board feet per year, dipping below the 120 million level only twice in those seventeen years. Thus Pacific Lumber's image as a small-town company belied its status as a diversified multinational conglomerate by the end of the 1970s. Pacific Lumber's traditional reputation won it many allies in the worker and local press communities, but it was not as benevolent or conservative as activists, workers, and the press believed.[11]

While Pacific Lumber's promotion of its redwood conservation commitments and community patronage had long protected it from attacks on the North Coast, transformation into a multinational conglomerate opened it up to investor attacks from Wall Street. When Pacific Lumber became a publicly traded company, the Murphy family and other investors ceded control of the company shares to Wall Street investors. By expanding and acquiring a diverse array of businesses, the company placed itself on the radar of other investors. Finally, Pacific Lumber attracted investors by maintaining a large inventory of valuable assets in the form of giant redwoods, which decreased its debt to assets ratio.

John Campbell: Innovator

John Campbell was to a large degree responsible for the profitability of Pacific Lumber's timber operations after 1970, and it was the logging and milling that made the company attractive to Hurwitz and Maxxam in 1985. A cosmopolitan and entrepreneurial adventurer, Campbell was an unlikely migrant to the North Coast. A native Australian, he grew up on a family farm in the Burragorang Valley with the expectation he would become a "gentleman farmer," as he put it. However, "the government, in its wisdom," decided to build a dam downstream from the Campbell family farm, and their property was confiscated to make way for the project. The memory of that event seems to have had a profound effect on Campbell's view of government. In 1964, after traveling around Europe upon graduation from North Sydney Technical College—a trip that apparently included his introduction of surfing to the Cornwall coast of England—Campbell moved to New York City to work for the Australian consulate. Campbell and some friends decided to leave the city after the murder of a friend, and they rented a car to drive across the continent. In 1965, while in South Lake Tahoe, California, Campbell met Cynthia Carpenter. The two married in September 1966 and moved back to Sydney, where Campbell worked as a salesman during the day and owner/restaurateur of Sydney's first wine bar at night. Carpenter, however, wanted to move back to the United States, and Campbell, given his adventurous nature, did not object, so the young couple moved to her hometown of Scotia, California.[12]

Campbell's marriage to Carpenter and their subsequent move to Scotia were the first steps in a life that would become synonymous with redwoods and the battle over Headwaters Forest. Carpenter's father was Edward Carpenter, an executive at Pacific Lumber and later the company's CEO. Campbell accepted a job with Pacific Lumber's sales department in Chicago, deeming it more interesting than the options in Humboldt. Before he could work in sales, however, the company required that Campbell spend a year working in the lumber mill to learn the business. At the end of the year, the superintendent of production asked Campbell to stay and work in manufacturing rather than relocating to Chicago, commenting that he had a sharp mind and worked well with the loggers and mill hands. Campbell happily accepted the offer.

Campbell's primary responsibility in Scotia was to build a new mill to manufacture lumber made from second-growth redwood timber to take advantage of the fact that the redwoods growing on the land logged before World War I were now anywhere from sixty to one hundred years old. The task was a challenge because lumberyards were set up to evaluate and price only old-growth redwood lumber. Old growth was preferred because of its clear heartwood—lumber devoid of knots, porous wood grain, and other imperfections. Second-growth redwood, sometimes referred to as new growth, contains knots and bent tree rings, and the grain is less dense, because the trees grow faster in the direct sunlight of clear-cut areas. Old-growth redwood, with its heartwood dense and strong from centuries of slow growth, is insect and fire resistant, making it ideal for shingles and general construction. Builders did not know how to use second-growth lumber. Accordingly, Campbell's supervisors charged him with figuring out how to market second-growth lumber. The new mill opened in February 1972 with a brand-new computer system to track inventory but no market for its product, save for a local company that wanted to use second-growth redwood to build deck furniture and planter boxes.

Campbell, however, seized on a new construction trend that he thought was ideal for his second-growth lumber. People were moving to the Sun Belt or purchasing second homes in warm climates. "Outdoor living" was also gaining popularity across the nation. Campbell wanted to convince builders that second-growth redwood was useful for decks, hot tubs, and outdoor furniture—uses that did not require the strongest, cleanest timber. Second-growth lumber could be priced cheaper than old growth, making it a smart choice for those projects, Campbell surmised. To convince builders and homeowners that the lumber was appropriate, Campbell convinced the California Redwood Association to create product grades for second-growth lumber similar to the grading system for old growth. The system quantified the lumber based on wood type and relative degree of imperfection. Each grade was associated with appropriate uses, giving consumers a degree of confidence in their purchases. The new market took off, and by 1976, Campbell boasted that the mill netted $1 million per month. In 1979, after Campbell and two other managers had computerized the entire mill, the company promoted Campbell to the position of resident manager of Scotia, a job that is part mayor of the company town and part supervisor of the company's entire logging and milling operations.

As resident manager, Campbell developed and implemented many of the operational changes that made Pacific Lumber an attractive target for Charles Hurwitz as well as environmental activists. He convinced the board to modernize the old-growth mill in Scotia, despite the economic downturn of 1980–81, and he convinced the board to close the plywood plant due to increased competition from particleboard. His operating theory was that the timber industry would rebound and Pacific Lumber needed to keep cutting, milling, and expanding its inventory to be ready when the market turned upward again. The key to Campbell's strategy was land acquisition. In 1981, Campbell discovered that Louisiana-Pacific wanted to leave the North Coast. He purchased twenty-two thousand acres of their land near Rockefeller Forest in Humboldt Redwoods State Park and another tract outside Scotia, both properties adjacent to the existing bulk of Pacific Lumber property outside the company town. To provide unfettered access to the newly expanded land, Campbell also purchased an additional twenty-seven thousand acres from various small inholders whose property was surrounded by Pacific Lumber land.[13]

Campbell wanted to start clear-cutting again. Leaving behind some old giants instead of clear-cutting was a part of the traditional company strategy to hold on to old-growth trees and dominate the valuable old-growth market. Campbell, however, concluded that repeatedly entering the stands of residual old-growth redwoods actually threatened to destroy the company because it reduced the overall growth of the forest. To reach the residual giants, bulldozers and tractors had to penetrate a sea of young second-growth trees, knocking them to the ground as they built roads and trails. And when the giants fell, they too crushed young redwoods. In Campbell's estimation, the company was destroying too much in future harvests to access the residual old growth. To make his case, the lumber leader took the firm's directors on a field trip, pointing out the damage done during harvesting of residual old-growth redwoods. He wanted a company focused on new growth. He wanted to maximize the production of the new second-growth mills. He took the board to see an area that had been clear-cut much earlier. The trees in the grove were all of even age and size, and he pointed out how easy it would be to go in and clear-cut the area again, feeding the second-growth mills. Campbell advocated more or less turning Pacific Lumber land into the mythical tree plantation described by the *Saturday Evening Post* during the 1950s. The board agreed with Campbell, and in 1982, the company submitted to the Board of Forestry its first clear-cut plans in decades.[14]

When Hurwitz acquired Pacific Lumber in 1985, the timber firm had already begun to adopt the types of forest management that had prompted environmentalists to attack Georgia-Pacific and Louisiana-Pacific, as well as corporatism more broadly. The Hurwitz takeover simply accelerated the transformation of Pacific Lumber and drew activist attention for the first time in decades to what was thought to be a small, family lumber company. By 1985, Campbell had thirteen or fourteen clear-cut plans in the Department of Forestry system, and as vice president of forest products, he had established himself as the lumber leader of the Pacific Lumber Company. The timber executive had convinced the board of directors not only to allow him to clear-cut again but to increase the company's overall harvest levels. In September 1985, John Campbell and Bob Stephens, head of the forestry department at the company, proposed a 40 percent increase in the annual harvest, to 170 million board feet. Pacific Lumber had acquired several thousand acres of new land in the 1980s, and Campbell was increasingly convinced that the 1956 timber cruise, an aerial study of the forest contents, had underestimated the company's previous timber inventory. He could not have known at the time that the annual harvest levels and clear-cutting plans would become central issues in the Redwood Wars.[15]

Charles Hurwitz: Maxxam and the Hostile Takeover

Pacific Lumber came into the crosshairs of corporate raiders like Charles Hurwitz because the timber company's strong balance sheet, insufficient timber inventory, and undervalued stock fit the mold of a company that could be acquired cheaply and generate high returns. From 1980 to 1985, Pacific Lumber averaged $179 million in annual net sales revenue, brought in an 18 percent annual profit, and held a meager $24 million in long-term debt (for a 0.15 debt to assets ratio). The company's low debt, large inventory of assets, and stable yet unremarkable revenues had left Pacific Lumber stock undervalued by 1985. The undervaluation of the company, combined with the value of its assets, meant an investor could tender an offer higher than the company's trading price but still lower than an accurate valuation of the firm's assets and revenues. Selling off some underutilized assets could thus generate revenue to pay off the acquisition debt without jeopardizing future operations. Additionally, the takeover process itself would drive up the stock price due to the increased trading in Pacific Lumber shares required to gain control of the company. The higher stock prices would further increase the acquirer's financial gains. These strong financials induced Charles Hurwitz to explore a takeover of Pacific Lumber during the 1980s mergers and acquisitions movement.[16]

The long and controversial history of the business ventures of Charles Hurwitz complicated the takeover of Pacific Lumber when he set his plan in motion in 1985. Hurwitz was born and raised in Kilgore,

Texas, and in 1968, at the age of twenty-eight, he helped create one of the nation's first hedge funds, Hedge Fund of America. As his reputation in finance grew, Hurwitz wanted in on the mergers and acquisitions action of that era, so he left the hedge fund in 1971 and purchased his first company, the Summit Group. As would happen repeatedly leading up to, and including, the Pacific Lumber takeover, trouble rapidly emerged. The same year he purchased the Summit Group, Hurwitz agreed to a Securities and Exchange Commission consent decree enjoining him and his new company from further violations of antifraud securities laws. The decree stemmed from a complaint by the Hair Extension Center alleging that Hurwitz had disseminated false and misleading information about the company to drive down stock prices. In 1975 Hurwitz liquidated the Summit Group altogether because the New York insurance superintendent charged him and others with "improperly, illegally, and fraudulently siphon[ing]" funds from the company. Undaunted, Hurwitz, backed by $12 million in loans, acquired Federated Development Company in 1973 to continue his acquisition plans.[17]

In his next takeover venture, the acquisition of McCulloch Oil, Hurwitz established what became his foundational business and management strategies. In 1978, the then thirty-eight-year-old financier launched what would become a long career of complex mergers, acquisitions, and reorganizations by purchasing a 13 percent share of McCulloch Oil. It was a cheap way into the energy business. The conglomerate produced chainsaws and housing developments in addition to oil. Most famously, McCulloch had built Lake Havasu City, Arizona, and in 1968 the company had purchased London Bridge from England and relocated it to Lake Havasu. Leading up to the Hurwitz takeover, legal problems related to its myriad developments had besieged McCulloch, and the company was saddled with debt. Hurwitz must have seen a company primed for reorganization because he quickly insinuated himself into the management, though not smoothly. Reorganization after an acquisition or merger usually entails selling off unprofitable factories and products, coupled with streamlining administrative overhead. Both of those actions typically produce layoffs and employee anxiety.

Just as Pacific Lumber and other acquisition targets would subsequently, the McCulloch management team resisted the takeover effort, arguing that Hurwitz's past legal problems made him and his representatives inappropriate board candidates. Hurwitz fought back, and by August 1978, he was a director, he had placed two additional representatives on the board, and Hurwitz and an associate were appointed to the executive committee. In 1980 Hurwitz became CEO and chairman of McCulloch Oil and appointed his associate, William Leone, as president. As CEO, Hurwitz changed the company's name to MCO Holdings, sold its energy holdings, passed nearly insurmountable antitakeover measures, reduced the size of the board from thirteen to seven members, and successfully replaced the entire board with his own representatives. In 1981, Hurwitz further consolidated control when he swapped 850,000 common stock shares for preferred shares, giving him control of 45 percent of the voting shares. MCO subsequently purchased 23 percent of United Financial Group, the parent company to the second largest savings and loan in Texas, United Savings of Texas. The later failure of the Texas savings and loan company became problematic during the battle over Headwaters Forest because of Hurwitz's involvement in the collapse of the savings and loan industry.[18]

That basic pattern characterized all Hurwitz takeover bids. He would identify a vulnerable company that was either struggling or greatly undervalued. Hurwitz and his companies would then begin to purchase stock. When they owned enough stock, they would tender an offer to acquire control of the target firm. The management and board of directors of the company being acquired would resist, recalling Hurwitz's past dealings and controversies. Hurwitz would fight back and win, then reorganize the management structure and the board of directors. To consolidate his control, he then would sell off assets to pay off any acquisition debts and purchase even more shares of the company. Finally, he would direct the board to impose ironclad antitakeover measures to protect his authority and ownership. As John Campbell said, Hurwitz was "Old Testament"; he could not be intimidated, and when fired upon, he retaliated with greater force.[19]

By the time Hurwitz targeted Pacific Lumber, he had built a reliable team of lieutenants and takeover tools. One of the most important tools was the transformation of MCO into Maxxam. In May 1982 MCO and Federated Development announced they had reached an arrangement to purchase 33 percent of Simplicity Pattern Company. Hurwitz replaced the Simplicity CEO and chairman with himself, and again placed his trusted colleague Bill Leone, along with Barry Munitz, chancellor of the Business School at the University of Houston and vice chair of MCO, on the Simplicity board. Most of Simplicity's assets were sold off, including the core pattern-making business, and Hurwitz renamed the company Maxxam, a subsidiary of MCO.

Hurwitz continued to attempt additional acquisitions, and he again found himself accused of securities fraud—a pattern that would be repeated several more times in the 1980s and 1990s. In 1984, Hurwitz tried to acquire Castle and Cook, a division of Dole Foods. The company sued Hurwitz, alleging that his efforts to acquire stock through multiple related companies were designed to disguise his takeover intentions. They further argued that the use of the savings and loan violated securities law by using "excessive unsecured loans to bankroll" the takeover effort. A Hawaii court temporarily enjoined Hurwitz and associates from buying more Castle and Cook stock, and in May, the company bought back Hurwitz's shares for $71 million—a $15 million profit for Hurwitz and his companies. Another company levied the same accusations at Hurwitz the following year during a failed takeover bid. They alleged Hurwitz was attempting to sneak up on companies by fraudulently evading the requirement that an investor publicly announce any intentions of a takeover. The press accused Hurwitz of greenmail, a disingenuous strategy of initiating a takeover bid only to scare board members into buying back shares at a premium. Similar accusations of fraudulent stock purchases would frustrate his efforts to acquire Pacific Lumber, increasing the climate of uncertainty on the North Coast and raising the stakes in the Redwood Wars.[20]

Hurwitz, like Campbell, planned to expand his operations in 1985, and the synergy of the plans eventually dragged Pacific Lumber into the Redwood Wars. In the spring, Maxxam filed papers with the Securities and Exchange Commission to offer at least $225 million of subordinated notes through Michael Milken's shop at Drexel Burnham Lambert. The risky, low-grade bonds issued by Milken became known as junk bonds and were central to the insider trading scandals of the late 1980s as well as Hurwitz's financing of hostile takeovers. On Monday, September 30, 1985, Pacific Lumber discovered that it was Charles Hurwitz's next target. At six in the morning, Hurwitz personally called Pacific Lumber president Gene Elam and told him that Maxxam Group was making a tender offer at thirty-six dollars per share, financed by the junk bonds, a nearly ten-dollar increase on the current trading value of Pacific Lumber stock.

Hurwitz was fortunate he didn't have to offer a higher price. Pacific Lumber trading activity had been increasing throughout the spring as Hurwitz anonymously acquired large numbers of shares, and the price continued to rise during the week ending September 27. However, Hurricane Gloria had closed the New York Stock Exchange on the 27th, forestalling further price increases and allowing Hurwitz to ready his tender offer. After listening to Hurwitz and shaking off his surprise at the early morning phone call, Elam balked, and the company acted to place the excess pension fund reserves out of reach of any acquirer. After news of the tender offer broke, Pacific Lumber stock jumped to thirty-nine dollars. Analysts asserted the company was worth closer to fifty dollars per share, especially given the sharp increase in cutting and welding earnings in 1984. A few days later, Hurwitz increased his offer to $38.50 per share, while the company flew in potential white knights—friendly investors who might beat Hurwitz's bid and leave the company intact, something the Pacific Lumber board did not think Hurwitz would do based on his past takeovers. On October 23, however, the board unanimously accepted a forty-dollar per share merger deal from Hurwitz for a total of $864 million.[21]

In the end, Pacific Lumber's board of directors capitulated rather quickly, but the deal was not uncomplicated, contributing to the firestorm that later swirled around the company and Headwaters Forest. Campbell believed that three important forces drove the board to sign off on the merger. Some members of the Murphy family wanted the merger approved, and though in 1985 they were minor shareholders, their voices carried historical weight. At a meeting at Jack's Restaurant in San Francisco, some members of the extended Murphy clan met with Ed Beck, Pacific Lumber's general counsel, and told him not to let Hurwitz get away. Other shareholders worried that the current Pacific Lumber board was not doing enough to reverse the undervaluation of the company and were simply happy to sell their shares at prices much higher than the stock exchange. Observers other than Campbell pointed to a possible Maxxam countersuit as an additional factor in the board's decision. When the board rejected Hurwitz's original offer, they approved additional poison pill measures requiring 80 percent shareholder approval of the sale of any assets, vesting the $60 million pension surplus in the employees and retirees, and increasing the board's severance packages. On October 18, Maxxam sued Pacific Lumber over the new measures and threatened to eliminate the board's severance packages altogether. Capitulation was swift.

The quick acquiescence to Hurwitz's bid and threats provides evidence that there simply was not enough shareholder will to hold out, especially when they could earn such a healthy return on their stock sales. In particular, Campbell was surprised that management and the board never discussed using Hurwitz's greenmailing strategy against him. Campbell thought the company could have bought off Hurwitz for $100 million if they wanted to, and they had the resources to absorb a payment of that size. For instance, the company could have used the $60 million surplus in the pension fund because, according to Campbell, the IRS had told Pacific Lumber it had to stop depositing funds into the account because regulations didn't allow companies to shelter assets from taxes by placing them in pension fund surpluses. And with such low long-term debt, the firm could easily have borrowed the other $40 million Campbell thought necessary to buy off the corporate raider. The board, however, decided they couldn't beat Hurwitz and wanted the shareholders to get out with a profit, even if some shareholders vehemently disapproved of the sale. During the first week of December 1985, Maxxam accepted 13.1 million shares of Pacific Lumber stock—approximately 60 percent of the total—and planned to buy the remaining shares in early 1986. One of the earliest, if not the earliest, hostile takeover backed by Michael Milken junk bonds had been completed, but objections to the takeover were not finished. In fact, they had only just begun.[22]

While the fight over the merger played out, Campbell prepared for the coming changes, hoping to execute his production plans. For the timber executive, the merger turned into his best opportunity to implement his industrial vision. In October, before the board even approved the merger, Campbell had ordered a new shipping building in Scotia to store additional lumber products, and he ordered additional tractors and bulldozers to increase the capacity of the lumber mills. He assumed the acquisition attempt, even if unsuccessful, would lead to further increases in harvests to drive up the stock price and make the company less vulnerable. Accordingly, in 1986, Campbell bought a mill from Louisiana-Pacific in Carlotta, at the doorstep of what would become known as Headwaters Forest. Early in the winter, Campbell and another manager, Tom Malarkey, met in San Francisco with longtime Maxxam executives Robert Rosen and Bill Leone. Campbell requested a new timber inventory and a modern computer inventory system for the timber products division, including a geographic information system. Leone agreed, and the inventory revealed that the property could handle an annual cut of 226 million board feet, compared with the old limit of 130 million board feet. For Campbell, the new owners must have seemed like a blessing.[23]

Anxiety marred much of the transition to the new ownership, however. Hurwitz visited Scotia in December 1985 and drew the ire of employees and the community with his ill-fated attempt at humor—the infamous "he who has the gold rules" comments at an all-employee meeting. Company employees subsequently took out a full-page ad in the *Times Standard* objecting to the takeover, and some of them unsuccessfully attempted to unionize. Though the union effort failed, it was clear that Maxxam's leadership did not inspire trust among the workers. By June 1986, the company had hired three hundred additional employees and announced plans to log 45 percent more old-growth acreage than in previous years, and even more second-growth trees. Though this would entail a short-term employment boon, some workers continued to worry that Maxxam planned to log the forest quickly and leave town. Adding to those fears, in 1987 the company refinanced its junk bond debt with additional non–investment grade notes and sold "substantial numbers of raw logs" to generate cash flow until the new harvests were ready to be milled, apparent signs that the takeover had severely strained the finances of both companies. Finally, Maxxam sold Palco Industries for $320 million. The massive junk bond debt and the Palco sale stoked escalating fears that Hurwitz intended to dismantle the company and the forest for cash and then shut down operations.[24]

As with previous Hurwitz deals, allegations of fraud surfaced almost immediately. Federal regulators, Congress, and journalists all investigated the takeover and concluded that rules and laws had been broken or evaded. In addition to dragging Pacific Lumber into the Redwood

Wars, the SEC investigation unearthed a large and lucrative network of insider trading that dominated the national news during the late 1980s. Very early on, the SEC was aware of some suspicious activity. In December 1986, the New York Stock Exchange recommended that the SEC investigate the activity of Herbert Gordon, a music producer in Westport, Connecticut, who commuted into New York City with Robert Rosen of Maxxam. Gordon had purchased 16,900 shares of Pacific Lumber in September 1985, just before the tender offer. Regulators suspected that Rosen had given Gordon inside information about the impending takeover. Gordon, however, was only a minor player in the insider trading of the 1980s. The same month that investigators began looking into the Gordon transactions, *Time* featured unsavory investing practices on its cover, the beginning of a two-year process that shattered the image of Wall Street and sent several individuals involved with the Pacific Lumber takeover to jail.[25]

An SEC investigation of a network of transactions centered on Ivan Boesky and Michael Milken pulled Charles Hurwitz and Pacific Lumber into the national limelight. Boesky became the face of Wall Street greed when he graced that December 1986 *Time* cover with the caption "Wall St. Scam" next to his face, above the moniker "Ivan the Terrible." Boesky specialized in betting on corporate takeovers and had made hundreds of millions of dollars since the late 1970s. Michael Milken was the banker at Drexel Burnham Lanham in Los Angeles who invented and sold the junk bond. The bonds offered high interest rates in exchange for high risk, and there was a market for high-risk, high-reward investments as the stock market climbed during the mid-1980s. Hurwitz and other takeover artists used the junk bonds to finance highly leveraged corporate takeover bids—bids financed with large amounts of debt and very little capital. Those ventures were risky because the large debt put a strain on the revenue streams of the acquired companies and could force management to follow a strategy that would produce short-term cash while damaging the long-term prospects of the company. If the company failed, the junk bond debt went unpaid, costing investors millions of dollars. The Pacific Lumber takeover was just that sort of deal.

Both Boesky and Milken were heavily involved in the Pacific Lumber takeover, adding to the attention drawn to the deal by the suspicious Gordon transactions. Congress and the SEC rapidly identified the timber deal as central to their work. In January 1987, the agency asked for the records of a New York accounting firm to review payments made by Ivan Boesky to Drexel Burnham. The investigators believed Boesky had been paying Milken and his team for insider trading tips, including information about Hurwitz's designs on Pacific Lumber. As they tracked Boesky's activity, they discovered a series of unusual transactions involving a number of companies recently acquired by larger firms. The SEC subpoenaed Maxxam Group, Diamond Shamrock Corporation, Lorimar-Telepictures, and Turner Broadcasting System—all firms that had orchestrated recent takeover bids underwritten by Milken and Drexel Burnham. Boesky also happened to own numerous shares in each of the acquired companies. It seemed unrealistic that a single trader like Boesky could have so accurately foreseen so many takeover efforts. For the SEC and Congress, the Pacific Lumber takeover was thus critical to the rapidly unraveling insider trading scandal because it potentially marked the earliest coordination among investors, traders, and bankers.[26]

When Congress began investigations into Wall Street corruption, more information emerged that helped North Coast opponents paint the takeover and Hurwitz as illegitimate. In May 1987, Congressman John Dingell from Michigan held the first congressional hearing regarding Milken and Boesky, focused on their role in the Pacific Lumber takeover. Dingell was a powerful Democrat who served in the House of Representatives for fifty years, starting in 1965. Author of the Endangered Species Act and a champion of workers' rights since his first election, Dingell was concerned about the impact of the mergers and acquisitions frenzy on American workers. In October, Dingell's committee concluded that Boyd Jefferies, a longtime West Coast trader and investor, secretly bought and held Pacific Lumber stock in early 1985 at Boesky's instruction so that Hurwitz could buy the stock at a later date. So-called parking stock is illegal because it allows the intended buyer, Hurwitz in this case, to accumulate stock without triggering SEC notification requirements, which dictate that after acquiring 5 percent of the shares of a company, an investor must notify the SEC whether an acquisition bid is planned.

By parking stock and using various subsidiaries of Maxxam to purchase additional shares, Hurwitz could disguise his intention to take over the timber firm, thus surprising Gene Elam, Pacific Lumber's president, with that early morning phone call on September 30, 1985. Hurwitz denied that his September 27 purchase of 539,600 shares of Pacific Lumber stock from Jefferies for below market price was set up in advance. Milken, Boesky, and Jefferies, however, were convicted of insider trading violations. Milken and Boesky were sentenced to federal prison terms, paid fines of $100 million and $600 million respectively, and were banned from stock activity for life. Jefferies paid a large fine, was sentenced to probation, resigned from his company, and was banned from stock activity for a number of years. The Public Broadcasting Service aired a thirty-minute documentary about the Pacific Lumber takeover and the insider trading scandal, further placing the company on radar of the public and North Coast activists. As in the past, Hurwitz escaped prosecution, but not without cost.[27]

Maxxam's takeover of Pacific Lumber had thus unintentionally driven the company with the small-town image into the national spotlight, marking yet another period of transformation in the Redwood Wars. New owners ran the Pacific Lumber Company, and not a single Murphy sat on the board. In their place was a group of Texans and New Yorkers with a long history of controversy and animosity. A junk bond debt of hundreds of millions of dollars weighed down the firm's finances. The notoriety drew scrutiny from local constituencies as Pacific Lumber suddenly started to look just like other industrial logging firms. Some workers viewed the new owners as hostile outsiders intent on dismantling the century-old Pacific Lumber Company. The fact that convicted criminals had orchestrated the takeover stoked activist fears that the new owners intended to liquidate the forest to pay off the junk bond debt. Plans by John Campbell and the former board to increase harvest levels and to begin clear-cutting were not well known immediately following the takeover. Those harvest plans became clear enough to activists within two years, however, and the Maxxam takeover would further increase logging activity on Pacific Lumber property. Activists on the North Coast grew increasingly agitated by the seemingly ever-expanding industrial logging by companies in Redwood Country, leading to more aggressive campaigns in more locations, especially on Pacific Lumber property. The stakes were also higher for the timber companies: they needed to pay off debts, compete with international logging operations, and contend with an expanding environmental protection regime. But it was the activists who initiated the battle.

EARTH FIRST! RETURNS

A new migration wave of activists energized the North Coast environmental movement with their own brand of nontraditional beliefs, and the Pacific Lumber takeover pulled them together as a movement. Those activists were largely responsible for the widespread adoption of direct action on the North Coast, the increasingly hostile tone of the activist community, and the unprecedented legal assault on development-focused forestry regulation, or de facto corporatism. Like the migrants of the late 1960s and early 1970s, most of the newer activists had been raised in midwestern or eastern middle-class homes. They were college graduates who had come to the North Coast in search of an alternative society. All shared an uncompromising constitution and a desire to confront corporate power. Their organizing, research, and media skills helped expand the popularity of the redwood preservation movement on the North Coast and beyond. Their visibility and unyielding positions made them easy targets, and frequently made coalition work and conflict resolution with state and corporate actors nearly impossible. This second wave of migrants, like the first, advanced the experimental and aggressive nature of the campaigns just as David Brower had changed the nature of public land campaigns during the 1950s and 1960s. The new migrants embraced hard-hitting positions, rhetoric, and visuals, just as Brower had when he published *The Last Redwoods* and publicly opposed Save the Redwoods League during the 1960s in the fight over Redwood National Park.[28]

The decision by North Coast Earth First! to escalate a direct action campaign on the North Coast made the Redwood Wars a national story—and ultimately protracted the conflict. Pacific Lumber's turn to clear-cutting after the Maxxam takeover was particularly troubling to the activists, especially after they discovered Headwaters Forest. John Campbell realized in October 1985 that the Maxxam takeover would bring change to his world, and indeed it did. Pacific Lumber transformed its logging operations, and that transformation changed the company's relationship with the redwood preservation movement. In 1984, the company harvested 3,701 acres; in 1985, they harvested 5,188 acres, evidence of Campbell's assertion that he had planned to increase production well before the merger. But the merger led to even greater increases: it logged 9,447 acres in 1986 and 10,436 acres in 1988. Of that total acreage, Pacific Lumber had traditionally harvested about 1,000 acres of old growth annually. In 1988, 7,811 acres of the 10,436 total were old-growth harvests; in 1989, 5,487 acres of the 8,206 total were old growth. Campbell claimed the company never doubled the rate of logging, but the evidence is clear. In the early 1980s, Campbell acquired additional land, but he did not double the size of the property, and he added no old-growth or ancient forest. But regardless of the actual rate increase, the increased acreage of old-growth harvests being cut was enough to fuel massive environmental opposition, adding Pacific Lumber to Georgia-Pacific and Louisiana-Pacific as the top environmental enemies.[29]

Despite the success of the Sally Bell Grove actions, activists had not pursued direct action and civil disobedience on the North Coast. But it didn't take long for the tactic to resurface among redwood preservation activists—certainly nothing like the time that elapsed between the 1924 Laura Mahan protest and those at Sally Bell. Once tree-sits, road blockades, and public trespassing were firmly established on the North Coast, the area remained awash in nearly daily direct actions and rallies for more than a decade. The intensity, frequency, and style of the actions delivered unprecedented media coverage—and industry backlash—to the Redwood Wars. The first actions after 1985 helped the movement garner great public support because they were largely media stunts, much like Andrew Hill's photographs during the Big Basin campaign at the turn of the twentieth century or the Sierra Club's films and books during the Redwood Park campaign. The events were aimed at publicity and not backwoods warfare.

Earth First! and direct action exploded on the North Coast after 1985 as a result of Darryl Cherney's arrival in Humboldt County and his encounter with Sonoma native and investigative reporter Greg King. Cherney, a slender man with bushy, dark hair, was in many ways a natural entertainer, though he described himself as a late bloomer— "the last kid on the block to kiss a girl and smoke pot." Cherney was gregarious, however, with a presence stereotypically described as "New York," utilizing sarcasm and a biting sense of humor to make his points. His talents in communication served him well as he worked to resurrect North Coast Earth First! Cherney's roots in media went back to his Manhattan childhood, where, at age five, he worked with advertisement creator Tony Schwartz, most famous for the "Daisy" television ads Lyndon Johnson ran in his campaign against Barry Goldwater in 1964. Cherney moved to Garberville in November 1985 after stints in marketing with the National Football League and Capital Sports Marketing. Cherney said he fell in love with the redwoods in 1970 on a family vacation and dreamed of one day living among them. The New Yorker's environmentalism was thus born of the awe that trip to the redwoods inspired in him, as well as his developing critique of consumer capitalism. Frustrated with city life and the materialism he saw around him every day, Cherney packed up his Dodge Sportsman camper van and left for California in late 1985 to fulfill his childhood dream.

Cherney moved west to reinvent himself and to figure out how to help save humanity from itself. He did not lack self-confidence. He was convinced that consumerism was destroying not only the planet but human morals and mental health. En route to San Francisco, Cherney picked up a hitchhiker named Kingfisher along the Oregon coast, and his plans changed dramatically. Kingfisher led Cherney to Garberville because he said that was where people were really living off the land—and working to save it. Almost immediately, Cherney located the EPIC office, where he immersed himself in redwood logging issues. Cherney asked a local activist, Mokai, about the Earth First! sticker on EPIC's front door and was told that the organization was "just a bunch of people who do things." In the office he found a copy of *Deep Ecology*, written by Humboldt State University professor Bill Devall. The book was a seminal work on environmental ethics, which had just come out that year and had captured the imagination of environmentalists looking to support their ethical stances with ecological principles. The basic tenet of deep ecology, often referred to as biocentrism, is that the earth and its nonhuman inhabitants have an inherent value independent of, and equal to, humanity, and that humans have a moral duty to protect and promote the survival of the earth's systems as living environments. The philosophy questioned the value of industrial society, consumerism, and the social focus on increasing economic standards of living rather than quality of life. The philosophy immediately spoke to Cherney.[30]

The North Coast activists around Garberville embraced the philosophy of deep ecology first articulated by Arne Naess in 1976, made popular in the United States by Bill Devall and George Sessions, and put into political action by Earth First!. Deep ecology resonated with Earth First! activists around the country because it provided a moral foundation for their ideas regarding wilderness protection and the ills of industrial society and population growth. The popularity of deep ecology gave rise to the activist-oriented scientific field of conservation biology, which bolstered environmentalists' arguments about the importance of protecting biodiversity and ecosystem health even as it challenged traditional forms of preservation like national parks. For Cherney, biocentrism was a nontechnical way to understand the need to protect species and forests. However, while Earth First! members who followed Dave Foreman's instructions more strictly adhered to the biocentric worldview, often to the point of misanthropy, Cherney and other North Coast activists incorporated social justice values into their environmentalism. That melding of social and environmental concerns set the actions of the North Coast apart from other radical environmental groups and helped turn out massive crowds at their public events.[31]

Though a small Earth First! group existed at Humboldt State University in the mid-1980s, the group disappeared from the Garberville area after EPIC won the Sally Bell court case. Cherney, however, was intrigued by the sticker and Devall's book. He asked Mokai how one joined Earth First! and how one obtained approval to act. Mokai told him, "You just go ahead and do it; it's cool." Cherney did not seize the opportunity right away. Instead, he did office work for EPIC for five dollars an hour, until 1986, when he participated in his first illegal direct action. From that March day until the early twenty-first century, Earth First! defined Cherney's identity.[32]

Fittingly, Earth First! was officially reborn on the North Coast in March 1986 at the site of its original appearance: Georgia-Pacific property near the Sinkyone. Richard Gienger and Mark Mullens organized locals to illegally plant approximately three thousand Douglas firs and redwoods on a Georgia-Pacific clear-cut near the Sally Bell Grove. Cherney asked if the guerrilla planting could be an Earth First! action, and when Mokai agreed, Cherney sent out a press release. A photograph of the action ran in the local paper, the *Redwood Record*. The day of the action, Greg King, a reporter from the *West Sonoma County Paper* who was unaware of the tree planting action, pulled into the EPIC parking lot to ask for directions to the Sinkyone. King was a fourth-generation North Coaster; the King Range was named after his ancestors, most of them loggers. The reporter had recently won an award for an article on industrial logging in Sonoma, and he wanted to see the Sally Bell Grove. When King pulled into the EPIC lot driving a four-wheel-drive truck, Cherney walked up to him and said, "I'm Darryl Cherney. Can we borrow your car?" King agreed to give Cherney and other activists a ride to the tree planting, and when they arrived, King headed into the forest for a hike. The reporter hiked by himself through the Sally Bell Grove and out into a Georgia-Pacific clear-cut, a scene that convinced him the logging of ancient forests had to be stopped.[33]

King and Cherney corresponded over the subsequent months (Cherney did not have a phone in the geodesic dome he rented for $125 a month), and they soon became organizing partners on a mission to protect Headwaters Forest. King lived in Guerneville in Sonoma County and was working on an article about Louisiana-Pacific's plans to clear-cut the company's remaining twenty thousand acres in Sonoma and sell the cutover land to real estate developers. He told Cherney the company's foresters were threatening him. For his part, Cherney was looking into Maxxam and the implications of the Pacific Lumber takeover. He asked EPIC, the North Coast Environmental Center in Arcata, and the Redwood Chapter of the Sierra Club to help him investigate Pacific Lumber activities, but they were all busy with other work and told Cherney he needed to take it on himself. During the late spring of 1986, Cherney called King, who had decided it was time for Earth First! to meet again. King had a copy of the 1986 Maxxam prospectus that detailed the financing of the takeover as well as the plan to harvest Pacific Lumber's remaining old growth within the next two decades. King was determined to stop Maxxam. In June, approximately twenty activists met at Annwfn (pronounced "On-a-van"), a piece of land owned by the Church of All Worlds, a pagan church in Greenfield

Ranch, just north of Ukiah in central Mendocino County. King and Cherney attended the meeting, as did Gary and Betty Ball from Mendocino County.[34]

Betty Ball was another recent transplant. She came from Milwaukee, the daughter of a YMCA director and a special education teacher. During the late 1960s, after graduating college, Ball worked as the program director for Hull House, the famous Progressive Era institution founded to assist immigrants, women, and the poor to assimilate in Chicago. Betty Ball, like Woods, was a countercultural reformer. She participated in the 1968 Democratic Convention protests, and she resigned from Hull House after the board decided to add middle-class programs like dance and theater to generate additional funding; her heart had grown more committed to radical social reform. Ball moved to Boulder, Colorado, where she married Gary Ball. She worked at a resource center for transients and at the National Institute for Criminal Justice and Community Relations. Looking for something else to do after a failed partnership in an optical retail business with Gary's father, the couple went on vacation to the Lost Coast. While on vacation, they decided they wanted to open an environmental center in California to help local activists coordinate so they wouldn't compete for resources. In the spring of 1986, the couple moved to California, and within a year they had moved to Ukiah and opened the Mendocino Environmental Center, which would become a primary nerve center for the redwood preservation movement.[35]

At the Annwfn meeting, attendees decided some of them would go to the annual Round River Rendezvous of the national Earth First! movement. The Round River Rendezvous was a camping retreat for Earth First! activists where they could learn about each other's work, successes, failures, and experiments. Part workshop and part team building, the retreat was a rowdy affair, where drinking, singing, and pot smoking helped build bonds. That year's retreat produced a national plan to focus the organization's efforts on Maxxam and its plans to log the redwood forest. The decision to focus on Maxxam proved wise because it opened possibilities to harness broader community concerns about the takeover to activists' concerns about the fate of North Coast redwood forests. Once the actions began, North Coast Earth First! grew in size and reputation, as the organization publicized what its leaders saw as the common enemy of the activists and the loggers: Maxxam. The activists also tapped into broader concerns about the fate of rain forests and biodiversity that had emerged out of recent scientific research about biogeography and species extinction rates. Such concerns had led Mike Roselle to leave Earth First! in 1985 to found the Rainforest Action Network, based in San Francisco.[36]

The first actions targeting Pacific Lumber were rallies that simply alerted Pacific Lumber to environmental opposition to its land management. In September 1986, Earth First! and Rainforest Action Network organized a national day of action focused on Pacific Lumber and its old-growth redwood forest. North Coast Earth First! organized a rally in Arcata. Alone, the small rallies might not have caused much concern within Pacific Lumber; however, the actions occurred at a time when logging seemed threatened across the West. More than one hundred national forest management plans were held up in courts over NEPA's environmental impact statement requirements. In addition, Earth First! in Oregon had recently halted logging inside part of the Willamette National Forest by conducting a six-month tree-sit two hundred feet in the air, and the US Forest Service had proposed banning logging on more than half a million acres in Oregon to protect the dwindling northern spotted owl population. The environmental protection developments were more broadly causing conservative political groups to wring their hands over "the specter of environmentalism" and its impact on businesses. Coming on the heels of conflicts over Alaska, western wilderness processes, and emerging concerns within the government over the long-term economic model of industrial forestry, the fall 1986 actions commanded Pacific Lumber's attention, especially when the hits kept coming from the radical locals.[37]

Following up on those first rallies, Cherney and others attempted, largely unsuccessfully, to build an alliance with workers in the battles against industrial logging and multinational corporate power. Their early efforts were often theatrical, in the hope that workers would be inspired by the same rallies and theater that drew environmentalists. In October 1986, after a regional Earth First! rendezvous near Santa Cruz, many California activists rallied at Pacific Lumber headquarters in San Francisco to protest the new logging regime. The centerpiece of the protest was a bit of street theater during which Tyrannosaurus rex blew up the Maxxam monster. Cherney played Charles Hurwitz. The show included a love story between a logger and an Amazonian-style forest activist. Mike Roselle played the logger, and he fought Hurwitz/ Cherney after being handed a pink slip, a clear attempt to woo loggers. In December, Cherney organized a rally in Scotia near the Pacific Lumber mills. "Paul Bunyan" spoke at the rally, while attendees held signs that read, "Will Jobs Be Gone in 20 years?" Prior to the rally, Cherney sent "Save the Loggers League" pamphlets to all the post office boxes in Scotia, the Pacific Lumber company town where its loggers and mill workers lived. The rallies may have piqued worker interest, but there was no mass movement toward an alliance with the radical environmentalists.[38]

Undeterred, North Coast Earth First! continued to stage loud, colorful rallies and protests designed to convince local residents of all stripes that Maxxam ownership of Pacific Lumber spelled certain doom for the rural society. In March 1987, Greg King, having purchased a single share of Maxxam stock, led activists to a Maxxam shareholders meeting in Houston to voice their concerns, thus following in the footsteps of Richard Gienger. North Coast Earth First! organized a protest at a Board of Forestry meeting in Eureka that month, where Cherney wore a chimpanzee mask and held a sign that read, "Monkeywrench the Monkey Business," referring to Edward Abbey's novel *The Monkeywrench Gang*, in which four friends destroy old trains, tractors, and other tools of development across the desert Southwest. Dave Foreman and Earth First! embraced monkeywrenching, or ecotage, as a tactic with the capacity to irritate industrial operations and cause them to lose money. Cherney hoped to eventually "kick Hurwitz out of Humboldt."

While Cherney developed a campaign strategy, Greg King, Kurt Newman, and Larry Evans decided they would trespass onto Pacific Lumber land in the dark of night to map the ancient forest reserves held by the company, an effort that led to the discovery of Headwaters Forest. The three men had connected at the September 1986 Arcata rally and believed local activists needed to understand the ramifications of Pacific Lumber's plan to liquidate its old-growth trees and turn its land into a young-growth forest. Nobody knew what Pacific Lumber owned because, unlike the Lost Coast, there were no homesteaders or small communities near the heart of Pacific Lumber property. They would sneak onto the land and start mapping it to ensure that Maxxam wasn't destroying any ancient forest.[39]

It seemed like the activists were building momentum, but in May 1987 events conspired to undermine their credibility with workers and other North Coast residents. George Alexander, a Louisiana-Pacific mill worker in Cloverdale, was nearly decapitated when the blade of his mill saw hit a large nail buried in a log. The nail caused the giant saw blade to rip loose from its axle, striking Alexander in the throat and leaving him lying, near death, on the floor of the lumber mill. Alexander survived, but local and state headlines proclaimed, "Eco-Terrorists Focus of Mill Accident Probe" and "Tree Spiking Terrorism." Tree spiking was in fact a tactic promoted by Dave Foreman and used by some Earth First! activists in the Pacific Northwest to stop timber sales on federal land. Activists would sneak into a forest and drive large nails into the bark of some trees. The nails did not threaten the trees' health, but if a chainsaw hit the nail, the chain could fly off and seriously injure a logger. The activists did not want to harm the loggers; they wanted to stop logging. Thus, after spiking an area, the activists would call the US Forest Service to warn them that some trees contained large nails. Logging could not move forward in the area without knowing which trees had been spiked. The tree in the Cloverdale tragedy was a small second-growth tree—not a giant ancient redwood—and it was later determined that the likely culprit was a mentally unstable landowner in the area, but that didn't matter at the time. The image of the North Coast activists never fully recovered.[40]

Despite the Cloverdale tragedy, the direct action campaign continued as planned. In May, King and Evans announced they had discovered a vast ancient forest in the middle of Pacific Lumber's property. The forest was in the northern part of the property, not far from Eureka, the largest city on the North Coast. The public had no idea that the area contained an ancient forest covering tens of thousands of acres. The men were awestruck when they stumbled across the ancient groves set back miles from the coast up in the hills. As Greg King said in a 1989 *Rolling Stone* article, hiking into Headwaters Forest was akin to "being dropped into a world totally apart from this planet." It was not a picturesque grove along an alluvial flat filled with giant redwoods of both girth and height; rather, it was a vast upland forest covered by a sea of tall, ancient redwoods of substantial but not mammoth diameter. They named it Headwaters Forest because numerous streams originating in the old-growth groves fed the major rivers of the region, including the Eel and Elk Rivers. Small streams and creeks seemed to emerge out of the rugged terrain on all sides. The activists described six groves of ancient forest in a sea of second-growth trees and clear-cuts. They named the largest stand Headwaters Grove because several streams and creeks originated there. King described the Little South Fork of the Elk River, which runs through the redwood complex, as "probably the finest redwood stream in the world. . . . [I]t's like a little microriver." His reverence and love for the groves was clear: "These trees are good friends of mine, as dear to me as any person." In naming the forest and its groves, the activists followed the conservationist tradition of giving places an identity as a means of generating traction with the broader public.[41]

Immediately, the North Coast activists at EPIC and Earth First! decided to make a top priority of stopping the Maxxam logging plans. On May 18, approximately 150 people gathered outside a Pacific Lumber logging road to thwart the company's efforts to harvest the old-growth groves. Fisher Road gate, outside Carlotta, was on the Louisiana-Pacific land Campbell had purchased, and the road led directly to Headwaters Forest. Six women were arrested for climbing up on a logging deck, and Mokai led a relatively unsuccessful three-person tree-sit in a stand of ancient trees that King's team had named All Species Grove. In late August, Greg King and Mary Beth Nearing climbed two trees in Elk-head Springs Grove and then All Species Grove. Those tree-sits garnered great attention from *Outside*, drawing mainstream press coverage to the Headwaters campaign and firmly establishing direct action as a primary tactic in the Redwood Wars.[42]

The Redwood Wars expanded in the late 1980s after Pacific Lumber refused to back down, deciding instead that it would mount a counter-attack. North Coast Earth First! had ramped up its tree-sitting efforts and was touring the state holding small grassroots fund-raisers to pay for their attacks on Pacific Lumber. In response to their activities, John Campbell told his woodsmen to call the sheriff rather than confronting the activists. However, he added, it was okay to have a little fun with the activists to discourage them from returning after the sheriffs escorted them off the property. Thus, when activists held rallies at Scotia in front of the Pacific Lumber offices, Campbell turned on the sprinklers. And in the fall of 1988, Pacific Lumber employees rubbed honey on the trunk of a tree below a sitter to attract bees and bears. The playfulness ran alongside serious hostility, however. Loggers in the woods yelled and cursed at the sitters, and sent climbers up trees to scare them and threaten to cut their ropes. To turn public opinion against the radicals, the company began to refer to Earth First! as a terrorist group during press interviews. The battle over Headwaters Forest was not going to be resolved through genteel negotiations.[43]

The relationship between activists and Pacific Lumber never went beyond mutual hostility because both sides refused to compromise. The activists believed protections offered by the 1970s environmental laws prohibited Pacific Lumber from logging the areas, and they weren't interested in compromise. Enough ancient trees had been logged. Pacific Lumber believed the new laws were ill conceived, and management looked at the activist challenges to their property rights as an existential threat to the company. Like the radicals, Pacific Lumber was in no mood to compromise. The company seemed confident that the California tradition of official and de facto corporatism would once again allow the timber industry to log private land as it wished. Not only could the industry lean on de facto corporatism, but it also had resources that were vastly superior to both the activists and the state district courts. And despite the series of judgments against corporatism, the state government certainly must have seemed like a more favorable venue for timber interests than the federal government in 1987.

Timber executives had observed the compromises forged in Congress as a result of industry losses in federal court. When activists challenged clear-cutting in national forests in the *Monongahela* case, Congress stepped in to legislate a compromise. In 1976, the National Forest Management Act specifically legalized clear-cutting. The law also mandated that the US Forest Service develop sustainable logging plans every ten years for all of the national forests. Those studies and plans would take time to develop and were certainly intended to slow logging on federal land, reducing profits for the timber industry. The following year, the Supreme Court heard its first case involving the 1973 Endangered Species Act, stopping a federal dam project. Congress had approved a new dam on the Telico River, part of the New Deal Tennessee Valley Authority hydroelectric power system. The dam project had brought electricity and construction jobs to the poor, rural region. It also, however, had displaced many farmers. Some of those farmers, working with environmentalists, discovered the rare snail darter fish in the Telico River. The Supreme Court ruled that the government had to abort the dam project, although the project had already begun and halting it would mean the loss of millions of dollars. The Endangered Species Act had proved a powerful tool in stopping development because its tough requirements excluded economic considerations when making decisions about protecting species threatened with extinction.

As they had done after the *Monongahela* ruling, development interests convinced Congress in 1978 to amend the Endangered Species Act, and again, Congress would forge a series of compromises granting short-term victory to industry with accompanying long-term costs. The 1978 amendments allowed the president to convene a so-called "God Squad" of cabinet heads and gave it the authority to overrule court orders and authorize a project that threatened a listed species. The amendment additionally allowed the executive branch to consider national economics when applying the Endangered Species Act. Flexibility was again added to the process in 1982, when Congress passed provisions enabling landowners to apply for an Incidental Take Permit that would allow destruction of endangered species habitat. In exchange, the permit holder needed to develop a Habitat Conservation Plan for the property that would provide for future increases in the threatened species' population. The Endangered Species Act compromises created new opportunities for development, but they came with a high price tag— long-term restrictions and obligations to the federal government. Pacific Lumber was determined not to allow activists to force them into such compromises over their land in Redwood Country. Thus, on the North Coast, timber firms and activists alike sought to contain the conflict to the local region rather than draw the attention of the federal government, whose compromise strategy was undesirable to both groups. As a result, battles in the local courtrooms increased in number and duration as the combatants continued to fight over the State of California's regulations for logging on private property.[44]

The initial confrontations in the Pacific Lumber woods in 1987 were only one part of the activist strategy to dismantle industrial logging on the North Coast. The success of the Sally Bell case (*EPIC v. Johnson*) convinced activists that litigation could serve as a powerful tool to permanently transform the North Coast. Before the Pacific Lumber tree-sits, Greg King and Darryl Cherney had already convinced Robert Sutherland, known as the Man Who Walks in the Woods, to sue Maxxam after they discovered two harvest plans for the newly identified Headwaters Forest complex. Woods, the charismatic cofounder of EPIC, was highly intelligent and, like Cherney, not lacking in self-confidence. He too believed that consumerism and capitalism were making humanity ill. As Woods described it, people were too accustomed to worshipping money as a form of "manna." He viewed the reform of logging practices and the reduction of corporate power as two steps on the path to reducing overconsumption. As EPIC's litigation coordinator and cofounder, Woods did not want the organization to work on issues outside southern Humboldt, but he went along with King and Cherney's proposal anyway. EPIC activists had begun monitoring Pacific Lumber harvest plans, and he wanted to expand the use of the *EPIC v. Johnson* case. To that end, Woods had already written a new brief for the then moot second Sally Bell lawsuit, so while a Maxxam suit was not in line with his vision for EPIC, the suit did fit into his broader plan to reform timber practices, which involved extensive use of the courtroom to "hit the donkey" until it moved.[45]

EPIC's first case against Pacific Lumber, *Maxxam I*, further undermined de facto corporatism and opened the floodgates for a tidal wave of lawsuits against the redwood lumber giant. In 1987, EPIC requested writs of mandate against three Pacific Lumber harvest plans, including two plans within Headwaters Forest. A writ of mandate invalidates a decision by a public agency on the basis of procedural violations; the agency then has an opportunity to resubmit its decision once it has remedied the errors or violations. According to EPIC, the logging plans lacked a CEQA-required cumulative impact analysis of the logging on the watershed and wildlife. Furthermore, none of the plans included provisions to mitigate environmental damage. Despite previous rulings that Timber Harvest Plans needed to follow CEQA guidelines, the Department of Forestry had signed off on three clearly deficient plans. Pacific Lumber and the forestry agency were determined to continue to push back against environmentalism.

The activists saw in the plans something even more sinister than the defiance of state law. The two Headwaters Forest plans prescribed clear-cutting ancient forest along Salmon Creek and the South Fork of the Eel River, and the third plan proposed clear-cutting old-growth Douglas fir in the Mattole River watershed east of the Lost Coast. The activists substantively objected to the company's plan to clear-cut its old-growth trees. The Salmon Creek plan would have, as Greg King wrote, "ripped the [Headwaters Grove] stand in half." The activists concluded that the company intended to fragment the grove of ancient trees specifically to reduce its value as habitat and thus prevent challenges to future clear-cuts in the area based on endangered species policy. The activists, probably correctly, viewed the proposed harvests as a grand version of the "shoot, shovel, and shut up" defense against the Endangered Species Act, which entailed secretly killing any endangered species found on one's property. The North Coast activists were determined to prevent Pacific Lumber from degrading the forest before the public even knew what the forest contained.

During the *Maxxam I* case, the Department of Forestry tried a new strategy to insulate itself from environmental protection laws. The agency argued that its hands were tied because the Timber Production Act superseded the environmental protection laws. State law had zoned the land for timber harvesting, making other uses illegal. The agency argued that CEQA and the California Endangered Species Act could not be applied to Timber Harvest Plans because the laws would effectively rezone the land for a different purpose. Thus, even though the harvests would cause significant environmental harm, the agency argued that it could not stop Pacific Lumber from logging its property. The judge disagreed. In November, a Humboldt Superior Court judge ruled that the courts had previously determined that Timber Harvest Plans must fulfill all CEQA requirements, regardless of timber production zoning. The judge added that the Department of Forestry had abused its administrative discretion when it "rubber-stamped" harvest plans and intimidated other agencies. In truth, the Department of

Forestry often approved incomplete logging plans and had contacted California Fish and Game biologists to prevent them from filing objections to plans that did not contain any scientific information about the presence of species of concern, such as the marbled murrelet, a small seabird that nests in old-growth redwoods and Douglas fir. The ruling in *Maxxam I* thus bolstered the court's *Johnson* decision and further discredited the Department of Forestry. It did not by itself, however, halt Pacific Lumber's logging plans; the plans were simply returned to the company and the agency for revision.[46]

A pattern was developing by the end of 1988: EPIC would challenge old-growth harvest plans based on the *Johnson* model, local Earth First! activists would stage direct actions to delay logging activity, Pacific Lumber would attempt to log the areas before the courts intervened, and when in court, Pacific Lumber and the Department of Forestry would experiment with defense arguments that might reverse existing precedent. For example, EPIC filed another lawsuit in 1987 that challenged two more 1987 Pacific Lumber logging plans within Headwaters Forest, as well as one Simpson Timber plan (*EPIC v. Maxxam II*). Simpson Timber withdrew its plan rather than go to court, but Pacific Lumber fought the writs of mandate. On April 1, a Humboldt judge denied EPIC a temporary restraining order for the harvest plan, but on April 25, the judge accepted a new petition for a restraining order. However, Pacific Lumber had been able to log most of one harvest area during the delay. In a letter to the Department of Forestry, John Campbell, the head of Pacific Lumber logging operations, outlined a new legal strategy. Instead of challenging CEQA's application to logging, the company planned to challenge California Fish and Game's assertion that the old-growth forests were important habitat for species of concern. Pacific Lumber argued that the wildlife agency never should have concerned itself with the species on company land because none of them were dependent upon old-growth redwood groves. Thus, on the North Coast, the science of habitat boundaries and population projections began to dominate environmental law and policy, as it had nationally. The company also claimed the state already owned enough redwood land to maintain viable populations of species dependent on old-growth redwoods. In May, Judge John Buffington placed a preliminary injunction on the contested harvest plans, and the logging ended.

On July 13, the Department of Forestry and Pacific Lumber reached a settlement: Pacific Lumber could remove the trees it had harvested in April, but the company would stop logging the harvest area.

The argument that the state already owned enough redwoods, which grew directly out of the fights over Redwood National Park in the 1960s and 1970s, remained a mainstay for timber companies for a decade. The timber firms had had enough. All across the United States, logging companies felt under attack in the wake of President Jimmy Carter's creation of the Alaska conservation lands and the growing spotted owl conflict over old-growth Douglas fir forests in the Pacific Northwest. Logging on federal land was declining, and the large owners of private timberland saw the same thing happening on their property. The creation of sixteen new wilderness areas in the East was further proof, they thought, that environmentalists were determined to drive them out of business. The industry reacted to the national trends by organizing citizens in defense of property rights and by challenging the science of environmentalists, on the North Coast and around the nation.[47]

EPIC v. Maxxam II created an initial, seemingly reluctant, split between the timber industry and the Board of Forestry. Despite the settlement between Pacific Lumber and the Department of Forestry, the trial judge eventually ruled against Maxxam and again accused the state's foresters of "rubber-stamping" and intimidation. In response, the Department of Forestry adopted emergency regulations covering old-growth timber plans, marbled murrelet and northern spotted owl habitat, and cumulative impact analysis. An appellate judge later strengthened the legitimacy of EPIC's litigation efforts by forcing Pacific Lumber to pay attorney fees for the case. Financial relief allowed EPIC to file additional lawsuits. The pressure of the litigation caused the agency to stray from the hard-line position that CEQA did not apply to Timber Harvest Plans, as evidenced by the agency's creation of the new regulations without a direct court order. The new regulations played a key role in breaking down development-focused corporatism because the agency had responded to citizens and courts, not to the wishes of the timber industry, and the rules recognized the agency's responsibility to noneconomic forestland resources. For the activists, the shift in agency policy was a major victory. One goal of the litigation was to destroy the traditional alliance between the forestry agency and the timber companies. Another goal was to force the agency to change its practices in order to better protect ecosystems. The *Maxxam II* ruling had finally forced the Department of Forestry to accommodate citizen demands instead of the timber company.[48]

1989: RECKONING

The activists of North Coast Earth First! seemed to hit their stride in 1989, but they faced a growing backlash, including physical violence—with near-deadly ramifications. The activists were publicly threatening to expand their challenges to industrial logging. The timber industry fought back. In 1987–88, Woods put the industry on notice. He drafted a manual, "How to Sue CDF," to help EPIC train the public to challenge Timber Harvest Plans. At a meeting of the California Licensed Foresters Association, he excoriated the Department of Forestry, accused the legislature of corruption, and called on professional foresters to work with environmentalists. At the 1988 convention of the National Association of State Foresters, Woods railed against the intimidation efforts of the Department of Forestry, referred to private property rights as the "merest legal fiction," and characterized the Redwood Wars as a "crisis of character" for society. In 1988 Woods was the face and voice of the North Coast movement to the media, and he both irritated timber executives and forestry officials and steeled them for battle the following year. Woods's messages made it clear that the activists expected not only to stop the logging of old growth, but also to transform the North Coast by evicting what they saw as cancerous corporate domination. In its place, they hoped to erect a community-oriented system of forestry and economics.[49]

For Greg King, the former journalist turned activist, 1989 began not in the trees but in meeting rooms. He had put together a slide show of photographs he had taken while trespassing on Pacific Lumber land, and he traveled the state to increase the visibility of, and public support for, the campaign to protect Headwaters Forest. Back in Humboldt, the tree-sits continued. Activists hung banners in the woods and over the Highway 101 overpass near the Fisher Road exit where Pacific Lumber loggers entered the Headwaters Forest complex. It was during that time that Cherney met Judi Bari while working on a poster at the Mendocino Environmental Center. Bari and Cherney fell in love, and Bari entered the fray on behalf of Earth First!, changing the direction of the North Coast activists' efforts to again emphasize broader social and forestry reform.

Judi Bari brought organizing experience and a fiery spirit to the campaign, reinvigorating activist efforts in Mendocino County and further widening the Redwood Wars. The thirty-seven-year-old's political style was rough and unyielding, a style she had cultivated on the East Coast during her college years. Bari was a native-born Marylander who had attended the University of Maryland, College Park. She described her major as "anti-Vietnam rioting." After leaving college early, Bari worked in a bakery, where she was fired for decorating a cake with a hammer, sickle, and the caption, "U.S. Get Out of the War." The bakers union successfully fought her dismissal, and a few years later, when the bakers struck, Bari led fellow picketers onto the property at night, sealing door locks with liquid steel and letting the air out of managers' tires. Bari unsuccessfully attempted to overthrow the same bakers union, then left to work as a package handler at the US Post Office. At the Postal Service, Bari eventually consolidated several unions into one, with herself at the helm. She was confident and not afraid of conflict. In 1979, Bari moved to California after meeting fellow union organizer Mike Sweeney at a labor conference. Sweeney lived in Sonoma County, just south of Mendocino. Bari married Sweeney and moved to Sonoma County. By 1988 the marriage had failed, leaving Bari with two girls.

Bari's environmentalism grew out of a commitment to labor organizing and social justice. She worked as a carpenter in Mendocino County, raised her daughters, and developed an urge to stop the last ancient redwoods from falling at the hands of loggers and corporations as she built homes out of the forest. She had grown concerned about the health of the planet her children would inherit, and she worried about the economic future of her fellow North Coast laborers. She feared that multinational corporations were going to leave the North Coast scarred and damaged, ecologically and economically. Bari certainly wasn't alone on that score, but she was the most forceful advocate on the North Coast who worked on the intersection between sustainable forestry, worker rights, and economic inequality. She understood the lives of timber workers because she was a lifelong blue-collar worker and union organizer. She understood connections between the loggers and the forest because she too worked with the fruits of the forest. She had experienced the unequal balance of power in industrial settings, and she did not trust corporate executives. She wanted to strip them of their power so that local people might make decisions for themselves about the future of their community.[50]

Bari and the other activist leaders on the North Coast empathized with the workers and seemed to truly desire a rural society with room for loggers, fisherman, farmers, and homesteaders. Quite unintentionally, the timber executives of the region initially assisted the activists' efforts to recruit timber workers. In addition to Maxxam's Charles Hurwitz, Louisiana-Pacific president Harry A. Merlo made himself an easy target for Judi Bari. In early 1989, Merlo told *Press Democrat* reporter Mike Geniella that the company was "chewing everything up and putting it back together. . . . We don't need a big tree [because we're making waferboard]. . . . We need everything that's out there. We don't log to a ten-inch top, or an eight-inch top, or a six-inch top. We log to infinity. Because we need it all. It's ours. It's out there and we need it all. Now."[51]

The *Press Democrat* was published in Santa Rosa in Sonoma County, but it was the major newspaper for residents of Mendocino County as well, and Merlo's statement was received in the same fashion as Hurwitz's statement that those with the gold do in fact rule. Judi Bari used that Merlo quote as fodder to recruit and motivate activists in her region, as well as to make inroads with Mendocino loggers worried about their jobs. Her efforts were aided by Louisiana-Pacific's November 10 announcement that it was building a $100 million mill in Mexico to process redwood logs, a plan protested by Earth First! and mill workers alike. The activists had begun to run up against the forces of globalization, which would connect their efforts to workers and environmentalists around the nation. In April, *Corporate Finance* discussed a burgeoning alliance between loggers and environmentalists on the North Coast, and in the fall, Bari represented Georgia-Pacific loggers and mill workers as the International Workers of the World representative in Fort Bragg. Also that fall, Pacific Lumber workers Peter Keyes and John Maurer began publishing *Timberlyin'*, an underground alternative to the company newsletter, *Timberline*. However, economic interests and environmental values were uneasy bedfellows in the post-war era, and the intersection of interests between the two groups of North Coasters was largely ephemeral.[52]

With energy drawn from Bari, Cherney, and Greg King, Earth First! expanded its actions in 1989, and violence reared its head—a sign of the expansion and protraction of the wars. At the annual Round River Rendezvous in 1989, the national movement decided to organize a national tree-sit week to highlight industrial logging and forestry issues around the country. With support from the national organization, Cherney, Bari, and King organized their first mass base camp for launching the tree-sits and other direct actions. The base camps, typically located at public campgrounds in national forests or state parks, served as home base, not unlike a military field camp. The radicals received supplies, hatched plans, held strategy meetings, and trained each other to climb trees and resist nonviolently. From that first base camp, North Coast activists put on three of the seven nationwide tree-sits: an all-women's tree-sit, a tree-sit in the famous drive-through redwood on Highway 128 in southern Humboldt, and a seventeen-person tree-sit in the walnut tree at the Arcata home of assembly member Dan Hauser because they wanted the legislator to act on their behalf in the legislature, and they knew they could easily draw media coverage sitting in a legislator's tree.[53]

The increasing frequency of protests and direct actions, while generating media attention, also began to fray the fragile worker-activist bonds that Bari, Cherney, and Earth First! had cultivated. By April, a reporter already was describing Scotia as a town "torn apart by a blaze of protests, lawsuits, and counter-charges." In June, King and Cherney organized a rally at Calpella, a mill town in Mendocino where Louisiana-Pacific was experimenting with chipboard/waferboard production. At the rally, a logger punched King and knocked him to the ground. Afterward, Dave Galitz, chief spokesman for Pacific Lumber, wrote John Campbell a memo: "Enclosed is an article on Cherney and King's latest stunt. As soon as we find the home of the fine fellow who decked Greg King, he has a dinner invitation at the Galitz Residence."[54]

The violence escalated in August as the activists grew bolder. North Coast Earth First! set up a road blockade at Whitethorn, along Lost Coast at the Humboldt-Mendocino border, to stop Lancaster Logging, which neighbors complained was logging late at night outside its approved boundary. At the Lancaster blockade, Mrs. Lancaster and Judi Bari exchanged blows, and the oldest Lancaster son hit fifty-year-old Mem Hill, knocking her down and breaking her nose. It was the second time Hill had been knocked down while protesting logging; the first was at Sally Bell nearly five years prior. When Greg King began to photograph the action, Lancaster threw him to the ground. King responded by standing up and punching the logger. Dave Lancaster, the owner's eighteen-year-old son, arrived with a shotgun and fired it into the air, scattering the activists. Two days later, on August 18, Cherney and Bari organized a roadblock near Navarro in Mendocino to stop logging trucks. The next day, just east of Navarro in Philo, a logging truck rear-ended the car carrying Bari, Cherney, another activist, and four children. It was the same driver Bari and friends had blocked the prior day, and there were no skid marks. The driver got out of his truck yelling, "I didn't see the children!"[55]

Despite the tensions with workers, the North Coast environmental movement gained momentum as it aggressively expanded its direct action and litigation campaigns. In October 1989, Bari organized a road blockade on federal land near Cahto Peak, near the South Fork of the Eel River, and staged a protest at the Mendocino offices of the Bureau of Land Management, temporarily shutting down the agency's operations. That same month, tree hugging shut down logging in the Sanctuary Forest of northern Mendocino. Six weeks after Bari's first action, an informant sent a letter to the Ukiah police accusing her of inciting violence and offering to provide additional information. The letter included a photograph of Bari holding an Uzi, a photo she and Cherney claimed was a spoof. Regardless, it became clear that like environmentalists nationwide, the North Coast activists would not be allowed to act unopposed. On the North Coast, however, the retributions were more personal than political and had clearly intensified by late 1989.[56]

On the ground a guerrilla war was developing in the forest. The activists and the companies tracked each other's movements, confronted each other physically, and adjusted their strategies accordingly. Earth First! placed scouts in the forests to monitor logging activity, while Campbell's security team worked to intercept people and messages. Pacific Lumber once found Earth First! walkie-talkies in the woods, which allowed the company to determine which radio channel the activists used and remotely track activist activity. After a number of inexplicable run-ins in the forest, Earth First! began using cell phones to communicate. The battle for Headwaters Forest was becoming, in many ways, a field battle to control territory.[57]

While confronting the growing field and legal battles, Pacific Lumber found itself in the middle of a battle with its employees and the public as well. The troubles began in February 1988, when a Maxxam division defaulted on $46.6 million in bank debt. In March, Maxxam announced it would acquire KaiserTech, a large metal manufacturer on the West Coast. The combination of the default and the acquisition fueled fears on the North Coast that Maxxam was solely interested in mergers and asset sales, not in running companies. In March, the *New York Times* ran an article about the takeover and the subsequent doubling of logging activity. The article described how John Maurer quit the company to protest the new logging regime, and how employee George Garibay thought the company was "destroying the future." The same article described employees getting new pickup trucks and large paychecks as a result of sixty-hour workweeks, but it also noted that employees were worried about Humboldt County becoming "another Appalachia." Finally, an attorney for the Murphy family was quoted as saying, "They [some workers] feel Maxxam is raping the land and dismembering the company." In October, some members of the Murphy family filed a $2.25 billion lawsuit in federal and state courts on behalf of former shareholders to invalidate the Maxxam–Pacific Lumber merger due to the fraudulent activities of Milken, Boesky, and Jefferies. Even the business press had turned against Maxxam. *Business Week* ran an article praising the effectiveness of 1980s takeovers that resuscitated laggard companies, but described the Maxxam takeover of Pacific Lumber as a "horror story about the consequences of excess leverage" because Maxxam was cutting down old growth to repay its junk bond debt. Throughout the swirl of press in 1988, Pacific Lumber's name and benevolent image were effectively subsumed by the callous Wall Street image of Maxxam.[58]

The bad press, combined with two new EPIC lawsuits and yet another harvest plan rejected by the Department of Forestry, led the company to voluntarily reverse its accelerated harvest of ancient forests.

David Galitz told the press that the company would cease clear-cutting inside ancient forests, a decision prompted by public concerns and the intervention of state senator Byron Sher and assembly member Dan Hauser, whose front yard had been the site of one of Earth First!'s national tree-sits. Earth First! dismissed the change as a public relations stunt, as did Save the Redwoods League.[59]

Pacific Lumber's reputation plummeted even further in 1989, often led by the business press and encouraged by the actions of the North Coast activists. In February, Maxxam sold three Kaiser facilities, feeding the cut-and-run fears in Humboldt County. Activists and workers feared Maxxam would do the same to Pacific Lumber and its mills once all the ancient redwoods had been harvested. *Corporate Finance* subsequently described a tenuous alliance between workers and environmentalists in an article titled "Angry Harvest." *Fortune* ran "A Raider's Ruckus in the Redwoods," which described the new logging regime as "felling trees so fast that barren clear-cut patches, covered only with sluglike tracks of huge log haulers, blot the landscape for miles." The article also claimed that "environmental extremists have declared holy war," while mainstream groups filed lawsuits. The *Fortune* article trumpeted the fragile worker-environmentalist alliance, but it was prophetic only with respect to the "holy war." The press had misread the relationship between EPIC and Earth First!, not recognizing the degree to which they were communicating. In fact, they were a part of the same movement, unlike the national environmental movement that kept Earth First! at arm's length.[60]

The popular press continued to undermine Pacific Lumber's carefully crafted, century-old paternal image. The *Sacramento Bee Magazine* coined the phrase "Redwood Wars" in an article chronicling the back-to-the land migrants working in forest restoration and activism. *Rolling Stone* ran "Milken, Junk Bonds, and Raping the Redwoods" by environmentalist author Bill McKibben. *Reader's Digest* published "California's Chainsaw Massacre" in November. The basic narrative of all these articles was that Pacific Lumber had been a good employer and steward of the land until a greedy Texan backed by dubious junk bonds bought the company and forced it to clear-cut its ancient forests to pay off a debt to Michael Milken. In all the articles, Campbell defended his logging regime and declared he had decided to clear-cut and expand production well before Maxxam entered the picture. He, of course, was correct on that point. Campbell and Hurwitz both explained that they believed clear-cutting was good for the forest because it replaced old trees that didn't grow fast with young trees that did. Hurwitz and Campbell's arguments largely fell on deaf ears, however, as the actions of the press, the activists, and the state proved over the next several years. The workers would support Campbell as one of their own, but Hurwitz was another story. The North Coast activists trusted no industrial logging leader and continued to file lawsuit after lawsuit to—as Woods had said during the Sally Bell conflict—"get the donkey moving."[61]

Despite the mounting legal losses, direct action, and old-growth regulations, the Board of Forestry and Pacific Lumber continued to challenge the lower courts' rulings. On April 18, 1988, the Department of Forestry had rejected two new Pacific Lumber harvest plans because they did not include marbled murrelet surveys, which the agency wanted to assess the impacts of the harvest plans on the tiny seabird. The agency told the press the decision amounted to a three-month moratorium on the approval of any harvest plan proposed in old-growth groves. Outraged by the moratorium, Pacific Lumber, like Chenoweth Lumber in 1976, appealed the decision directly to the Board of Forestry, claiming it did not have to provide survey information because such a survey was not specifically required by the rules. Following their corporatist tradition, the Board of Forestry overruled its state foresters and approved the plans.[62]

EPIC and the Sierra Club immediately filed for a writ of mandate to rescind the board's approval on the basis that the murrelet surveys were necessary to determine the appropriateness of the plan's wildlife mitigation measures. With *Sierra v. Board of Forestry*, EPIC teamed up with the Sierra Club, beginning what would become a long-standing alliance in which EPIC litigated and the two groups split the costs. Humboldt's Judge John Buffington denied the initial writ, but on July 1, 1988, an appellate court overruled the decision, and on remand in February 1989, Buffington returned the Timber Harvest Plans to the Board of Forestry and asked it to assess the impact of the proposed logging on wildlife. His instructions included a requirement to consider additional mitigation options and to produce a cost-benefit analysis for each alternative.

The back-and-forth between the Board of Forestry and the lower courts continued and eventually drove a wedge between Pacific Lumber and the Board of Forestry. On March 20, 1989, the Board of Forestry convinced Judge Buffington that the revised harvest plans would not have any significant impact on wildlife, and the judge once more denied a new writ of mandate. EPIC and the Sierra Club appealed the decision, and the appellate court again overturned Buffington. When Pacific Lumber appealed the case to the California Supreme Court, the Board of Forestry withdrew its support. Too many appellate rulings over the previous decade had upheld the statutory requirement that Timber Harvest Plans fulfill environmental impact statement requirements for the Board of Forestry to continue its challenges. The case had not yet been decided, but already it was clear that citizen litigation had destabilized the traditional relationships between the forestry agency and the timber industry. The Department of Forestry had begun to take CEQA's environmental impact report requirements seriously by requiring wildlife surveys, and the governing Board of Forestry finally took a step away from de facto corporatism by refusing to support Pacific Lumber's appeal to the Supreme Court.[63]

The person leading EPIC's litigation efforts was Cecelia Lanman, a member of the 1970s migrant community. Lanman was a local landowner, another San Francisco Bay Area refugee, and an EPIC activist. From 1969 to 1972, Lanman had studied political science at the University of Cincinnati and worked as an intern on political campaigns. In her early twenties, she and her then husband, Gil Gregori, moved to California, where she worked as the East Bay coordinator for the United Farm Workers during the grape boycott. After that campaign, she resumed her political science studies at California State University Hayward. The Grigoris were not environmental activists, but they did attend the very first EPIC meeting in 1977 while hunting for land in the area. Later in 1977, the couple and their daughters, Megan and Mariah, moved to a ranch house on the Mattole River near Ettersburg in Humboldt County, just west of Garberville. On the North Coast, they owned forestland as well as an organic apple and chestnut orchard, and Lanman worked in stream restoration, forest thinning, and tree planting.

Like Gienger, Woods, and so many other North Coast activists, Lanman's knowledge of the local landscape developed through her work on the land, and her passions grew from those experiences. In 1982, Lanman and her husband had begun working with EPIC to expand the Sinkyone Wilderness, with Cecelia serving on EPIC's board of directors. She quickly became a pivotal figure in the organization. In 1986, Lanman mediated the settlement among Georgia-Pacific, the Trust for Public Land, and local Sinkyone activists for the Sally Bell purchase. That year she was named president of EPIC as a result of her leadership qualities and a rift between Woods and some members of the board over the best use of the *Johnson* attorney's fees. Woods wanted the funds to be held in escrow and used only for litigation. Others wanted to use the money to more broadly fund EPIC's environmental activism. As an EPIC board member and president, Lanman seized the litigation reins from Woods just as the group embarked on the first *Maxxam* cases, and she helped build EPIC into a full-time litigation, research, and advocacy organization for the North Coast. In 1987, *California Journal* named Lanman the number one opponent of CDF director Jerry Partain, firmly establishing EPIC as a statewide political player.[64]

EPIC and the Sierra Club filed additional cases in the late 1980s that chipped away at the corporatist leanings of the Board of Forestry and the property rights arguments of Pacific Lumber. The most important Pacific Lumber harvest plans they challenged were again within the Salmon Creek watershed in Headwaters Forest, near Owl Creek Grove (*Sierra and EPIC v. CDF [Salmon Creek]* and *Sierra and EPIC v. Imboden*). EPIC argued that the Department of Forestry was still not adequately considering the cumulative impact on the marbled murrelet population of California, nor was the agency implementing all "feasible" alternatives and mitigations to protect murrelet habitat as required by CEQA. The Owl Creek cases would eventually drag the US Supreme Court and President Clinton into the quagmire. Challenging Pacific Lumber plans to liquidate its old-growth forests was, of course, only part of the attack on industrial logging on the North Coast. EPIC and the Sierra Club were also determined to demonstrate that the Department of Forestry willfully ignored CEQA requirements as a matter of official policy and not just a matter of incompetence. Accordingly, in 1989, the two groups filed a suit challenging sixty-five Timber Harvest Plans from various timber companies across the North Coast. Through the case, they hoped to demonstrate that because the Department of Forestry repeatedly failed to assess the cumulative impact of logging on watersheds and wildlife, and repeatedly waited until after they had approved harvest plans to issue legally required responses to public comments, the agency had a de facto policy of ignoring CEQA. Like all other cases except *Maxxam I*, the *Native Salmon* case—so called because one of the plaintiffs was Californians for Native Salmon and Steelhead Association—dragged on into the mid-1990s. The case was a part of the broader campaign to overhaul logging practices across Redwood Country.[65]

The 1980s ended with the North Coast timber industry on unstable ground. Old growth was nearly impossible to harvest, the Department of Forestry and Board of Forestry were under intense scrutiny by the courts, and activists were flooding the woods with eyes and bodies to monitor logging plans and logging activities. In addition, the growing spotted owl conflict to the north and increasing popular concern over tropical rain forests and global biodiversity created a national environment the industry felt was hostile to its interests, despite its strong allies in the White House.

• • •

The developments on the North Coast during the 1980s illustrate the bottom-up character of the Redwood Wars, how different valuations of forestland and society clashed, and how state and private institutions responded. Some local residents disapproved of the industrial logging regimes on the North Coast's private lands, and they took action. Though they had moved north to escape a consumerist culture, they were quite familiar with political action and used their experience to defend their vision for North Coast society. Following the precedents set by past conservation campaigns, they attended hearings, wrote to regulators and legislators, filed suits, and put their bodies in harm's way to stop timber harvesting where they felt it was immoral and illegal. New waves of migrants moved to the area and infused the movement with heightened intensity and urgency. Charles Hurwitz's orchestration of the takeover of Pacific Lumber in 1985 was a public relations windfall for these activists, marking a major turning point in the Redwood Wars. Hurwitz was the ultimate villain, against whom they could juxtapose their vision of sustainable forestry, community control of institutions, a stable working environment, and the protection of biodiversity and ecological health. Timber workers were caught in the middle. They appreciated the employment offered by increased logging, but they also feared that the new regime would eventually shut down logging on the North Coast. The workers had a similar relationship with the environmentalists. They appreciated the idea of a sustainable future for the industry, but they feared too much regulation might destroy the industry—in the short and long term.

As a result of the Pacific Lumber takeover, the Redwood Wars zeroed in on the battle over Headwaters Forest. The battle over that old-growth forest epitomized the war raging between multinational corporations and local activists. The villain threatening the giants was a seemingly callous outsider to Redwood Country with a history of greed and deception. Opposing him was a band of colorful characters who utilized much more combative tactics, and who were unrelenting and resistant to compromise. In truth, the battle was more complex than any David and Goliath narrative. The complexity of the issues surrounding ancient redwood preservation, sustainable forestry, corporate power, governmental regulation, appropriate activist tactics, and ecosystem management created uncertainty among the public and lawmakers. The growing mutual animosity among the combatants created a nearly intractable situation.

Thus the battles in the woods and the courtroom continued unabated, leading to violence. The public hostility of the Headwaters conflict exemplifies the militancy and populism of postwar environmental politics. Across the country, local groups such as the Oregon Natural Resources Council, Forest Watch, and the Clamshell Alliance challenged federal agencies to take seriously the responsibilities imposed on them by the Wilderness Act, the National Environmental Policy Act, the National Forest Management Act, the Endangered Species Act, and the myriad 1970s environmental laws. Likewise, North Coast activists continued to challenge California's agencies to meet their statutory responsibilities, and they continued to doggedly pursue a strategy to radically reform logging in Redwood Country. The battle over Headwaters Forest shows how multinational corporations fought back against citizen activists during the 1980s and 1990s: they used the media to promote fear of economic collapse, and they used their access to lawmakers to forestall reform. And they successfully turned workers against environmentalists to a large degree. The battle was not entirely intractable, however. Because the Redwood Wars were fought on private land, the public acquisition strategy remained a viable tool to relieve political and social pressure in the region.

FOUR

BURSTING OUT

ON MAY 24, 1990, THE NOW INFAMOUS BOMB EXPLODED BENEATH Judi Bari's seat, leaving a massive hole in the carriage. The bomb was rudimentary but powerful: it fractured Bari's pelvis, crushing her tailbone, and seriously damaged her nervous system and soft tissues. Bari and Cherney were in Oakland on their way to Santa Cruz to recruit students for protests and direct actions over the summer. The idea for the protests had developed in January 1990. According to Darryl Cherney, Walking Rainbow, a "white guy who wore a robe and beard, and was full of himself, and a little psychotic, maybe," showed up at Gary and Betty Ball's Mendocino Environmental Center asking to speak with Bari. When the two met, Walking Rainbow told Bari about his vision: that they should recruit people to the North Coast for a summer of activism like Freedom Summer. Despite the off-putting demeanor of the relative stranger, Bari loved the idea of a Redwood Summer, and she and Cherney hatched plans to publicly shame timber companies and draw attention to the plight of the northern forests.[1]

That spring, as university final exams approached, East Coast transplants Bari and Cherney planned to organize and attend rallies, sing their humorous protest songs, and sign up students to spend their summers volunteering behind the Redwood Curtain. The bomb halted all those plans. On that May morning, FBI agents accompanied Oakland police to the bombing location, and the two activists were placed in police custody while in the hospital and charged with transporting a bomb. The Oakland Police and FBI immediately presumed the bomb was Cherney and Bari's. Cherney was treated and released, but Bari remained in the hospital. The police guarded her room in the intensive care unit and searched her home in Mendocino. Two months later, the Alameda district attorney dropped the charges against the activists due to lack of evidence. A year later, frustrated by the absence of any investigation into the bombing and a year's worth of FBI harassment, Bari and Cherney filed suit against the FBI and Oakland Police Department for false arrest. In 2002, a federal jury granted Cherney and the estate of Judi Bari $4.4 million and ruled the FBI and Oakland police had committed fraud against the two activists. As of 2015, the identity of the bomber was still unknown, though Darryl Cherney was still working to obtain DNA testing of the evidence held by the FBI.[2]

The bombing helped to bring national attention to the Redwood Wars. It was part of a pattern of protracted conflict and increasing violence in Redwood Country. Those conflicts occurred in the woods, on the streets, in the courtrooms, in the legislatures, and in the media. And as local North Coast institutions proved incapable of resolving the seemingly intractable battles between the timber industry and North Coast environmentalists, the combatants looked outside the region for political and legal leadership. North Coast environmentalists looked to the legislative process to permanently protect ancient redwoods and to reform logging practices. They enlisted supporters around the state to provide money and to work to block logging efforts in the woods. They used the media to publicly embarrass timber companies. And eventually, the activists would look to the federal courts and the Endangered Species Act for help in stopping the Pacific Lumber Company from logging its old-growth reserves. At the same time, the timber companies worked toward their own legislative solution. They tapped into a national network of anti-environmentalists to galvanize their workers, and they used the media to undermine the environmentalists' efforts. Eventually, Pacific Lumber also looked to the federal courts to end the Redwood Wars.

National and international developments generated support for the activists. In the late 1980s and 1990s, scientists and the media warned of an impending extinction crisis, and space imagery documented the massive loss of forests around the globe since 1970. Scientists estimated that as many as one thousand species were disappearing from the earth each year, threatening the biodiversity of the planet. The ability to manage ecosystems was disappearing, they argued, along with the loss of life and knowledge. Many of the extinctions occurred in the tropical forests, where ranching, farming, and logging annually destroyed millions of acres of rain forest. As a result of those warnings, the need to protect rain forests and biodiversity drove public support to environmental groups. Many Americans grew concerned that potential medicines would be lost if the rain forests disappeared or that such massive losses of biodiversity would wreak havoc on the earth's natural systems, threating humanity's survival. Closer to home, Americans needed only to look at the redwoods to find their own threatened temperate rain forest with untold undiscovered species and ecosystems. Those concerns about ecological health were broad enough that Reagan's heir apparent, George H. W. Bush, ran for president in 1988 as the "environmental president."[3]

On the heels of those warnings, some of the original Earth Day organizers organized twentieth anniversary events in April 1990, with an estimated 200 million people participating in more than 140 countries. The day of rallies and protests focused on biodiversity, rain forests, and the effects of consumerism on ecological health. Many activists criticized the events as mainstream and superficial, saying they seemed like window dressing rather than activism. However, Earth Day 1990's success in attracting participants underscored broad concern for environmental problems. According to a Gallup poll, 71 percent of Americans thought environmental protection should take priority over the economy. In 1992, 68 percent of Americans thought the U.S. government was not doing enough to protect the environment. The deforestation of the Amazon rain forest thus developed into a cause célèbre, and international leaders gathered in Brazil in 1992 for the United Nations Earth Summit to discuss global deforestation, biodiversity, climate change, and sustainable development. It was in that context that North Coast activists worked to expand their challenge to industrial logging in the redwoods, as industrial and conservative political leaders tried to undermine public support for environmental protection.[4]

While many Americans rallied around environmentalism, others ratcheted up their efforts to roll back environmental protection laws. Those individuals and organizations had begun working on the North Coast to oppose forestry reforms. Under the banner of "Wise Use," property rights activists and resource users organized western residents to resist grazing and mining regulations, as well as protections for endangered species. By 1990, Wise Use organizers, largely funded by conservative foundations and resource extraction firms, were distributing yellow ribbons to ranchers, timber workers, and miners to wear as symbols of their anti-environmentalism. Timber and mining companies gave employees paid days off to attend public hearings about public land issues, providing transportation and lunches. One of the earliest efforts to organize workers against environmental protection occurred in Yellowstone National Park. The National Park Service wanted to coordinate logging and development activities in the Greater Yellowstone area to protect the ecological health of the region. Wise Use activists viewed restrictions on their economic activities as threatening their livelihoods, rural culture, and Fifth Amendment property rights. At one hearing, a woman called one park superintendent a Nazi. Also in 1990, Wise Use activists began the "Adirondacks rebellion" to protest plans to increase environmental protections for that park. Activists fired flaming arrows at park offices, organized a Minuteman Brigade, threatened to burn down state forest reserves, and even burned down activists' homes from New Hampshire to Arkansas. Violence was on the rise across the nation when the bomb exploded inside Judi Bari's car.[5] While the nation may have broadly supported environmentalism, environmental protection was also an increasingly polarizing issue.

On the North Coast, tensions ran equally high. The activists and timber companies continued to escalate the conflicts in the redwoods. As the controversy grew more intense, violence increased and any willingness to negotiate disappeared. Instead of talking, the two sides looked to institutions with expansive authority to resolve the battles over logging the redwoods. Activists used a three-pronged strategy: If the timber industry would not comply with state court rulings, then the activists would use the legislative process to protect old growth and reform logging practices. Second, they would escalate their direct actions to frustrate logging efforts and generate broad public support for their cause. Finally, EPIC would continue to provide legal protection for threatened groves through continued legal challenges of specific logging plans. The three tactics worked concurrently. Pacific Lumber led industry resistance. Eventually, the battlegrounds of the Redwood Wars encompassed statewide elections, the woods of the North Coast, the halls of Congress, and finally the federal courts.

GOING ABOVE THEIR HEADS:
FORESTS FOREVER AND LEGISLATIVE ACTION

One of the more important developments in the expanding Redwood Wars was the reemergence of activists who had migrated to the North Coast during the 1960s and 1970s. That group decided to see if they could convince California voters to eliminate both corporatism and industrial logging in the state. They were frustrated by the still expanding industrial logging operations on the North Coast and the stubborn corporatist tradition enabling that logging regime to thrive. By 1989, EPIC was winning lawsuits against the Department of Forestry and Pacific Lumber, and the national press had taken up the cause of vilifying Charles Hurwitz, Maxxam, and their logging practices. However, logging rates remained high. In 1988, Pacific Lumber logged 10,436 acres in the redwood forest, more than any year since at least 1979. Frustration also grew because the court cases took many years to conclude, and state agencies did not seem inclined to change their policies or relationships.[6]

A group of older activists, including EPIC cofounder Woods (formerly Robert Sutherland), decided to bypass the forestry agency and the state legislature, placing an initiative on the ballot for citizen approval. As Darryl Cherney, Judi Bari, and North Coast Earth First! built their organization and generated press coverage and backlash, the older activists worked to make sustainable forestry and forestry policy statewide issues. Their 1990 ballot initiative, in combination with Redwood Summer, provided the movement with an enormous boost. With a bit of luck, a lot of voter outreach, some good theatrics, and a lot of bravado, the activists mounted a major campaign for significant reform that captured the attention of the state for a brief while. Most importantly, the campaign drew older, experienced activists back into the Redwood Wars to work with the more recent migrants. That coalition continued to press its social vision of the North Coast for more than a decade, especially regarding the fate of Headwaters Forest.

What became known as the Forests Forever initiative complicated the narrative of the Redwood Wars told by timber companies and landowners. In early 1989, the *Sacramento Bee Magazine* ran an article entitled "The Redwood Wars," in which Pacific Lumber accused EPIC of blackmailing the timber company with its lawsuits. In the same article, Eel River Sawmills claimed Earth First! protesters were trying to run timber companies in Humboldt County out of business. And it wasn't just timber spokesmen who were critical of the environmentalists. A rancher from Humboldt was quoted as saying that Earth First! activists "get on welfare and grow pot and make good money at it. I think the buggers ought to go get real jobs." Thus the conflict was established as pitting the rural working class and the timber industry against a group of activists who largely rejected traditional middle-class life, the sanctity of private property, and the benefits of stable institutional employment. Activists were painted as being absolutely hostile to logging. But the article also subtly laid out a different aspect of the story, which involved 1970s back-to-the-landers doing battle with "titans of consumptive society." The article outlined the political organizing backgrounds of activists such as Woods and Cecelia Lanman (then Cecelia Gregori) and described their political, legal, and restoration work. The older generation's emphasis on sustainable logging ran counter to the portrayal of the activists as anti-logging and anti-logger. This group counted loggers in their original ranks, including Jim DeMulling, who had named EPIC.[7]

Kathy Bailey was one of those experienced organizers whose impact was immediately felt when she engaged with the sustainable forestry campaign. Bailey had noticed that more logging trucks had appeared in the 1980s near her rural home off route 128 in central Mendocino. One day in the spring of 1989, a logger acquaintance told Bailey she "wouldn't believe what they're doing in the woods," referring to the massive clear-cuts by Georgia-Pacific and Louisiana-Pacific, the morass of tractor trails, and the erosion caused by those logging techniques. The logger was also referring to the fact that the timber companies were harvesting second-growth stands too early to use the trees as timber. Instead, they were feeding the particleboard mills. The result was an increasingly treeless, clear-cut landscape back in the hills. The Redwood Wars were pulling Kathy Bailey back into politics to defend her neighborhood.[8]

The war in Vietnam had sparked Bailey's activism in the 1960s. The Minnesota native first became aware of the war in Vietnam in 1966, during her second semester at the University of New Mexico. Her reaction was immediate and visceral, inspiring her to join a "five-person SDS [Students for a Democratic Society] group" on campus. She organized a demonstration near campus, then was invited to a leadership program in Sevier County, Tennessee, run by the Southern Conference Educational Fund. The training involved organizing poor, rural whites during the election year. Instead of going back to New Mexico afterward, she moved to New York City to pursue antiwar activism, then enrolled in Franconia College in New Hampshire to continue her studies and antiwar work.

Seemingly on a whim, she and her then-husband moved to the San Francisco Bay Area in 1968, and Bailey began work with Todd Gitlin's newspaper, *The Dock of the Bay*. After a brief stint with Gitlin's paper—and in the wake of the bombing of the Chase Manhattan building, the raid on the Oakland Black Panthers, and the rise of the Weather Underground—Bailey was burned out and ready for a change. Shaken by the movement's infighting and violence, she reached the point where she "couldn't leave the house not stoned." After separating from her husband, Bailey left the Bay Area in 1969 and moved to New Orleans with a friend. During the spring of 1970, a Bay Area friend invited Bailey to help her set up a commune in Mendocino County. Bailey accepted and, like Richard Gienger and Woods, moved to the North Coast to live a simpler life.

When Bailey first arrived in Mendocino County, she struggled to get by, working at a local farm for subminimum-wage pay and a box of surplus government food, and writing for the *Anderson Valley Advocate*. In an effort to improve her finances, Bailey obtained a real estate license. She had a "few lucky moments" as a real estate agent, including a sale to the Navarro Vineyards. Bailey used the money to buy some land. She continued to write for the *Advocate*. In 1976, Gail Lucas, a volunteer with the California chapter of the Sierra Club, pitched Bailey on a story about timber company use of Agent Orange, a defoliant containing known carcinogens that had been used extensively in Vietnam. The timber companies were spraying the chemical out of helicopters to prevent the growth of weeds and shrubs on clear-cut land. Logging companies planted redwood saplings on clear-cuts, and they didn't want weeds and shrubs competing for nutrients. It was a toxic practice, and it increased erosion by eliminating root systems on the hillsides. Bailey had a seven-month-old boy; as she recalled, her motherly instincts took over and she began working to ban the use of Agent Orange. Bailey organized a county ballot initiative, and in 1979, the county passed an ordinance banning aerial application of pesticides and herbicides on timberland. Though successful, her foray into local environmental politics was brief. She married a local lawyer, and they had a daughter together. After her daughter started school, Bailey won a seat on the school board, which she held for six years.

Once again, female leadership had emerged on the North Coast, as talented, experienced organizers committed to protecting their communities by turning back the tide of industrial logging and harvesting of ancient redwoods. By the late 1980s, Bailey, Judi Bari, Cecelia Lanman, and others had joined the long tradition of female leadership in redwood politics that extends back to the late nineteenth century, including the work of the Garden Clubs of America, the Women's Federation, and Laura Mahan, who in the 1920s led residents into the woods to stop Pacific Lumber logging operations. The female North Coast activists were not unique in the environmental movement, yet the tradition of female leadership and the infusion of 1960s activism and countercultural values seem to have encouraged women on the North Coast. They brought diverse talents, flaws, and styles to their work. Bailey thrived in activist processes such as public comments, ever attentive to the politics of the possible as well as the politics of the ideal. Bari was tough, unyielding (some might say caustic), and charismatic. She brought media and citizen-organizing savvy to the movement. Lanman, too, was charismatic and worked well with the media. She was also adept at managing people and organizations, increasing EPIC's litigation prowess. Bailey was now reentering that world, and she left an indelible mark on the Redwood Wars.[9]

After the conversation with the logger about the Louisiana-Pacific clear-cuts in the spring of 1989, Bailey called Meca Wawona (an adopted name in the tradition of many North Coast migrants), whom she knew from the pesticide initiative of the 1970s. Meca told Bailey about a meeting at Grapevine Station, north of Laytonville in Mendocino, to discuss a possible ballot initiative to reform North Coast logging practices. John Lewallen had developed the idea, and the Man Who Walks in the Woods, who was phasing out his EPIC work, had organized the meeting. Woods, Bailey, Cecelia Lanman, Darryl Cherney, Jama Chapin (an EPIC volunteer), Gary and Betty Ball of the Mendocino Environmental Center, Lewallen, Bill Mannix, Eric Swanson, and a few others attended the Grapevine Station meeting. They decided Woods, Lewallen, and Mannix would develop the language of the initiative. At another meeting, at Eric Swanson's home west of Willits in Mendocino, the group held hands and stood in a circle to brainstorm names for their new group. Someone blurted out "Forests Forever," and the name stuck. That fall, Woods, Bailey, and a few other Forests Forever activists took their draft initiative to the annual Planning and Conservation League (PCL) conference in Sacramento. PCL was an influential statewide environmental group, and many current and former Department of Forestry leaders attended the conference. Forests Forever showed the initiative to a group that included former Board of Forestry member Phillip Berry, former Department of Forestry director David Pesonen, and former California Resources secretary Huey Johnson. They tentatively agreed not to oppose the initiative if it qualified for the 1990 ballot.[10]

The Forests Forever initiative was a comprehensive set of reforms to the management of forests in Redwood Country. The text referred to a "new approach to forestry," echoing the calls for a "New Forestry" coming from biologists in the federal government. Jerry Franklin, an ecologist who began his career with the US Forest Service before moving into university positions, had been working since the 1970s on "a kinder and gentler forestry that better accommodates ecological values, while allowing for the extraction of commodities." Franklin and his colleagues in Oregon were developing forestry practices to "minimize fragmentation" of old-growth areas and avoid clear-cuts adjacent to old-growth groves. The goal of New Forestry was to produce forests that could regenerate old-growth habitat over time to maintain high levels of biodiversity. The forestry approach prescribed by the activists was based on providing "maximum protection for the environment" using the "best available biological information." The major sections of the initiative included a prohibition on exporting raw logs from California, a near ban on clear-cutting, and a ban on removing timber from riparian zones. Banning raw log exports would decrease demand for timber and prevent multinational corporations from sending mill jobs overseas. The other provisions were designed to prevent erosion, elevated stream temperatures harmful to salmon, and even-aged tree farms that did not encourage biodiversity. Additionally, the initiative proposed a forest restoration program to remove logging roads and required 150-year sustained yield plans to be crafted by every timber owner such that for any ten-year period, timber harvests would not exceed tree growth.[11]

The Forests Forever initiative also proposed large-scale command-and-control regulations designed to eliminate the negative environmental and social impacts of industrial logging. Activists included in the initiative a Timber Workers Compensation and Retraining Fund and an Ancient Forest Protection Fund, along with major changes to the Board of Forestry designed to reduce the timber industry's influence over logging regulations. The Board of Forestry was to immediately acquire the Headwaters Grove inside Headwaters Forest, using the power of eminent domain if necessary, and to subsequently compile a list of other stands of ancient redwoods to acquire. The Forests Forever initiative was thus a direct effort to legislatively reinforce the growing number of California court rulings favorable to conservationists and to hasten the demise of corporatism in the forestry agencies.[12]

The activists had tentative political support, but they lacked resources. However, later in the fall of 1989, Forests Forever got lucky. Hal Arbit, an investor from San Mateo, told the forestry expert at the Natural Resources Defense Council, David Edelson, that he wanted to contribute to a campaign to protect old-growth redwoods. According to Kathy Bailey, Edelson pitched Arbit on what was known as the Big Green initiative. The Big Green initiative was put together by organizations including the California Public Interest Research Group and PCL, and was supported by state senator Tom Hayden and former San Francisco mayor Dianne Feinstein. Big Green addressed greenhouse gas emissions, pesticide use, toxic waste cleanup, and clear-cutting. Arbit didn't think that initiative did enough for ancient forests, so

Edelson arranged a meeting with Woods, Bailey, Lanman, Lewallen, and Mannix to discuss the Forests Forever initiative.[13]

That meeting changed the fortunes of the North Coast activists. Arbit agreed to finance the campaign so long as his contributions remained anonymous. Back north, however, Richard Johnson, proprietor of the very small *Mendocino Environmentalist*, convinced Lewallen to allow him to reveal the identity of the anonymous donor on the basis that it was wrong to hide that information from the public. Lewallen was removed from the steering committee. Arbit remained committed, but he never truly trusted the country folk again, and he grew less interested in their ideas and input. In early 1990, the secretary of state accepted the ballot language, and Forests Forever formed a statewide campaign committee to qualify and pass the initiative, hiring professional signature-gathering and campaign experts to carry out the on-the-ground operations.[14]

Despite the generally sympathetic press coverage, the Forests Forever activists confronted a series of early obstacles in 1990. John Campbell of Pacific Lumber, and the timber industry more broadly, tied the initiative to Earth First! in an attempt to convince voters that the Forests Forever initiative was too radical. Simultaneously, Pacific Lumber argued that the initiative was unnecessary. In early February 1990, state senator Barry Keene, state assembly member Dan Hauser, and congressman Doug Bosco reached a voluntary agreement with Pacific Lumber and Louisiana-Pacific. Forests Forever, EPIC, and Earth First! referred to it derisively as the "Boskeenhauser" deal. According to the deal, Pacific Lumber agreed to a two-year moratorium on logging in the three-thousand-acre Headwaters Grove, and Louisiana-Pacific agreed to limit the number of raw logs it exported to its newly constructed Mexico mill. Both companies agreed to a moratorium on clear-cuts in old-growth groves, but announced they would selectively log ancient groves. The elected officials, in exchange, agreed not to support the Forests Forever initiative. In the face of those obstacles, Forests Forever activists grew weary of Leo McElroy, the Sacramento-based campaign manager hired to run the initiative, who seemed unable to coordinate all the moving pieces of the campaign and was determined to convince Forests Forever to denounce Earth First!.[15]

Perceived links between Redwood Summer and Forests Forever

dogged the initiative's prospects. The Forests Forever campaign developed nearly concurrently with plans for Earth First!'s Redwood Summer protests, and the combination created a maelstrom on the North Coast. The Wise Use movement drove deeper into Redwood Country, distributing fliers in Humboldt claiming that the Forests Forever initiative would end logging in Humboldt, eliminating thousands of jobs. Redwood Summer was painted as anti-logging and anti-logger. In May 1990, as the qualifying signatures for the Forests Forever initiative were filed with the secretary of state, the car bombing rocked the efforts of both Forests Forever and Earth First!. Hal Arbit refused to believe Bari and Cherney were innocent, McElroy continued to obsess over the perceived connection between Earth First! and the initiative, and Woods left for Siberia after Arbit objected to Woods's statements to the media about what he regarded as the fallacy of private property rights. Woods believed communities had a right to dictate the best use of all land to protect future generations and that environmental degradation was a "crisis of character" rather than a question of economic strategy. Arbit didn't think Woods's ideas best promoted the campaign. The prospects of the Forests Forever initiative seemed bleak given the internal tension.[16]

The initiative's fortunes found new life when the campaign hired Steve Glazer to replace McElroy in early summer. Glazer was an experienced initiative manager from Southern California, and though he agreed that associating the initiative with Earth First! was not helpful, he recognized that Earth First! was not directly involved with Forests Forever and dropped the issue. Instead, Glazer focused on courting moderate and conservative endorsements and refocusing the campaign on the various forestry initiatives: Forests Forever, Big Green, and an initiative crafted by the timber industry. However, Kathy Bailey, Glazer, Arbit, and others were concerned about the potential impact of Redwood Summer on the initiative, and they were pleasantly surprised when no violence erupted on the North Coast and no media tied Earth First! to the ballot initiative. For its part, the Forests Forever group focused on delivering the message that their initiative was better than that proposed by the timber industry, for both the workers and the forest. They hand-delivered pamphlets across the North Coast. With the help of Arbit and Frank Wells of the Disney Company, they hired Sidney Galanty to produce several television ads, and a San Francisco television station aired a sympathetic documentary, "The Forest through the Trees," leading up to the election. For the activists, the comparison was straightforward: their initiative provided for the purchase of the three-thousand-acre Headwaters and Elkhead Springs Groves in Humboldt, banned clear-cutting statewide, required wildlife surveys for all harvest plans in old-growth stands, protected workers, required every timber company to develop a Sustained Yield Plan, and reduced the number of seats on the Board of Forestry dedicated to timber industry representatives, among other reforms.[17]

The Forests Forever campaign needed both to win a majority of votes and to defeat the timber industry's initiative, because the industry initiative contained a provision invalidating the Forests Forever initiative. The campaign thus evolved into convincing the public that the industry measure was a wolf in sheep's clothing. Primarily, Forests Forever emphasized that the industry initiative—the Global Warming and Clear-Cutting Reduction, Wildlife Protection and Reforestation Act of 1990—provided for the acquisition of only 1,600 acres of old-growth redwood forest that weren't even within Headwaters Forest, included no funding mechanism to purchase ancient redwood groves, and was a sham because it only limited clear-cutting in old-growth stands to ten acres at a time with no restrictions on time or distance between clear-cuts. They hammered away at a provision limiting the Department of Forestry's supervision of individual Timber Harvest Plans. Forests Forever painted the industry initiative as a boon to timber companies and a retrenchment of traditional corporatism.

Those late-summer efforts paid enormous dividends. Kathy Bailey recalled that, as she stood next to former California governor Jerry Brown at a bar in Oakland early on election day, an industry lobbyist congratulated her on her impending victory. In the end, neither initiative passed. Forests Forever garnered 48 percent of the vote (by comparison, Big Green garnered just 34 percent), probably a last-minute victim of the Republican sweep of statewide elections that day. Bailey and Woods argued that McElroy's obsession with Earth First! and the diminished influence on Arbit of the "country folk" played large roles in the defeat, causing management to move too slowly in defining and publicizing the initiative.[18]

The initiative experience provided valuable lessons in campaign management and increased the activists' power on the state level. The Forests Forever activists learned how to raise money and work with donors. They honed their public relations skills. They amassed a network of campaign professionals and mainstream environmentalists. The relationship between the North Coast and Sacramento environmentalists was never easy, but it lent the redwood activists additional credibility and access to decision makers. The North Coast country folk disliked insider politics and preferred to think of their work as dismantling the political system. They were confident that their vision was righteous, and this belief often led to an unwillingness to compromise. The mainstream groups had grown used to compromise, working to make the best possible deals to protect the environment. Those tensions between the North Coast activists and the mainstream groups would become more problematic as the Redwood Wars expanded.[19]

The most pressing issue after the November 1990 loss, however, was how to capitalize on the initiative's near success. The campaign had dramatically elevated forestry and redwood preservation issues across the state. After the failure of the initiative, Hal Arbit, Kathy Bailey, and others continued to pursue comprehensive forestry reform in the state legislative arena, but they were only successful at blocking harmful bills. The activists had failed to resolve the Redwood Wars using California's legislative apparatus. However, the Forests Forever campaign had forced the timber industry to recognize the widespread unpopularity of their practices. Timber executives grew more irritated and less willing to engage with the activists. Redwood Summer exacerbated those tensions.

ACTIONS FOR THE MASSES AND MASSIVE ACTIONS

Redwood Summer

The Forests Forever initiative, though it failed in the end, boosted the fortunes of North Coast Earth First! by increasing the relevancy of Redwood Summer. Likewise, Redwood Summer boosted the fortunes of forestry reform by generating national attention and creating a more sophisticated working relationship among the activists. The various organizations worked symbiotically. EPIC researched Timber Harvest Plans and identified those that threatened ancient redwoods and old-growth habitat, then filed suit to stop the logging. Forests Forever and Sierra Club California (via Kathy Bailey) generated public comments on proposed logging plans and worked to advance legislative reforms. Earth First! and related affinity groups generated media attention and frustrated logging efforts by interfering with the work of loggers in the woods. But the lines were never that clean. Darryl Cherney had helped form Forests Forever, EPIC and Earth First! filed public comments, and they all worked with the media. They also relied on tight communication with each other. The relationships were not, however, always harmonious or beneficial.

The activities of North Coast Earth First! grew more brazen, confrontational, and hostile to mainstream politics in 1990. During the Forests Forever campaign and leading up to Redwood Summer, Earth First! began organizing road blockades and trespassing expeditions, and they occupied a few ancient redwood groves to prevent logging. The strategy garnered national publicity as the activists tried to shame timber companies, just as the civil rights movement had discredited southern state governments in 1964. Those efforts gained popular support from environmentalists across California and the nation, but they did not endear the group to the workers or the timber companies, especially since the initiative seemed to threaten workers' livelihoods. Equally important, Earth First! began to design other rallies and actions to recruit a broader set of activists. Combined, the confrontational actions and mass rallies led to a county-under-siege mentality.

Activists on the North Coast had decided they could no longer trust local politicians, leading to an atmosphere of hostility and a turn to disruptive actions. When Mendocino district attorney Susan Massini refused to prosecute Dave Lancaster for breaking Mem Hill's nose at Whitehorn in August 1989, Earth First! occupied her office. Darryl Cherney and Judi Bari tried to appeal to local timber workers' self-interest by performing at an American Federation of Labor rally protesting Louisiana-Pacific's plans to open a mill in Mexico. Most dramatic, however, were the February actions. After Pacific Lumber and Louisiana-Pacific announced the "Boskeenhauser" deal on February 8, 1990, more than seventy-five activists stormed the Eureka offices of the politicians. The next day, approximately fifty activists surrounded Don Nolan's Pacific Lumber logging truck while five activists chained themselves to logs after Nolan was quoted in a *Sacramento Bee* article as saying that environmentalists were his worst enemy. The urgency of the activists increased dramatically when trespassers discovered what became known as "Death Road," a thirty-foot-wide access road on Pacific Lumber land piercing the center of the Headwaters Grove. It was clear to activists that Headwaters Forest was in serious jeopardy and that elected officials could not be trusted to embrace their vision for reforming North Coast logging practices. Instead, they turned to the workers.[20]

North Coast Earth First!'s attempt to include timber workers and other environmentalists in their movement differentiated them from other radical groups, including other Earth First! groups. In March 1990, Judi Bari's presentation at the Public Interest Environmental Law Conference in Eugene, Oregon, divided the national Earth First! movement. The academic conference at the University of Oregon had become an important meeting ground for government workers, environmental lawyers, and activists to share research and debate issues. David Brower, the former leader of the Sierra Club, and Dennis Hayes, the organizer of the first Earth Day, were among that year's keynote speakers. Darryl Cherney was on a panel with Sea Shepherd captain Paul Watson to discuss civil disobedience. Bari was on a panel discussing the gap between union and environmental interests. Bari's goal was to make clear that she supported making peace with timber workers. Across the West Coast, tensions between environmentalists and timber workers had increased dramatically in recent years. In 1988, the US Fish and Wildlife Service had decided the spotted owl was not a threatened species, but a federal judge overruled the agency. In 1989, federal courts blocked more than one hundred logging projects in the national forests of Oregon due to the proposed listing of the spotted owl as a threatened species. As mills closed and timber firms laid off workers, logging towns protested loudly—including Colburg, Oregon, where one restaurant added "pickled spotted owl egg" to its menu. Angry loggers and environmentalists packed public hearings held by the Fish and Wildlife Service to discuss plans to protect the endangered owl.[21]

At the end of Judi Bari's presentation, mill worker Gene Lawhorn challenged her to demonstrate her sympathy toward workers by publicly denouncing tree spiking. Though this practice endangered workers' lives, Dave Foreman and others in Earth First! had argued that tree spiking was a legitimate form of nonviolent protest because they warned the company or agency when a grove had been spiked. Spiking thus prevented logging while doing no harm to the trees or workers, some activists argued. The 1989 near-beheading of George Alexander in Cloverdale had raised the stakes, however. In response to Lawhorn's challenge, Bari denounced tree spiking, angering Earth First! activists outside northern California. For Bari and many in North Coast Earth First!, however, the decision was easy, and likely necessary as they worked to organize support for Redwood Summer among mainstream groups and college students.[22]

Bari's denouncement of tree spiking and the organizing work for Redwood Summer did not dampen the enthusiasm for confrontation within North Coast Earth First!, however. Later in March, activists hung a banner on an Okestrom feller buncher at the annual Redwood Region Logging Show in Ukiah that read, "This Thing Kills Jobs & Forests." The new feller bunchers were mechanical clippers on cranes, operated by a single logger, that could snip a tree at its base, grab the trunk, and carry it to a log landing in one series of motions. They cost $700,000 at the time, and a few weeks later, one was found burned in the woods. When asked if Earth First! burned the feller buncher, Bari replied, "I didn't do it, I was home in bed with five witnesses." It appeared Bari was trying to simultaneously secure the allegiance of radicals and more mainstream activists.[23]

Despite the rhetorical bone Bari threw to the more radical elements of Earth First! through her defiance and sexual innuendo, the more organizing-focused North Coast Earth First! divided the national movement as preparations for Redwood Summer moved forward. Timber companies had been warning that the county would be overrun by radical outsiders and hippies, and the activists moved to shore up local support. On April 11, North Coast Earth First! held several press conferences to denounce tree spiking, an effort to preserve what worker sympathy remained in the wake of the Alexander incident, reduced timber harvests in the region due to the "Boskeenhauser" deal, and numerous EPIC lawsuits. Additionally, they hoped the announcement would, in Cherney's words, "take the wind out of the timber industry's publicity sails" leading up to Redwood Summer and the November elections, which would determine the fate of Forests Forever. Later in April, Earth First! activists—including Bari—along with International Workers of the World members and Louisiana-Pacific workers attended a Mendocino Board of Supervisors meeting to protest layoffs at Louisiana-Pacific and demand that the county seize the company's property. Actions like that led many in the national Earth First! movement to regard the North Coast chapter as too anthropocentric, leftist, and "hippie-dippy." Dave Foreman himself argued that Earth First! was never supposed to be about anti-corporate activism and, referring to the infiltration of the North Coast "class struggle/social-justice left," wrote, "We are inconsistent when we castigate Charles Hurwitz for destroying the last wilderness redwood forest, yet feel sympathy for the logger working for him."[24]

As much as they tried, the North Coast radicals in Earth First! were too strident, too irreverent, and too inconsistent to bridge the gap with local workers. The denunciation of tree spiking seemed disingenuous when Bari had smugly evaded answering questions about the sabotaged feller buncher. Cherney, Bari, and Greg King began to receive death threats. Fliers calling for violent protests during Redwood Summer, falsely attributed to Earth First!, were distributed to mill workers by timber companies. Louisiana-Pacific installed barbed wire around its mill. Local officials had also turned against Bari, Cherney, and King. In her memoirs, Bari recounted one Mendocino Board of Supervisors meeting where a "gyppo" (contractor) logger called for violence against the Redwood Summer activists. When Bari showed Supervisor Marilyn Butcher the death threats she had received, Butcher allegedly retorted that Bari had brought the violence on herself. After the meeting, Bari met with the gyppos to prevent violence during the summer demonstrations.[25]

Then the car bombing took place. The bombing and subsequent arrests of Cherney and Bari drove the mainstream environmental groups to Bari and Cherney's defense, attracted national media to Redwood Summer, and created a leadership void in the preparations. The bombing also led Greg King to quit Earth First! and move back to Sonoma. He was exhausted and scared.[26]

Despite the loss of King, the bombing strengthened the movement over the long term as mainstream groups started to take an interest in the North Coast. More immediately, it forced North Coast Earth First! to develop a broader base of leaders. With its main three organizers absent, others picked up the reins, including Karen Pickett, Anna Marie Stenberg, Naomi Wagner, Mokai, Zack Stentz, Tracy Kattleman, Betty Ball, and Sequoia, all of whom would play major roles in the Redwood Wars for years to come. Redwood Summer began in June 1990. One group organized a rally at the export docks in Sacramento to protest the exportation of raw logs and mill jobs, and the related increases in harvest levels. Humboldt Earth First! organized cat-and-mouse actions on Pacific Lumber property, disrupting logging operations by placing "civilians" in harm's way. The Squirrel Affinity Group organized a tree-sit on Pacific Lumber property in what they named Murrelet Grove; they were promptly arrested. Several women were arrested for trespassing at Maxxam's Marin County offices. On July 18, tipped off by a local resident, more than twenty Redwood Summer activists hiked into Osprey Grove on Louisiana-Pacific property in Mendocino to halt the harvest of old-growth trees. Over two days, twenty-two activists were arrested in Osprey Grove, but within a week, a judge issued a temporary restraining order halting the logging. On June 20, seven hundred people rallied at the Samoa docks of Louisiana-Pacific between Eureka and Arcata. Forty-four activists were arrested for blocking trucks at the docks. After the rally, small woods actions persisted, but the majority of participants went to the mills to engage workers or marched in Mendocino's Fourth of July parade with banners denouncing clear-cutting.[27]

Redwood Summer activists then settled into Mendocino and prepared for the main event: a rally in Fort Bragg culminating with a march through town to the Georgia-Pacific mill. On July 21, an estimated two thousand environmental activists marched through Fort Bragg chanting, "Earth First! Profits Last!" Waiting at the other end of town were approximately 1,500 supporters of the Yellow Ribbon Coalition, founded by timber interests to rally loggers and supporters against the proposed spotted owl protection plan for federal land in Oregon and Washington. When the two crowds met, sparks flew. The logging supporters yelled and cursed at the activists. Cherney tried to defuse the situation by inviting the hecklers to use the Earth First! sound truck to air their concerns. Few took up Cherney on his offer, but no violence occurred either. After the Fort Bragg rally, seventeen activists were arrested at a Pacific Lumber logging gate, and angry officers shaved the heads of the jailed activists.[28]

Tensions escalated again when the actions moved back to Humboldt and Pacific Lumber in late August. The largest action was in a section of Headwaters Forest named Murrelet Grove. Fifty to seventy activists snuck into the grove in the middle of the night, awaiting sunrise and the arrival of the logging crews. The activists unveiled a new tool and a new willingness to take chances. They used Kryptonite bike locks to chain themselves to logging equipment, and one man stopped a logger from turning on his chain saw by placing his hand under it. Other activists surrounded an old-growth tree to keep the loggers away. Judi Bari reported that one activist was run over by a truck and that others were chased by bulldozers. Earth First! also organized a seventy-person rally outside a meeting between Humboldt State University professors and timber executives. The crowd surrounded John Campbell's car, and one activist, Serina, lay on the hood and refused to let go. Campbell drove down the drive with the activist on the hood until the police arrived to remove her. With Serina in jail for four months, Earth First! established a noisy round-the-clock vigil at Campbell's home, forcing Campbell and his wife to travel with a police escort.[29]

The events of Redwood Summer brought attention to the timber wars and briefly halted some logging operations. The summer's most lasting effect, however, was an escalation in the vitriol coming from the industry and its allied workers. Aside from the hostility of the Fort Bragg Yellow Ribbon supporters, loggers at Murrelet Grove, police officers, timber executives, county supervisors, and other residents amplified their opposition to Earth First! and its campaign. Shep Tucker of Louisiana-Pacific symbolized the increasing hostility when he suggested to a USA Today reporter that the activists were a "terrorist group." More ominously, police arrested two men carrying rifles at a counterprotest in Fortuna. Another symptom of the growing frustration was the creation of Mother's Watch, a pro-timber women's group, by Candace Boak. Cherney and Bari charged Boak with originating the death threats they received. In July, Mother's Watch organized a "Dirty Tricks Workshop" to teach members how to harass environmentalists and feed false information to the press. Those types of workshops were invented by Wise Use activists to harass environmentalists across the West. Boak commented that "it was just harmless stuff that added some humor to the summer." However, one of her associates was arrested for throwing a fake bomb in the Arcata Earth First! office. The North Coast, and Humboldt County in particular, was increasingly a county under severe strain.[30]

Moving North to Headwaters

In what appeared to be an effort to tamp down growing animosity in the local worker community, Earth First! stopped directly confronting loggers and mill workers. Instead, they targeted timber company executives. In September 1990, Cherney, with 125 others, rallied outside Maxxam's Houston headquarters. In October, Earth First! organized a protest at Louisiana-Pacific chief Harry Merlo's house near Cloverdale. The activists hung banners, dumped wood chips in the driveway, and played Cherney's music at top volume. At one point, a group of activists jumped into Merlo's hot tub. In December, activists calling themselves the Corporate Fallers descended on Campbell's house to deliver presents of ash and sawdust while singing "endless" renditions of "Hang Down Your Head, John Campbell" to the tune of the folk song "Tom Dooley." The caroling was brought to an abrupt halt when Candace Boak showed up with a crew of supporters and chased the activists off the Campbell property. Things then settled down a bit until the summer of 1991.[31]

Earth First! lost much of its national appeal in the 1990s due to the splinters running through the anarchic movement and the loss of Dave Foreman after he was arrested in 1989 for colluding with a group of Earth First! activists attempting to destroy power lines in Arizona. Foreman subsequently assumed a low profile. Around Garberville in southern Humboldt, where EPIC and many other activists were based, North Coast Earth First! continued to attract supporters and develop new campaigns. Leib Ostrow and Linda Dillon, proprietors of Music for Little People, a recording studio and store in Garberville that had just sold half its business to Warner Bros., started the Trees Foundation. As Ostrow described it, the couple wanted to "'tithe' some of the money." The foundation supports local grassroots environmental activism, using its resources to fund leadership training and meeting facilitation, among other coordinating and consulting services. Trees Foundation grew particularly interested in funding geographic information system technology to map Pacific Lumber land in order to develop credible land management proposals for Headwaters Forest. The maps and technical assistance provided EPIC with evidence for its lawsuits. During the 1990s, Trees Foundation developed into a major force in the Redwood Wars.[32]

The activists who took the reins of Redwood Summer in 1991 took greater risks than ever before. Redwood Summer II in 1991 was also known as Ecotopia Summer, a reference to *Ecotopia*, the 1975 novel by Ernest Callenbach that imagined the new nation formed when Oregon, Washington, and northern California secede from the United States. In the novel, the area secedes to escape the destructive use of technology by postwar American society. For the young activists organizing the 1991 Earth First! actions, the idea of forcefully resisting multinational corporations and what they saw as a corrupt government was appealing. One popular environmentalist bumper sticker of the era proudly proclaimed, "U.S. out of Humboldt County."[33]

Despite the momentum of Redwood Summer, the follow-up plans lacked mass appeal, likely the result of losing Bari, Cherney, and King. Bari was working on her lawsuit against the FBI, Cherney was off on a campus tour to generate media, and King had quit the movement due to exhaustion. The two major actions of Ecotopia Summer 1991 took place deep inside Pacific Lumber property, away from the public and the media. John Campbell and his team had prepared for the activists, equipping the loggers with diamond saw blades to cut through the Kryptonite locks used by activists to chain themselves to bulldozers. Campbell authorized the loggers to capture trespassers and hold them until the sheriff arrived. This was a disaster for the activists, and even those who escaped capture were far from roads, help, and safety. Furthermore, the actions failed to stop logging operations, and there were no media to publicize the drama in the woods. These were not the kinds of actions that had generated attention and support in the past; these covert actions were directed solely at Pacific Lumber and its employees, and they only generated frustration.[34]

After the disasters in the woods, Bari re-engaged with Earth First!, though she was badly handicapped. Her shattered pelvis and broken coccyx left her dependent on a cane. More than that, her damaged nerves caused persistent pain that, as one close friend put it, "ranged from mercifully mild at times to debilitating, and would flare up for any number of reasons, cold temperatures, exhaustion, over-exertion, etc." Thus, Bari could not hike into the backwoods, march around, or live at a base camp. She certainly could not work as a carpenter. Despite her disabilities, neither she nor her peers seem to have questioned that she would rejoin the fights against corporate logging. On that score, she seemed determined: she could work with other activists to strategize and organize. She hosted meetings, helped recruit activists, and reached out to the media and small donors. Unsurprisingly, Earth First! moved the remaining summer actions to safer, more public locations largely out of Humboldt County and out of the woods.[35]

The most important event of 1991, however, was the arrival of Alicia Littletree Bales on the North Coast. She helped bring order to Earth First!'s planning, focusing on recruiting activists rather than orchestrating daring backwoods adventures. Littletree was a seventeen-year-old high school student when she arrived on the North Coast in early July with an affinity group from Sacramento, where she went to school. Attracted by the stories of friends who had participated in the disastrous actions deep in Pacific Lumber land, Littletree stayed at the Ecotopia base camp, swam, and listened to people play music. She participated in her first action in July at the state capitol in Sacramento. Littletree and four other women, naked and covered with mud, created a distraction outside while other activists locked themselves to the statue of Columbus inside the capitol and another group hung a banner over the second floor rotunda. Littletree was arrested and taken to a juvenile detention center. Her mother convinced the police not to press charges, but she also refused to allow Littletree to return home. Littletree subsequently moved to Garberville and found work as an administrative assistant at the Institute for Sustainable Forestry. In the fall, Littletree enrolled at Whale Gulch Independent School, tucked back in the community, upslope from Shelter Cove off a dirt road near the Sinkyone Wilderness.[36]

Littletree spent much of her time at Earth First! meetings, however, and quickly became a fixture in the North Coast organization. During the fall and winter of 1991–92, approximately fifteen people regularly attended the meetings. The main cohort included Bari, Cherney, Naomi Wagner, Dave Biebe, and Mary Corte, and they talked a lot about Louisiana-Pacific and Harry Merlo. That winter, Littletree also experienced the dysfunctional side of Earth First! at a movement conference in Portland, Oregon. Bari, Littletree, and other North Coast Earth First! activists at the conference were disturbed by the inability of the attendees to run a coherent meeting or make decisions due to the number of disruptions. The North Coast group left the conference concerned about the state of the national movement and wondering whether "agents or assholes" were the source of disruption, as Littletree explained. Such concerns probably contributed to the ever-increasing time and energy Bari put into the bombing lawsuit, as she was convinced the FBI had infiltrated the organization.[37]

Littletree adopted a more visible role that spring, and North Coast Earth First! also made a major splash, again propelling the Redwood Wars to prominence in California. In February 1992, Louisiana-Pacific began logging near Albion, on the Mendocino Coast, close to what was known as Enchanted Meadow, a popular spot for picnics and hikes. North Coast Earth First! organized a nine-week campaign, including daily actions for fifty-four consecutive days. The organization set up roadblocks in the woods that attracted young and daring activists, and they organized sixteen tree-sits. One activist, Dark Moon, sat in a tree for thirty consecutive days. The actions became known as the Albion Uprising, and they effectively shut down Louisiana-Pacific's logging plans in the area. Littletree and Cherney were both tree-sitters. In fact, Littletree did the first nude Earth First! tree-sit, sitting in a tree for nine days talking to paddlers and the media from a very visible location on the river.[38]

After the Albion Uprising, Littletree became the primary Earth First! organizer in Humboldt and helped draw attention and resources to the Headwaters conflict. Living with Judi Bari, Littletree studied politics and organizing with the elder stateswoman of the movement as she helped prepare the court case against the Oakland Police Department and the FBI. In June 1992, Pacific Lumber began illegally logging the Owl Creek Grove of Headwaters Forest, one of the Timber Harvest Plans under court restriction since 1989. Later that summer

Littletree moved north because of her affinity for Humboldt as the place she moved to when she left home. Kurt Newman, one of the activists who had discovered Headwaters Forest with Greg King in 1987, took her deep into Pacific Lumber land to witness the figure-eight-shaped road the company had cut into the ancient grove. Little-tree recalls that the road was so steep she could hardly walk on it, and the silt and dust was nearly a foot deep and littered with dead "critters." On the hike, Littletree and an EPIC activist photographed the road, logging zones, and log decks. EPIC later used the photos in pamphlets and supporting documents for their 1992 alternative writs in *Sierra v. Board of Forestry*, the 1989 case challenging the logging of Owl Creek Grove, in which the Board of Forestry refused to support Pacific Lumber's appeal to the California Supreme Court. Littletree organized nightly hikes into Owl Creek to publicize the campaign and monitor logging. Her group called itself the Owl Creek Protection Association to avoid the Earth First! stigma while recruiting a broader base of activists in the college town of Arcata.

Pacific Lumber entered Owl Creek Grove again over Thanksgiving weekend 1992, apparently in violation of a court order. Earth First! activists rushed into the woods to impede the logging until the courts could intervene. Littletree estimated that thirty activists hiked into the woods to prevent the felling of ancient trees. Police and loggers awaited the activists. Littletree was in Sacramento at her mother's house when she received the call. Against her mother's wishes, Littletree immediately drove north and entered the woods, where she, along with a "truckload" of activists, was arrested and taken to Eureka. On Monday, November 30, 1992, EPIC and the Sierra Club obtained a temporary restraining order against Pacific Lumber, and on December 1, an appeals court granted the environmentalists an emergency stay halting all logging in the area pending completion of *Sierra v. Board of Forestry*.[39]

The activists and timber companies both were clearly frustrated by the uncertainty on the North Coast. By 1992, the Forests Forever and Redwood Summer campaigns had elevated the profile of the Redwood Wars, resulting in broad sympathy for the environmentalists outside of Redwood Country. However, the Forests Forever effort had failed to bring permanent reform to North Coast land management, and the expanded direct actions associated with Redwood Summer had failed to break the resistance of the timber companies. EPIC was seriously limiting opportunities to log giant redwoods, but companies continued to clear-cut hillsides and cut down the giants as opportunities arose— legally or not. The Department of Forestry continued to resist fully embracing their responsibilities under the California Environmental Quality and Endangered Species Acts. Pacific Lumber, in particular, was determined to defeat the activists. The company's defiant logging in Owl Creek combined with their aggressive suppression of Earth First!'s backwoods actions turned them into enemy number one for the activists. Amid the uncertainty and frustration, the activists and the Pacific Lumber Company gradually began to look to the federal government for resolution to the increasingly hostile conflicts over the redwoods.

OUT OF CALIFORNIA AND INTO WASHINGTON, DC

The election of environmentalist Dan Hamburg to Congress in 1992 convinced the North Coast activists to move the fight over Headwaters Forest to a larger stage. Dan Hamburg grew up in the Midwest, raised in a liberal Democratic household in Saint Louis where General Dwight D. Eisenhower was referred to as "old bubble head." When Hamburg began college at Stanford, he dove headfirst into student politics. Hamburg joined a group of campus radicals and organized against the Vietnam War. Through his activism, Hamburg developed his political skills and forged a lifelong friendship and working relationship with California native Kate Anderton, who would become his chief of staff.

Deeply involved in radical politics, Hamburg slowly came to environmental politics. His first recollection of concern for humanity's impact on the planet was from his senior year at Stanford. While hiking in the mountains above Palo Alto, he noticed how much more developed and polluted the city had become during the four years he had lived in the area. After graduating in 1970, Hamburg moved to Ukiah, the county seat of Mendocino, as a part of the back-to-the-land movement. Like Richard Gienger, the Man Who Walks in the Woods, and Kathy Bailey, Hamburg belonged to that generation of activists who moved to the North Coast after experiences in the social movements of the 1960s. He wasn't sure what he wanted to do with his life after college, and some friends, including Anderton, had moved to Mendocino to establish the Mariposa School in Ukiah. In 1971, Hamburg purchased thirty-eight acres and began teaching at an alternative school in central Mendocino. That year, he met Carol "Carrie" Blood and her three children, and the couple married in 1974. Community politics was never far away, however. In 1972, Hamburg and friends staged the first Ukiah antiwar demonstration in front of the courthouse. After Hamburg unsuccessfully ran for the Ukiah City Council in 1975, a friend on the council appointed him to the County Planning Commission, where he worked to prevent so-called leapfrog developments extending beyond city infrastructure. In 1977, the Hamburgs worked with Kathy Bailey on an initiative to eliminate Agent Orange use in Mendocino. During the campaign, Hamburg suddenly became aware of the vast forest "out there" in the hinterlands. In 1980, he was elected to the Mendocino Board of Supervisors, and his experience as a board member eventually pulled him into the forestry arena.

On the board of supervisors, Hamburg saw the timber industry's influence on local politics and noted the increased logging in the late 1970s and early 1980s. His opposition to shopping mall and subdivision development put him at odds with the other supervisors, but it was his failure to support the timber industry that had the most dramatic impact on his political career. In early 1981, Hamburg and another supervisor took their sons to a congressional hearing on wilderness designation in Weaverville. Hamburg spoke in favor of protecting roadless areas in the national forests, and the assembled crowd was not pleased. According to Hamburg, he and his fellow supervisor left the hearing with their sons clutched tightly and in fear for their lives. Hamburg spent the next four years focusing on timber and fishing issues, especially efforts to prevent the conversion of agricultural areas and timberland into residential and commercial developments. In 1985, he left the board to pursue other interests.[40]

Hamburg's return to politics in 1992 thus offered North Coast environmental activists new hope for protecting Headwaters Forest, and they swiftly forced the issue onto the national stage. Hamburg had been elected on a broad platform of universal health care, reduction of the defense budget, and social justice. As Hamburg explained, his campaign was caught up in the enthusiasm for Democratic presidential candidate Bill Clinton. Hamburg had strong liberal bona fides, and he was

handsome and well spoken, even labeled a "big hunk" by *People Maga-*
zine in its "50 Most Beautiful People" issue after his election. Hamburg
chose the right time to make a run at a Republican incumbent. He was
able to run unopposed in the Democratic primary, presumably because
the national party had forced Doug Bosco to back out of the campaign
after his involvement in the congressional bank scandal of 1992. (Pacific
Lumber later employed Bosco as a lobbyist on forestry issues.) Though
the Redwood Wars were not part of Hamburg's campaign platform, he
sensed the Headwaters conflict would be an issue for his office because
other California representatives had in recent years introduced bills to
address the Headwaters conflict.[41]

It was the North Coast activists who forced Hamburg and Congress
to take up the Headwaters issue. After unsuccessful efforts at the state
level, the North Coast activists, frustrated by the local power of the timber industry, poured energy and resources into bringing the Headwaters conflict to the attention of the federal government. Shortly after his
election, Hamburg traveled to Arcata for an interview with Humboldt
State University's radio station. A caller asked when he was going to
introduce a Headwaters Forest protection bill. Hamburg replied that he
intended to, but wanted to take time to develop a bill that could actually
pass. His response opened the door for North Coast activists. In January 1993, Hamburg began meeting with Kathy Bailey, Darryl Cherney,
Judi Bari, Woods, Cecelia Lanman, and other North Coast activists.
The activists took on the task of writing a federal legislative proposal,
and Larry Evans—who had discovered Headwaters Forest in 1987 with
Greg King and Kurt Newman—worked on computer-generated maps
documenting the changes in the Headwaters Forest landscape since
the Maxxam takeover. The activists divided up the responsibilities
for crafting the proposal, with Kurt Newman in charge of the acreage
committee, Lanman working on the land management specifics, Bari
focused on a worker's package, and Cherney leading the committee to
develop a funding mechanism. Hamburg's office would put the proposal
into legislative language.[42]

The time was ripe for a new strategy in the Redwood Wars. From
1987 until 1993, court after court in California had halted Timber Harvest Plans, undermined de facto corporatism, and made logging ancient
redwoods extremely difficult, especially after the US Fish and Wildlife

Service listed the marbled murrelet as a threatened species in 1992 and declared the Headwaters Forest complex critical habitat. Pacific Lumber fought back, in the courtroom and in the woods. Nationally, tensions were also high. When the spotted owl controversy generated hostile confrontations in Oregon after the US Forest Service canceled timber sales across that state, the Clinton administration nervously waded into the breach, holding a timber summit in Portland in April 1993. In that volatile milieu, the activists went to work writing legislation.[43]

The new federal strategy developed by the activists was the Legislative Action Plan for Headwaters Forest. While ecologist Jerry Franklin, US Forest Service chief Jack Ward Thomas, and other foresters in the agency worked out the contours of the New Forestry on public lands in Oregon in an effort to balance spotted owl habitat and logging, North Coast activists proposed aggressive restoration, job creation, and preservation for 73,000 acres of Pacific Lumber property. The Headwaters Legislative Action Plan (HLAP) differed in significant ways from the Northwest Forest Plan developed by the Clinton administration in response to the spotted owl conflict. The HLAP dealt specifically with the regulation of private land. Rather than focusing on timber sales, the HLAP sought to restore "pre-disturbance biological health and diversity" across the entire complex. As such, the HLAP mandated intensive landscape management to achieve and maintain old-growth forest habitat.[44]

The plan involved three programs addressing some of the pressing concerns about environmental protection broadly and forestry specifically: cultural hostility, economic uncertainties, and developments in ecology and biology that prioritized biodiversity. The core of the plan featured a ten-year restoration proposal, a jobs program to "heal the wounds" between environmental activists and rural workers, and a plan to grant control of the forest to local residents. The biological diversity and health restoration plan was based on the expertise of North Coast activists, who had participated for decades in stream and forest rehabilitation. Its specific shape took form due to the work of Pacific Watershed Associates, an ecological restoration and engineering firm established in 1989 and hired by the initiative to help craft the restoration plans. Restoration involved removing roads, repairing watercourses, improving fisheries, removing exotic plant species, and managing second-growth stands to "hasten successional rates and to speed the re-establishment of . . . old growth character." The proposal did not specifically prescribe timber harvesting, but it did explicitly state that timber harvests might be appropriate on a 150-year rotation.

One significant feature of the plan, developed by Judi Bari, dealt with jobs and the local economy. The federal government, the activists proposed, as part of its acquisition of Headwaters Forest, would provide training and relocation opportunities for timber workers to find jobs of "equivalent opportunity," along with early retirement packages, loans to create small businesses in Humboldt County focused on value-added forest products, and priority hiring for all restoration work in Headwaters Forest. The HLAP envisioned all restoration and future timber harvesting work to be carried out by an employee owned and operated company utilizing an employee stock ownership plan (ESOP).[45]

The Headwaters Legislative Plan thus represented a radical departure from business as usual in Redwood Country. Too often radical environmentalists have been described by their opponents, and many scholars, as monolithically anti-worker and anti-development. The rhetoric of Earth First! founder Dave Foreman and his followers has often been used to define the goals of all radicals. Foreman may have wanted to create a large Paleolithic wilderness park across the American West. He may have wanted that land occupied by diverse fauna and small bands of hunter-gatherers. But the North Coast activists were not interested in closing the redwood forest to humans and human activity. Their Headwaters proposal was neither a plan for a new park nor a piece of forestry reform legislation. It was a plan to end corporate control of Headwaters Forest. The workers and the North Coast community would own and manage the forest for timber and habitat. They may have been naïve in their understanding of the risks timber workers were willing to assume, or in thinking that Congress would take up legislation that turned corporate land over to an ESOP. The activists, however, were genuine in their efforts. The persistent efforts to include worker packages into their plans underscore their commitment to workers. Their repeated efforts to evict Maxxam and Pacific Lumber from the forest provide additional support to their claims, as do their recorded oral histories. They unanimously spoke with great earnestness about sustainable forestry, anti-corporate politics, and the maintenance of their rural blue-collar community. They shared a radical vision for local control that was based not on maximizing profit but on maximizing equality, opportunity, and sustainability.[46]

Rumors about Hamburg's impending bill and other congressional action buzzed through the dense North Coast air throughout the spring and summer of 1993, forcing the logging and activist communities to fully enter the federal fray. John Campbell told the Associated Press that Hamburg was a "captive of the special interests of the radical environmental community" and had no regard for workers on the North Coast. The company hired former congressman Doug Bosco, at the rate of $15,000 a month, to lobby against the bills. The *Humboldt Beacon* described Hamburg as arrogant and callous, accusing him of developing his proposal without input from Humboldt residents. Pacific Lumber had apparently prepared for congressional intervention. In December 1992, after the Thanksgiving debacle in Owl Creek, Pacific Lumber had reorganized its operations so that the mills, the old-growth groves, and the town of Scotia remained Pacific Lumber property, while a new wholly owned subsidiary, Scotia Pacific Holding Company, owned the second-growth forest. According to activist analysis, the filings included a provision ensuring that the proceeds of a Headwaters Forest sale would be used to pay the bond debt—a sure sign, they believed, that Hurwitz intended to sell Headwaters and dismantle the company. The activists' analysis was partly corroborated by the press. In early August 1993, *Wall Street Journal* reporter Charles McCoy wrote an article about Hurwitz asserting that the Maxxam chief wanted the federal government to purchase 4,500 acres of Headwaters Grove for hundreds of millions of dollars. Otherwise the company would log the grove. With Hurwitz and the North Coast activists watching Congress, most of the Redwood Wars revolved around Washington, DC.[47]

At the center of the fray was the office of Dan Hamburg. The Headwaters Forest Act (HR 2866), written by Hamburg's office and introduced in August 1993, closely reflected the Headwaters Legislative Action Plan. It required the federal government to acquire approximately forty-four thousand acres of Pacific Lumber and Elk River Timber lands, closely matching the Fish and Wildlife Service's designation of murrelet critical habitat rather than the more expansive activist proposal. The acquired land would be included in Six Rivers

National Forest, with a portion assigned to the National Wilderness Preservation System. The bill prohibited logging of old-growth redwood and provided for restoration of logged forest. Unemployed timber and commercial fishery workers were to conduct the restoration work. The bill also provided annual payments to Humboldt County and the State of California to compensate for lost timber yield tax revenues. Finally, the bill required separate federal study of an additional fourteen thousand acres to identify additional old-growth forests and endangered species habitat, bringing the total of potentially protected land to approximately sixty thousand acres. The ESOP plan was not included in the final bill.[48]

Not specifically in the bill but endorsed by Hamburg was a plan to fund the acquisition with a so-called debt-for-nature swap, an idea given prominence by Darryl Cherney. In 1992, the Federal Deposit Insurance Company had informed United Financial Group, parent company to the failed United Savings Association of Texas (USAT), that the company and its former officers were liable for any breach of fiduciary duty. Charles Hurwitz was the CEO of United Financial, and Maxxam was a major shareholder. USAT had regularly purchased junk bonds from Michael Milken, including some used to finance the Pacific Lumber acquisition in 1986. The debt swap idea, promoted by the newly formed Rose Foundation in Los Angeles, was to force Hurwitz to give up Headwaters Forest in exchange for some of the more than $1 billion in claims against USAT in the savings and loan failure. Hamburg and the North Coast activists believed the debt-for-nature swap was the best way to acquire Headwaters because it required no appropriation and exacted justice on Hurwitz for his role in the Texas savings and loan failure.[49]

Despite Cherney and Bari's involvement with the bill, or maybe because of it, Alicia Littletree organized the Week of Outrage in response to Dan Hamburg's bill. The bill did not meet Earth First!'s expectations because it failed to turn over the forest to the community and only guaranteed protection for some forty-four thousand acres of the Headwaters Forest complex. Pacific Lumber was actively logging in Headwaters Forest, and Earth First! wanted more forest protected than the bill authorized. On August 21–28, 1993, Littletree organized daily actions protesting Pacific Lumber's logging and promoting an Earth First! counterproposal to protect ninety-eight thousand acres of forest.

One day, Pacific Lumber employees discovered one of their gates entirely entangled in yarn and fifth-generation logger Ernie Pardini sitting in a tree near Headwaters Grove. At the same time, a group of activists blocked another entrance to the harvest area and hung a banner reading, "Blame Hurwitz, Not Spotted Owls." The Week of Outrage signified a significant shift in Earth First! strategy to appeal to a broader audience, a shift that benefited the local movement in the long run. Actions were once again designed as public demonstrations to draw attention to the company and its operations. The message changed as well, focusing on demonizing Hurwitz rather than on sustainable forestry or forest protection. That change was a conscious decision to appeal to the common fears and grievances of environmentalists, Pacific Lumber workers, and other Humboldt residents. After the Week of Outrage, Earth First! activity declined as Hamburg's bill moved through Congress, EPIC and the Sierra Club successfully blocked key harvest projects in court, and Littletree traveled to Guatemala for a much-needed respite. There was little urgency to develop large-scale campaigns.[50]

The movement of the Headwaters bill through Congress was urgent, however. Congress held hearings on Hamburg's bill in October 1993, and the North Coast radicals and Pacific Lumber were ready for the national stage. John Campbell expressed the company's outrage that the bill required Congress to acquire the land regardless of the company's willingness to sell. He argued that the Redwood National Park purchase decades earlier had already left Redwood Country in economic ruin and that Hamburg's bill would crush Humboldt County's largest remaining private employer by confiscating nearly 30 percent of its land. The company contended that since enough ancient redwoods were already protected in state and national parks, the bill was ecologically unnecessary in addition to being too expensive for taxpayers during a time of enormous budget deficits. Finally, Campbell suggested that the company was willing to sell 4,500 acres—the Headwaters Grove and a surrounding buffer—at a price equivalent to the value of the logs on the property. The "Boskeenhauser" deal's two-year voluntary moratorium on logging Headwaters Grove had expired, and Campbell told the committee that unless an agreement could be reached, the company would be forced to log Headwaters due to its responsibility to its shareholders.[51]

Hamburg and the activists countered Campbell's attacks. They argued that fair market value was not equivalent to the value of the logs because many of them could not be harvested due to the restrictions of the Endangered Species and Forest Practices Acts. Mostly, however, they described the urgency they believed was necessary to prevent ecological and economic disaster on the North Coast. Sierra Club's Kathy Bailey and EPIC's Cecelia Lanman testified about the need to protect the last ancient redwood groves in private hands; the crucial role the Headwaters complex played for the marbled murrelet, northern spotted owl, and salmon; and the need to reform timber practices to more sustainably harvest the forests of the North Coast. The activists and Hamburg leaned heavily on wildlife biologists to make their cases, particularly allied biologists Peter Moyle and Kim Nelson. They relied on descriptions of the illegal Owl Creek timber operations in 1992 and press accounts of the doubled rate of logging to vilify Maxxam and Hurwitz. Bailey particularly focused on the company's logging, pointing out that of the forty-four thousand proposed acres in the bill, Pacific Lumber had logged more than twenty-three thousand acres since 1986, of which only nine hundred were second growth. She argued that if any ancient and residual old-growth groves were to be saved, immediate action was necessary. Lanman highlighted the inaction of California's forestry agency, the resistance of Pacific Lumber to court and agency orders, and the company's use of a new harvest pattern to evade wildlife laws by surrounding ancient forest with clear-cuts and puncturing ancient groves with roads, thus reducing their value to wildlife. What she described recalled 1968, when Miller Timber Company had logged around and through a property designated for discussion as a part of the Redwood National Park proposal.[52]

The action surrounding the Headwaters Forest Act quickened after the hearings, driven by North Coast residents. Had their influence not been as great, and had Hamburg not embraced their agenda, the issue probably would have died before then. They were coming up on an election year, and political operatives and North Coast supporters believed the congressman needed to avoid a campaign referendum on the Headwaters issue; it was too volatile. However, the North Coast activists formed the Headwaters Forest Coordinating Committee (HFCC)— another reference to the civil rights movement—to coordinate efforts to pass Hamburg's bill before the election. The effort was extraordinarily successful given the locals' lack of federal experience. Kathy Bailey, Darryl Cherney, Cecelia Lanman, Jill Ratner from Rose Foundation, EPIC attorney Tom Lippe, and others orchestrated the advocacy efforts.

Neither the activists nor Pacific Lumber was particularly pleased with Hamburg's bill, but the activists were even less pleased that Congress might allow Hurwitz to log the old-growth forest. To put pressure on Congress and Pacific Lumber, the Headwaters Forest Coordinating Committee produced its own acquisition proposal for the Headwaters Forest complex. It was similar to the Hamburg bill, though HFCC wanted to explicitly include a debt-for-nature swap, and they wanted to acquire additional lands over time using private funds, including the so-called Northern Headwaters Grove from Elk River Timber, which was owned by Sierra Pacific, the largest private landowner in California. The HFCC proposal made Hamburg's bill look modest by comparison. The HFCC was so serious about their proposal that they assigned a negotiating team to work with Red Emerson of Elk River Timber, telling Emerson he could avoid an EPIC lawsuit if he entered into the negotiations. Pacific Lumber was also active in the legislative process. Later in the spring of 1993, the PALCO Family Defense Fund—an organization created by the company to combat the Hamburg bill—signed a contract with the DC-based American Land Rights Association to organize national opposition to the Hamburg bill. Meanwhile, Bailey, Lanman, Cherney, and others from HFCC spent considerable time in Washington trying to convince national environmental groups and members of Congress to support Hamburg's bill.[53]

In that busy environment, the Headwaters Forest Act moved through the House committees and onto the floor. In early April 1994, the Agriculture Committee's Subcommittee on Special Crops and Natural Resources, and the Natural Resources Committee's Subcommittee on National Parks, Forests and Public Lands each approved the bill. On May 11, the full House Natural Resources Committee marked up the bill and scheduled a voice vote. At that point, John Campbell and other timber industry executives started to lobby against the bill and even donated heavily to Hamburg's opponent in the Democratic primary, former congressman Doug Bosco. Campbell and his wife reregistered as Democrats so they could try to unseat Hamburg and derail the bill. Douglas Thron—a student at Humboldt State University who, in 1992, began trespassing on Pacific Lumber land to photograph the forest and logging sites—summoned the ghost of Andrew Hill of 1900 Big Basin fame and embarked on a summer tour using his photographs to drum up public support and congressional cosponsors for the bill. Pacific Lumber had former congressman Bosco, Democratic lobbyist Tommy Boggs, and President Clinton's advisor, Vernon Jordan, working to defeat the bill. On August 9, with no vote on the calendar, Hamburg and Hurwitz met in DC. On August 15, Pacific Lumber reversed its position and publicly endorsed a new version of the bill. Hamburg had agreed to insert "willing seller" language into the bill. John Campbell said they just wanted to end the conflict and get paid for giving up company land. That same day, many of the national environmental groups joined EPIC, Sierra Club California, and Earth First! in their Washington lobbying efforts.[54]

Though the bill had the support of Pacific Lumber and the North Coast activists, it failed to reach the president's desk. At 4:40 p.m. on September 21, 1994, the House approved the amended Headwaters Forest Act with a vote of 288–133. The amended bill included "willing seller" language, a $200,000 purchase cap, and a provision allowing the Forest Service to acquire land as it became available for sale instead of requiring that the land be purchased all at once. It appeared that Hamburg and the activists were about to snare a victory. However, on the last day of the Senate session, Senator Malcolm Wallop of Wyoming filibustered California Senator Dianne Feinstein's California Desert Lands Act, with Majority Leader George Mitchell calling senators back to town to vote before they went home to finish their re-election campaigns. At 5:11 p.m. the filibuster broke, the California Desert Lands bill passed, and the Senate adjourned. The Desert Lands Act, covering various degrees of protection for six million acres, was a major priority for national environmental groups and the California delegation, especially Feinstein, who faced re-election that fall. Headwaters had no such powerful champions.

On that final day of the Senate, Kathy Bailey and Darryl Cherney sat in the galley of the Senate, watching impotently as the Senate adjourned without voting on the Headwaters bill. Any hope of reintroducing the bill in 1995 died when Hamburg lost his re-election bid to Republican Frank Riggs. Cherney's presence, and his subsequent focus on Senator Barbara Boxer as the one he suspected of killing the bill, often distracted the North Coast activists from positive campaign work. The efforts of the locals—company leaders and activists—had pushed the Headwaters conflict out of the North Coast forests and courtrooms and into the national arena. The countercultural activists achieved that feat with a combination of radical and traditional ideas and tactics. Though defeated, the Hamburg bill highlighted the power of the locals to influence national debates.[55]

SPIRALING TOWARD THE FEDERAL COURTS

The North Coasters had forced Californians and Congress to weigh in on the Redwood Wars, and they eventually forced the federal courts into the battles as well. By the end of 1994, after four years of public relations, legislative, and legal attacks on its policies and practices, the Board of Forestry and the Department of Forestry had taken steps to cut their corporatist ties, yet they remained under attack from North Coast activists who wanted the agency to take even greater action, especially after the California Supreme Court validated their legal arguments once and for all. After the death of Hamburg's bill, the activists and Pacific Lumber returned their attention to the courts. With a combination of Sierra Club funding and the past attorney fees awarded by the courts, EPIC ramped up its efforts.

The chaotic litigation over logging Owl Creek eventually caused activists to look to the federal Endangered Species Act and federal courts to protect the giant trees and valuable marbled murrelet habitat. Logging, oil spills, and gill net fishing during the twentieth century had reduced the marbled murrelet's population in the Pacific Northwest to approximately twenty thousand individuals, as a result of a roughly 5 percent annual decline. The birds spend much of the year at sea hunting small fish and crustaceans. Each spring they nest on platforms in old-growth conifers near the shore. The nesting pairs are solitary, but scientists found clusters of murrelet nests, indicating a need for large unfragmented forests as nesting grounds. The murrelet females lay only one egg per year, making each nest critical to maintaining the overall population. Male and female birds alternate shifts hunting and incubating. The hunter leaves the nest at dawn, from high up in a tree under the cover of thick canopy, and heads out to sea to forage, returning at dusk. Traveling out into the open sky at low light affords the tiny birds some protection against predators like crows, jays, and owls. The rapid clear-cutting of Redwood Country, especially after the Great Depression, badly fragmented the coastal old-growth forests of California, Oregon, and Washington. By the 1990s, the US Fish and Wildlife service could find only twelve nesting sites in all of California's remaining seventy thousand acres of old-growth redwood forest habitat, which was less than 5 percent of the old-growth redwood forest acreage in 1850. Pacific Lumber owned approximately ten thousand of those acres, including Owl Creek and the main Headwaters Grove. For the North Coast activists and biologists, the plight of the murrelet, like that of the giant redwoods, was a symptom of the dangers industrial logging posed to Redwood Country. Through their earlier cases against Pacific Lumber, the activists had forced the Department of Forestry to request wildlife surveys from timber owners before approving Timber Harvest Plans. Pacific Lumber resisted the new responsibility.[56]

The fate of Owl Creek was thus critical to the marbled murrelet as well as the course of the Redwood Wars. Owl Creek was located in the eastern part of Pacific Lumber property, due north of Humboldt Redwoods State Park and southeast of the main Headwaters Grove. It was thus essential in connecting the two larger old-growth forests. And it was the place where Alicia Littletree had organized nightly hikes after the illegal logging in June 1992. The legal challenges to Pacific Lumber's plans to log Owl Creek date back to 1989, when EPIC challenged the company's original harvest plan for the area in *Sierra v. Board of Forestry*, which was still pending in 1992. Pacific Lumber had appealed to the California Supreme Court to overturn court orders prohibiting logging in the area until Pacific Lumber conducted proper wildlife surveys. Predicting defeat for Pacific Lumber, the Board of Forestry had withdrawn its support, and it had further distanced itself from corporatist tradition by approving the agency's new regulations limiting logging in old-growth areas to protect the marbled murrelet. The two Board of Forestry actions demonstrate the success of citizen litigation in destabilizing the traditional relationship between the board and industry.[57]

In 1994, the California Supreme Court ruled against Pacific Lumber in the Owl Creek case, delivering a staggering blow to industry independence and property prerogatives. Like previous lower courts, the court ruled that the Board of Forestry had to comply with the California Environmental Quality Act and the Forest Practice Act, and that the board had the authority to require timber companies to conduct wildlife surveys. The court further underscored the Board of Forestry's nontimber responsibilities when it argued that *not* requiring timber companies to submit enough information to assess and *prevent* environmental damage violated CEQA. This victory for EPIC and the Sierra Club forced the Board of Forestry to further reform its practices regarding ancient redwoods and to recognize its responsibilities toward old-growth-dependent species. For ten years after *EPIC v. Johnson*, citizen litigation had exposed and discredited the de facto corporatist regime, destroyed the autonomy of the Board of Forestry and the industry, and widened the growing divide between industry and the agency. However, legal battles over nontimber resources escalated when the agency, and especially the timber industry, yet again failed to embrace the high court's ruling. Therefore, as the court ended one conflict, it escalated another by increasing legal demands on the industry and the Board of Forestry to protect nontimber forest resources.[58]

Owl Creek Grove continued to play a crucial role in the litigation campaign of North Coast activists because Pacific Lumber continued to try to log the area, before and after the Supreme Court ruling. While *Sierra v. Board of Forestry* worked its way through the courts, EPIC decided to use the state and federal Endangered Species Acts to permanently stop the logging. Three things had changed in northern California that made federal courts appealing. On October 1, 1992, the US Fish and Wildlife Service listed the marbled murrelet as a threatened species, granting the bird protection under the federal Endangered Species Act along with its earlier protection under California law. Pacific Lumber seems to have decided it could no longer count on the Board of Forestry to protect its interests and thus grew more aggressive and independent in its actions, increasing the activists' anxiety. Finally, lower state courts began to rule against EPIC more regularly in cases against Pacific Lumber.[59]

The ugliness of the legal cases surrounding Owl Creek Grove prompted activists to pursue federal remedies before Hamburg's election and well before the California Supreme Court ruled in their favor. The California decision only confirmed for the activists that they should seek a permanent solution to prevent logging in Owl Creek and the other old-growth groves inside Headwaters Forest. The so-called Thanksgiving Massacre of 1992 was the tipping point for activists. On November 24, 1992, California Fish and Game had warned Pacific Lumber not to log in Owl Creek without complying with federal endangered species law, and the company agreed to consult with US Fish and Wildlife biologists. Despite Earth First! activists conducting nightly hikes to Owl Creek to monitor logging activity, Pacific Lumber resumed logging on November 28, over Thanksgiving weekend, without consulting any agency. It was the first time in the sixteen-year career of Pacific Lumber's chief timber operations manager, Dan McLaughlin, that he could recall the company logging over Thanksgiving, and he asserted that Owl Creek was the only area harvested. The next day, Fish and Wildlife sent EPIC a letter informing it that the harvest constituted a "taking" in violation of the Endangered Species Act. On December 1, 1992, the California appeals court issued an emergency stay of logging operations in Owl Creek.[60]

Frustrated that the state court proceedings in *Sierra v. Board of Forestry* were stalled in countless motions and counter motions and horrified that Pacific Lumber was so willing to flout the law and agency instructions, EPIC pondered its options. Since harming a threatened or endangered species violates section 9 of the federal Endangered Species Act, Macon Cowles, an environmental attorney involved with the Exxon Valdez oil spill, suggested that EPIC sue in federal court. Cowles had read Charles McCoy's 1993 *Wall Street Journal* article about the conflict over Headwaters Forest and thought the situation warranted federal action under the Endangered Species Act. EPIC attorney Sharon Duggan agreed that the claimants had a better shot in federal court because the Humboldt County judges were growing weary of EPIC and Pacific Lumber in their courtrooms and the superior courts did not have the time or resources to thoroughly review the massive administrative records in the cases. On April 16, 1993, EPIC filed suit in federal court against Pacific Lumber, the Department of Forestry, the Board of Forestry, the California Department of Fish and Game, the US Fish and Wildlife Service, and secretary of the interior

Bruce Babbitt, arguing that all the parties were responsible for allowing "harm" to the threatened marbled murrelet in Owl Creek during the two illegal logging operations in 1992—one in June and the other in November. The case was tried in August and September 1994, while Hamburg's bill was moving through Congress. A ruling would not come down until early 1995.[61]

• • •

By the mid-1990s, the Headwaters Conflict had thus achieved great notoriety, and the stakes had grown enormously high. The North Coast activists pursued new strategies and developed new tactics in their dogged pursuit of logging reform and ancient redwood protection, highlighting their commitment to active land management and human integration in their biocentrist vision. Their proposals included provisions to protect ancient redwoods, implement sustainable forestry operations, and create worker relief and assistance programs. The activists believed that corporate control of the forest had led to liquidation logging and that timber workers and the broader community would make better land management decisions. These campaigns reflect the flexibility and resourcefulness of the activists, who worked the traditional avenues of power to protect the forest and their rural community. The success of the direct actions and litigation forced the state and the industry to attend to the issues, undermining de facto corporatism. Their failure is testimony to the resources and political effectiveness of Pacific Lumber and the timber industry.

EPIC's litigation continued to break the log jams piling up in the uncertainty of the Redwood Wars. The impending federal case and the failure of the federal bill had created a combustible situation: Pacific Lumber might lose the timber in Owl Creek if the courts continued to rule against them, but they might be able to log Headwaters Grove itself since there was no longer a potential buyer and the so-called "Boskeen-hauser" moratorium had expired. In 1995, the federal courts prohibited logging in all marbled murrelet habitat; the aftershocks pulled President Clinton into the orbit of the Redwood Wars. Pacific Lumber had been preparing a nuclear option in case of such a defeat and filed suit against the State of California and the US government. The Clinton administration, determined to avoid a costly court battle, worked to negotiate a deal with Pacific Lumber. The intervention of the executive branch would transform the way the environmental protection regime affected private landowners.

FIVE

THE TRANSFORMATION

KATHY BAILEY SHOULD HAVE BEEN ELATED. THE CALIFORNIA LEG-islature was about to take the final step to evict Charles Hurwitz and Maxxam from Headwaters Grove. Bailey had worked for the past decade to acquire the greater Headwaters Forest complex from the Pacific Lumber Company to prevent the logging of the world's largest privately owned old-growth redwood forest. Sometime after 7 p.m. on March 1, 1999, Kathy Bailey retired to her room at the "Capitol Punishment Inn"—a moniker given to the Sacramento hotel by North Coast activists, who despised their visits to the statehouse. Later that night, thanks in large part to her efforts, the State of California would pass an appropriations bill to acquire the Headwaters Forest Reserve from Pacific Lumber.[1]

For nearly two decades, a small group of rural Americans had forced a multinational corporation, the State of California, and the United States government to accommodate local environmental concerns. California and the US government had agreed to pay Pacific Lumber nearly half a billion dollars for approximately ten thousand acres of redwood forest. Pacific Lumber had also completed the nation's first multispecies Habitat Conservation Plan, an agreement with the federal government restricting logging activities on the private timberland to better protect the habitat of the northern spotted owl, the murrelet, the Pacific martin, the salmon, and other threatened species. It was a historic night for ancient redwoods, endangered species policy, and environmental politics more broadly.

"The Deal" was emblematic of the Redwood Wars during the 1990s, and it left an indelible imprint on national environmental politics. Activists had filed dozens of lawsuits challenging North Coast clear-cut plans, many of them on Pacific Lumber land. The goal of the suits was to permanently protect the groves by applying environmental protection laws to private land management, destroying California's development-oriented corporatist traditions. By 1996, the lawsuits had frustrated Pacific Lumber enough to turn the forest over to the public. To complement the litigation, radical activists escalated their direct actions and public protests, garnering national attention and infuriating Pacific Lumber. Pacific Lumber grew impatient and began to aggressively look for ways to log its land—both legally and illegally. The company tested the state's regulatory and enforcement systems. When California's public institutions failed to offer the consistent reforms and protections sought by the activists, they turned to federal courts and the Endangered Species Act. Pacific Lumber also looked to federal institutions, filing its own case against the United States to force federal officials to end the conflicts and compensate the company for lost revenue. The final terms of "the Deal" reflected the respective power of the activists and the company. The Clinton administration, Congress, the California legislature, and the state and federal agencies were forced to accommodate those varied local interests.

Government negotiators were responding to national circumstances that compelled them to intervene in what had become the longest and most violent episode of the Redwood Wars. In 1994, Republicans led by Newt Gingrich took control of Congress and launched an assault on the nation's environmental protection laws. The attacks galvanized public support for mainstream environmental organizations and contributed to the success of the movement's campaigns to defend the Endangered Species Act, toxic waste cleanup laws, and the Clean Air and Clean Water Acts. Combined with the ongoing spotted owl conflict, the Republican attacks led the Clinton administration to fear it might lose its reelection bid as well as the scaffolding of environmental protection policy that had done much to clean the nation's air, water, and landscapes. The president evaded Congress by negotiating an administrative resolution to the spotted owl conflict in 1994 through the Northwest Forest Plan, a federal land management plan negotiated with timber companies that reopened limited logging in the national forests of the Pacific Northwest and created a series of old-growth reserves for the northern spotted owl. The Clinton administration hoped its initiative would undercut Republican popularity and avoid risky litigation to defend the Endangered Species Act against timber companies and landowners. While federal agencies worked to implement the Northwest Forest Plan, the federal courts addressed the Redwood Wars. On the North Coast, Earth First! and Pacific Lumber confronted one another in the woods. Together, the activists and timber leaders forced President Clinton to intervene in the Redwood Wars as he had the spotted owl conflict, though the results were quite different.

Kathy Bailey, however, was in no mood to celebrate "the Deal" in 1999 and did not even stay in the capitol to hear the votes. Instead, she sat in solitary silence and "drank quite a bit," dozing in and out of sleep while watching *Natural Born Killers*, starring Woody Harrelson. It seemed only fitting. Woody Harrelson was, as Bailey commented, "one of the funnier side dodges we had [during the Headwaters Campaign]. At some point, Woody came and lobbied at the capitol [in Sacramento] and I shepherded him around, and it was the funniest thing, I mean people would just flock to him. . . . At some point he was invited to dinner with Hurwitz in Texas, and Woody went, and he described it as just a very strange dinner, and so to have his movie on the tube was just bizarre." For Bailey and others, the Deal was indeed bizarre. Yes, Headwaters Grove, Owl Creek, and a few other groves on public property were now protected. Yes, there were now legal agreements limiting the types of logging the company could do on its private property. However, she was convinced the protections and limitations were not enough—for the old-growth redwood ecosystem or the species dependent on it. And she was angry that Charles Hurwitz had seemingly succeeded in holding his redwoods hostage to get a massive public bailout, just like he had received in the 1980s after the collapse of the Texas savings and loan industry. Those concerns were just the tip of the iceberg for Bailey and her colleagues, many of whom had fought the Deal until the very end of that day in March 1999, and would continue to fight for years to come.[2]

The Deal had divided friends and colleagues on the North Coast, especially its land management provisions. That night in March, Bailey had not even sought out her longtime colleagues. Bailey was staying across the street from EPIC's Kevin Bundy and Cecelia Lanman, but she didn't want to face them. They were going to be angry about the vote. She instead placed a note on their car before heading into her private vortex. The note read, "So long, been good to know you," a reference to a Woody Guthrie song. Kathy Bailey was sad, assuming her friendships with Bundy and Lanman were gone. The two EPIC leaders, along with Darryl Cherney, had been lobbying to kill the California appropriation because of the Habitat Conservation Plan (HCP) included in the deal to acquire the largest grove of ancient redwoods within Headwaters Forest. Habitat Conservation Plans were a conservation tool developed in the 1980s, and they were usually attached to Incidental Take Permits (ITP), which permitted the deaths of endangered species. The plans allow a landowner to engage in behavior that would likely kill some individuals of an endangered population in exchange for a long-term plan to increase habitat and population numbers.[3]

The plans and permits were a part of the compromise Congress had made with industries and major landowners in 1982 in the face of the far-reaching power of the Endangered Species Act. The act prohibited all activity that might result in the death of an endangered or threatened species—on private as well as public property. The US Supreme Court had ruled that economics and financial losses did not trump the law's strict prohibition on harming endangered species. In 1981, a federal court had ruled that deforestation and the destruction of critical habitat violated that prohibition. The HCP amendment to the Endangered Species Act was supposed to encourage public and private stakeholders to collaborate on species protection issues rather than litigate. Additionally, Congress hoped to eliminate the perverse incentives landowners had to rid their properties of endangered species for fear that the law would limit their economic prerogatives.

The activists, including Kathy Bailey and many others in the environmental community, believed the impending threat of population crashes of the murrelet and other species due to the Pacific Lumber HCP was greater than the likelihood of success. The activists simply did not believe that state and federal agencies, along with Pacific Lumber, would execute adequate plans to save the threatened species and restore old-growth habitat across the forest complex. However, unlike many other activists, Bailey did not want to allow the opportunity to pass; without the Deal, she believed Hurwitz would log the entire forest. Bailey recalled John Burton, president pro tem of the California Senate, "at his podium with his cell phone waiting for Carl's okay." Carl Pope, executive director of the Sierra Club in 1999, was in turn waiting for Bailey to call with her approval of the appropriation language. At the time, Bailey felt like she had done everything possible to maximize protections for the trees, the salmon, and the marbled murrelet, but she didn't think it was enough. Not in the long run, anyway. This sense of unfulfilled potential nagged at the North Coast activist community both before and after the Deal.[4]

John Campbell and Pacific Lumber also felt a nagging uncertainty and unease. Campbell was weary of fighting and negotiating. He was fed up with being painted as the villain or, worse, the villain's henchman. In the final run-up to the California appropriation, he had been forced to agree to stricter restrictions on his logging practices than he felt were necessary or appropriate. Campbell worried about whether his company could remain profitable and able to employ hundreds of Humboldt residents. He had hoped the Deal would end the Redwood Wars and enable him to run his timber company. But he knew that on March 1, 1999, the fight was probably not over. Many of the North Coast radicals were not willing to accept the Deal, and he knew that, at a minimum, they would try to derail the Habitat Conservation Plan during the public review periods.[5]

A TRAIN WRECK FOR THE NORTH COAST

Years of fighting between warring factions of activists over the scope of the Endangered Species Act had left a situation ripe for executive branch intervention. Throughout the spotted owl conflict in the Pacific Northwest, environmentalists and government officials had accused the George H. W. Bush administration and the timber industry of avoiding resolution in the hope that endangered species law and timber economics would collide, creating a crisis over timber profits and jobs. The theory posited that the industry and conservative lawmakers hoped the "train wreck" would generate enough backlash to gut the Endangered Species Act. The 1994 Northwest Forest Plan was designed to avoid such a train wreck. Pacific Lumber seems to have initiated its own version of the train wreck strategy with the hope of evading judges and activists by catapulting its conflict up to the executive branch.[6]

In late 1994 the North Coast awaited US district judge Louis Bechtle's ruling in the Owl Creek case, which EPIC had filed after Pacific Lumber twice logged Owl Creek in 1992 without approval. In *Marbled Murrelet v. Pacific Lumber*, EPIC argued that the clear-cuts had destroyed marbled murrelet habitat, in violation of the federal and state Endangered Species Acts. The trial ended on September 7, 1994, just before the failure of Hamburg's Headwaters bill. Before the judge could issue his ruling, Pacific Lumber harvested what they could under a salvage logging exemption, which allows the property owner to remove dead, diseased, or dying trees across most of their property to prevent forest fires and the spread of disease. A salvage permit is technically an exemption from filing standard Timber Harvest Plans, so there is no public review period. Though the Department of Forestry cannot grant salvage exemptions for areas containing threatened species, it granted Pacific Lumber a salvage permit for most of its property, excluding Headwaters Grove proper. On November 29, the California Department of Forestry informed the company it was violating the exemption by removing healthy trees in addition to dead ones.[7]

Undeterred, the company convinced the forestry agency to grant a new salvage exemption for its entire holdings; the Department of Forestry was apparently convinced that Pacific Lumber had learned its lesson and would avoid disturbing murrelet habitat. Because they now had legal and regulatory authority to log inside Headwaters Forest, Pacific Lumber had regained much of the leverage in the conflict. Pacific Lumber began to log and log, putting pressure on the activists and the state. Pacific Lumber's leverage with the state foresters was exactly what had led activists to demand stricter regulations for logging on private land in the first place. North Coast activists would again act to further regulate timber operations, but in 1996, they turned to the federal government to acquire the threatened land, as they had in 1968 and 1978.[8]

The North Coast activists quickly responded to Pacific Lumber's salvage operation with their own train wreck strategy. The plan was to expand litigation and direct action, forcing the Department of Forestry to ban all logging in ancient and residual old-growth groves. In January 1995, EPIC asked Kathy Bailey, then the volunteer state chair of forestry for Sierra Club California, to convince her organization to once again join EPIC's litigation against the Department of Forestry. The litigation strategy developed by Brian Gaffney attacked the agency's continued failure to address the cumulative effects provisions of CEQA. The plan had three important components: EPIC and Sierra Club would file a new breed of suits aimed at the logging of residual old-growth stands—where partial logging had left some old-growth trees—inside Headwaters Forest. If successful, the cumulative judgments would leave the Department of Forestry no alternative but to reject all old-growth and residual grove harvest plans due to their serious cumulative impacts on salmon and murrelets. In addition, the suits would seek enforcement of the Endangered Species Act, including designation of critical habitats and recovery plans for threatened and endangered species on the North Coast. The ultimate goal was to reignite the great debate over the economic and social implications of North Coast logging practices by creating a massive legal gauntlet that would make old-growth logging practically impossible. Gaffney's plan indicated that EPIC was gearing up for a major round of fights. The small organization was going to challenge the legitimacy of salvage exemptions and residual old-growth logging, and hoped to block a rumored Pacific Lumber application for an Incidental Take Permit from the US Department of the Interior that would allow the company to log endangered species habitat.[9]

That strategy—an incredibly ambitious escalation of the "hit the donkey" strategy initiated by Woods a decade earlier—recognized that old-growth groves were virtually off limits for Pacific Lumber due to the success of EPIC lawsuits and moved the target to residual groves. The plan applied legal arguments from the federal *Marbled Murrelet* case to the entire Headwaters complex. EPIC argued that residual old-growth trees were also crucial to murrelet recovery because the birds needed large expanses of nesting sites in and near old-growth groves. In addition to the litigation plan, Bailey and EPIC courted national and western organizations to pressure the Clinton administration into acquiring the forest outright. The major national groups urged Clinton's chief of staff, Leon Panetta, to pursue a debt-for-nature or land swap to remove the forest from Pacific Lumber control.[10]

Their efforts paid quick dividends. When Congress reduced the endangered species enforcement budget by $2 million, assistant secretary of the interior George Frampton Jr., a former president of the Wilderness Society, announced plans to pursue more public-private land partnerships. Frampton's strategy was presumably a means of avoiding the Gingrich Congress. In California, the activists began to use growing concern over the plight of salmon runs to pressure timber regulators to change forestry practices near North Coast salmon streams. By the end of 1995, EPIC had filed eight lawsuits challenging state and federal policies, twelve harvest plans, and two salvage exemptions. The new strategy recognized the predicament the Clinton administration faced with the Gingrich Congress and sought to expand legal efforts to choke off Pacific Lumber's old-growth logging.[11]

On February 27, 1995, Judge Bechtle ruled in favor of EPIC in *Marbled Murrelet v. Pacific Lumber*. The court placed a permanent injunction on the Owl Creek harvest area, finding that "EPIC [had proved] by a preponderance of evidence" that murrelets occupied Owl Creek Grove. He also ruled that Pacific Lumber had tried to minimize detection of the birds by neglecting scientific protocols for conducting surveys, intimidating surveyors, sending fraudulent data sheets to state and federal agencies, and intimidating government witnesses. The ruling was devastating for the company and de facto corporatism because the permanent injunction was the first time the Endangered Species Act had been used to stop logging on private land. Bechtle's decision reinforced the responsibility of California's forestry agencies to protect endangered species habitat—an issue the anti-corporatist campaign had pressed for more than two decades in California. The precedent-setting ruling also broadened the definition of the Endangered Species Act. Bechtle ruled that one could "harm" and "harass" a threatened species if there was "reasonable certainty" of "imminent" injury or death, meaning that a plaintiff did not need to discover an actual injured or dead animal to substantiate violations of the Endangered Species Act. The *Murrelet* ruling meant Pacific Lumber could no longer log in Owl Creek and potentially prohibited logging in their other old-growth redwood groves. More than that, the ruling had troubling implications for other landowners across the country because it further limited development near endangered species habitat.[12]

Federal protection of the marbled murrelet under the Endangered Species Act had empowered activists to pursue a permanent prohibition on logging particular areas. Their legal strategy since the 1985 *EPIC v. Johnson* ruling had been to force the Department of Forestry to follow proper administrative procedures in its fact-gathering duties. The activists believed that foresters would make decisions to protect watersheds, salmon, wildlife, and giant redwoods once they began to accumulate the appropriate information and took seriously their responsibility to mitigate environmental damage. They believed biodiversity would be protected and forestry made sustainable if only corporatism could be destroyed and citizens asserted the authority granted to them in the 1970s state environmental protection laws. However, by 1992 the timber companies had demonstrated their ability to resist state efforts to reform logging practices, as Pacific Lumber used every available avenue to log Headwaters Forest, including illegal logging and salvage exemption applications. The activists' reliance on enforcing administrative procedure also meant that court rulings didn't offer protection for any particular forest. Timber companies could revise and resubmit their Timber Harvest Plans, hoping to convince, or pressure, the state foresters to eventually approve them, as had happened with the Sally Bell and Owl Creek groves. Under the Endangered Species Act, however, if EPIC could prove a forest was inhabited by a protected species, the courts, along with the federal land and wildlife agencies, would be forced to permanently prohibit logging in the area. Thus, the *Murrelet* ruling laid the foundation for further escalation.

Pacific Lumber seemed undeterred by the loss in federal court; in fact, the company appeared to be emboldened by the judgment. On March 2, 1995, Pacific Lumber launched a counteroffensive with a surprise announcement that it intended to begin logging the main Headwaters Grove using a new salvage exemption. John Campbell told the press, "After nearly eight years of [voluntary] delay, it's time for us to move forward." Within hours, Earth First! sent out a call to arms over the Internet for "full-fledged occupation" of Headwaters Forest. The tensions that had simmered for so long finally came to a boil. On March 15, the Department of Forestry approved the salvage exemption for 5,994 acres within Headwaters Grove. Importantly, the exemption included a moratorium on logging inside murrelet habitat during the breeding season: April 1 to September 15.[13]

The activists continued to lash out at Pacific Lumber over the next few days. EPIC sent out a press release declaring that the Pacific Lumber salvage logging plans violated the Endangered Species Act because the new plan was based on the same "incredulous" murrelet surveys rejected by the federal court. Pacific Lumber still claimed Headwaters Grove was not critical to marbled murrelet breeding. Cecelia Lanman told the press, "This is a bid to cut every bit of murrelet habitat before they are stopped." Essentially, the North Coast activists argued that the salvage plans were a backdoor effort to enter the ancient groves of Headwaters Forest and remove old-growth trees. Even the snags, they argued, were important for old-growth habitat. One could not salvage logs without destroying habitat, thus violating the *Murrelet* decision. In response, Pacific Lumber published an op-ed in the *San Francisco Chronicle* proclaiming its right to manage company land as they had for a hundred years. Littletree, Bari, and Cherney began preparing a mass protest at the entrance of the logging road leading into Headwaters Forest. In doing so, the activists fell into a trap John Campbell had set: he needed logging activities restricted in order to use his nuclear option.[14]

Anticipating an expansion of hostility, activists and the company looked for allies and public support. Campbell told the press he'd be willing to swap Headwaters Grove for federal or state land. Kathy Bailey wrote to Pete Wilson, the second-term Republican governor of California, to warn him that Pacific Lumber's salvage logging exemptions had backed the activists into a corner with no option but to sue the Department of Forestry. She pointed out that current California law did not allow for "known sites of . . . threatened or endangered species [to] be disturbed, threatened or damaged." The governor effectively told the legislature and activists to figure out how to quickly buy the land because the state was going to ensure Pacific Lumber could log as quickly and easily as possible.[15]

True to historic patterns set in 1924 at Dyerville and cemented in 1969 in the *Bayside* case and again during the Sally Bell campaign, EPIC and the Sierra Club worked to delay logging plans in the main Headwaters Grove. The organizations filed a state lawsuit challenging Pacific Lumber's Headwaters salvage logging exemptions. EPIC and the Sierra Club argued that salvage exemptions violated CEQA because permits are issued without public review or environmental impact reports to assess environmental damage. Simultaneously, EPIC filed a federal lawsuit against Pacific Lumber and the US Fish and Wildlife Service, challenging not only Pacific Lumber's salvage logging permit but also eight other logging plans. EPIC argued that the Fish and Wildlife Service should not have approved any of the plans because all destroyed habitat for both the marbled murrelet and the spotted owl. The lawsuits challenged the legality of all salvage logging exemptions and all Habitat Conservation Plans. EPIC believed HCPs and salvage logging exemptions prevented the recovery of endangered populations because recovery required time and expanded habitat. Instead, salvage logging and HCPs result in decreases in both population and habitat. On March 27, Pacific Lumber agreed not to log the ancient groves until a judge could review the cases. Unknowingly, the activists had set up Pacific Lumber to file its own lawsuit against the federal and state governments for loss of economic property.[16]

The March 28 Carlotta rally at the entrance to Headwaters ushered in an April dominated by brinksmanship and hostility. Five hundred protesters demonstrated in Carlotta. However, the Department of Forestry quickly approved five new Pacific Lumber harvest plans in residual old-growth groves of the Yager Creek drainage of Headwaters Forest. The watershed was important to activists because it supported one of the last coho salmon and steelhead trout runs on the North Coast. Salmon populations were declining, like those of the marbled murrelet and the spotted owl, and activists had petitioned the government to list salmon as threatened under the Endangered Species Act. EPIC, local photographer-activist Doug Thron, and other local environmental groups filed suit alleging the plans violated murrelet, spotted owl, and bald eagle protections. After a local judge issued a temporary restraining order stopping the five Timber Harvest Plans, the company closed its old-growth mill and laid off 105 mill workers. Pacific Lumber then recruited the laid-off workers to attend an April 28 hearing for the Yager Creek case. The company had clearly learned from the tactics of the Wise Use movement and Oregon timber firms, who regularly utilized similar tactics to combat limitations on logging. To make matters worse for the company, Judge Bechtle had awarded EPIC $1.1 million in attorney fees from the *Marbled Murrelet* case, money that would fund additional challenges to the company's logging operations.[17]

The situation on the North Coast was a mess. Pacific Lumber was playing hardball with the state, activists were invading the forest, EPIC had five cases pending against Pacific Lumber, and it seemed civil authority had disappeared in Humboldt County: there were no available judges due to recusals, legislative interventions had failed, and the state and federal executive branches were not acting either. Nonetheless, the Yager Creek harvest plans were under a restraining order until June, and the main Headwaters Grove was also temporarily off limits, offering some possibility of a respite during the late spring. Instead, the activists continued their assaults on the company's property rights, further galvanizing the company and its sympathizers. The activists wanted to choke off Pacific Lumber in court and force the forestry agencies to address industrial logging once and for all. The company challenged the state's loyalty by logging aggressively, almost begging EPIC to tie it up in court so it could file a takings suit and force the chief executives of California and the United States into action.[18]

HEAD-ON COLLISION

The North Coast activists were coordinating their actions tightly but did not always maintain a united front. In early 1995, the Headwaters Forest Coordinating Committee had been revived, and in May it was decided to run a joint campaign to raise $1 million from individual donors, other environmental groups, and charitable foundations. The goal was to acquire sixty thousand acres of Headwaters Forest, and HFCC immediately looked to the federal government as the best available purchaser. Sixty thousand acres would encompass the area local activists and allied foresters and scientists had determined was necessary to restore the largest possible contiguous old-growth forest surrounding the six main groves of ancient redwoods on Pacific

Lumber property. Kathy Bailey, however, suggested that the national Sierra Club organization push California senators to propose exchanging federal land or federal timber contracts with Pacific Lumber for the ancient groves owned by the Salmon Creek Corporation. Salmon Creek had been created in 1993 as a wholly owned subsidiary of Pacific Lumber and owned approximately ten thousand acres, including the main Headwaters Grove and other ancient groves. Bailey agreed with the sixty-thousand-acre goal, but she saw no "clear path to the greater goal" and wanted some group working to at least acquire what Forests Forever had proposed in the 1990 ballot initiative.[19]

On the North Coast, the conflict ebbed and flowed over the summer. In mid-May, EPIC's state trial challenging the Pacific Lumber salvage exemptions began, adding to the anxiety of activists who were preparing to challenge as many as twenty-six harvest plans, many in the residual old-growth groves of Headwaters Forest, including the Yager Creek drainage. In mid-June, a California appellate court lifted the temporary restraining order on a harvest plan inside the Yager Creek drainage. Pacific Lumber spokesperson Mary Bullwinkle told the press the case proved that "state-approved harvest plans meet all obligations required by law . . . and that properly regulated timber harvest activities do not have significant adverse impacts on the environment." The statement must have driven North Coast activists mad: it ignored the many prior rulings to the contrary, and it positioned Pacific Lumber on the side of the law, a position once held by the activists. Pacific Lumber continued to work to generate support with the public, heavily publicizing the release of forty-two thousand king salmon into the Yager and Lawrence Creek watersheds and aggressively blaming activists and the weather for the closing of the mill in April. With a few deft maneuvers, the company attacked the activists' new salmonid habitat strategy and upended activist claims to being the allies of timber workers.[20]

North Coast activists responded, aided by the stalling tactics of Earth First! in the woods. As was true in 1983 and throughout the Redwood Wars, direct action and litigation formed a powerful toolkit for the activists. In the midst of the legal wrangling, North Coast Earth First! occupied the forest, organized rallies and protests, and directed actions toward the Department of Forestry and Pacific Lumber alike. Activists were arrested for blocking a logging road by chaining themselves to a bridge over Blanton Creek. On June 26, the First District Court of Appeals in California placed an emergency stay on Blanton Creek logging after EPIC filed suit against the company for violations of the Unfair Business Practices Act. Later in the summer, Littletree and others planned a series of actions to block road gates, lock down activists in the backwoods, occupy Department of Forestry offices, and conduct a mass arrest event on Pacific Lumber property.[21]

Earth First! tried desperately to regain public support and frustrate Pacific Lumber, but the organizers had misjudged public sentiment. They seem to have believed they could continue to challenge Pacific Lumber property rights and Department of Forestry authority through backwoods actions and still appeal more broadly to the public via civil disobedience displays. The result was great national sympathy for their cause but little local support. On July 5, thirty-four protesters were arrested for trespassing and shutting down the Department of Forestry office in Fortuna, and nine activists were arrested in the Yager Creek drainage. The police used pepper spray on a group of activists blocking the road leading out of the Department of Forestry offices. The *Times-Standard* in Eureka published the names, ages, and hometowns of the arrestees. Activists criticized the published list and the use of pepper spray as attempts to intimidate supporters of the redwood movement. Pacific Lumber continued to try to shift public support away from the activists, telling the press that Earth First! civil disobedience was a drain on county resources. After the July actions, Earth First! orchestrated several more actions to "highlight the group's return to mass politics," as Cherney wrote. In addition to civil disobedience, Earth First! launched a nationwide boycott of all redwood products. The Earth First! strategy was clearly two-pronged: to frustrate Pacific Lumber and to generate national attention.[22]

The actions did in fact generate attention and frustrate the Department of Forestry and Pacific Lumber, but momentum abruptly swung in Pacific Lumber's favor due to the overwhelmingly negative press coverage. As their support waned, a group of activists, including EPIC and Doug Thron, entered into mediation with Pacific Lumber and the Department of Forestry. The mediation failed, however, and the company used the opportunity to again paint the activists as unreasonable obstructionists. John Campbell had other plans to end the conflict, though. Campbell had met with US Senator Dianne Feinstein in March 1995 and asked her to be, as he told it, the "ombudsman" for a round of real estate negotiations between Pacific Lumber and the state and federal agencies. Feinstein had agreed, but the plan had not proceeded any further.[23]

Momentum continued to run hard against the activists, driven by an aggressive Pacific Lumber public relations campaign and EPIC losses in court. In addition to rejecting requests for preliminary injunctions against logging plans, one local judge required EPIC to post a $10,000 bond for Pacific Lumber's defense costs in exchange for an emergency stay. Campbell told the press, "It is unfortunate that EPIC and Doug Thron continue to raise money from the public in order to pursue dilatory and wasteful litigation." Pacific Lumber went even further, charging the activists with harassing endangered species by flying planes low over Pacific Lumber land to assess the company's logging efforts. Indeed, Mark Harris, an Arcata attorney and member of the legal team in the federal *Marbled Murrelet* case, had learned to fly in 1992 specifically so he could monitor the company's compliance with court injunctions. The nonprofit group LightHawk, a network of volunteer pilots who support environmental efforts, had also flown over Headwaters Forest on numerous occasions to take aerial photographs of the Pacific Lumber property. The activists used those photographs to generate maps of the forest and to monitor logging activity and its effects on the canopy. Campbell's strategy appeared to be working, but the North Coast activists' attempt to compel the federal government to acquire Headwaters Forest evolved as well.[24]

Activists hoped a massive rally could turn the tide of public opinion and command the attention of decision makers. The Headwaters Forest Coordinating Committee had been planning a protest for September 15, 1995, the day the moratorium on salvage logging during murrelet breeding season expired. The various Earth First! splinter groups on the North Coast prepared backwoods actions to follow the rally. On the day of the rally, outside the log decks in Carlotta and the Fisher Road gate leading into Headwaters, more than two thousand people rallied to protest the salvage logging exemption and the logging of ancient redwoods. The protestors were flanked by angry loggers. Motivated by Bonnie Raitt, Bob Weir and Mickey Hart from the Grateful Dead, Darryl Cherney, and Ed Begley Jr., among other speakers and performers, two hundred people were arrested during a symbolic trespassing event, as the rally launched Alicia Littletree's backwoods action campaign. Adding to the rally's symbolic power, the California Senate passed a bill the same day mandating that Governor Wilson negotiate the acquisition of Headwaters Grove. Even before the assembly could vote, however, Wilson promised to move ahead without legislation.[25]

The aftermath of the rally was even more dramatic than the events of September 15th. North Coast Earth First! activists launched an unprecedented two-month base camp that produced press coverage, an astronomical escalation in arrests, and a resurgence of violence against the activists. From September 17 to October 9, Humboldt police arrested nearly four hundred activists on Pacific Lumber and Elk River Timber property. Red Emmerson, owner of Elk River Timber, which held the property adjacent to the northern border of Headwaters Grove, was one of the largest landowners in California, and the timber firm had recently submitted a Timber Harvest Plan to log a second-growth tract along the perimeter of Pacific Lumber property. The HFCC had been trying to include that second-growth forest to protect the riparian zone of the South Fork of the Elk River, which flowed out of Headwaters Grove, because it was critical to spawning salmon. The police reported that activists blocked logging roads deep in the woods with abandoned cars and locked themselves to gates and logging equipment. Loggers responded with threats of violence. Sheriff Dennis Lewis recalled one logger telling the police to "go have some donuts and coffee, and be happy—that he had his rifle and would take care of things himself. . . . And he wasn't joking." By October 11, the arrest total had reached 550, and the Humboldt County Board of Supervisors requested emergency aid from President Clinton. On October 14, two Earth First! tree-sitters climbed down after a six-day sit, and Elk River Timber reportedly announced they were ready to negotiate. The new strategy of Earth First! appeared to be working with Red Emmerson at least.[26]

The pressure was mounting for Pacific Lumber as well as for Humboldt County officials. After nearly ten years, Maxxam settled the shareholder lawsuit filed by former shareholders, including some of the Murphy family, agreeing to pay them $17 million ($10 per share).

Maxxam and its investment banks each contributed to the settlement fund, along with the convicted inside traders Michael Milken and Ivan Boesky, a tacit acknowledgment of the fraudulent handling of the Maxxam takeover. A week later, the Department of Forestry finally rejected the so-called Death Road plan to pierce the center of Headwaters Grove, which Pacific Lumber had refiled along with the Headwaters salvage exemption nearly a year prior. Adding to the company's woes, Senator Dianne Feinstein began working to get Vice President Gore to agree to the debt-for-nature scheme.[27]

The train wreck appeared imminent. The *Murrelet* case had made logging Owl Creek impossible and threatened to prohibit logging in all six ancient groves. However, Pacific Lumber worked around the ruling using salvage logging exemptions and continued to test the Department of Forestry by filing additional logging plans inside the Headwaters complex. California delivered mixed messages on Pacific Lumber's right to log inside Headwaters Forest. The local courts, weary of the incessant hearings and motions, had begun to rule against EPIC. However, despite approving the salvage logging exemptions, the Department of Forestry hesitated to approve additional controversial Timber Harvest Plans. And the governor and state legislature offered nothing of value to resolve the chaotic confrontations on the North Coast. EPIC continued to file lawsuits, tying up court resources and Pacific Lumber time. The September 15 rally had drawn major celebrities, two thousand people, and a lot of media to publicize the imminent salvage logging of Headwaters Forest, set to begin the following day. And Earth First! was creating dangerous and frustrating situations in the backwoods that impeded Pacific Lumber's ability to log anywhere near old-growth redwoods. Everyone involved, it seems, was frustrated.

TRANSFORMING AMERICAN ENVIRONMENTAL POLITICS: "THE DEAL"

Given the situation on the North Coast, the local combatants in the Redwood Wars picked just the right moment to thrust the Headwaters Forest conflict into the arms of the executive branch of the federal government. A presidential election was at hand in 1996, and President Clinton wanted to solidify his eroding support among environmentalists.

In July 1995, Clinton had signed a bill to provide relief to victims of the Oklahoma City bombing by right-wing militia earlier that spring. Attached to the bill was a rider to dramatically expand salvage logging in the national forests and require the Forest Service to open up logging in areas currently blocked by court order and the Northwest Forest Plan. Clinton eventually admitted that approving the rider was a mistake, but the damage was done in the eyes of environmentalists. In the fall, the federal government shut down twice as the president and the Republican Congress battled over Medicare funding reductions and the reach of the Endangered Species Act, among other issues. Throughout the year, the Headwaters conflict looked like the best opportunity for the president to increase his support among environmentalists. The administration's collaboration tools might also stave off further congressional attacks on the Endangered Species Act.[28]

Pacific Lumber was poised for a major power grab early in 1996, first at the state level and then at the federal level. In early January, the company sent a letter to the California Department of Forestry threatening to sue unless it approved the Death Road Timber Harvest Plan. If the company couldn't get approval for the road into Headwaters Grove, it effectively couldn't log any of its old-growth trees. Charles Hurwitz himself then contacted the Department of the Interior and arranged a meeting in Washington, DC, that included himself; John Campbell; Red Emmerson; Terry Gorton, deputy director of the California Resources Agency; Michael Mantell of the California Department of Natural Resources; Phil Dietrich from the US Fish and Wildlife Service; and John Garamendi, deputy secretary of the interior. The participants discussed public acquisition of Headwaters and Elk Head Springs Groves—the approximately three thousand acres Campbell had repeatedly announced the company was willing to sell.[29]

The high-level discussions over Headwaters Forest resolved nothing, however. In early April 1996, the Department of Forestry again levied a fine on Pacific Lumber for violations of forestry regulations inside Headwaters Forest. On April 22, the Board of Forestry denied the company's appeal of the Death Road harvest plan. Pacific Lumber, as threatened, filed a reverse condemnation, or regulatory takings, lawsuit against the State of California. Since 1985, conservative legal scholars and property rights activists had made the case that property owners qualified for compensation under the Fifth Amendment if government regulations diminished the economic value of their property. Proponents of that legal interpretation argued that government had effectively used its powers of eminent domain by prohibiting economic activity on the land. Landowners subject to such a regulatory "taking" were entitled to monetary compensation just as if eminent domain had been used to seize their property for a park, they declared. In 1987, the US Supreme Court ruled twice in favor of property owners seeking compensation. In 1992, in *Lucas v. South Carolina Coastal Commission*, the court clarified Fifth Amendment jurisprudence to date when it ruled that a regulation constituted a taking if it prevented the owner from exercising any economic activity on the property. Pacific Lumber hoped it might convince the increasingly conservative court that if all economic activity was prohibited on a portion of their property, the Fifth Amendment also applied. On May 7, the Ninth US Circuit Court of Appeals upheld the permanent injunction on Owl Creek but ruled against EPIC's suit challenging the legality of the Pacific Lumber salvage logging exemption. Logging in murrelet habitat was thus prohibited, but salvage logging remained viable. Moments later, however, Pacific Lumber filed a takings suit against the United States, a clear indication that the lawsuit had been prepared well in advance of the ruling.[30]

In one fell swoop, the Pacific Lumber takings suit had derailed the activists' local campaigns and forced them to accept the federal executive branch as a new stakeholder in the Redwood Wars. The Clinton administration wanted to negotiate a way to end the takings lawsuit. In response, the activists mounted a complex effort to pressure the government to acquire the full sixty-thousand-acre Headwaters complex. Their efforts were aided by the US Fish and Wildlife Service, whose critical habitat ruling in 1995 had designated 3.9 million acres in Oregon, California, and Washington as critical habitat for the marbled murrelet, noting that Pacific Lumber land was especially important— approximately forty-four thousand acres of company land, the same land included in the 1993 Hamburg acquisition bill. The habitat designation and takings suits offered the activists a way into the official negotiations as public policy commenters. HFCC assigned its member groups varying responsibilities to generate public support and governmental pressure, directing them to meet with officials from the Department of the Interior and petition as interveners in the federal takings suit. The Department of Interior balked at the activists' demands, however. Over the next few months, the activists embarked on a door-to-door and telephone outreach operation in the San Francisco Bay Area; developed full-page ads for the *New York Times* and other papers; distributed Headwaters Forest videos, brochures, and postcards; developed a North Coast media campaign; and began organizing another massive public rally, set for September 15, 1996—the day the annual logging ban for murrelet nesting season ended. Meanwhile, Earth First! planned base camps to disrupt Pacific Lumber's salvage logging efforts and support the September 15th rally.[31]

A three-way version of brinksmanship thus emerged after the two July meetings between Pacific Lumber and the administration, as the Department of Interior, the company, and the activists each tried to generate the leverage needed to close the negotiations in their favor. In the *New York Times*, the deputy secretary of the interior suggested that the pressure was on Pacific Lumber to accept a land swap because Hurwitz would face an angry public if he logged the groves. The secretary told a reporter, "He [Hurwitz] is the one who is going to incur the wrath of anyone who knows anything about Headwaters if he goes in and logs." The statement appears to be a direct reference to the North Coast activists' backwoods actions as well as the public relations nightmare Hurwitz had experienced since taking over Pacific Lumber.[32]

The activists continued to press the federal government to purchase the entire sixty thousand acres they deemed necessary for murrelet and salmon habitat. They convinced David Brower, the nation's best-known postwar environmental activist, to write an op-ed for the *Los Angeles Times* stating that he would not vote for Bill Clinton if the president supported land deals that administratively weakened the Endangered Species Act. Later in the month, HFCC ran a full-page advertisement in the *New York Times*, designed and submitted by Dan Hamburg, urging President Clinton to use a debt-for-nature swap to acquire all sixty thousand acres of Headwaters Forest. The ad stated, "We need a forest, not a tree museum." The message from the activists was that the battle over Headwaters Forest was not simply about protecting the grandest grove of giants in the forest; rather, it was, as it always had been, about protecting an entire ecosystem and its residents. In fact, many North Coast activists would have preferred to kill the deal rather than accept a much smaller purchase that enriched Hurwitz. The activists also convinced Ralph Nader, whom pundits trumpeted as a real threat to Clinton's electoral votes, to send Clinton a letter demanding that the president orchestrate a debt-for-nature swap for the full sixty thousand acres. Nader subsequently placed an advertisement to that effect in the *New York Times* leading up to the Democratic Convention in Chicago.[33]

John Campbell and Charles Hurwitz knew they had the upper hand, however, and the company's August and September strategy was born of the option to walk away and log under its salvage logging exemption. On August 5, 1996, the firm announced it would begin salvage logging on the first lawful day—September 16—unless the government picked up the pace of negotiations and sealed a deal before then. The government was simply moving too slowly for Hurwitz's taste. When the August congressional recess began, Campbell met with Senator Feinstein in San Francisco and again asked her to help in the negotiations. She agreed and convened weekly meetings with the company, the Clinton administration, and California officials. Pacific Lumber was in control of the negotiations.[34]

The activists scrambled—in both constructive and not so constructive ways—to gain traction in negotiations conducted without them. They had created the conflict and largely driven the action to that point, and to be shut out was especially hard to swallow. The frustration of a few anonymous North Coast residents boiled over on Labor Day weekend. Campbell's house was vandalized with "Save Headwaters" graffiti, and his pool was covered with gasoline and set ablaze. The press speculated that the culprits were either environmentalists or individuals inside the timber industry who wanted to sully the reputation of the activists. Either way, frustration then led activists down a perilous path. Shut out of the official negotiations, the activists enlisted new tactics to undercut the power of Pacific Lumber. The North Coasters recruited mainstream Washington-based groups to pressure Clinton not to concede the authority of the Owl Creek injunction or the Endangered Species Act. To aid that effort, the activists stopped targeting Clinton directly in the press and refocused on vilifying Hurwitz.[35]

Though government officials balked at the company's payment demands, Pacific Lumber held firm because it had nearly all the leverage. The Clinton administration was cornered: If negotiations failed, Americans would be outraged that ancient redwoods fell or the government would be forced to fight a takings suit in a Supreme Court increasingly siding with property owners. And since the Gingrich Congress was clamoring to dramatically reform the Endangered Species Act, a federal victory in the takings suit, or a deal offensive to landowners, might provide Republicans with the capital to push a reform bill through Congress. On Friday, September 13, 1996, the company again announced it planned to begin logging on Monday, and Governor Wilson pleaded with Pacific Lumber to delay cutting until a deal was concluded. The Wilson and Clinton administrations, along with Campbell and Senator Feinstein, huddled in Washington over the weekend. The company agreed to postpone logging for two weeks.[36]

The North Coast activists used the September 15 rally to repeat their demand for public acquisition of sixty thousand acres. An estimated five thousand people attended the rally in Carlotta, with three hundred to four hundred, including Bonnie Raitt, arrested in a symbolic crossing of the Pacific Lumber property line. The sheer size of the rally—the largest forestry-related protest in US history—must have attracted the attention of the negotiators. The massive protest was just the beginning of the next round of the Redwood Wars. Earth First!, as planned, launched a number of multiweek actions to disrupt logging and publicize their sixty-thousand-acre demand. The actions, once again organized to a large degree by Alicia Littletree, included activists locked to every gate leading to Headwaters. They used handcuffs inside metal pipes set into cement-filled oil drums to secure themselves to, and around, the logging gates and placed an old Toyota in front of one logging gate, complete with activists handcuffed to the car. Forty people were arrested during the first four days of the actions, costing the county an estimated $10,000 a day.[37]

The situation turned increasingly tense over the subsequent week. Negotiations among the Clinton administration, Hurwitz, and Director Douglas P. Wheeler of the California Department of Natural Resources resumed in Washington on Friday, September 20. The North Coast activists submitted requests to participate in the negotiations, but county officials and residents continued to be locked out of the process. Meanwhile, Senator Barbara Boxer of California pleaded with Governor Wilson to stop the impending salvage logging in Headwaters. And in the woods, Earth First! was in the midst of a ten-day tree-sit at Owl Creek that included ten sitters and five tree platforms. On September 18, local police hired a tree climber to remove half the tree-sitters and much of their supplies. The police were accused of injuring activists during various backwoods actions, as they had been throughout the 1990s. In Sacramento, state officials met with Red Emmerson of Elk River Timber to include North Headwaters Grove in the deal with Pacific Lumber. Emmerson agreed to temporarily halt operations in the grove. By September 26, the negotiations had arrived at a crossroads. Campbell and the agencies met for eighteen hours on Thursday and Friday. The government negotiators threatened to walk out when the company refused to reduce its asking price, and Pacific Lumber came out of the negotiations announcing it would begin logging Monday if no deal was reached.[38]

Finally, on Saturday, September 28, 1996, what became known as "the Deal" was finally announced, outlining the price and process for completing an unprecedented land acquisition and endangered species habitat management agreement. The federal and California governments agreed to purchase 7,470 acres of Pacific Lumber land, including the Headwaters and Elk Head Springs Groves, for $380 million. Part of the cash would be used to purchase 9,600 acres from Elk River Timber, of which Pacific Lumber would receive 7,755 acres. As part of the acquisition, Pacific Lumber agreed to file a federal Habitat Conservation Plan and a California Sustained Yield Plan to govern logging and development on the rest of its property. The company also agreed to suspend its takings suits against the United States and California. Finally, Pacific Lumber agreed not to log the 7,470 acres for ten months while the financing was negotiated. North Coast activists immediately criticized the deal as insufficient for the ancient redwoods and its inhabitants.[39]

The HCP was the first multispecies conservation plan approved under the 1982 amendments to the Endangered Species Act, and it opened the door for a new Clinton administration strategy to resolve private land conflicts outside of the courts and Congress. The Clinton process had begun with the Northwest Forest Plan to resolve the spotted owl conflict on federal lands, where federal agencies had direct control of the land. The Headwaters deal extended the administrative strategy to private land, where no agency could directly control the land outside of restrictions imposed by the Endangered Species Act. The activists' strategy to force the acquisition issue had succeeded, but they had failed to secure their goals for the forest complex and the reformation of industrial logging. The Deal demonstrated the power of local actors, but it also underscored the limits of activist influence when up against a multinational corporation. Cumulatively, the direct actions, mass rallies, and litigation had driven the conflict into federal hands, but it had also, in the end, shut the activists out of the negotiations.[40]

As had happened in the past, the announcement of a proposed resolution to part of the conflict only re-escalated the wars. Although the press—and undoubtedly the negotiating parties—viewed the preliminary agreement as an end to the Redwood Wars, nearly all local and national environmental groups objected to the Deal, and HFCC worked relentlessly over the next two and a half years to amend the agreement and influence the financing. Earth First! launched a barrage of actions—the backwoods actions lasting for the better part of those same two and a half years—to protest the Deal and protect the forest that had not been included. Pacific Lumber began its salvage operations in the parts of Headwaters Forest not included in the provisional Deal, provoking a backlash from federal and state agencies, as well as the public.[41]

Earth First!, historically an asset to EPIC, the Sierra Club, and HFCC, reacted so strongly to the Deal that it almost derailed the new campaign before it got off the ground. On September 29–30, Darryl Cherney, against the advice of Kathy Bailey and other HFCC leaders, organized rallies in San Francisco, Arcata, and Scotia to protest the Deal and demonize Senator Feinstein. One thousand five hundred protestors attended the San Francisco rally and march to Feinstein's office. Locally, approximately three dozen Earth First! activists invaded the Eureka headquarters of the Democratic Party to spread cow manure and feathers about the office. The California press characterized the Earth First! activists as arrogant, Cherney as whiny, and their actions as detrimental to their allies. Despite the criticism, Earth First! continued to organize daily actions in the backwoods: tree-sits, road blockades, rallies, and reconnaissance efforts to identify and stop old-growth logging on Pacific Lumber land. More than 1,200 activists were arrested between September 15 and the end of November, including Woody Harrelson, who climbed the Golden Gate Bridge to hang a banner.[42]

Meanwhile the Headwaters Forest Coordinating Committee developed a new strategy to ensure that the final deal would protect endangered species and ancient redwoods. Stubbornly, they remained committed to protecting the full sixty-thousand-acre complex from unsustainable forestry. The activists wanted the final deal to bolster the Endangered Species Act and provide for restoration of the entire forest complex—and to remove the corporate owners from the county once and for all. To achieve their goals, they revised their strategy from a focus on stopping individual Timber Harvest Plans to an attempt to build public support for the purchase of Headwaters Forest. An HFCC consultant believed the groups needed to stop attacking the Deal and instead encourage all efforts to protect Headwaters Forest, even if they thought the efforts didn't provide adequate protection. To some degree, Kathy Bailey agreed, but she thought it was HFCC's job to work toward the best plan for managing the forest, not the one that was most politically expedient.[43]

During the fourteen months following the announcement of the Deal, the conflict over Headwaters Forest focused on the financing of the acquisition and management proscriptions for the portion of the Headwaters complex left under Pacific Lumber control. Pacific Lumber played into the hands of the environmentalists in October when it resumed salvage logging in the complex. The company also submitted new Timber Harvest Plans for old-growth and residual old-growth groves. Senator Feinstein and the Clinton administration pleaded with the company and the Board of Forestry to halt old-growth logging during the final negotiations. The Board of Forestry rejected the appeals, and Pacific Lumber forged ahead with its operations, no doubt hoping the final negotiations would conclude quickly.[44]

STALEMATE: 1997–1999

After Pacific Lumber submitted its Habitat Conservation Plan to the EPA for comment, it seemed like the Deal might be finalized quickly.

However, the California legislature still needed to appropriate its share of the acquisition funds, and the North Coast activists had far greater access and leverage in Sacramento than they did in Washington. Rather than quickly completing the final agreements in 1997, the process dragged on until early 1999. The long stalemate was partly due to the relentless advocacy efforts of North Coast activists and partly due to Pacific Lumber's tough negotiating strategy. EPIC and HFCC developed a sophisticated campaign to influence the Habitat Conservation Plan. The strategy was twofold: Federal agencies must consider significant public comments before amending and approving any plans. Hence, EPIC coordinated a campaign to generate comments from the public as well as in-depth analysis by noted scientists. Second, HFCC utilized the analyses to convince the California legislature to force Pacific Lumber to make significant concessions to wildlife and ecological advocates before authorizing any appropriation.

As had been the case for the past three transformations of the Redwood Wars, a new set of migrants to the North Coast stepped into leadership roles and helped define the three years following the announcement of the Deal. The first wave brought the Man Who Walks in the Woods, Richard Gienger, Dan Hamburg, Cecelia Lanman, and Kathy Bailey to the North Coast—activists with deep social justice roots and a commitment to the rural community. The second wave of migrants included Judi Bari and Darryl Cherney, activists who would radicalize the Redwood Wars. The third wave ushered in Alicia Littletree and other young activists who embraced direct action with conviction. The developments leading up to and following the Deal drew in a new group of activists who would master the policy and technical requirements of Sacramento and Washington. Of that group, two stand out: Paul Mason and Kevin Bundy played major roles in EPIC and in the HFCC's efforts to challenge the terms of the land management plans. In doing so, the activists forced the legislature to accommodate their demands once again.

Kevin Bundy, who developed into one of EPIC's primary legislative analysts, was critical to convincing the California legislature that it could impose restrictions on Pacific Lumber through appropriations bills. Bundy, a self-described high school misfit, was born in Casper, Wyoming, in 1970. Though he was involved in anti–nuclear bomb protests at an early age, Bundy became politically active only after he graduated from Oberlin College in 1993 and moved to Garberville with his wife. The couple split up in 1995, and Bundy found a new home in the Earth First! movement. His first meeting was a planning session for the first September 15 demonstration in 1995. When a friend decided to participate in the civil disobedience portion of the demonstration—ceremonially crossing onto Pacific Lumber property—Bundy signed up to be her jail support person. The woman got arrested on three consecutive days. As Bundy told it, he was "pretty much in love" with her at that point, and his involvement in the movement grew steadily. Bundy knew in those early days that he was not prepared to physically challenge loggers and get arrested, so he continued to support arrestees while working at Music for Little People, the children's music studio and catalog owned by Trees Foundation cofounder Leib Ostrow. Seeing his work in the woods and in town, Tracy Kattleman of the Trees Foundation approached Bundy to join the Trees board of directors, and in January 1996, Bundy accepted a job as office manager for EPIC. He remained involved with Earth First! as well, though he was careful to retain "clean hands" so as not to jeopardize EPIC lawsuits. During the following summer, Bundy went nearly sleepless as they prepared for the September 15, 1996, rally amid rumors of the deal between Pacific Lumber and the federal government. In 1997, Bundy became the media point person for EPIC as well as one of the group's primary lobbyists in Sacramento, positions he held until early 1999, when he "needed to get out of town" due to fatigue and frustration.[45]

Paul Mason emerged alongside Kevin Bundy to lead EPIC's efforts. Mason was born in Massachusetts in 1972 but grew up in Vermont, moving to Humboldt in 1993 after three semesters at the University of Vermont and a year in Lake Tahoe working ski jobs and fighting forest fires with the US Forest Service. While at the Forest Service, Mason witnessed, as he stated, "the terrible conditions" in the Tahoe area's forests after nearly a century of fire suppression. Tired of the transient community in the ski town, Mason visited the North Coast and thought Humboldt State University would be a wonderful place to finish his undergraduate degree and fulfill his new interest in forest policy. He enrolled at the College of the Redwoods in Eureka, a community college just a few miles from Headwaters Forest. While there, Mason came across an EPIC insert from the *Earth First! Journal* about the Headwaters Forest conflict. When he transferred to Humboldt State, Mason developed his own major, natural resource policy, and began working part-time for EPIC doing local and online outreach to generate support for the Headwaters campaign.

With only a few classes remaining but the Headwaters Forest conflict nearing a crisis, Mason began working for EPIC full-time in Garberville, continuing outreach and coordinating the litigation efforts. In 1996, after the Deal was announced, Mason coordinated the massive campaign to influence the details of the Habitat Conservation Plan, recruiting dozens of experts to submit scientific comments on the Pacific Lumber HCP. By March 1999, Cecelia Lanman was ready to end her tenure as EPIC's leader, and the board elected Mason as executive director, a new position created to guide the organization into the twenty-first century.[46]

Bundy and Mason were critical to HFCC's efforts to radically change the terms of the Deal. For two years, lawmakers and local combatants debated the public and private valuation of Pacific Lumber land and the nature of private property rights. The price of the public land acquisition and the relative values of salmonids, ancient trees, murrelets, owls, and shareholder wealth were contested. The goals and reach of the Endangered Species Act were debated. And the role of private individuals and corporations in promoting the public good was challenged. Those were the same issues that had framed the Redwood Wars from their inception, and the negotiation of the final Headwaters deal simply offered a platform to focus on those issues. Additionally, the more than two years beginning on September 15, 1996, with the massive rally and the late fall arrest of Woody Harrelson on the Golden Gate Bridge, provided some of the most enduring images of the Redwood Wars.

In September 1996, the North Coast activists decided they needed, and could get, a sixty-thousand-acre public forest that would protect both timber production and endangered species habitat. The clearest description of their vision was the Headwaters Forest Stewardship Plan, a citizens' proposal coordinated by the Trees Foundation. The plan, intended to convince the government to hand over management of

Headwaters Forest to a local nonprofit organization, included a long-term land management plan based on aerial photography and GIS mapping software. It also included financing options, annual logging plans, and employment forecasts. In support, Earth First! remained in the woods to physically protect the ancient groves. The articulation of the activists' ideas and goals was important for them because the negotiations that led to the Deal had taken place without their participation. Like the earlier Forests Forever initiative and the Headwaters Legislative Action Plan, the Headwaters Forest Stewardship Plan reflected an abiding concern for sustainability—economic, social, and ecologic. The plan reflected the influence of years of conflict over the Endangered Species Act in the West, as well as the rising tide of free-market trends in environmental policy circles.[47]

The intense, and in some ways neoliberal, management proposal was driven by frustration with the legacy of park and forestry traditions on the North Coast. Corporatism in California—de jure and de facto—combined with two decades of corporate consolidation and the traumatic spotted owl conflict had left Redwood Country mired in a seemingly intractable conflict over the proper regulation of private land. The Deal only exacerbated activists' fears because it continued the tradition of setting aside small park groves surrounded by private property under the management of large corporate timber companies with minimal, erratic, or inconsistent agency oversight. Thus, the myriad activist groups on the North Coast remained committed to a future without Maxxam Corporation, and the 1998 Headwaters Stewardship Plan centered on demonstrating that conservation biology offered a management system that would better benefit the landscape and its inhabitants—human and nonhuman. Reed Noss, a redwood ecologist, noted conservation biologist, and Earth First! sympathizer, was prominently featured in the proposal. Noss had written numerous articles for the *Earth First! Journal* since the mid-1980s, and his ideas on ecological restoration resonated with the North Coast activists, especially his principle that forests be managed to represent "all example communities/ecosystems for biodiversity and sustainable human use." In many ways, the ideas in the proposal continued the stream of ideas articulated by Jerry Franklin, the ecologist who had helped develop New Forestry and the Northwest Forest Plan. The activists wanted to eliminate the industrial logging that scarred the landscape with roads, tractor trails, clear-cuts, and burned-over soil. They envisioned more selective harvests, an end to the logging of giant old trees, and more aggressive post-harvest restoration work to protect streams from siltation and mass-wasting. However, the Headwaters Forest Stewardship Plan diverged from New Forestry in that the North Coast activists tied land management practices to changes in institutional ownership and to ecocentric restoration: leaving some land alone for long periods as a means of restoration.[48]

Thus the Headwaters Forest Stewardship Plan was at its core a business plan designed to convince a broad array of constituents that intense management of Headwaters Forest could protect ancient groves, restore old-growth habitat, and provide economic sustainability if local people controlled the operation. Their vision was an operation that improved the "integrity of the redwood ecosystem" and demonstrated the "viability of timber-related jobs and revenue" in Redwood Country. They envisioned a future forest with three management "mosaics": core reserves, riparian reserves, and a long-term management area. The core reserves would be constituted around the six ancient groves; this section was designed to expand the range of redwood forest with old-growth characteristics. Lying among those ancient groves were clear-cuts and residual groves that would be added into the core over time. The ancient groves were to be off limits for timber harvesting and surrounded by six-hundred-foot buffers called habitat recovery zones (HRZ). Both the HRZ and remaining residual forests were to undergo intensive restoration to re-create old-growth habitat characteristics. To protect salmonids and amphibians, the riparian reserves included buffers ranging from one hundred to six hundred feet depending on the size of the watercourse. The buffers were designed to provide shade for the streams and to prevent sediment runoff, because salmonids require cool temperatures and clear water for breeding and spawning. Like the core reserves, the riparian reserves would undergo intensive restoration and then be protected from timber harvesting. The long-term management area (LTMA) was designed to produce sustainable revenue from timber harvesting. The model was based on a Sustained Yield Plan informed by the tenets of conservation biology, whereby harvest never exceeds growth. The goal was to restore the LTMA to old-growth characteristics and to maintain those characteristics via a legacy tree program, which would cut no more than one-half to two-thirds of the growth in any harvest area. Most of the local economic benefits would come from two sources: massive restoration efforts across the entire sixty-thousand-acre forest and timber harvests inside the LTMA. However, the model included additional revenue streams as well.[49]

The secondary pieces of the eighty-year economic development plan reflected the activists' investment in an inclusive vision of localism that included workers, Native Americans, and other rural residents. The activists projected that the forest could sustain more than one hundred permanent timber-related employees in addition to more than 150 restoration jobs during at least the first decade after acquisition. Restoration and timber harvesting would provide the bulk of employment, with former Pacific Lumber workers receiving priority placement. The activists also laid out a vision for "value-added" employment crafting finished products from the hardwoods and other forest species removed during restoration. They deemed recreation a potentially significant growth opportunity for the region, echoing the work of economist Tom Power on the value of protected forests. While concerns about jobs and local economics defied the popular perception of radical environmentalists on the West Coast, their anti-corporate positions certainly were in line with their radical peers in other parts of the country. What was different was the North Coast activists' enthusiasm for creating a community organization to harvest timber, coordinate other forest products, and restore past ecosystems rather than simply "locking up" tracts of land from development. Thus the stewardship plan proposed creating a nonprofit organization with a board of directors composed of local timber workers, Native Americans, residents of local watersheds, local conservationists, and local foresters. The forecasts and margins were tight, but the proposal built a convincing case.[50]

The Headwaters Forest Stewardship Plan, along with EPIC's in-depth and rigorous scientific comments on the Habitat Conservation Plan, gave the North Coast activists credibility in the state legislature. They could point to specific issues where they thought their ideas were better than those of Pacific Lumber or the federal land and wildlife agencies. They could point to scientific comments to substantiate their claims. And they had maps and photos to document the reality inside the forest. Though fellow activist Josh Kaufman derisively referred to public comments as playing the "agency game," for Mason and EPIC, the scientific comments were a natural and indispensable continuation of their litigation work. They intended to build an irrefutable administrative record documenting the flaws in the HCP, which was necessary for any future litigation.[51]

Pacific Lumber held firm, however. The company had been able to drive a hard bargain with the state and federal governments because it could walk away and begin logging any time it chose. The leverage provided by the salvage exemption explains why Pacific Lumber filed its taking lawsuit when it did. The *Murrelet* ruling prohibited the company from generating revenue on part of its property and thus substantiated its claim to a regulatory taking. The takings lawsuit put pressure on the government to negotiate with the company to avoid a court challenge. The simultaneous ruling against EPIC in the salvage logging case allowed Pacific Lumber to continue to log its old-growth forests, increasing its power in the acquisition negotiations.

While details of the final agreement between the state and Pacific Lumber were ironed out and EPIC worked on its strategy to amend the HCP, Earth First! and related activists dramatically expanded direct actions. The activists intended to highlight the destructive logging practices of Maxxam/Pacific Lumber and to place their bodies in front of loggers to protect old-growth trees and endangered species such as the coho salmon and marbled murrelet. The small size of the proposed land acquisition and the inclusion of a Habitat Conservation Plan created a sense of urgency among the activists because they believed the Deal would not prevent degradation of the ancient redwood ecosystem or the local community. During 1997–98, activists expanded their tree-sits to protect residual old-growth groves within and without the sixty-thousand-acre Headwaters complex, and they ramped up their installation of road blockades. The move outside the Headwaters Forest complex only gave credence to the media portrayal of them as obstructionists determined to stop all Pacific Lumber logging. For the activists, the moves reflected their intention to end industrial clear-cut logging as a practice. The changes in strategy also demonstrated their commitment to ecological restoration—turning residual old-growth groves into true old-growth habitat over time. However, their actions fueled unsympathetic local press coverage.[52]

Part of the trouble for Earth First! during those years stemmed from the anarchic nature of the group. Various affinity groups struck out on their own with mixed results. For every incident that tilted public opinion in their favor, another action erased the gains. For example, a December 31, 1996, mudslide originating from a Pacific Lumber clear-cut that buried nearly the entire town of Stafford increased working-class frustration with Pacific Lumber and aided environmentalists. The mudslide eventually led to a 738-day tree-sit by Julia "Butterfly" Hill that drew national attention to the protests over the Deal but also alienated many workers and activists who viewed the tree-sit as distracting and self-aggrandizing. Even the death of Judi Bari in 1997 had negative unintended consequences. Bari continued to be instrumental in the massive September 15 rallies and in grassroots fund-raising until her death. Her death from breast cancer seemed so sudden when it came in March 1997 that the California Senate adjourned for the day in her honor. Bari's death left Earth First! rudderless. Afterward, Littletree and Cherney increasingly focused on the car bomb litigation against the FBI. The loss of their leadership opened the door for splinter groups with uncoordinated efforts and messages, a distraction the movement could not afford in those heated times.[53]

Finally, use of pepper spray by Humboldt County sheriffs to remove locked-down, peaceful protesters drew the ire of the California attorney general as well as the national public. On at least two occasions, Humboldt County sheriffs rubbed Q-tips soaked in pepper spray in the eyes of activists whose hands were locked inside steel tubes or to logging gates, including one fourteen-year-old girl. The subsequent heckling of Congressman Riggs at a Veterans Day event over his support for the pepper spray tactics, however, diminished public support for the activists. By the end of 1998, with Bari gone and Cherney and Littletree largely absent from the Earth First! movement on the North Coast, backwoods actions were directed by myriad smaller cohorts often without using the Earth First! moniker. The new action groups were inventive and reckless, leading to the death of David "Gypsy" Chain in September 1998 when a logger felled a tree in his direction and it landed on the activist. Chain's death occurred during cat-and-mouse actions near Grizzly Creek in southern Humboldt, north of Highway 101 and Humboldt Redwoods State Park. The activists were on the Pacific Lumber land to stop the logging of an area they hoped to get included in the final deal.[54]

As eye-popping as some of the confrontations on the ground were, the movement's most powerful tool in the late 1990s was HFCC's public advocacy, as litigation had been from the 1970s through the mid-1990s. This phase of the campaign demonstrates the lasting influence of the 1950s Dinosaur Monument fight, when conservationists first challenged federal agencies on technical and scientific grounds. It is also a legacy of what Samuel Hays has referred to as the 1970s and 1980s development of the politics of administration. HFCC's most creative tactic was to lobby the California legislature to impose its own strict land management guidelines on the entire Marbled Murrelet Conservation Area and the forest's coho salmon runs—separate from those prescribed by the federal government in the Habitat Conservation Plan. The legislature might then attach its management prescriptions to California's appropriation for the Deal. If those efforts failed, EPIC prepared to challenge the HCP in court under the Endangered Species and National Environmental Policy Acts. That the activists achieved what they did in 1998–99 is miraculous, given the power wielded by Pacific Lumber and the conflicts within HFCC over tactics and their members' divergent analyses of the Deal and the HCP.[55]

The California legislature became the central arena of the battle in 1998 when President Clinton signed the all-cash federal appropriation on November 14, 1997. Under the appropriation, the federal government would contribute $250 million toward the acquisition of the agreed-upon groves, and the State of California would contribute the remaining $130 million. California had not yet appropriated its share of the funding, however, and there was limited support for the Deal in the legislature. Until the acquisition was consummated by all three parties, Pacific Lumber could walk away and start logging. Thus Pacific Lumber could effectively hold Headwaters Grove hostage to obtain the most favorable parameters for the still outstanding Habitat Conservation Plan. On top of all that, the activists were badly divided about whether to support the Deal, complicating their efforts to improve the HCP and severely straining relationships. How the stalemate broke is testament to the power of the North Coast activists even when faced with great disunity. The end of the stalemate also indicates how badly Pacific Lumber wanted to sell Headwaters Grove and enter a more certain regulatory future under the prescriptions of the Habitat Conservation Plan.[56]

BREAKING THE STALEMATE:
POLICY INNOVATIONS AND CASH

The California legislature was hung up on three basic points: the level of protection afforded to salmon runs, how to best rehabilitate logged areas into marbled murrelet habitat, and the fate of the four old-growth groves not included in the purchase plan. Legislative leaders had warned President Clinton that unless an additional 2,300 acres of old growth were protected, they couldn't get the votes to pass the California appropriation. Despite the uphill battle, state senator Byron Sher introduced a Headwaters appropriations bill in the summer of 1998, dividing North Coast activists. Sher's bill increased the no-logging buffers along streams to levels above Pacific Lumber's draft HCP but below those prescribed by the Federal Ecosystem Management Asset Team, which had developed the Northwest Forest Plan. Sher's bill also prohibited logging in Owl Creek until California could figure out how to acquire that grove, and the bill stipulated that the company could not log old-growth trees inside the Marbled Murrelet Conservation Area for fifty years. Kathy Bailey and Sierra Club California decided they would work to improve the legislation with an eye toward supporting the bill. EPIC, Earth First!, and others wanted to kill the bill because the official draft HCP had not yet been released, and they thought that offered a better opportunity to improve the overall land management schemes. Pacific Lumber also rejected the terms of the bill, and in early August the California budget passed without the Headwaters appropriation. At that point, it looked like the Deal was dead.[57]

Undeterred by the activists' tepid responses, Senator Sher introduced his bill again (AB 1986) with an additional appropriation of $100 million to acquire the Grizzly Creek and Owl Creek groves on the eastern portion of Pacific Lumber property. The additional money swayed

Pacific Lumber in the end, and Governor Wilson signed the appropriation into law. The Deal was not out of the woods yet, however, largely due to the persistence of the activists, who relentlessly pursued further murrelet and salmon protections. Primarily, the activists were not convinced the stricter stipulations in the California appropriation were enforceable because the HCP had the force of federal law. They decided to devise a contract between the California Wildlife Conservation Board (WCB) and Pacific Lumber as their enforcement tool. The WCB was tasked with acquiring all wildlife conservation land for California, and was thus the signatory to the land deeds with Pacific Lumber. In February 1999, legislators and activists convinced Democratic governor Gray Davis and the WCB to craft a contract enforcing the terms of the California Headwaters appropriation. Simultaneously, the state and federal agencies were attempting to reduce the annual allowable timber harvests in the HCP. Pacific Lumber rejected their demands, and just days before the federal appropriation was set to expire, the company threatened to walk away from the deal. Senator Feinstein leapt into the void and convinced the company to accept reduced harvest totals in exchange for an "adaptive management" clause in the HCP allowing the company to revise harvests in the future without going through the normal agency bureaucracy, including environmental reviews. Pacific Lumber relented and accepted the new terms of the draft HCP, but the battle was not complete.[58]

Kathy Bailey told Senator Sher the Sierra Club was prepared to publicly oppose any deal if the WCB contract was insufficient. Sher took her words to heart and, as a personal supporter of the North Coast activist positions, worked to complete the WCB contract. On February 25, 1999, the WCB unanimously approved a deed contract that banned logging in the Marbled Murrelet Conservation Area groves for fifty years and widened the watercourse protections delineated in AB 1986. John Campbell was uncharacteristically silent. At the same time as the WCB was finalizing its proposed contract for Pacific Lumber, Richard Wilson, the Department of Forestry chief, steeled himself to force Pacific Lumber into agreeing to another reduction in annual harvests— a nearly 30 percent reduction. Meanwhile, the Department of Interior altered the language of the adaptive management plan to make it more difficult for Pacific Lumber to implement future changes to the HCP.

The scientific comments collected by EPIC had seemingly persuaded the agencies that the draft HCP was insufficient. Hurwitz announced the deal was off.[59]

On the final day of the federal appropriation, Pacific Lumber's power was on full display, as was the company's desire to close the Headwaters chapter of its history. On February 27, the three federal wildlife agencies each sent letters to Richard Wilson pressuring him to lower his new demands on Pacific Lumber for the Sustained Yield Plan required by California law. On March 1, an apparently angry Wilson sent John Campbell a letter agreeing to an approximately 15 percent reduction in planned annual harvests instead of 30 percent. The same day, the Department of Interior sent Campbell a letter assuring him that the agencies would devote enough resources to the adaptive management process to accommodate reasonable requests for changes to the plan. The department also offered the personal availability of the assistant secretary of commerce and the general counsel for interior, on a quarterly basis, to ensure that the company could meet its now-approved annual timber harvest of 176,000 board feet. Just before midnight—some allege it was hours after midnight because legislators physically stopped the state house's clock at midnight so they could complete the negotiations—the deeds, permits, and agreements were signed and exchanged, including the WCB contract.[60]

• • •

The final deal was an important development in the political history of American environmental protection. It helped transform the way land conflicts were handled, not only in Redwood Country but on all private land across the nation. Federal and state agencies had completed the complicated and tense negotiation of the nation's first multispecies Habitat Conservation Plan. The plan was designed to assist the recovery of the marbled murrelet, the northern spotted owl, the American bald eagle, the western snowy plover, and eight other terrestrial species. It would also ensure the viability of the Pacific Lumber Company. The Pacific Lumber HCP would serve as a collaborative model for implementing the Endangered Species Act on private land without lengthy, costly, and frustrating rounds of litigation.

The Deal also demonstrated the power of the North Coast activists, who forced Pacific Lumber to agree to restrictions on its logging operations stricter than those authorized by the federal government, including protections for salmon streams. Late nineteenth- and early twentieth-century redwood conflicts had been resolved privately, and early postwar conflicts had been resolved legislatively—some after court orders pursued by citizen activists. The Headwaters Deal was administrative and public. In the end, the activists and the company backed the Clinton administration into a corner through relentless and often unconventional pursuit of conflict resolution. Their efforts paved the way for future administrative action to avoid such protracted conflicts.

The final agreement included numerous transactions. The federal and state governments paid $380 million for 7,470 acres of company land, including 3,000 acres of old growth. The land was transferred to the Bureau of Land Management and named the Headwaters Forest Reserve. Because of the legacy of nineteenth-century land sales in Redwood Country, the US Forest Service did not have a large presence in Redwood Country. However, the Bureau of Land Management at the time supervised Gilham Butte Reserve in southern Humboldt, between the Lost Coast and Humboldt Redwoods State Park. Activists had positive experiences with the BLM staff, so they pressed California leaders to hand the reserve over to the BLM. California agreed to pay an additional $100 million for approximately 1,600 acres of old growth in Grizzly Creek and Owl Creek. Pacific Lumber, in addition to cash, received 7,755 acres of second-growth forest from Elk River Timber Company. The federal government agreed to approve the HCP and Incidental Take Permit, allowing the company to log in residual old-growth areas. The ancient groves still owned by Pacific Lumber would be off limits to logging for fifty years to help the murrelet recover. The state approved the Sustained Yield Plan governing the company's long-term timber harvests. And Pacific Lumber signed the WCB contract and agreed to drop its takings lawsuits. [61]

The Deal was expansive and contested, and President Clinton and secretary of the interior Bruce Babbitt firmly believed it provided a model for resolving other private land conflicts. Before 1994, when the federal government first actively engaged the Headwaters conflict, only thirty-nine HCPs had been produced since the passage of the 1982 Endangered Species Act amendments, which had been created specifically to avoid the kinds of adversarial conflicts generated by the act. The *Palilla* cases in the early 1980s raised the anxiety of private landowners that they, too, were accountable to the Endangered Species Act. Soon after the 1982 amendments were passed, Californians in the San Bruno Mountain area near San Francisco had hammered out the first Habitat Conservation Plan to protect the mission blue butterfly. But there were few other successful negotiations until the mid-1990s. The spotted owl conflict first convinced Clinton and Babbitt of the desirability of more collaborative, less adversarial procedures using HCPs as their main mechanism.

In the mid-1990s, the Clinton administration aggressively pursued Habitat Conservation Plans to forestall additional crises. From 1994 to 1998, the federal government negotiated more than 230 HCPs. Indeed, even before the Deal was consummated, Clinton used it as the impetus for negotiating eighteen million acres' worth of HCPs in 1997 alone. The administration also developed new tools to aid in negotiations with private landowners. Safe Harbor Agreements preclude the government from further restricting activity on a property should conservation efforts attract additional endangered species to the property in the future. No Surprises Policies assure signatories to Habitat Conservation Plans that no additional land use restrictions will be applied to their land in the future. These policy innovations were designed to encourage landowners to voluntarily comply with the Endangered Species Act and species recovery plans in exchange for legal and financial certainty in the future. It was precisely those kinds of uncertainties that had created the mutual hostility between activists and timber companies during the Redwood Wars.[62]

However, it wasn't the landowners in Redwood Country that forced the Redwood Wars onto the radar of state and federal officials; it was the persistent activism of North Coast residents working to transform their local communities. The locals had been willing to press forestry reforms, at times using radical means. Their social and ecological values drove them to utilize all available means to challenge an entrenched system, including conventional tactics such as litigation and lobbying. From 1968 to 1999, the activists pushed the state to dramatically transform North Coast logging, and while they were largely displeased with the final deal and continued to challenge its terms well into the twenty-first century, most of the activists took some solace in permanently protecting the Headwaters Reserve and forestalling logging in other ancient groves on Pacific Lumber property.

EPILOGUE

Continuity and Vanguard

THE CONSUMMATION OF THE HEADWATERS DEAL MEANT THE RED-
wood Wars had ended as far as the national government, press, and
national environmentalists were concerned, but on the ground on
the North Coast, the battles among the state, activists, and timber
companies continued. Nearly ten months after the Deal was finalized,
Julia "Butterfly" Hill climbed down from Luna, the approximately
thousand-year-old redwood she had lived in, two hundred feet off the
ground, for more than two years. Luna is visible from Highway 101 on
the hillside across from Pacific Lumber's company town, Scotia. Hill
had decided to occupy the lone giant on the slope to protest the terms
of the Deal as federal and state agencies negotiated the final terms of
the Habitat Conservation Plan with Pacific Lumber. On the last day
of 1996, just three months after the agreement was signed, massive
winter storms had caused a mudslide and debris flow that covered the
town of Stafford, located at the base of the mountain that supported
Luna. The slide originated from a recent Pacific Lumber clear-cut,
providing further evidence to North Coast activists that the terms
of the Deal were insufficient. The agreement did not protect enough
ancient redwoods. It did not provide adequate protection to salmon
streams. And it did nothing to reform logging practices on the North
Coast. Activists continued to argue that communities were at risk,
as the residents of Stafford watched their town fill up with mud and
debris.

Hill's tree-sit was the most visible event of the Redwood Wars, even though it began well after the Deal had been announced to the public. Her tree-sit kept the spotlight on the Redwood Wars while North Coast activists worked to influence the final contours of the historic land agreement. In the end, her efforts protected a mere three acres of land. However, they illuminate the characteristics of activist resistance to industrial logging during the Redwood Wars: dramatic confrontations, a commitment to sustainable logging reforms, an insistence that the rural communities—not corporations—should dictate their own future, and a belief that ancient redwoods should be spared from the chainsaw and preserved as monuments to an ancient past. From the activists' perspective, the Deal would not, and could not, be the end of the wars.[1]

Despite North Coast activist resistance, the impact of the Redwood Wars on national politics diminished after the government purchased the Headwaters Forest Reserve, but their effects on the North Coast continued to evolve, as did the wars' influence on a new generation of anti-globalization activists. North Coast activists continued to innovate, and they achieved success regarding both Headwaters Forest and logging reform. Their innovations followed a previously defined path: investigate local developments and concerns, then pursue all available legal, political, and extralegal means of addressing those concerns. In their efforts to continue to transform North Coast logging, the activists returned to the courts, calling on the Endangered Species Act to protect salmon habitat in old-growth forests but also increasingly in second-growth forests. They also turned to a new ally to help them enforce the Endangered Species Act—the California Water Quality Control Board, which had jurisdiction over logging operations that affected rivers and streams. For its part, Pacific Lumber went through another transformation, entering the second decade of the twenty-first century with a new lease on life after it filed for bankruptcy and was once again taken over by new owners. On March 1, 1999, President Clinton, California governor Gray Davis, Charles Hurwitz, and John Campbell had hoped the Redwood Wars were finished, but in fact the Deal marked the end of only one discrete battle in the war over industrial logging in the north. The relentless activists continued to challenge Timber Harvest Plans and the now completed Deal.

Even before the Deal was complete, North Coast activists had embarked on a plan to undermine it. In January 1999, in line with their counterparts in the Pacific Northwest, they continued their shift toward using salmonid habitat to restrict logging on Pacific Lumber land and the rest of the North Coast. Throughout the later 1990s and early 2000s, activists across the Northwest, including northern California, pressed the National Marine Fisheries Service (NMFS) to list myriad salmonid species as threatened and to provide protection for their habitats via logging and irrigation reforms. In the Central Valley of Oregon and northern California, tribal organizations, environmentalists, commercial fishermen, utility companies, and agricultural landowners all fought over the diversion of the Klamath River in California and Oregon and the volume of water remaining in the river. The protests, lawsuits, hostility, and agency actions all swirled to create what became known as the Salmon Wars. North Coast activists engaged in the fights over listings and critical habitat, but they remained focused on logging reforms and their impact on salmon spawning grounds closer to the Pacific Ocean. Thus, in January 1999, before California had appropriated its portion of the Headwaters funding, EPIC filed suit against NMFS to compel the agency to designate critical habitat for the coho salmon, which they hoped would force Pacific Lumber to create wider buffer zones along the waterways inside Headwaters Forest, reducing logging levels and changing logging practices.[2]

Once the Headwaters purchase was complete and the land management plans approved, the activists immediately set out to impose additional restrictions on Pacific Lumber logging. At the end of March 1999, EPIC and the Sierra Club filed suit against the state for approving a Sustained Yield Plan for Pacific Lumber that lacked cumulative impact analyses. The suit also challenged a Streambed Alteration Permit and the Incidental Take Permit because California law forbade incidental takes altogether and the logging plans would disrupt murrelet and salmon breeding grounds. That spring the activists vowed to continue to pursue their goal of acquiring all sixty thousand acres of Headwaters Forest, and before 1999 ended, they had filed suit in federal court arguing that EPA and NMFS had violated the National Environmental Policy Act (NEPA) and the Endangered Species Act with respect to the Pacific Lumber HCP—the first time activists had used NEPA in the

Redwood Wars. Their main argument was that the approval of the HCP constituted a federal agency action, and thus NEPA required an environmental impact statement for salmonid habitat and other endangered species. The activists at EPIC clearly had not accepted the full terms of the Clinton pact with Pacific Lumber.[3]

Julia Butterfly Hill's continued tree-sit in 1999 also highlighted activists' anger about the Deal and the lack of protections afforded to the broader redwood forest and its human communities. Even as she descended, however, splinter groups of Earth First! flocked to the backwoods of Pacific Lumber land to continue thwarting logging along salmon streams and in mature groves of redwoods and Douglas firs. Activists associated with Earth First! began to occupy stands of trees along the Mattole River on Pacific Lumber property, working to prevent access to the old-growth Douglas fir groves along the salmon streams just outside the Lost Coast. The occupations lasted for years, until in 2012 the California Department of Forestry finally approved new procedures for logging in the Mattole watershed.[4]

In addition to their tried and true tactics, the activists' strategy also evolved over those ensuing years. The most successful new strategy was to attack North Coast timber operations via the Regional Water Quality Control Boards. The boards were not signatories to the Headwaters Deal, and they used their authority to further restrict logging operations near streams, leading to charges by Pacific Lumber that the State of California was violating the terms of the agreement and forcing the company to reduce its annual timber harvests well below those spelled out in the California Sustained Yield Plan. By 2008, frustrated by lost revenue, continuing litigation, and new regulatory hurdles, Pacific Lumber had filed for bankruptcy and was under new ownership. The California Supreme Court had invalidated the company's Sustained Yield Plan and forced it to work on a new plan. The new owners of Pacific Lumber's land and mills, the Humboldt Redwood Company—owned by the Fisher family, who created the Gap retail stores—vowed not to harvest trees less than two hundred years old. Consequently, the last tree-sitters inside Headwaters walked out of the forest. North Coast residents accepted all the news of 2008 with a sigh of relief and a nervous optimism that the wars would die down and that some sense of stability would prevail.[5]

Many activists were not content, however, in the absence of comprehensive logging reform. Some North Coast activists continued to press the Board of Forestry to abandon its corporatist and development-focused traditions via lawsuits, regulatory proposals, and legislative action, and direct actions continued, though increasingly targeting other timber companies, as they had in the 1980s. Green Diamond Resource Company became the object of a four-year occupation beginning in August 2008. Green Diamond was a part of the old Simpson Timber Company on the North Coast, and they proposed logging the McKay tract, just east of Eureka, which was designated for residential development in the future. Earth First! established "Ewok Village" in the redwood forest to prevent the logging and protect the giant redwoods and the salmon spawning grounds of Ryan Creek. Hundreds of activists participated in the tree-sits and ropes course high above the ground. In June 2012, after trying to wait out the activists instead of engaging in hostile confrontations, Green Diamond, Trust for Public Land, and the State of California agreed to a conservation easement for the tract that created the Humboldt Community Forest. The tenor of the conflicts over timber harvesting was slowly changing. Timber companies had grown reluctant to fight it out in the woods, deciding instead to bide their time and slowly work with less confrontational activists to develop compromises.[6]

The post-Deal history of the Redwood Wars thus largely reinforces the historical patterns of pre-Deal history. Sustainable forestry, habitat protection, and preservation of ancient redwoods remained top priorities for North Coast activists. Unsatisfied with the Habitat Conservation Plan and the Sustained Yield Plan, they continued to agitate and press their demands at the local, state, and federal levels. Like William Dudley, they were interested in the fusion of preservation and conservation ideals. Also true to historical forms established by John Muir, Andrew Hill, John Merriam, Madison Grant, William Kent, Newton Drury, and David Brower, the activists innovated in response to the Deal. When the HCP made it impossible to use the Endangered Species Act, they turned to the Regional Water Quality Control Board to assert local authority over timber operations—a tactic never before used on private timberlands. At stake was what became known as the "Hole in Headwaters," a 705-acre second-growth forest of eighty-year-old redwoods along the South Fork of Elk River. After the state purchased the Elk River Timber property on the north side of the main Headwaters Grove, Pacific Lumber had no road access to the stand of trees, so it filed a Timber Harvest Plan for helicopter logging. Activists recruited the Water Quality Control Board to submit comments on the proposal, and the board recommended ongoing water quality testing to ensure that any logging activity damaging the river could be quickly halted. In response, Pacific Lumber filed suit against the government alleging that it had breached the terms of the Deal and that the Regional Water Quality Board had no jurisdiction. In March 2004, a California court of appeals ruled in favor of the activists and the Water Quality Control Board. Another new tool for the activists was the Clean Water Act. EPIC filed suit against Pacific Lumber and the EPA in 2001, arguing that the "pipes, ditches, culverts," and other sources of water discharge around the company's property qualified as point sources of pollution and required EPA permits and monitoring. The case was dismissed during the bankruptcy hearings after 2007. That spirit of innovation and response had propelled the Redwood Wars onto the national scene in the late 1980s, extended them for decades, and gave them a wide influence on state and federal agencies.

Finally, the post-Deal events reinforce the independence, and often the radical ideas, of the North Coast activists. When faced with a nationally praised deal, they fought back, using all available tools, because it did not conform to their vision for the North Coast. Maxxam still owned Pacific Lumber. Only a handful of the ancient groves were permanently protected. Salmon runs were not as well protected as they hoped. They believed the Sustained Yield Plan was not truly sustainable for the forest or the workers. In response, the activists commented on and litigated the terms of the Deal. They rushed back into the forests to stop logging at the point of production. When the last tree-sitter emerged from Headwaters Forest in 2008, detente had been reached in one part of the North Coast, but not everywhere. Just as they had in the past, the activists seeking broad regulatory reform looked to protect sites they deemed threatened. That was the way activists had propelled the Redwood Wars and the way subsequent conflicts over land management were handled.

Due to their longevity and evolving character, the Redwood Wars offer many historical lessons. Of particular importance are lessons about the power of rural people in an increasingly corporate and global world economy, the role of federal executive branch authority at the turn of the twenty-first century, and the nature of the independent and often radical actions of North Coast residents, which undermine oft-told narratives about environmentalism. Despite political and social transformations, four generations of redwood activists remained committed to conservation methodology, demonstrated by their persistent work to promote the long-term feasibility of North Coast timber operations as part of their more preservationist activism. They also developed successful private land acquisition strategies that remained a reliable source of temporary conflict resolution. The intensity of the conflicts and the final forms of the compromises, however, were most powerfully influenced by the interactions between local industry leaders and local activists over the development of specific plots of land.

The conflicts over the redwoods were continually pushed and prodded by North Coast women in independent actions that challenged corporatist development and traditional private property rights. The importance of female leadership on the North Coast is an important detail in itself. Women played a leading role on the North Coast, not just in the postwar world but throughout the history of the region. Those facts do not separate North Coast activists from the broader history of environmentalism, because the environmental community has always heavily relied on female leadership and rank-and-file activists— as historians are increasingly noting and studying. Women played an especially important role in the Redwood Wars because the community of activists never resisted female leadership. There was no tradition of male leadership in North Coast activist circles to block female leaders. They were all committed to counterculture values, gender equality, and social justice, and that made a difference in the culture of the North Coast redwoods movement. Finally, women on the North Coast seized the reins of the movement because of their talent and ambition, and primarily due to their deeply held belief that old-growth redwood forests had to be protected from logging. Because of the prominence of female activists, a study of gender in the Redwood Wars and the sustainable forestry movement deserves its own book.

The relief and anxious hope in 2008 was nothing new for the North Coast. Past generations were similarly relieved each time a crisis in Redwood Country was averted. Thus, the 2008 sentiment was similar to the relief felt by of the Murphy family and Laura Mahan earlier in the twentieth century. It was similar to the feelings of Miller Redwood, Louisiana-Pacific, and Pacific Lumber after Congress authorized the Redwood National Park purchase in 1968 and again in 1978. And it was similar to the relief felt by the Sempervirens Club and William Kent in the first decade of the twentieth century. If nothing else, the long history of strife in Redwood Country is the story of seemingly irrepressible conflict over the value of the redwoods—standing and fallen—and over competing social visions for the North Coast. At each moment of crisis, the conflict bound Redwood Country to the broader political and economic trends of the nation, while highlighting the local nature of the conflicts over redwoods because it was people on the North Coast driving the conflicts—activists and timber leaders. The Headwaters activists, like so many other twentieth-century environmentalists, had re-created and revised the campaign strategy developed during the Big Basin conflict, another example of the long and broad reach of redwood politics. The Sempervirens Club had physically hiked the groves of ancient trees, mapped their boundary, documented the landscape, and developed a photographic presentation for public and legislative viewing. In short, they used modern publicity to generate public and governmental support. The prewar redwood movement raised funds privately to acquire ancient redwood groves and then donated the lands to the state for public management. In that way, the early movement was directly aligned with that part of the progressive movement committed to private-public partnerships and corporatism, which became known as associationalism in the 1920s. Similarly, that early strategy linked the redwood preservation movement to the national conservation movement led by wealthy white male professionals including Madison Grant, John C. Merriam, and John D. Rockefeller Jr.

The Redwood Wars of the last third of the twentieth century were also linked to broad national and international trends. The intractable nature of the conflict was a product of the activists' stubborn commitment to environmental and social justice ideals, their resistance to corporate power, their willingness to explore tactics and strategies, and their success in implementing those strategies, especially litigation. It is not a surprise that the conflict over Headwaters Forest helped transform national environmental politics, pushing the executive branch to the forefront of environmental policy making. Since the redwoods have long held sway as symbols of American exceptionalism, garnering a statewide or national audience was an easy task. Because the Redwood Wars involved private land, they easily prompted political opposition from business leaders and conservative politicians. The situation in the 1990s was ripe for the expansion of executive power. While ecological health was popular with the public, the two major political parties had increasingly diverged with respect to environmental policy. Democrats generally favored environmental protection and Republicans did not. Thus, the legislative system deadlocked over environmental protection because neither party could control Congress for long periods or with a clear majority. At the same time, the local combatants pushed the Headwaters Conflict to the center of the federal fray.

Executive influence on the environmental protection regime progressively increased under President Clinton, influenced by the spotted owl conflict and the Redwood Wars. Clinton asserted direct control over endangered species policy in 1994 when he and Vice President Al Gore convened a conference in Portland, Oregon, to negotiate a compromise plan for the national forests affected by spotted owl habitat designation. Pacific Lumber's takings suit then drove the Clinton administration to intervene in the Redwood Wars, furthering the encroachment of the executive branch in environmental policy making. For endangered species law, that process had begun with the 1982 congressional amendments to the Endangered Species Act authorizing executive branch negotiations with private landowners. Those provisions were rarely used before the Headwaters Deal. President George H. W. Bush asserted executive authority over the law when he convened the "God Squad" to deal with the spotted owl conflict on public land in the Pacific Northwest. President Clinton pushed executive power by personally negotiating administrative compromises to end conflict and ward off congressional attacks on the Endangered Species Act. Clinton was not the first president to use his executive powers to protect landscapes, but he wielded his powers differently from his predecessors. Clinton, like Carter and many other presidents, used the Antiquities Act to protect large swaths of public land, such as the Grand Escalante Staircase in Utah. Presidents now routinely designate national monuments at the end of their terms to enhance their conservation legacies. The spotted owl and Headwaters agreements were different, however. Clinton's executive interventions were designed to create compromise; they were not attempts to simply avoid Congress when politics and the judiciary made compromise impossible. The Clinton administration worked to create collaborative tools in an effort to bring industry, workers, and the public together on environmental issues. Those efforts were not entirely successful on the North Coast, but they were significant nonetheless because they opened up new pathways for activists and timber leaders.

The Headwaters Deal was the Clinton administration's response to the first federal court order to halt logging on private land because of endangered species policy. The North Coast activists and the Pacific Lumber Company had backed Clinton into a corner. State courts had not resolved the Redwoods Wars. The California legislature and Congress had both failed to legislate a resolution to the conflict over the fate of the last ancient redwoods and their old-growth forests. When the Redwood Wars began to peak, merging concerns over giant trees and endangered species, Clinton faced both a noisy congressional opposition to reauthorization of the Endangered Species Act and a takings suit filed by Pacific Lumber—to be heard by a court that had a much more conservative outlook than many others in the postwar era. The Deal was thus a major experiment with Clinton's No Surprises and Safe Harbor Agreement rules, designed to encourage landowners facing endangered species restrictions to negotiate with the federal government. Under Clinton, the use of administrative tools to implement and alter Endangered Species policy exploded, including a dramatic increase in Habitat Conservation Plans and Incidental Take Permits. Again, part of the administrative strategy was to stave off attacks by the Gingrich Congress on the Endangered Species Act and to prevent a high-stakes court battle over regulatory takings in a conservative Supreme Court. The Clintonian expansion of executive power included designation of individual de facto wilderness areas via national monument designation, and the designation of wilderness writ large via the Roadless Rule in 2000, which prohibited development on nearly sixty million acres of national forests.

In the end, however, only the collapse of Hurwitz's Pacific Lumber and the accommodation of the North Coast activists' demands by the new owners quelled the Redwood Wars, a testimony to the powerful influence of the North Coast activists who skillfully, if gruffly, navigated the structures of power they had tried to avoid by moving to the North Coast. The anxious peace may not last, though there is hope. Unlike Pacific Lumber, Humboldt Redwood Company (HRC) has adopted a less antagonistic approach with the activists, and has worked with EPIC and others as they revised logging plans for their property. That kind of collaboration had disappeared during the Redwood Wars, as activists and corporate executives focused on building power for their own institutions. It was that kind of collaboration the Clinton administration tried to encourage through the use of its administrative powers, though only between property owners and the government; environmentalists were only indirectly engaged. HRC has directly engaged with activists, and the initial results are positive. Most of the tree-sitters came down, and litigation decreased dramatically. Despite their collaborative efforts and patience with the few remaining tree-sitters, Humboldt Redwood Company may eventually face the same pressures that John Campbell and Charles Hurwitz confronted: maximizing revenue and profits for investors. If that time comes, HRC leaders will likely be tempted to harvest some, or all, of the giant redwoods it still owns, risking the end of the détente. That the resolution of the battle over Headwaters Forest is so tenuous and riddled with nervous optimism reflects the reality that the modern environmental protection regime had not, as of 2012, adequately defined the obligations of private landowners to endangered species and other ecological values.

A final legacy of the North Coast activists who created the Redwood Wars concerns the global movement challenging private property prerogatives. In 1999, when labor, environmental, and human rights activists gathered in Seattle to protest global capitalism and the undermining of local sovereignty to serve multinational corporate profit margins, North Coast activists played prominent roles. They carried anti-Hurwitz and anti-Maxxam placards, and they marched with the steelworkers with whom they had begun to collaborate to oppose Maxxam's sell-off of Kaiser Aluminum assets. The "Battle for Seattle," as it came to be known, pulled together disparate activists who experienced the frustrations North Coast activists had felt since at least 1985. The activists in Seattle shared an aesthetic and tone with the North Coast activists. The cartoonish representations of corporate leaders, the emphasis on sustainability and jobs, and the vehement opposition to distant ownership and control resembled the protests of Redwood Summer and the annual anti-Maxxam rallies on September 15. Here, then, was another important legacy of the Redwood Wars, and another suggestion of the complexity behind the activism that drove them.[7]

NOT YOUR AVERAGE ACTIVISTS

The colorful North Coast activists are not easily pinned down and defined. They were at once hippies, "country folk," scientists, mystics, conservatives, radicals, progressives, and neoliberals. The early activists were part of a constituency swept up in the rising tide of environmental activism of the late 1960s. In most histories, the high tide of insurgent, grassroots environmentalism was Earth Day 1970. However, activists on the North Coast retained and even increased their demands on society during subsequent decades. They worked conservatively to protect their bucolic, small-town society and the health of the landscape, which they defined as one rich in biodiversity. They sought to rid North Coast logging of large corporate owners—distant, eastern, absentee landlords in their minds. Their numbers were certainly not as large as those mobilized by the first Earth Day, but their persistence provides evidence that the narrative of the nationalization and professionalization of environmental politics unravels when viewed from the North Coast instead of Washington, DC.

Despite their radicalism and anti-industrial attitudes, the activists remained committed to the evolution and incorporation of sustained yield forestry. Due to the persistence of those conservation goals, the Redwood Wars complicate our understanding of the perceived conservation-preservation split by inserting forestry techniques and landscape management more aggressively into historical discussions of landscape protection. The North Coast activists repeatedly pursued both preservationist actions and conservationist land management plans. Accordingly, the continuity of Pinchotian and Muirian influences in the fights over Redwood National Park and Humboldt Redwoods State Park stands out in stark relief against the once-standard narrative of a transition from "conservation to environment." More historians are highlighting the continuities between the pre- and postwar eras in American environmental politics, and the North Coast conflicts offer powerful examples of such continuity. The conflict over Bull Creek in the 1950s was the result of the Sierra Club's insistence that the state regulate logging operations on private land to protect ancient forests in the state park system. Similarly, the 1978 expansion of Redwood National Park was the result of litigation over the impacts of logging on private land adjacent to the park. In both instances, the local activists were determined to reform private logging operations on the North Coast despite the acquisition of additional parkland designed to end the conflicts. The North Coast activist goal was for humans to work in the forests to supply timber and rehabilitate slopes and streams to protect traditional rural lifestyles.

Though the activity on the North Coast was contemporaneous with the passage of the Wilderness Act and Roderick Nash's seminal work on the intellectual history of wilderness ideas, the North Coast activists' ideas and goals with respect to redwood preservation did not fit comfortably into Congress's or Nash's definition, but were closer to the interwar activists who founded the Wilderness Society. Aldo Leopold, Benton MacKaye, Robert Sterling Yard, and Robert Marshall viewed roadless wildlands—their notion of wilderness—as resources worthy of conservation, alongside timber and water. Leopold, in particular, envisioned landscapes as matrices of myriad land uses, including roadless areas. As a group, they saw in wilderness places where humans could escape cars and industrial society to rejuvenate their souls. In that way, their motivations were similar to that of John Muir, who also viewed preservation as a means to offer Americans respite from industrial society. They saw in wilderness places where *men* could challenge themselves and retain survival instincts. MacKaye saw the Appalachian Trail as a way to physically connect rural working communities in ways that reinforced their connections to the land. Similarly, across almost a century of activism, North Coast activists have consistently defied the conservation-to-environment narrative.[8]

Concern with logging methodologies, sustainable development, and ecological health remained the hallmark of North Coast activists during the Redwood Wars. Though biocentrism and deep ecology were major influences on the activists in the Redwood Wars, the local North Coast cohort strayed dramatically from the often misanthropic views of the founders of Earth First!. The North Coast Earth First! activists blended prolabor, anti-corporate, feminist, and biocentric ideals into their work, aiding their mass movement goals. Their tactics and faith in science were decidedly progressive, but their goal was inherently conservative: protecting the rural and wild landscape of the North Coast from industrialization.

The successes of the late twentieth-century activists in North Coast Earth First!, EPIC, and Forests Forever thus at least partially undermine the narrative of middle-class professional organizations and their Capitol Hill counterparts implementing the modern environmental protection regime. The migrants and native-born residents who led the citizen movement to break corporatism and reform timber operations were largely individuals who rejected middle-class work, politics, and culture. Some wanted to live out their counterculture goals and values. Later migrants wanted to escape corporate work and culture. They were largely people who moved to the North Coast precisely because it lacked (or at least seemed to lack) a strong commitment to cultural conformity. At the very least, the North Coast offered refuge to those seeking alternative lifestyles. They lived off dirt roads, some without electricity. Many rejected consistent, regular employment. They were not independently wealthy; they moved to the North Coast because they rejected consumer culture and the materialism of modern American society. They bartered and work-traded, and they earned wages as needed to secure a material lifestyle of their choosing. Their criticism of industrial capitalism led many of the activists of the North Coast to enthusiastically embrace direct action at the point of production as a means to achieve their forestry and political goals, many to the point of syndicalism. Often their actions crossed the boundaries of "good taste," and at other times they performed civil disobedience.

The trajectories and strategies of the Redwood Wars did not come from middle-class activists working for well-funded, established organizations. Nor were the Redwood Wars the product of policy entrepreneurs in Washington, DC. The Redwood Wars, especially the battle over Headwaters Forest, were legally, legislatively, and promotionally the product of North Coast activists. Most of the activists were not anarchists; they were organizers. The older generations, especially, brought civil rights and labor organizing experience to the movement, but they also recognized the value in using traditional political avenues to push their goals, including lobbying and policy making. Because of the influence of the organizers, the North Coast activists became tactical pragmatists, however unwilling they were to compromise their vision for North Coast society and landscapes. Kathy Bailey, Woods, and others took their Forests Forever proposal to Sacramento and then forced their issues into the voters' consciousness. Likewise, North Coast activists pressed Dan Hamburg to adopt their congressional resolution for the battle over Headwaters Forest. North Coasters advocated their cause in DC and organized a nationwide constituency; they pursued their vision for North Coast society and their vision for the redwood forests wherever a potential decision maker resided. Their paths, despite personal preference, led them higher and higher up the hierarchy of government as the conflict stretched out. Because of their persistence, the state and national governments were forced to accommodate North Coast actors more often than the North Coast was forced to accept edicts handed down to them. In many ways, the process was similar to the way rural residents of the Pacific Northwest—loggers and activists alike—drove the spotted owl conflict onto the national stage.

In the end, the Redwood Wars speak to a persistent tension over private property rights, the growing criticism of globalization, and the local roots of the development of American politics. They were long and sometimes bloody wars, and in the end, though the North Coast activists transformed environmental politics, nobody won. Pacific Lumber went bankrupt, Louisiana-Pacific and Georgia-Pacific left the area, vast parts of Headwaters Forest were harvested, mudslides buried towns and choked salmon runs, new corporations took ownership of the forest, and North Coast counties were left holding their breath.

But through it all, North Coast activists persisted, and their example suggests that modern environmentalism has often been a powerful bottom-up social movement that successfully transformed state and national environmental politics.

NOTES

INTRODUCTION

1   Judi Bari, "The Earth First! Car Bombing," *Earth First! Journal*, February 2, 1994.

2   Mike Geniella, "Bari Trial Pressed over FBI Problems," *Eureka Times Standard*, April 7, 1997, EPIC archives, Redway, CA; Evelyn Nieves, "Environmentalists Win Bombing Lawsuit," *New York Times*, June 12, 2002 (www.nytimes.com/2002/06/12/us/environmentalists-win-bombing-lawsuit.html); *Judi Bari and Darryl Cherney v. FBI Agents Stockton Buck, Frank Doyle, John Reidkes, and Phillip Sena, and Oakland Police Officers Clyde M. Sims, Robert Chenault, and Michael Sitterud*, No. C 91–01057 CW, US District Court, Northern District of California (June 11, 2002); *Bari and Cherney v. FBI*, 14 F.3d 457 (January 12, 1994; http://law.justia.com/cases/federal/appellate-courts/f3/14/457/613523).

3   David Harris, *The Last Stand: The War between Wall Street and Main Street over California's Ancient Redwoods* (New York: Times Books, 1995). See also Alston Chase, *In a Dark Wood: The Fights over Forests and the Myths of Nature* (New Brunswick, NJ: Transaction, 2001).

4   The dominant narrative has largely been crafted through journalistic and polemic accounts. David Harris wrote the only journalistic book that deals solely with the Headwaters conflict (*The Last Stand*). The journalistic and polemical treatments that attend briefly to the Headwaters conflict include Chase, *In a Dark Wood*; David Helvarg, *The War against the Greens: The "Wise-Use" Movement, the New Right, and the Browning of America* (Boulder, CO: Johnson Books, 2004); Christopher Manes, *Green Rage: Radical Environmentalism and the Unmaking of Civilization* (Boston: Little, Brown, 1990); Jacqueline Vaughn, *Green Backlash: The History and Politics of the Environmental Opposition in the U.S.* (Boulder, CO: Lynne Rienner, 1997); and Susan Zakin, *Coyotes and Town Dogs: Earth First! and the Environmental Movement* (Tuson: University of Arizona Press, 1993). A few scholarly books that are focused on environmentalism briefly mention the Headwaters conflict: Douglass Bevington, *Rebirth of Environmentalism: Grassroots Activism from the Spotted Owl to the Polar Bear* (Washington, DC: Island Press, 2009); Alessandro Bonanno and Douglas H. Constance, *Stories of Globalization: Transnational Corporations,*

Resistance, and the State (University Park: Pennsylvania State University Press, 2008); Samuel Hays, *Wars in the Woods: The Rise of Ecological Forestry* (Pittsburgh, PA: University of Pittsburgh Press, 2007); Carolyn Merchant, *Radical Ecology: The Search for a Livable World* (New York: Routledge, 2005); Rik Scarce, *Eco-Warriors: Understanding the Radical Environmental Movement* (Walnut Creek, CA: Left Coast Press, 2006); and Richard Widdick, *Trouble in the Forest: California's Redwood Timber Wars* (Minneapolis: University of Minnesota Press, 2009). Both Hays and Merchant erred in reference to the timber company name and the name of the forest, respectively. Bonanno and Constance repeat the morality play narrative, while Bevington and Widdick briefly offer more nuanced interpretations of Pacific Lumber Company's history. Some firsthand accounts include Judi Bari, *Timber Wars* (Monroe, ME: Common Courage Press, 1994); Joan Dunning, *From the Redwood Forest: Ancient Trees and the Bottom Line: A Headwaters Journey* (White River Junction, VT: Chelsea Green Publishing, 1998); Dave Foreman, *Confessions of an Eco-Warrior* (New York: Harmony Books, 1991); and Julia Butterfly Hill, *The Legacy of Luna: The Story of a Tree, a Woman, and the Struggle to Save the Redwoods* (New York: HarperCollins, 2000).

5   David Harris, interview by the author, Mill Valley, CA, May 1, 2007 (recording and notes in possession of author).

6   See William Cronon, "The Trouble with Wilderness," in *Uncommon Ground: Rethinking the Human Place in Nature,* ed. William Cronon (New York: W. W. Norton, 1996), 69–90; William Dietrich, *The Final Forest: The Battle for the Last Great Trees of the Pacific Northwest* (New York: Penguin Books, 1993); Kathie Durbin, *Tree Huggers: Victory, Defeat, and Renewal in the Northwest Ancient Forest Campaign* (Seattle: Mountaineers, 1996); Ramachandra Guha, "Radical American Environmentalism and Wilderness Preservation: A Third World Critique," in *The Great New Wilderness Debate: An Expansive Collection of Writings Defining Wilderness from John Muir to Gary Snyder,* ed. J. Baird Callicott and Michael P. Nelson (Athens: University of Georgia Press, 1998), 231–45; Kevin R. Marsh, *Drawing Lines in the Forest: Creating Wilderness Areas in the Pacific Northwest* (Seattle: University of Washington Press, 2007); Reed F. Noss, ed., *The Redwood Forest: History, Ecology, and Conservation of the Coast Redwoods* (Washington, DC: Island Press, 2000), 87 (regarding old-growth definition); James Morton Turner, *The Promise of Wilderness: American Environmental Politics since 1964* (Seattle: University of Washington Press, 2012); and Stephen Lewis Yaffee, *The Wisdom of the Spotted Owl: Policy Lessons for a New Century* (Washington, DC: Island Press, 1994).

7   *Corporatism,* as used here, refers to the definition Ellis Hawley used in his classic article, "The Discovery and Study of a 'Corporate Liberalism,'" *Business History Review* 52, no. 3 (Autumn 1978): 309–20. Hawley defines corporatism as a system whereby industries are guided by "officially recognized, non-competitive, role-ordered occupational or functional groupings . . .

where the state properly functions as a coordinator, assistant, and midwife rather than director or regulator."

8   Turner, *Promise of Wilderness*, 248–52, 273–89, 315–40.

9   For a fuller discussion of the history of globalization, workers, and environmentalism, see Erik Loomis, *Out of Sight: The Long and Disturbing Story of Corporations Outsourcing Catastrophe* (New York: New Press, 2015).

10   The narrative of nationalization and professionalization is largely the product of Samuel Hays's and Roderick Nash's classic books and the reactions to them: Samuel P. Hays, *Beauty, Health, and Permanence: Environmental Politics in the United States, 1955–1985* (Pittsburgh, PA: University of Pittsburgh Press, 1987); Roderick Nash, *Wilderness and the American Mind* (New Haven, CT: Yale University Press, 1973). For more on the development of modern environmentalism and its professionalization, see especially Gary C. Bryner, *Blue Skies, Green Politics: The Clean Air Act of 1990 and Its Implementation* (Washington, DC: Congressional Quarterly Press, 1995); Michael P. Cohen, *The History of the Sierra Club, 1892–1970* (San Francisco: Sierra Club Books, 1988); Stephen Fox, *The American Conservation Movement: John Muir and His Legacy* (Madison: University of Wisconsin Press, 1985); Paul Hirt, *A Conspiracy of Optimism: Management of the National Forests since World War Two* (Lincoln: University of Nebraska Press, 1994); Robert Gottlieb, *Forcing the Spring: The Transformation of the American Environmental Movement* (Washington, DC: Island Press, 1993); Mark W. T. Harvey, *A Symbol of Wilderness: Echo Park and the American Conservation Movement* (Seattle: University of Washington Press, 1989); Samuel P. Hays, *A History of Environmental Politics since 1945* (Pittsburgh, PA: University of Pittsburgh Press, 2000); Michael E. Kraft, *Environmental Policy and Politics* (New York: Pearson Longman, 2007); Richard J. Lazarus, *The Making of Environmental Policy* (Chicago: University of Chicago Press, 2004); Dennis C. Lemaster, *Decade of Change: The Remaking of Forest Service Statutory Authority during the 1970s* (Westport, CT: Greenwood Press, 1984); J. Michael McCloskey, *In the Thick of It: My Life in the Sierra Club* (Washington, DC: Island Press, 2005); Adam Rome, *The Bulldozer in the Countryside: Suburban Sprawl and the Rise of American Environmentalism* (Cambridge: Cambridge University Press, 2001); Christopher C. Sellers, *Crabgrass Crucible: Suburban Nature and the Rise of Environmentalism in Twentieth-Century America* (Chapel Hill: University of North Carolina Press, 2012); Paul Sutter, *Driven Wild: How the Fight against Automobiles Launched the Modern Wilderness Movement* (Seattle: University of Washington Press, 2002); Turner, *Promise of Wilderness*; Edgar Wayburn, *Your Land and Mine: Evolution of a Conservationist* (San Francisco: Sierra Club Books, 2004); and Thomas R. Wellock, *Preserving the Nation: The Conservation and Environmental Movements, 1870–2000* (Wheeling, WV: Harlan Davidson, 2007). Rome, Sutter, Turner, and Wellock each argue there was greater continuity between the pre- and postwar environmental movements than what Hays and Nash

found. Sellers revitalized the argument that there was a marked difference between the pre- and postwar environmental movements, as well as noting the important role suburban activism played in postwar environmentalism.

11   Regarding the origins of scientific forestry, see Henry E. Lowood, "The Calculating Forester: Quantification, Cameral Science, and the Emergence of Scientific Forestry Management in Germany," in *The Quantifying Spirit in the 18th Century*, ed. Tore Frangsmyr, J. L. Heilbron, and Robin E. Rider (Berkeley: University of California Press, 1990), 315–42. Regarding the fusion of preservation and conservation ideology, see Samuel P. Hays, *Conservation and the Gospel of Efficiency: The Progressive Conservation Movement, 1890–1920* (Cambridge, MA: Harvard University Press, 1959); Hays, *Beauty, Health and Permanence*; and Cohen, *History of the Sierra Club*, 2, 4–16, 114–19. In particular, Cohen highlights the ways Muir's views of landscapes were often anthropocentric, desiring a "partly wild and partly tame Sierra," 12. See Emily Wakild, *Revolutionary Parks: Conservation, Social Justice, and Mexico's National Parks, 1910–1940* (Tucson: University of Arizona Press, 2011); and "Border Chasm: International Boundary Parks and Mexican Conservation, 1935–1945," *Environmental History* 14 (July 2009): 453–75, for a wonderful discussion of how ideas and practices involving wilderness, work, local interests, tradition, and conservation intermingled during Mexico's interwar national park boom. In many ways, the situations in Mexico and California were similar due to the need to contend with private property rights and the traditional practices of rural populations.

12   See Richard White, "Are You an Environmentalist or Do You Work for a Living? Work and Nature," in Cronon, *Uncommon Ground*, 171–85.

13   For a discussion of radical environmentalism, wilderness, and the critiques of both, see Cronon, "The Trouble with Wilderness"; and all of the essays in J. Baird Callicott and Michael P. Nelson, eds., *The Great New Wilderness Debate: An Expansive Collection of Writings Defining Wilderness from John Muir to Gary Snyder* (Athens: University of Georgia Press, 1998), especially Guha, "Radical American Environmentalism." The classic texts covering the wilderness debate are Callicott and Nelson, eds., *The Great New Wilderness Debate*; Cronon, *Uncommon Ground*; Gottlieb, *Forcing the Spring*; Nash, *Wilderness and the American Mind*; Nancy Langston, *Forest Dreams, Forest Nightmares: The Paradox of Old Growth in the Inland West* (Seattle: University of Washington Press, 1995); and Joseph Sax, *Mountains without Handrails: Reflections on the National Parks* (Ann Arbor: University of Michigan Press, 1980).

14   Other scholars have similarly looked at local case studies and how environmental policy was implemented, including Bedford, Durbin, Marsh, Sellers, and Wakild. Henry F. Bedford produced a wonderful study of the local activism in New Hampshire regarding NEPA's impacts on the nuclear industry: *Seabrook Station: Citizen Politics and Nuclear Power* (Amherst: University of Massachusetts Press, 1990).

15   See Thomas Andrews, *Killing for Coal: America's Deadliest Labor War* (Cambridge, MA: Harvard University Press, 2010); and Bonanno and Constance, *Stories of Globalization*.

16   Hirt, *Conspiracy of Optimism*; and LeMaster, *Decade of Change*, are great studies of the transformation of federal land management after World War II. Some of the recent treatments of local forestry activism as it relates to federal laws, such as the Wilderness Act of 1964, the Endangered Species Act, and the National Forest Management Act, include Dietrich, *The Final Forest*; Durbin, *Tree Huggers*; Marsh, *Drawing Lines in the Forest*; and Hays, *Wars in the Woods*. Some of the best examples of studies about the interest-group jockeying and scientific and political confusion involved in the spotted owl conflicts are Chase, *In a Dark Wood*; Hays, *Wars in the Woods*; Langston, *Forest Dreams, Forest Nightmares*; Victor M. Sher, "Travels with Strix: The Spotted Owl's Journey through the Federal Courts," *Public Land Law Review* 14 (Spring 1993); Brendan Swedlow, "Scientists, Judges, and Spotted Owls: Policymakers in the Pacific Northwest," *Duke Environmental Law and Policy Forum* 13 (Spring 2003); John Lowe Weston, "The Endangered Species Committee and the Northern Spotted Owl: Did the 'God Squad' Play God?" *Administrative Law Journal of the American University* 7 (Fall 1993/Winter 1994); and Yaffee, *The Wisdom of the Spotted Owl*.

1. DEEP ROOTS

1   Michael Barbour, Sandy Lydon, Mark Borchert, Marjorie Popper, Valerie Whitworth, and John Evarts, *Coast Redwood: A Natural and Cultural History* (Los Olivos, CA: Cachuma Press, 2001), 1–2, 88; and Noss, ed., *The Redwood Forest*, chapter 1.

2   Four excellent sources about the natural history of the coast redwoods are Barbour et al., *Coast Redwood*; Jared Farmer, *Trees in Paradise: A California History* (New York: W. W. Norton, 2013); Noss, ed., *The Redwood Forest*; and Richard Preston, *The Wild Trees: A Story of Passion and Daring* (New York: Random House, 2008). Preston, in particular, tells the story of Stephen Sillett and the other botanists who began to explore the redwood canopy after 1987.

3   Barbour et al., *Coast Redwood*, 7–9; John O. Sawyer, Jane Gray, F. James West, Dale A. Thornburgh, Reed F. Noss, Joseph H. Engbeck Jr., Bruce G. Marcot, and Roland Raymond, "History of Redwood and Redwood Forests," in Noss, *The Redwood Forest*, 7–24, 39.

4   Barbour et al., *Coast Redwood*, 10, 39–41.

5   Barbour et al., *Coast Redwood*, 58–74; John O. Sawyer, Stephen C. Sillett, William J. Libby, Todd E. Dawson, James H. Popenoe, David L. Largent, Robert Van Pelt, Stephen D. Veirs Jr., Reed F. Noss, Dale A. Thornburgh, and Peter Del Tredici, "Redwood Trees: Communities, and Ecosystems: A Closer

Look," in Noss, *The Redwood Forest*, 81–118; Allen Cooperrider, Reed F. Noss, Hartwell H. Welsh Jr., Carlos Carroll, William Zielinski, David Olson, S. Kim Nelson, and Bruce G. Marcot, "Terrestrial Fauna of Redwood Forests," in Noss, *Redwood Forest*, 124–33 (for description of mammalian residents).

6   Barbour et al., *Coast Redwood*, 80–90.

7   The subsection title refers to the classic book by Lynwood Carranco and John T. Labbe, *Logging the Redwoods* (Caldwell, ID: Caxton, 1975), which describes in detail the history of logging, logging technology, and timber companies in Mendocino and Humboldt counties.

8   Henry Sadler, "Winter Damage in Redwood Parks," *Sierra Bulletin* 41, no. 8 (October 1956): 12–18; Peggy Wayburn and Edward Wayburn, "Bulletin Board," *Sierra Bulletin* 44, no. 9 (December 1959).

9   Peggy Wayburn and Edward Wayburn, "Our Vanishing Wilderness," *Sierra Bulletin* 42, no. 1 (January 1957): 6–9; and George Ballis, "Havoc in Big Trees," *Sierra Bulletin* 42, no. 5 (May 1957): 10–11. See also Cohen, *History of the Sierra Club*, 299–310.

10   For compelling analysis of the roles of women in the environmental movement more broadly, see Susan R. Schrepfer, *Nature's Altars: Mountains, Gender, and American Environmentalism* (Lawrence: University of Kansas Press, 2005); and Nancy Unger, *Beyond Nature's Housekeepers: American Women in Environmental History* (New York: Oxford University Press, 2012).

11   Carranco and Labbe, *Logging the Redwoods*, chapters 3–4; Susie Van Kirk, "Humboldt County: A Briefest of Histories," in *Shades of Humboldt Project*, Humboldt County Library, 1999, Humboldt County Historical Society archives, http://www.humboldthistory.org/bHumboldtHistory.html.

12   Carranco and Labbe, *Logging the Redwoods*, chapters 4–5; Van Kirk, "Humboldt County." See also Farmer, *Trees in Paradise*, 50–56.

13   Carranco and Labbe, *Logging the Redwoods*, chapters 6–8.

14   Barbour et al., *Coast Redwood*, 91–95; Carranco and Labbe, *Logging the Redwoods*, 112; "Business," *Los Angeles Times*, October 26, 1897, 12; "Big Lumber Deal," *Los Angeles Times*, September 24, 1902, 1; Widdick, *Trouble in the Forest*, 107–11. The "Reports of the President to the Shareholders" were also incredibly helpful, especially page 5 of the 1917 report, regarding early claims about the company's competitive position (Pacific Lumber Company, "Report of the President to the Shareholders, 1917," in *Selected Historical Annual Reports*, available at the Library of Congress).

15   Carranco and Labbe, *Logging the Redwoods*, 112; and Lowell S. Mengel II, "The Murphy Family and T.P.L. Co.," *Humboldt Historian* 25, no. 4 (July–August 1977): 1.

16   "Big Lumber Deal"; Harris, *The Last Stand*, 10–18; Mengel, "The Murphy Family and T.P.L. Co.," 1; "Report of the President to the Shareholders," 1, 5–6.

17   Harris, *The Last Stand*, 3, 16, 18; "Report of the President to the Shareholders,

1917," 6; Le Roy Joffers, "A Highway Menaces Great Redwoods," *New York Times*, November 15, 1925, 7.

18   Hays, *Beauty, Health, and Permanence*, chapter 1; Hirt, *A Conspiracy of Optimism*, chapter 2; William J. Novak, *The People's Welfare: Law and Regulation in Nineteenth Century America* (Chapel Hill: University of North Carolina Press, 1996); Daniel T. Rodgers, *Atlantic Crossings: Social Politics in a Progressive Age* (Cambridge, MA: Harvard University Press, 1998); Robert H. Wiebe, *The Search for Order, 1877–1920* (New York: Hill and Wang, 1967); Michael Williams, *Americans and Their Forests: A Historical Geography* (Cambridge: Cambridge University Press, 1989), 393–425.

19   Samuel Hays provides the classic interpretation of conservationism and progressivism in *Conservation and the Gospel of Efficiency*, chapter 13. Hays argues that progressivism and conservationism were motivated by the efficient use of resources via the central guiding hand of executive branch scientific experts, not by "people versus the interests" politics. The Board of Forestry in California was similar, but different, in that the board was composed of not scientific but industry experts. The state forester, overseen by the board, provided technical analysis and advice. Stephanie S. Princetl, *Transforming California: A Political History of Land Use and Development* (Baltimore, MD: Johns Hopkins University Press, 1999), argues that the progressive boards and commissions created during the Progressive Era directly contributed to land use and ownership patterns in the twentieth century because the regulatory boards were composed of business experts focused on development. See C. Raymond Clar, *California Government and Forestry from Spanish Days until the Creation of the Department of Natural Resources in 1927* (Sacramento: Division of Forestry, Department of Natural Resources, State of California, 1959), 96–98, 74.

20   Clar, *California Government and Forestry*, 214, 225–49, 268–69, 297, 402, 411, 433, 445; Barbour et al., *Coast Redwood*, 132–33; and Samuel Trask Dana and Myron Krueger, *California Lands: Ownership, Use, and Management* (Washington, DC: American Forestry Association, 1958), 64, 68.

21   See Widdick, *Trouble in the Forest*, chapter 4, for a good analysis of the early conflicts over property and culture on the North Coast.

22   Barbour et al., *Coast Redwood*, 8, 94, 122–24; Susan R. Schrepfer, *The Fight to Save the Redwoods: A History of Environmental Reform, 1917–1978* (Madison: University of Wisconsin Press, 1983), 6–7, 15–16; Walt Whitman, "Song of the Redwood-Tree," *Harper's Monthly Magazine* 48 (February 1874): 366–67; Cameron Binkley, "'No Better Heritage Than Living Trees': Women's Clubs and Early Conservation in Humboldt County," *Western Historical Quarterly* 33, no. 2 (Summer 2002): 3; Roderick Nash, "John Muir, William Kent, and the Conservation Schism," *Pacific Historical Review* 36 (November 1967): 423–33.

23   Barbour et al., *Coast Redwood*, 124–28; and Clar, *California Government and Forestry*, 116–17.

24   See Barbour et al., *Coast Redwood*, 128–29; Clar, *California Government and Forestry*, 116–17. While Muir was devoted to recreation and spiritual endeavors in the wild, as Michael Cohen points out, he too believed that "forest management must be put on a rational, permanent, scientific basis, as in every other country." John Muir quoted in Cohen, *History of the Sierra Club*, 15.

25   See Cohen, *History of the Sierra Club*, 10–18; Hays, *Beauty, Health, and Permanence*, chapter 1; Rodgers, *Atlantic Crossings*; Martin J. Sklar, *The Corporate Reconstruction of American Capitalism, 1890–1916* (Cambridge: Cambridge University Press, 1988).

26   See William R. Dudley, "Forestry Notes," *Sierra Bulletin* 2, no. 4 (June 1898): 244–45, regarding Dudley's comments; and Dana and Krueger, *California Lands*, 62, regarding all public land sold except ten thousand acres for schools.

27   See Barbour et al., *Coast Redwood*, 128–29; Schrepfer, *Fight to Save Redwoods*, 18; William R. Dudley, "Forestry Notes," *Sierra Bulletin* 2, no. 2 (May 1900): 182–88; and F. L. Clarke, "The Big Basin," *Sierra Bulletin* 3, no. 2 (May 1900): 218–23.

28   Barbour et al., *Coast Redwood*, 130; William R. Dudley, "Forestry Notes," *Sierra Bulletin* 3, no. 3 (February 1901): 262–70; Schrepfer, *Fight to Save Redwoods*, 11; and Carrie Stevens Walter, "The Preservation of Big Basin," *Overland Monthly and Out West Magazine* 40, no. 4 (October 1902).

29   Barbour et al., *Coast Redwood*, 129–30; Clarke, "The Big Basin," 218–23; William R. Dudley, "Forestry Notes," *Sierra Bulletin* 3, no. 2 (May 1900): 182–88; ibid., 3, no. 3 (February 1901): 262–70; ibid., 4, no. 3 (February 1903): 246–52; Schrepfer, *Fight to Save Redwoods*, 11; and Stevens Walter, "The Preservation of Big Basin." On wilderness and parks and the public/national interest, see Aldo Leopold, "Wilderness as a Form of Land Use," in Callicott and Nelson, *Great New Wilderness Debate*; Robert Marshall, "The Problem of Wilderness," in Callicott and Nelson, *Great New Wilderness Debate*; and Sigurd Olson, "Why Wilderness?" in Callicott and Nelson, *Great New Wilderness Debate*; Alfred Runte, *National Parks: The American Experience* (Lincoln: University of Nebraska Press, 1997); and Turner, *Promise of Wilderness*.

30   Barbour et al., *Coast Redwood*, 136–39; and Schrepfer, *Fight to Save Redwoods*, xiii, 12, 15–18.

31   Barbour et al., *Coast Redwood*, 139–40; and Schrepfer, *Fight to Save Redwoods*, xiii, 12, 20, 30, 24, 72. See Runte, *National Parks*, for the best discussion of the East Coast elite community's promotion of the national parks, including John D. Rockefeller Jr., Stephen Mather, Franklin Lane, and William Kent.

32   See Gary Gerstle, *American Crucible: Race and Nation in the Twentieth Century* (Princeton, NJ: Princeton University Press, 2001).

33   Barbour et al., *Coast Redwood*, 136–42; Schrepfer, *Fight to Save the Redwoods*, 12–15, 18–38; Binkley, "No Better Heritage," 5–9. Cohen also describes the professional and business orientation of 1910s and 1920s conservation

philanthropy in California and New York (*History of the Sierra Club*, 11, 53–56).

34   Barbour et al., *Coast Redwood*, 139–42; Binkley, "No Better Heritage," 2–9, 10, 12. Again, see Schrepfer, *Nature's Altars*; and Unger, *Beyond Nature's Housekeepers*, for a discussion of the broader trends nationally of women in the conservation movement.

35   Barbour et al., *Coast Redwood*, 139; Dana and Trask, *California Lands*, 63–64; and Schrepfer, *Fight to Save Redwoods*, 23–25.

36   Barbour et al., *Coast Redwood*, 140; and Schrepfer, *Fight to Save Redwoods*, 29–33

37   Binkley, "No Better Heritage," 12–14.

38   Barbour et al., *Coast Redwood*, 140–42; Binkley, "No Better Heritage," 12–14; "Dyerville Flat Redwoods Fall," *Humboldt Times*, November 25, 1924, 1; "League Acts to Save Dyerville Flat," *Humboldt Standard*, November 25, 1924, 1; Schrepfer, *Fight to Save Redwoods*, 74; and Robin W. Winks, *Laurance S. Rockefeller: Catalyst for Conservation* (Washington, DC: Island Press, 1997), 85. In addition to Schrepfer, Farmer, *Trees in Paradise*, 60–72, recounts the origins of the Save the Redwoods League and the creation of the early parks.

39   For some excellent discussions of the ways women in America opened up the public domain during the Progressive Era, see Glenda Elizabeth Gilmore, *Gender and Jim Crow: Women and the Politics of White Supremacy in North Carolina, 1896–1920* (Chapel Hill: University of North Carolina Press, 1996); Robyn Muncy, *Creating a Female Dominion in American Reform: 1890–1935* (New York: Oxford University Press, 1991); Schrepfer, *Nature's Altars*; and Unger, *Beyond Nature's Housekeepers*.

40   Lizabeth Cohen, *Making of a New Deal: Industrial Workers in Chicago, 1919–1939* (New York: Cambridge University Press, 1990), is a great investigation of how welfare corporatism developed and was instituted.

41   Widdick, *Trouble in the Forest*, chapter 5.

42   Widdick, *Trouble in the Forest*, 107–20; Pacific Lumber Company, "The Pacific Lumber Company and the Redwood Parks," ca. 1970, Pacific Lumber Company file, Forest History Society Library, Durham, NC. Additionally, see Pacific Lumber Company, "Rising from the Ashes," accessed January 30, 2008, www.palco.com.

43   Dana and Krueger, *California Lands*, 68; "Report of the President to the Shareholders, 1917"; John Campbell, interview with the author, Fortuna, CA, April 24, 2008 (tapes and notes in possession of author); and Farmer, *Trees in Paradise*, 74–78.

44   See Schrepfer, *Fight to Save the Redwoods*, 18–37; National Park Service, "Redwood National and State Parks: Area History," accessed July 10, 2015, http://www.nps.gov/redw/learn/historyculture/area-history. htm#CP_JUMP_551084.

45   Ralph W. Hidy, Frank Ernest Hill, and Allan Nevins, *Timber and Men: The Weyerhaeuser Story* (New York: MacMillan, 1963).

46 See Wink, *Laurance S. Rockefeller*, 86, regarding Reagan's alleged comments. See Hirt, *Conspiracy of Optimism*, chapter 6, regarding the postwar timber boom.

47 Joseph Zaremba, *Economics of the American Lumber Industry* (New York: Robert Speller & Sons, 1963), 1, 7, 16–20, 84–90; Paul V. Ellefson and Robert N. Stone, *U.S. Wood-Based Industry: Industrial Organization and Performance* (New York: Praeger, 1984), 25, 359. Additionally, every issue of the trade journal *Forest Industries* from the 1970s and 1980s included at least one article highlighting automation efforts and promoting automation.

48 See Mengel, "Murphy Family and T.P.L.," regarding land purchases.

49 Brooks Atkinson, "Critic at Large: Supporters of Park Exhort the Woodsmen to Spare That Tree, the Redwood," *New York Times*, August 4, 1964, 26; Frank J. Taylor, "Paradise with a Waiting List," *Saturday Evening Post*, February 24, 1951, 36–37, 103–4, 106–7; Jewel M. Larson, "Visit to a Redwood Sawmill," *Christian Science Monitor*, October 9, 1957, 17. See also Pacific Lumber Company, "1950–1998: Investing in the Future," accessed January 30, 2008, www.palco.com.

50 C. Raymond Clar, *California Government and Forestry-II: During the Young and Rolph Administrations* (Sacramento: Division of Forestry, Department of Conservation, State of California, 1969), 36–37, 52, 121–25, 148–50, 189–274. See also Princetl, *Transforming California*, 110, 162–65; Dana and Krueger, *California Lands*, 69–71, 187–88, 192–93; and Barbour et al., *Coast Redwood*, 188.

51 Samuel P. Hays and Roderick Nash provide classic discussions about the changing attitudes of the American public toward natural resources and landscapes during the nineteenth and twentieth centuries (Hays, *Beauty, Health, and Permanence*; and Nash, *Wilderness and the American Mind*). See also Cohen, *History of the Sierra Club*, 114–18 and chapter 4; Harvey, *A Symbol of Wilderness*, 5, 53, 35–57; Turner, *Promise of Wilderness*; and Sellers, *Crabgrass Crucible*. See Rome, *Bulldozer in the Countryside*, regarding influences other than wilderness that drove popular interest in the nonhuman world. See Princetl, *Transforming California*, 163, for a discussion of the protimber attitudes of North Coast residents after World War II.

52 See Cohen, *History of the Sierra Club*, 299–310; Princetl, *Transforming California*, 162–65, regarding the 1950s Sierra Club and Fish and Game complaints. S. B. Show, "Timber Growing Practice in the Coast Redwood Region of California," Technical Bulletin 283, March 1932, in *USDA Technical Bulletins Nos. 276–300* (Washington, DC: US Government Printing Office, 1932); Assembly Interim Committee on Natural Resources, Planning and Public Works, *Findings and Recommendations Related to the Forest Practice Act, 1961–1962*, quoted in Sharon Duggan and Tara Mueller, *A Guide to the California Forest Practice Act and Related Laws* (Point Arena, CA: Solano Press Books, 2005), 1; Assembly Subcommittee on Forest Practices and Watershed Management,

Man's Effect upon the California Watershed, 1965–1967, quoted in Duggan and Mueller, *Guide to the California Forest Practice Act,* 1–2; Committee on Salmon and Steelhead Trout, *An Environmental Tragedy, 1971,* quoted in Duggan and Mueller, *Guide to the California Forest Practice Act,* 2. The history of state legislators, agency employees, and environmentalists pushing these studies and reforms still needs to be told. For this study, the fact that they took place and the framework they set up are the most important aspects of that history because that framework led to changes in law during the 1970s that gave citizens greater access to the bureaucracy and courts.

53 Schrepfer, *Fight to Save the Redwoods,* 135–41, 210–15; Save the Redwoods, "Milestones," accessed July 2015, http://www.savetheredwoods.org/league/milestones.php.

54 See David Perlman, "The Local Boy Who Made Good," *Sierra Bulletin* 41, no. 1 (January 1956): 3–4; Richard M. Leonard, "Directors Hold February Meeting," *Sierra Bulletin* 35, no. 3 (March 1950): 14; Richard M. Leonard, "Board Holds Organization Meeting," *Sierra Bulletin* 35, no. 5 (May 1950): 11; and Richard M. Leonard, "Directors Hold Winter Meeting," *Sierra Bulletin* 35, no. 12 (December 1950): 5–9. McGee Young, "From Conservation to Environment: The Sierra Club and the Organizational Politics of Change," *Studies in American Political Development* 22 (Fall 2008): 183–203, argues that the Dinosaur controversy marked the emergence of a new Sierra Club with a focus on public organizing and a more militant position. McGee is correct for the most part, but he largely ignores the importance of the Hetch Hetchy conflict in the "new" tactics of the club. Muir led a national public relations and letter-writing drive in his effort to protect the Hetch Hetchy Valley, and he blasted opponents as purveyors of greed and selfishness. Looked at from that perspective, Brower simply resurrected Muir's tactics and added new arguments about the importance of ecosystems and ecology. Cohen, *History of the Sierra Club,* 17, 180–81, also recognized this 1950s trend.

55 The story of the Dinosaur National Monument controversy has been well documented by several authors, including Cohen, *History of the Sierra Club,* chapter 4; and Harvey, *A Symbol of Wilderness,* regarding the long fight over Echo Park and Dinosaur National Monument. Harvey argued that new tactics defined the Dinosaur Monument battle, but I see the Dinosaur campaign as revitalizing an older style of environmental politics with the addition of books and film. Susan Schrepfer (*Fight to Save the Redwoods*), Roderick Nash (*Wilderness and the American Mind*), and McGee Young ("From Conservation to Environment") also include discussions.

56 J. W. Penfold, "The Dinosaur Controversy," *Sierra Bulletin* 36, no. 10 (December 1951); Henry Sadler, "Winter Damage in Redwood Parks," *Sierra Bulletin* 41, no. 8 (October 1956): 12–18; Peggy Wayburn and Edward Wayburn, "Our Vanishing Wilderness," *Sierra Bulletin* 42, no. 1 (January 1957): 6–9; and George Ballis, "Havoc in Big Trees," *Sierra Bulletin* 42, no. 5 (May 1957): 10–11.

The ranger quote comes from Susan J. P. O'Hara and Dave Stockton, *Images of America: Humboldt Redwoods State Park* (Charleston, SC: Arcadia, 2012), 118. See also Cohen, *History of the Sierra Club*, 299–310.

57   "Board Adopts Policy Guide, Sets Budget," *Sierra Bulletin* 45, no. 1 (January 1960): 5; Peggy and Edward Wayburn, "Bulletin," *Sierra Bulletin* 44, no. 9 (December 1959); Peggy Wayburn, "The Tragedy of Bull Creek," *Sierra Bulletin* 45, no. 1 (January 1960): 10–11; Newton B. Drury, "Chapter II—Bull Creek Story: Redwoods and You," *Sierra Bulletin* 45, no. 4 (April/May 1960): 10–13; Schrepfer, *Fight to Save Redwoods*, 108–10, 112, 117, 144; and Francois Leydet, *The Last Redwoods and the Parkland of Redwood Creek* (San Francisco: Sierra Club, 1960).

2. THE WAR BEGINS

1   The quote can be found in numerous articles, including Ellen Schultz, "A Raider's Ruckus in the Redwoods," *Fortune*, April 24, 1989, 72; and John Skow, "Redwoods: The Last Stand," *Time*, June 24, 2001, accessed March 7, 2008, http://www.time.com/time/magazine/article/0,9171,1101940606–164513,00.html. The best description of the incident at Scotia is Harris, *The Last Stand*. Some good analyses of general postwar citizen group legal history are Hays, *Beauty, Health, and Permanence*, chapter 14; Lazarus, *The Making of Environmental Policy*; James Salzman and Barton H. Thompson, *Environmental Law and Policy* (New York: Foundation Press, 2003); Joseph L. Sax, *Defending the Environment: A Strategy for Citizen Action* (New York: Alfred A. Knopf, 1971); David B. Sicilia, "The Corporation under Siege: Social Movements, Regulation, Public Relations, and Tort Law since the Second World War," in *Constructing Corporate America: History, Politics, Culture*, ed. Kenneth Lipartito and David B. Sicilia (Oxford: Oxford University Press, 2004); and Richard B. Stewart, "A New Generation of Environmental Regulation?" *Capital University Law Review* 29 (2001): 21–182.

2   For context on globalization trends, see Loomis, *Out of Sight*. See also Hays, *Beauty, Health, and Permanence*; Rome, *Bulldozer in the Countryside*; Sellers, *Crabgrass Crucible*; and Turner, *Promise of Wilderness*.

3   Bonnano and Constance, *Stories of Globalization*, introduction.

4   Marsh, *Drawing Lines in the Forest*.

5   See Runte, *National Parks*, for a full discussion of the evolution of the parks.

6   Wayburn, *Your Land and Mine*, 97–110, 140–68; McCloskey, *In the Thick of It*, 66–80.

7   Schrepfer, *Fight to Save Redwoods*, 119–30; Barbour et al., *Coast Redwood*, 146.

8   Turner, *Promise of Wilderness*, 18, 26.

9   McCloskey, *In the Thick of It*, 66–80; Wayburn, *Your Land and Mine*, 140–71; Wink, *Laurance S. Rockefeller*, 85–94.

10   "Congress Clears Redwood National Park Bill," *CQ Almanac* 1968, 24th ed.,

11–434–11–439 (Washington, DC: Congressional Quarterly, 1969, accessed July 2015, http://library.cqpress.com/cqalmanac/cqal68–1284092); and Schrepfer, *Fight to Save Redwoods*, 130–61, offer very detailed accounts of the legislative and public campaigns to create Redwood National Park, in addition to the Wayburn, McCloskey, and Wink accounts. Regarding the history of park acreages and management, see "Redwood National Park Boundry Adjustment Act of 2004," S. Rep. 108–372 (2004), http://www.gpo.gov/fdsys/pkg/CRPT-108srpt372/html/CRPT-108srpt372.htm. John Campbell also described the long-term disillusionment the park bill instilled among timber executives and forest workers (Campbell interview)

11   Some good analyses of the postwar legal actions of citizen groups include Hays, *Beauty, Health, and Permanence*, chapter 14; Lazarus, *The Making of Environmental Policy*; Salzman and Thompson, *Environmental Law and Policy*; Sax, *Defending the Environment*; Sicilia, "The Corporation under Siege," 188–222; and Richard B. Stewart, "A New Generation of Environmental Regulation?" 21–182. The two 1972 court cases that opened up standing requirements to citizen groups were *Scenic Hudson Preservation Conference v. Federal Power Commission*, 407 US 926, 10; and *Sierra Club v. Morton*, 405 US 727, 25, 73.

12   Dan Walters, "Timbermen Stunned as Forestry Act Declared Void," *Eureka Times Standard*, September 21, 1971, 1; *Bayside Timber Co. v. Board of Supervisors (1971)*, 20 Cal.App.3d 1, 9; Sharon Duggan, "Citizen Enforcement of California's Private Land Forest Practice Regulations," *Journal of Environmental Law and Litigation* 8 (Spring 1994): 300–315.

13   Duggan, "Citizen Enforcement of California's Private Land Forest Practice Regulations." Duggan rightly argues that *Arcata* provided motivation for citizens to watchdog the timber harvest plan review process. However, *Bayside* marks the beginning of the citizen watchdog era because citizens and citizen groups pressured the County Board of Supervisors to reject a harvest plan and argue the unconstitutionality of the 1945 FPA on appeal.

14   "Ecologists and Timbermen Gird for Legislative Tug-of-War," *Los Angeles Times*, January 15, 1973, 3; William Endicott, "Senate OKs Stiff Rules on Logging," *Los Angeles Times*, March 1, 1973, A3; William Endicott, "Conservation Group Withdraws Support of Logging Control Bill," *Los Angeles Times*, July 20, 1973, A3; "An End to Logging Confusion," *Los Angeles Times*, September 14, 1973, B6.

15   Institute of Ecology at the University of California at Davis, *Public Policy for California Forest Lands* (UC Davis, 1972), quoted in Duggan, *Guide to the California Forest Practice Act*, 2–3. See Princetl, *Transforming California*, 167–68; and Barbour et al., *Coast Redwood*, 188–89. For a detailed review of the sections of the 1973 FPA (CA Pub. Res. Code sec. 4511 et seq.), see Duggan, *Guide to the California Forest Practice Act*, 6–9, 790–96.

16   See Turner, *Promise of Wilderness*, 119–66, with respect to the Alaska campaign by environmental groups; and also Hirt, *Conspiracy of Optimism*,

243–47. *Tennessee Valley Authority v. Hill* (437 US 153, 261) was the first lawsuit regarding the implementation of the Endangered Species Act, and *Lead Industries Association v. EPA* (647 F.2d 1130, 81) was the first litigation over the implementation of the Clean Air Act.

17　The citizen suit provision of the Forest Practice Act is in Public Resource Code section 4514.5. The ability to challenge discretionary actions is found in Code of Civil Procedure, sections 1085 and 1094.5. See Duggan, *Guide to the California Forest Practice Act*, 797–98, for a discussion of standing issues in California.

18　William H. Rodgers, Jr., *Environmental Law*, 2d ed. (Saint Paul, MN: West Publishing, 1994), 818, 836; *Calvert Cliffs Coordinating Committee v. Atomic Energy Commission*, 146 U.S.App.D.C. 33, 449 F.2d 1109, 1 ELR 20346 (1971); and *The Wilderness Society v. Hickel*, 325 F Supp. 422 (DDC 1970).

19　*National Resources Defense Council v. Arcata National Corporation and Lewis A. Moran, State Forester*, 59 Cal.App.3d 945 (1976); 58 Ops.Cal.Atty.Gen 250 (1975). The California Environmental Quality Act is California Public Resources Code (CA PRC), secs. 21000–21006, 21050, 21060–72, 21080–98, 21100–21108, 21150–54, 21156–59.9, 21160–62, 21165–77.

20　See Schrepfer, *Fight to Save Redwoods*, 194–200, for a discussion of the *Arcata* case and park expansion efforts. Regarding the expansion bill, see Kent W. Olson, Ronald L. Moomaw, and Richard P. Thompson, "Redwood National Park Expansion: Impact on Old-Growth Redwood Stumpage Prices," *Land Economics* 64, no. 4 (August 1988): 269–75; and Jimmy Carter, "Redwood National Park Expansion Bill Statement of Signing H.R. 3813 into Law," March 27, 1978.

21　See Turner, *Promise of Wilderness*, 187–91; and Hays, *Wars in the Woods*, 14–17, regarding the *Monongahela* decision and the National Forest Management Act. See Turner, *Promise of Wilderness*, 143–80, regarding the Alaska National Interest Lands Act campaign and President Carter's national monument declaration.

22　Barbour et al., *Coast Redwood*, 189–90; *Gallegos v. California State Board of Forestry*, 76 Cal.App.32 945 (1978).

23　In addition to the published court opinions and regulations, Sharon Duggan offers a detailed analysis of codes, laws, and rulings of the 1970s regarding CEQA, the Timberland Productivity Act, and the FPA. The article also provides analysis of a few of the subsequent rulings related to defining the laws regulating timber harvesting in California that this paper does not cover. See Duggan, *Citizen Enforcement of California's Private Land Forest Practice Regulations*.

24　See Schrepfer, *Fight to Save Redwoods*, 129–28, for a detailed account of the 1968 and 1978 efforts to create Redwood National Park.

25　Richard Gienger, interview with the author, Redway, CA, March 22, 2007 (tapes and notes in possession of author); interview with Greg King, "The

Econews Report," KHSU radio, March 1, 2007 (audio file archived at http://nec.streamguys.us/gregking.mp3).

26 Robert Sutherland, interview with author, Arcata, CA, April 22, 2008 (audio tapes and notes in possession of author); Gienger interview; Ruthanne Cecil, phone interview with author, January 6, 2016; and Ruthanne Cecil, e-mail message to author, January 6, 2016.

27 Sutherland interview.

28 "Organizational History and Goals," EPIC Publications binder, Environmental Protection Information Center, Redway, CA; Kathy Bailey, interview by the author, March 20–21, 2007, Philo, CA (tapes and notes in possession of author); Kevin Bundy, interview by the author, April 26, 2007, San Francisco, CA (tapes and notes in possession of author); Sharon Duggan, interview by the author, Oakland, CA, April 27, 2007 (notes and tapes in possession of author); Gienger interview; Paul Mason, phone interview with the author, February 16, 2007 (notes in possession of author); Sutherland interview.

29 David Cross, "Sally Bell Redwoods Protected! Sinkyone Coast Purchased for Park," *Earth First! Journal*, February 2, 1987, 1–4.

30 Cross, "Sally Bell Redwoods Protected!" 1–4.

31 Cross, "Sally Bell Redwoods Protected!" 4; Duggan interview and correspondence with author; Gienger interview. See Cohen, *History of the Sierra Club*, chapter 1; and Harvey, *Symbol of Wilderness*, 164–66, regarding the historical value of field trips.

32 Cross, "Sally Bell Redwoods Protected!" 4; Duggan interview and correspondence with author; Gienger interview. See Harvey, *Symbol of Wilderness*, 209, regarding David Brower and Bernard DeVoto's aggressive attacks irritating more moderate, genteel conservation groups in the 1950s.

33 *EPIC v. Johnson*, 170 Cal.App.3d 694, 4 and 12 (1985), regarding "keystone" determination; Harvey, *Symbol of Wilderness*, 6, 52–57, 95.

34 Gienger interview; Foreman, *Confessions of an Eco-Warrior*, 11–23; Scarce, *Eco-Warriors*, 67–78; Zakin, *Coyotes and Town Dogs*, chapter 7.

35 Zakin, *Coyotes and Town Dogs*, 231–60.

36 Duggan, Gienger, and Sutherland interviews and correspondence; Cross, "Sally Bell Redwoods Protected!" 4.

37 Cross, "Sally Bell Redwoods Protected!" 4; Ann Levin and Mari Ragan, "Environmentalists Ready to Chain Themselves to the Trees if It Will Save Redwoods," *Christian Science Monitor*, December 13, 1985, 3; Gienger interview; King interview, "The Econews Report." Gienger and 1990 car bomb victim Darryl Cherney would later purchase Maxxam stock to attend shareholder meetings in Houston so he could protest the logging of Headwaters Forest. Shareholder activism grew in the 1990s, used most prominently by activists working to stop attempts to drill for oil in the Arctic National Wildlife Refuge.

38 Duggan interview; Gienger interview; Sutherland interview.

39   Cross, "Sally Bell Redwoods Protected!" 4; Levin, "Environmentalists Ready to Chain Themselves," 3; Gienger interview; King interview, "The Econews Report"; and Darryl Cherney, interview with the author, Redway, CA, April 23, 2008.

40   *EPIC v. Johnson,* 170 Cal.App.3d 694, 4 and 12 (on "keystone" determination), 1–6 (on EPIC's arguments), and 9–12 (on CDF arguments and the court's analysis of the arguments) (1985). See pages 8–15 for the substance of the court's analysis.

41   The preceding two paragraphs draw on Cross, "Sally Bell Redwoods Protected!"; Levin, "Environmentalists Ready to Chain Themselves"; Gienger interview; King interview, "The Econews Report"; and Cherney interview.

42   "Memorandum of Points and Authorities in Support of the Petition for Writ of Mandate, Complaint for Injunction, Declaratory Relief and Attorneys' Fees," *Environmental Protection Information Center, et al. v. Ross Johnson, Resources Manager of the California Department of Forestry, et al.,* Superior Court of Mendocino County, Case No. 51969, March 28, 1986, unprocessed Archives of the Environmental Protection Information Center, Eureka, CA; "Epic v. Johnson II," in "Summary of EPIC Litigation," EPIC unprocessed archives, Eureka, CA; Cross, "Sally Bell Redwoods Protected!" 4; Levin, "Environmentalists Ready to Chain Themselves," 3.

43   Sharon Duggan cites *Gallegos* and *Seghesio v. County of Napa,* 185 Cal. Rptr. 224, 982, as the two previous THP challenges in "Citizen Enforcement," 12n55.

3. RADICALIZATION

1   Phil Garlington, "The Predator's Maul," *Outside,* December 1988, 38, EPIC archives, publication binder; Chase, *In a Dark Wood,* 241–43.

2   The Greg King quotes are from Bill McKibben, "Milken, Junk Bonds, and Raping the Redwoods," in *The Bill McKibben Reader: Pieces from an Active Life* (New York: Holt , 2008), 303–10.

3   Hays, *Beauty, Health, and Permanence,* chapter 9; Turner, *Promise of Wilderness,* 10, 253–67.

4   Hays, *Beauty, Health, and Permanence,* chapter 9; Gottlieb, *Forcing the Spring,* chapter 4; Helvarg, *War against the Greens*; Kraft, *Environmental Policy and Politics,* chapter 4; Lazarus, *Making of Environmental Policy,* chapter 6, for discussion of the 1980s federal attacks on the 1970s environmental regulations and laws.

5   Hays, *Beauty, Health, and Permanence,* chapter 15; and Turner, *Promise of Wilderness,* 204–9.

6   This popular narrative is so strong that Representatives Pete Stark and George Brown of California published an op-ed in the *New York Times* describing Pacific Lumber Company as a "model corporate citizen" before the takeover. George Brown and Pete Stark, "The Last Stand," *New York Times,* December 1, 1995, A33.

7   Also identifying transportation, automation, and conservation as the three major timber industry trends during twentieth century are Hidy, Hill, and Nevins, *Timber and Men*; Michael V. Namorato, "Lumber and Wood Products, 24.0," in *Manufacturing: A Historiographical and Bibliographical Guide*, ed. David O. Whitten and Bessie E. Whitten (Westport, CT: Greenwood Press, 2000), 117–31; Zaremba, *Economics of American Lumber*, 2–3; and Ellefson and Stone, *U.S. Wood-based Industry*, 359.

8   John Campbell interview with the author, Fortuna, CA, April 24, 2008; Pacific Lumber Company, *1981 Annual Report*, Washington, DC, Library of Congress; Pacific Lumber Company, *1982 Annual Report*, 5; Stanwood A. Murphy obituary, *New York Times*, August 10, 1972, 38; Pacific Lumber Company, *1976 Annual Report*, 1, 10; Pacific Lumber Company, *1980 Annual Report*, 6, 18.

9   Pacific Lumber Company, *1977 Annual Report*, 3; Pacific Lumber Company, *1978 Annual Report*, 3; Pacific Lumber Company, *1979 Annual Report*, 3; Pacific Lumber Company, *1980 Annual Report*, 2–3; Pacific Lumber Company, *1981 Annual Report*, 2, 3, 14; "Briefs: Debt Issues," *New York Times*, June 16, 1983, D8.

10   Pacific Lumber Company, *1980 Annual Report*, 4–16; Campbell interview. In 1988, Campbell told the *New York Times* that increased harvest levels were the industry norm and that clear-cuts were a responsible form of logging. Robert Lindsey, "Ancient Redwoods Fall to a Wall Street Takeover," *New York Times*, March 3, 1988, A16.

11   Pacific Lumber Company, *1980 Annual Report*, 4; Harris, *The Last Stand*, 45–47; John Campbell, interview with author, April 24, 2008. The company's annual reports are clear about their redwood strategy, divestiture efforts, and labor strategy. See Pacific Lumber Company, *1976 Annual Report*, 3; *1978 Annual Report*, 3; *1979 Annual Report*, 4; *1980 Annual Report*, 3, 4, 6; *1981 Annual Report*, 2; *1982 Annual Report*, 2; and "Brief," *Wall Street Journal*, February 20, 1985, 16.

12   Campbell interview.

13   The preceding paragraphs all draw on the Campbell interview.

14   The biographical detail in the preceding paragraphs come from Campbell interview; Bruce Weber, "John Campbell, Logging Chief, Dies at 67," *New York Times*, October 24, 2008, A29. In 1990, Campbell told the *Sydney Morning Herald* that he had always believed Pacific Lumber's job was to intensify management and grow more board feet (Wanda Jamrozik, "Black Future for Redwoods," *Sydney Morning Herald*, November 11, 1990, 79). Campbell relied on the argument that young-growth trees grow more each year than old growth, so a young forest produces more new board feet per year.

15   Campbell interview; Chris Bowman, "The Redwood Wars," *Sacramento Bee Magazine*, February 12, 1989, 10, EPIC archives, publications binder, Redway, CA; and Harris, *The Last Stand*, 45–47.

16   "Corporate Balance Sheet Scoreboard," *Business Week*, August 1, 1983, 64; Pacific Lumber Company, *1980 Annual Report*, 3,4, 6; Pacific Lumber Company, *1981 Annual Report*, 2; and Pacific Lumber Company, *1982 Annual Report*, 2.

17   "Biography," Charles Hurwitz website, http://charleshurwitz.com/leadership .html; S. C. Gwynne, "Tree Ring Circus," *Texas Monthly*, April 2006; Paula Kepos, "MAXXAM Inc." in *International Directory of Company Histories*, vol. 8 (Detroit: St. James Press, 1994); Stephen J. Sansweet, "Once Unwelcome as a Holder, Hurwitz Has Become McCulloch Oil Chairman," *Wall Street Journal*, March 27, 1980, 16; "McCulloch Oil Seen Losing a Board Seat to Hurwitz Interest over Its Opposition," *Wall Street Journal*, May 11, 1978, 4; "Federated Development Says SEC Is Studying SMR's Take-Over of It," *Wall Street Journal*, Dec. 18, 1973, 4.

18   "MAXXAM Inc.," in *International Directory of Company Histories*; Sansweet, "Once Unwelcome as a Holder"; "Black&Decker Sells McCulloch Oil Stake to Option Holder," *Wall Street Journal*, May 9, 1978, 18; "McCulloch Oil Corp.'s Management Loses Two Board Seats to Hurwitz's Candidates," *Wall Street Journal*, May 12, 1978, 12; "Inside the Times," *Los Angeles Times*, May 17, 1978, SD2; "McCulloch Oil Elects C. E. Hurwitz Director," *Wall Street Journal*, Aug. 9, 1978, 24; Al Degugach, "Texas Financier Settles Suit with Beverly Hills REIT," *Los Angeles Times*, January 29, 1979, D12; "McCulloch Oil Names Charles E. Hurwitz Chairman and Chief," *Wall Street Journal*, March 20, 1980, 29; Al Delugach, "Hurwitz Gets Strong Vote to Deter Take-over of McCulloch," *Los Angeles Times*, June 19, 1980, F1; "Company News," *New York Times*, July 10, 1980, D4; Pamela G. Hollie, "The Man Who Won McCulloch Oil," *New York Times*, July 13, 1980, F11; and "Business in Brief," *Los Angeles Times*, E2.

19   Campbell interview.

20   Mark Ivey, "Charles Hurwitz Doesn't Bark, He Just Bites," *Business Week*, December 10, 1984, 73; Charles E. Huwitz, "Charles Hurwitz Calls It a 'Soap Opera' Portrait," *Business Week*, December 31, 1984, 8; Thomas C. Hayes, "Hurwitz Group Buying 33% of Simplicity Stock," *New York Times*, May 11, 1982, D6; Janet Guyon, "Simplicity Halts Payout after 37 Years when Stormy Meeting Elects New Board," *Wall Street Journal*, July 27, 1982, 37; "What's News," *Wall Street Journal*, March 12, 1984, 1; David E. Sanger, "Bid Fought by Castle & Cooke," *New York Times*, March 12, 1984, D1; Mike Tharp, "Castle & Cooke Is Facing Tough Time; Concern Awaits Decision about Loans," *Wall Street Journal*, December 26, 1984, 5; "Investor Buys 6% of UNC," *Washington Post*, October 30, 1984, E3; "Houston Investor Raises Stake in UNC," *Washington Post*, November 12, 1984, 3; Elizabeth Ehrlich, "Behind the Amf Takeover: From Highflier to Sitting Duck," *Business Week*, August 12, 1985, 50; Nell Henderson, "Hurwitz Firm Buys 6.7% of UNC Resources," *Washington Post*, March 19, 1985, D5; Nell Henderson, "Hurwitz Adds to UNC Stake,"

Washington Post, April 29, 1985, 11; "Finance Briefs," *New York Times*, May 17, 1985, D11; "Briefs," *New York Times*, May 23, 1985, D21; Bill Richards, "Amsted Adopts 'Poison Pill' Step against Takeovers," *Wall Street Journal*, May 31, 1985, 8; and "MAXXAM Inc.," in *International Directory of Company Histories*.

21 Gene G. Marcial, "A Stock for Armchair Raiders," *Business Week*, June 10, 1985, 110; "Company Briefs," *New York Times*, July 9, 1985, D5; "Hurwitz Planning a Bid for Pacific Lumber Co.," *New York Times*, October 1, 1985, D19; Hank Gilman and Mike Tharp, "Maxxam Plans Bid to Acquire Pacific Lumber," *Wall Street Journal*, October 1, 1985, 2; Mark Walters, "California's Chain-Saw Massacre," *Reader's Digest*, November 1989, 144, EPIC archives, publication binder, Redway, CA; David Anderson, "PL Rearranges, Grows during Maxxam Decade," *Eureka Times Standard*, October 29, 1995, EPIC archives, Eureka, CA. See part 1 of Harris, *The Last Stand*, for a detailed journalistic account of the takeover and the events surrounding it.

22 Campbell interview; Harris, *The Last Stand*, 31–36; Schultz, "A Raider's Ruckus"; "Legal Proceedings on Maxxam Bid," *New York Times*, November 30, 1985, 30; Kenneth N. Gilpin, "Business People: Pacific-Maxxam Link Is Fought by a Family," *New York Times*, November 11, 1985, D2; John Goff, "Angry Harvest," *Corporate Finance*, April 1989, 53, EPIC archives, publication binder, Redway, CA; Walters, "California's Chain-Saw Massacre"; "Stock Plans by Maxxam," *New York Times*, December 2, 1985, D2; "Maxxam Gains Control of Pacific Lumber," *Washington Post*, December 6, 1985, F1; "MAXXAM Inc.," in *International Directory of Company Histories*; Allan Sloan, "Thrift Regulators Slipping and Tripping over One Another's Feet," *Washington Post*, April 16, 1991, D3. The *Washington Post* alleges the takeover was the first; the International Directory says one of the earliest.

23 Campbell interview.

24 Campbell interview; Schultz, "A Raider's Ruckus"; Pacific Lumber Company, Form S-2, Registration No. 33–56332, December 28, 1992, EPIC archives, Eureka, CA; "FINANCE: $680.5 Million Sale at Pacific Lumber," *New York Times*, July 2, 1986, D16; Leonard M. Apcar, "Maxxam to Sell Most of Palco for $320 Million," *Wall Street Journal*, August 18, 1987, 15; Peter H. Frank, "Palco's Acquirer Plans to Linger after the Deal," *New York Times*, August 21, 1987, D2.

25 Thomas E. Ricks, "Big Board Urged SEC in '86 to Examine Trading in Pacific Lumber, Panel Says," *Wall Street Journal*, October 6, 1987, 12.

26 Connie Bruck, *The Predators' Ball: The Inside Story of Drexel Burnham and the Rise of the Junk Bond Raiders* (New York: American Lawyer/Simon and Schuster, 1988); and Michael Lewis, *Liar's Poker: Rising through the Wreckage on Wall Street* (New York: W. W. Norton, 1989), remain two of the best descriptions of the 1980s insider trading scandals.

27 David A. Vise and Peter Behr, "SEC Subpoena Probes Boesky's Fees to Drexel," *Washington Post*, January 15, 1987, A1; Bailey Morris, "SEC Focus on

Boesky Payments," *Times* (London), January 16, 1987; Brian McTigue interview with author, May 9, 2009; "Denial Made on 'Parking,'" *New York Times*, October 6, 1987, D2; Thomas E. Ricks and Daniel Hertzberg, "Ex-Jeffries Aide May Have Parked Stock for Hurwitz, Congressional Report Says," *Wall Street Journal*, October 5, 1987, 3.

28 See Cohen, *History of the Sierra Club*, 304–7; Harvey, *Symbol of Wilderness*, chapter 8.

29 EPIC Summary Sheets for Pacific Lumber Timber Harvest Plans 1980–July 1990, papers of Kathy Bailey, Philo, CA; Kathy Bailey to Ed, "Re: Prop 130 Effects on Pacific Lumber," September 8, 1990, papers of Kathy Bailey, Philo, CA; Campbell interview.

30 Bill Devall and George Sessions, *Deep Ecology* (Salt Lake City, UT: G. M. Smith, 1985). Turner, *Promise of Wilderness*, 216, 272–73, discusses the connections among deep ecology, environmentalists, and scientists. Darryl Cherney interview.

31 Arne Naess, *Ecology, Community, and Lifestyle: Outline of an Ecosophy* (Cambridge: Cambridge University Press, 1989); Cherney interview; Sutherland interview; Kevin Bundy, interview with the author, San Francisco, CA, April 26, 2007 (all tape recordings and handwritten notes in possession of author). The groups of activists on the North Coast doing work under the name Earth First! operated under different names at different times, such as Redwood Action Team, Ecotopia Earth First!, Ukiah Earth First!, Humboldt Earth First!, the Albion Nation, and North Coast Earth First!. I use North Coast Earth First! when referring to the group writ large and only use the subnames when it is necessary to set some group or action apart from the whole. Roderick Nash, *The Rights of Nature: A History of Environmental Ethics* (Madison: University of Wisconsin Press, 1989); and Merchant, *Radical Ecology*, are two excellent studies of the concepts and influence of Naess, Devall, and Sessions.

32 Cherney interview.

33 Cherney interview; Harris, *The Last Stand*, 141–45; Greg King, Testimony to the Humboldt County Board of Supervisors, "Re: Emergency TPZ Ordinance," November 6, 2007, accessed July 28, 2009, at http://www.asje.org/documents/GregKingHumboldtSupes11_06_07.pdf.

34 Thomas Fields-Meyer, "Forest Gumption," *People*, November 11, 1996.

35 "A Few of the People & Groups," undated, anonymous memo, papers of Kathy Bailey, Philo, CA; Betty Ball, by Jennifer Davis, OH1233, interview transcript, Maria Rogers Oral History Program Collection, Carnegie Branch Library for Local History, Boulder, CO.

36 "National Conference Begins Today," *Miami Herald*, September 21, 1986, SH3; "Warning on Rain Forests," *San Francisco Chronicle*, September 22, 1986, 19; Garvey Winegar, "Doves Avoid Media, Frying Pan," *Richmond Times-Dispatch*, September 23, 1986, C5; Boyce Rensberger, "A Fear of Mass

Extinctions—Some Say Thousands of Species Are Vanishing," *San Francisco Chronicle*, October 22, 1986, A10.

37   Cherney interview; Fields-Meyer, "Forest Gumption"; Darryl Cherney, "History of Headwaters Campaign—an Outline, 1998, 2007," papers of Darryl Cherney, Redway, CA; King, Testimony to Humboldt County. For the broader environmental context, see Turner, *Promise of Wilderness*, 191, 222–23, 275, 283–85.

38   Cherney interview; Cherney, "History of Headwaters Campaign"; Earth First!, "Schedule—Scotia Rally, December 3, 1986," press release, EPIC archives, Eureka, CA.

39   Cherney interview; Cherney, "History of Headwaters."

40   Cherney interview; Cherney, "History of Headwaters"; Larry B. Stammer, "Eco-Terrorists Focus of Mill Accident Probe," *Los Angeles Times*, May 15, 1987; Eric Brazil, "Tree Spiking in Mendocino Splinters All Sides," *San Francisco Examiner*, June 21, 1987. The *Press Democrat* headline was "Tree Spiking Terrorism," and the *Times Standard* headline read, "Earth First! Blamed for Worker's Injuries." Bari, *Timber Wars*, 267–70.

41   The Greg King quotes are from McKibben, "Milken, Junk Bonds, and Raping the Redwoods."

42   Bari, *Timber Wars*, 267–70. See Harvey, *Symbol of Wilderness*, 6, 52–57, 95, 130–31, regarding crafting an identity for Dinosaur National Monument in the 1950s as one example; *The Last Stand: Ancient Redwoods and the Bottom Line*, dir. Holiday R. Phelan (Trillium Films, 2000), videocassette; Garlington, "The Predator's Maul"; Chase, *In a Dark Wood*, 241–43.

43   Campbell interview.

44   Campbell interview; Stanford Environmental Law Society, *The Endangered Species Act* (Palo Alto, CA: Stanford University Press, 2001), chapters 1 and 5.

45   Cherney interview; Sutherland interview.

46   Greg King, "Headwaters Forest Alert," *Country Activist* 6, no. 10 (November 1989): 8, EPIC archives, publications binder, Redway, CA; *EPIC v. Maxxam*, Humboldt Superior Court #79879, August 13, 1987, Judge Peterson, 2–4.

47   See Turner, *Promise of Wilderness*, for an excellent discussion of changing public land policies.

48   *EPIC v. Maxxam*, 4 Cal. App. 4th 1373 (1992). The marbled murrelet regulations are found in CA. Code Regs., title 14, sec. 895.1, 912, 919.13, and 919.14. The spotted owl regulations are in CCR, title 14, sec. 919.6(d)(1), 919.9, and 919.10. The cumulative impact regulations are in the FPR, sec. 985.1, 898, and 912.9.

49   Sutherland interview; the Man Who Walks in the Woods, "The California Forest Practices Act: Is It Tough Enough?" *Forest Watch Report*, December 1986 (published by CHEC, PO Box 3479, Eugene, OR 97403), 1; the Man Who Walks in the Woods, "How to Sue CDF," December 1987, EPIC archives;

Robert Sutherland, "Environmental Position on Sustained Yield and Old Growth," presentation to the annual convention of the California Licensed Foresters Association, Redding, CA, March 4, 1988; the Man Who Walks in the Woods, "Vision of Future Forestry in Mendocino County," presentation to the Forestry Forum, Willits, CA, April 23, 1988; Robert Sutherland, "Environmental Agenda for the Future of California Forestry," presentation to the National Convention of the National Association of State Foresters," Eureka, CA, September 12, 1988; the Man Who Walks in the Woods to Ruthanne Cecil, EPIC Board of Directors, October 4, 1985, EPIC archives, Eureka, CA; Bailey interview; Cherney interview. These sources can be found in the publications binder, EPIC Archives, Redway, CA.

50 Bari, "About the Author," in *Timber Wars*; Scarce, *Eco-Warriors*, 81; Nicholas Wilson, "Judi Bari Dies But Her Struggle Continues," *Albion Monitor*, March 2, 1997, accessed on July 15, 2009, www.monitor.net/monito/bari/barideath3.html.

51 Quoted in Kathy Bailey, "A Timeline History of Logging Reform in Mendocino County: DRAFT," memo for Sierra Club California, papers of Kathy Bailey, Philo, CA.

52 Untitled L-P factsheet, EPIC archives, publications binder, Redway, CA; Bailey, "Timeline History of Logging"; Charles Winkler, "Don't Go to Mexico, Signs Urge L-P," *Eureka Times Standard*, Thursday, December 28, 1989, 1, EPIC archives, publication binder, Redway, CA; Goff, "Angry Harvest," 53; Cherney, "History of Headwaters Campaign."

53 Cherney interview; Cherney, "History of Headwaters Campaign."

54 Bari, *Timber Wars*, 97–98.

55 Bari, *Timber Wars*, 10, 60; Cherney interview; Cherney, "History of Headwaters Campaign"; Harris, *The Last Stand*, 275–77.

56 Bari, *Timber Wars*, 290–91; Cherney interview; Cherney, "History of Headwaters Campaign"; Wilson, "Judi Bari Dies."

57 Campbell interview.

58 Caleb Solomon, "Small Energy Firm Could Spoil Record of Tough Financier," *Wall Street Journal*, February 4, 1988, 19; "Maxxam Will Buy Kaisertech Stake," *New York Times*, March 1, 1988, D5; Robert Lindsey, "Ancient Redwoods Fall to a Wall Street Takeover," *New York Times*, March 2, 1988, A16; Donald Worster, *Rivers of Empire: Water, Aridity, and the Growth of the American West* (New York: Oxford University Press, 1985), argues on behalf of viewing the American West of the twentieth century in eastern colonial terms with respect to water storage and hydropower. I see the Appalachia quote as evidence of North Coasters seeing themselves in colonized terms as well. "Don't Clamp Down on the Dealmakers," *Business Week*, March 21, 1988, 170; "Company Briefs," *New York Times*, March 25, 1988, D5; Danial Akst and Brenton R. Schlender, "MCO Holdings Agrees to Buy KaiserTech Ltc.," *Wall Street Journal*, May 24, 1988, 2; "Drexel, Milken, Boesky Sued by Ex-Holders

of Pacific Lumber Co.," *Wall Street Journal*, September 8, 1989, C8; David J. Jefferson, "Suit on Takeover of Pacific Lumber Tied to Drexel Case," *Wall Street Journal*, October 24, 1988, 5.

59   The first case was *EPIC v. Maxxam* (HUM 79879, June 4, 1987). The second case was *EPIC v. Maxxam* (HUM 81790, May 17, 1988). Dept. of Forestry denied THPs 1–88–65 and 1–88–74 on April 19, 1988, because the company did not include wildlife surveys. *Sierra Club and EPIC v. California Board of Forestry*, 4 Cal. App. 4th 982 (1992); Lawrence M. Fisher, "Company Eases Its Policy on Logging of Redwoods," *New York Times*, May 27, 1988, A13.

60   Goff, "Angry Harvest"; Schultz, "A Raider's Ruckus."

61   Bowman, "The Redwood Wars"; McKibben, "Milken, Junk Bonds, and Raping Redwoods"; Walters, "California's Chain-Saw Massacre."

62   Bailey interview. The other three major blows to corporatism were the *Bayside, Gallegos*, and *Johnson* cases. *Sierra Club v. California State Board of Forestry*, 7 Cal. 4th 1215, 18; Robert Lyndsey, "California Officials Limit the Harvesting of Older Redwoods," *New York Times*, April 22, 1988, A13.

63   *Sierra Club v. California State Board of Forestry*, 7 Cal. 4th 1215, 1, 4–7, 12, 18; Duggan, "Citizen Enforcement," 8; Kathy Bailey, memo to Chuck Powell, Cecelia Lanman, Paul Mason, and Kevin Bundy, Draft 1, August 19, 1997, papers of Kathy Bailey, Philo, CA.

64   Robert Sutherland, e-mail messages to the author, November 18 and 19, 2009; Bowman, "The Redwood Wars"; Cecelia Lanman, résumé, circa 1990, papers of Kathy Bailey, Philo, CA; "A Few of the People & Groups"; *Headwaters Forest Act: Hearing on H.R. 2866 before the Subcommittee on Specialty Crops and Natural Resources of the Committee on Agriculture*, 103rd Congress 42 (October 13, 1993); Robert Sutherland, e-mail message to author, July 15, 2009. See White, "Are You an Environmentalist or Do You Work for a Living?" White argues the modern environmental movement is largely based on middle-class values and an understanding of nature based on science, which tends to exclude the knowledge and values of workers. The North Coast activists don't really fit that bill. They valued science, local knowledge and tradition, participatory democracy, and their own experiences in the forest simultaneously.

65   During my interviews with EPIC staff members Richard Gienger, Sharon Duggan, and Kevin Bundy, they each expressed the anxiety EPIC felt about the size, direction, and scope of the Headwaters conflict, and each stated that EPIC wanted to continue its challenges to CDF even while Headwaters work consumed ever more time and energy. Kevin Bundy, April 26, 2007, San Francisco, CA (all tape recordings and handwritten notes in possession of author). See Settlement Agreement, CDF, Californians for Native Salmon and Steelhead Association, EPIC, and Fred "Coyote" Downy; and *Californians for Native Salmon and Steelhead Association v. Department of Forestry*; 221 Cal.App.3d 1419 (1990), EPIC unprocessed archives, Eureka, CA.

1   See Charles Payne, *I've Got the Light of Freedom: The Organizing Tradition and the Mississippi Freedom Struggle* (Berkeley: University of California Press, 1995).

2   Helvarg, *War against the Greens*, 240–51; Kathy Bailey, "A Timeline History of Logging Reform in Mendocino County: DRAFT," memo for Sierra Club California, unknown date, papers of Kathy Bailey, Philo, CA; Mike Geniella, "Bari Trial Pressed over FBI Problems," *Eureka Times Standard*, April 7, 1997, EPIC archives, Redway, CA; Cherney, "History of Headwaters"; Katherine Bishop, "2 Won't Be Charged in Bombing Case," *New York Times*, July 18, 1990, A14; Elliot Diringer, "Earth First Leaders Sue Authorities over Oakland Blast/Police Accused of Not Looking for Bomber," *San Francisco Chronicle*, May 22, 1991, A17.

3   Erik Eckholm, "Species Are Lost before They're Found," *New York Times*, September 16, 1986, C1; Andrew Pollack, "Not without the Rain Forests," *New York Times*, March 5, 1992, D9; Boyce Rensberger, "A Fear of Mass Extinctions—Some Say Thousands of Species Are Vanishing," *Washington Post*, October 22, 1986, A10; Edward O. Wilson, "Bulldozing Forests Costs Us Genetic Wonders," *San Jose Mercury News*, January 7, 1987, 7B.

4   Maura Dolan, "Organizers Put All the Elements into Worldwide Earth Day Series: Earth Day 1970–1990: The Environmental Movement Comes of Age," *Los Angeles Times*, April 20, 1990; Barry Meier, "It's Green and Growing Fast, But Is It Good for the Earth?" *New York Times*, April 21, 1990, 48; Michael Oreskes, "Earth Day 1990: Political Memo: G.O.P. Fears It Is Losing Points on Environment," *New York Times*, April 23, 1990, B12; Wolfgang Saxon, "On Earth Day, Plans to Make a Point: Tree Plantings, and Elephants Stomping Cans," *New York Times*, April 21, 1990, 8; Sharon Begley, Mary Hager, and Brook Larmer, "American Risks Being a Leader without Followers," *Newsweek*, June 22, 1992, 46; and Gallup Historical Trends/Environment, accessed July 26, 2015, http://www.gallup.com/poll/1615/environment.aspx.

5   Hays, *Beauty, Health, and Permanence*, chapter 15; Helvarg, *War against the Greens*, 47, 165, and chapter 9.

6   "EPIC Summary Sheets for Pacific Lumber THP's: 1980–July 1990," EPIC archives, Eureka, CA.

7   Chris Bowman, "The Redwood Wars," *Sacramento Bee Magazine*, February 12, 1989, 10, EPIC archives, publications binder, Redway, CA; Goff, "Angry Harvest"; Lindsey, "Ancient Redwoods Fall."

8   Kathy Bailey, interview by the author, March 20, 2007, Philo, CA (tape recordings and notes in possession of author).

9   Bailey interview; Robert Sutherland, e-mail message to the author, December 31, 2015.

10   Kathy Bailey to Ed, "Re: Prop 130 effects on Pacific Lumber," September 8,

1990, papers of Kathy Bailey, Philo, CA; Bailey interview; personal correspondence with Bailey, September 14, 2009; Sutherland interview.

11 Jerry F. Franklin, "Toward a New Forestry," *American Forests* 95, nos. 11–12
(November–December 1989): 37–44; and Anna Maria Gillis, "The New Forestry: An Ecosystem Approach to Land Management," *Bioscience* 40 (1990):
558–62.

12 Forests Forever Initiative, "Forest and Wildlife Protection and Bond Act of
1990," submitted January 12, 1990, personal papers of Kathy Bailey, Philo,
CA.

13 Bailey interview; personal correspondence with Bailey, September 14, 2009;
Andrew Pollack, "Logging Regulation Bill Vetoed in California," *New York
Times*, October 13, 1991; personal correspondence with Doug Phelps, chair-
man of the board, CALPIRG, October 1, 2009.

14 Bailey interview; Kathy Bailey, memo to Chuck Powell, Cecelia Lanman,
Paul Mason, and Kevin Bundy, Draft 1, August 19, 1997, papers of Kathy Bailey, Philo, CA; Kathy Bailey, e-mail to the author, September 14, 2009.

15 Mike Geniella, "Timber Tempest," *Press Democrat* (Santa Rosa), January 14,
1990, A1, EPIC archives, publication binder, Redway, CA; Jane Kay, "3 Competing Initiatives to Protect the Forests," *San Francisco Examiner*, January 21,
1990, EPIC archives, publications binder, Redway, CA; Jane Kaye, "North
Coast Split over Logging of Old Growth," *San Francisco Examiner*, January
21, 1990, A1; Bailey interview; Kathy Bailey, memo to Chuck Powell, Cecelia
Lanman, Paul Mason, and Kevin Bundy, Draft 1, August 19, 1997, papers of
Kathy Bailey, Philo, CA; Mark Rathjen, "Lawmakers Hopeful Agreements
Will End Local Timber Wars," *Eureka Times Standard*, February 9, 1990, EPIC
archives, Redway, CA.

16 Woods to Kathy Bailey, Betty Ball, Steven Day, Gil Gregori, Cecelia Lanman,
Pam Limpanson, Eric Swanson, January 26, 1990, papers of Kathy Bailey,
Philo, CA; David Edelson to Leo McElroy, March 14, 1990, papers of Kathy
Bailey, Philo, CA; Bailey interview; Sutherland interview; Robert Suther-
land, "Environmental Agenda for the Future of California Forestry," pre-
sentation to the National Association of State Foresters, September 12, 1988,
Eureka, CA, publications binder, EPIC archives; and Robert Sutherland,
"Envisioning California II," presentation at state capitol, Sacramento, CA,
February 10, 1990, publications binder, EPIC archives.

17 Bailey interview; Kathy Bailey to Hal Arbit, July 22, 1990, papers of Kathy
Bailey, Philo, CA; Forests Forever, "Forest and Wildlife Protection Initiative
Brief Summary," fact sheet, EPIC archives, publications binder, Redway, CA;
"Forests Forever Initiative: Summary," fact sheet, EPIC archives, publica-
tions binder, Redway, CA.

18 "The Global Warming and Clearcutting Reduction, Wildlife Protection and
Reforestation Act of 1990 (The Timber Association of California Initiative):
A Summary," EPIC archives, publication binder, Redway, CA; Vince Bielski

and Rick Sine, "Stumping for the Industry," *San Francisco Bay Guardian*, August 8, 1990, 17; Bailey interview; Sutherland interview; personal correspondence with Doug Phelps, October 1, 2009.

19   See also Bevington, *Rebirth of Environmentalism*, chapter 3, for additional analysis of the insider-outsider tensions between the North Coast and mainstream groups.

20   Bari, *Timber Wars*, 67, 69–70; Cherney, "History of Headwaters"; "PL to Log Headwaters!" *Mendocino Country Environmentalist*, March 1, 1995, EPIC archives, Redway, CA; Greg Lucas, "Logging to Resume in Humboldt," *San Francisco Chronicle*, March 3, 1995, EPIC archives, Redway, CA; Mike Geniella, "Plan to Log Headwaters," *Press Democrat* (Santa Rosa), March 3, 1995, A12, EPIC archives, Redway, CA.

21   "Grassroots Strategies for Our Global Future," Public Interest Law Conference program, 1990, accessed July 28, 2015, http://pielc.org/wp-content/uploads/2013/11/1990.pdf; Yafee, *Wisdom of the Spotted Owl*, chapters 4 and 5; Craig Welch, "A Brief History of the Spotted-Owl Controversy," *Seattle Times*, August 6, 2000, accessed July 28, 2015, http://community.seattletimes.nwsource.com/archive/?date=20000806&slug=4035697.

22   Cherney interview; Bari, *Timber Wars*, 70.

23   Bari, *Timber Wars*, 70.

24   Darryl Cherney, Judi Bari, and North Coast Calif. Earth Firsters!, "Tree-spiking Renunciation & Mississippi Summer in the Calif. Redwoods, memorandum from the authors to All Earth First! Groups, Chapters, Individuals, etc. . . . ," April 1990, accessed February 26, 2007, http://www.things.org/~jym/ef/tree-spiking-memo.html; Bari, *Timber Wars*, 71; Cherney interview; Foreman, *Confessions of an Eco-Warrior*, 31, 117–60, 218.

25   Bari, *Timber Wars*, 71, 98.

26   Kathy Bailey, "A Timeline History of Logging Reform in Mendocino County: DRAFT," memo for Sierra Club California, unknown date, papers of Kathy Bailey, Philo, CA. See Harris, *The Last Stand*, 324–35, for one version of King's postbombing trauma.

27   Redwood Summer 1990: Earth First!, Seeds of Peace, Industrial Workers of the World, "Redwood Summer Halts Logging at Osprey Grove, Mendocino Counties [sic] last Old-Growth," press release, July 19, 1990, EPIC archives, Eureka, CA; Bari, *Timber Wars*, 73–74; "10 Environmentalists Arrested/ Redwood Summer Event in Mendocino," *San Francisco Chronicle*, July 19, 1990, A6; "Old-Growth Logging Halted near Mendocino," *San Francisco Chronicle*, July 24, 1990, A2; Jay Matthews, "Environmentalists Attempt to Revive '60s Activism in Redwood Summer," *Washington Post*, July 8, 1990, A3; Maria Goodavage, "At Loggerheads in California; Timber Interests, Activists, Poised for Redwood, Summer," *USA Today*, June 20, 1990, 3A; Katherine Bishop, "One Result of Logging Protests: More Antagonism," *New York Times*, September 24, 1990, B8; Bill Barol and Lynda Wright, "Eco-Activist

Summer," *Newsweek*, July 2, 1990, 60; Katherine Bishop, "Militant Environmentalists Planning Summer Protests to Save Redwoods," *New York Times*, June 19, 1990, A18; Katherine Bishop, "Police Arrest 44 in Redwood Protest," *New York Times*, June 21, 1990, A16; Trip Gabriel, "If a Tree Falls in the Forest, They Hear It," *New York Times*, November 4, 1990, 34.

28 Dan Levy, "Redwood Summer Protesters Sue over Jail Head-Shaving," *San Francisco Chronicle*, September 7, 1990, A2; Jay Matthews, "Environmentalists Attempt to Revive '60s Activism in Redwood Summer," *Washington Post*, July 8, 1990, A3; Katherine Bishop, "One Result of Logging Protests: More Antagonism," *New York Times*, September 24, 1990, B8; Bari, *Timber Wars*, 74–75.

29 Bari, *Timber Wars*, 75–77; Chase, *In a Dark Wood*, 344–45. Chase's book is a polemic against modern environmentalism, but the chapter "Redwood Summer" chronicles many actions and protests not discussed in the preceding paragraphs.

30 "Humboldt Supervisor Says More Trees Were Spiked," *San Francisco Chronicle*, August 30, 1990, A2; Maria Goodavage, "At Loggerheads in California; Timber Interests, Activists, Poised for Redwood, Summer," *USA Today*, June 20, 1990, 3A; Katherine Bishop, "One Result of Logging Protests: More Antagonism," *New York Times*, September 24, 1990, B8; "Earth First! Replies to Mothers' Watch: We ARE Home!" *Anderson Valley Advertiser*, September 1, 1993, papers of Dan Hamburg, Ukiah, CA. Candice Boak is quoted in Helvarg, *War against the Greens*, 201.

31 Bari, *Timber Wars*, 77–81.

32 Leib Ostrow, "Trees Foundation: A Beginning," "Our History: 20 Years of Service," Trees Foundation website, accessed August 2, 2015, https://go.treesfoundation.org/about/history/.

33 On the struggles of Earth First! nationally after 1990, see Zakin, *Coyotes and Town Dogs*, 1–11, 273–342, 397–443; Cherney interview; Cherney, "History of Headwaters;" interview with Alicia Littletree Bales by the author, May 20, 2008, Ukiah, CA (all notes and audio files in possession of the author); *Chancellor Watch*, Winter '91–'92, Sacramento, CA, papers of Kathy Bailey, Philo, CA.

34 Cherney interview; Littletree interview; Bari, *Timber Wars*, 168–70.

35 Alicia Littletree, e-mail messages to author, July 30, 2015, and August 1, 2015.

36 Littletree interview.

37 Littletree interview; personal correspondence with Littletree, September 29, 2009; Bari, *Timber Wars*, 195–217.

38 Cherney interview; Littletree interview; Bari, *Timber Wars*, 226–30.

39 "Nightly Hiking Tours," flier, Ecotopia Earth First!, papers of Alicia Littletree, Ukiah, Ca; Littletree interview; *Sierra Club and EPIC v. California Board of Forestry*, Emergency Stay A059797, December 1, 1992, EPIC archives, Eureka, CA.

40 Dan Hamburg and Kate Anderton, interview with the author, Ukiah, CA, May 1, 2007; Dan Hamburg, interview with the author, Ukiah, CA, May 20, 2008 (all tapes and notes in possession of author).

41 Hamburg interview; "Dan Hamburg," *People Magazine*, May 3, 1993, http://www.people.com/people/archive/article/0,,20110326,00.html; William McBurn, "Rubber Congressman," *National Review*, April 13, 1992; HR 3818 by Pete Stark, November 21, 1989, EPIC archives, publications binder, Redway, CA; text of Stark bill with no HR number listed, faxed on Feb. 20, 1990, at 15:40, EPIC archives, publications binder, Redway, CA; "'Headwaters Forest Act' Introduced in Congress," *Wild California*, Fall 1993, 1, EPIC archives, Eureka, CA; "Riggs Slams Timber Land-Grab, Offers His Own 'Rational' Headwaters Bill," *Redwood Record* (Garberville), September 15, 1992, papers of Dan Hamburg, Ukiah, CA; "Congress' Neglect Kills Humboldt Tree Measure," *Contra Costa Times*, October 9, 1992, 15A, EPIC archives, Redway, CA; "A Headwaters Forest Chronology," fact sheet/fund-raising appeal/action alert, EPIC archives, Eureka, CA.

42 See Harvey, *Symbol of Wilderness*, chapter 7; and Nash, *Wilderness and the American Mind*, chapter 12, regarding the Dinosaur and Wilderness Act campaigns. Bailey interview; Hamburg interview; Darryl Cherney, "History of Headwaters"; "Re: Headwaters Legislative Team," confidential memorandum, March 9, 1993, papers of Kathy Bailey, Philo, CA; Pete Stark, "Let's Stop the Mining of One of Our National Symbols: The Majestic Redwood," extension of remarks, March 18, 1993, EPIC archives, Eureka, CA.

43 Yaffee, *Wisdom of the Spotted Owl*, chapters 4 and 5; and Sher, "Travels with Strix."

44 Jack Ward Thomas et al., "Forest Ecosystem Management: An Ecological, Economic, and Social Assessment," report of the Forest Ecosystem Management Assessment Team (Washington, DC: Gov. Printing Office, 1993); Headwaters Legislative Action Team, "Headwaters Redwoods Forest Complex: A Legislative Proposal," 1993, personal papers of Congressman Dan Hamburg, Ukiah, CA, 1.

45 "Summary of Qualifications," Pacific Watershed Associates website, http://www.pacificwatershed.com/company/summary-qualifications; the quoted text comes from Headwaters Legislative Action Plan, "Headwaters Legislative Proposal," 9, 11, 12.

46 For discussions of the critique of radical environmentalists, see Cronon, "The Trouble with Wilderness," in *Uncommon Ground*; Guha, "Radical American Environmentalism"; and White, "Are You an Environmentalist?"

47 Michael Spears, "Bosco Defends Lobbying Role for Timber Industry," *Napa Valley Register*, April 6, 1994, papers of Dan Hamburg, Ukiah, Ca; Charles Winkley, "Bosco Getting $180,000 as Headwaters Lobbyist," *Eureka Times Standard*, April 1, 1994, papers of Dan Hamburg, Ukiah, CA; "Rep. Hamburg Must Meet with North Coast Constituents," *Humboldt Beacon and Advance*,

July 1, 1993, papers of Dan Hamburg; Pacific Lumber Company, Form S-2, Registration No. 33–56332, December 28, 1992, EPIC archives, Eureka, CA; "MAXXAM Inc." in *International Directory of Company Histories*; Mike Geniella, "Pacific Lumber Cutting a Deal," *Press Democrat*, December 9, 1992, E1, EPIC archives, Eureka, CA; Judi Bari, "Charles Hurwitz Strikes Again," unknown publication, January 1993, EPIC archives, publications binder; and Charles McCoy, "Cutting Costs," *Wall Street Journal*, August 6, 1993, A1.

48 Hamburg interview; "Congressmen Seeking Purchase of Forest Land," *Napa Valley Register*, June 18, 1993, papers of Dan Hamburg, Ukiah, CA; Honorable Dan Hamburg, "Introduction of the Headwaters Forest Act," *Congressional Record* 139, no. 112 (August 4, 1993), papers of Dan Hamburg, Ukiah, CA.

49 Hamburg interview; Wade Lambert and Milo Geyelin, "United Financial Found Liable by FDIC," *Wall Street Journal*, May 22, 1992, EPIC archives, Eureka, CA; and Kathy Bailey, e-mail to author, October 15, 2009.

50 Glenn Franco Simmons, "Earth First! Wants 98,000; 4,500 Acres Tops, PL Says," *Humboldt Beacon and Advance*, August 26, 1993, papers of Dan Hamburg, Ukiah, CA; Littletree interview; "Week of Outrage against Maxxam," flier, Earth First!, August 1993, papers of Alicia Littletree Bales, Ukiah, CA; North Coast California Earth First!, "Headwaters Forest Wilderness Complex," EPIC archives, Eureka, CA; Mike Geniella, "Earth First! Protests Headwaters Logging," *Press Democrat* (Santa Rosa), August 24, 1993, papers of Dan Hamburg, Ukiah, CA; "Outrage against Maxxam," *Mendocino Country Environmentalist*, August 26, 1993, 1, papers of Dan Hamburg, Ukiah, CA; "Earth First! Replies to Mothers' Watch: We ARE Home!"; Cherney, "History of Headwaters Campaign."

51 The testimony of John Campbell can be found in *Headwaters Forest Act: Hearing on H.R. 2866 before the Subcommittee on Specialty Crops and Natural Resources of the Committee on Agriculture, House of Representatives*, 103rd Congress 168–84 (1993). Campbell interview with author.

52 The statements of Dan Hamburg and Pete Stark can be found in *Headwaters Forest Act*, 137–48.

53 Hamburg interview; Bailey interview; "Summary Outline of the Headwaters Acquisition Proposal," HFCC draft, faxed to EPIC on February 21, 1994, EPIC archives, Eureka, CA; James W. Sweeney, "Early Bosco TV Ads Rip Hamburg," *Press Democrat* (Santa Rosa), April 1, 1994, B1, papers of Dan Hamburg, Ukiah, CA; "Organization Hired to Fight Forest Bill," *Eureka Times Standard*, May 5, 1994, papers of Dan Hamburg, Ukiah, CA; Josh Kaufman to Dan Hamburg and Kate Anderton, "Re: Meeting with Red Emerson's attorney," papers of Kathy Bailey, Philo, CA; "'Headwaters': A Public Scam," PALCO Family Defense Fund, Scotia, CA, 1994, papers of Dan Hamburg, Ukiah, CA.

54 Derrick DePledge, "Committees Vote to Protect More Humboldt Forest," *San Francisco Examiner*, April 3, 1994, papers of Dan Hamburg, Ukiah, CA;

Clyde Weiss, "Headwaters Bill Passes Another Hurdle," *Ukiah Daily Journal*, May 14, 1994, papers of Dan Hamburg, Ukiah, CA; Charles Winkler, "PL Chief Joins Democrats," *Eureka Times Standard*, May 3, 1994, papers of Dan Hamburg, Ukiah, CA; Steve Tetreault, "Different Camps Back Hamburg, Bosco," *Ukiah Daily Journal*, June 2, 1994, papers of Dan Hamburg, Ukiah, CA; Kathy Bailey to Ken Miller, "Re: Headwaters Video," July 27, 1994, papers of Kathy Bailey, Philo, CA. See Harvey, *Symbol of Wilderness*, 164–67, regarding Harold Bradley home movie. See Schrepfer, *Fight to Save Redwoods*, 11; and Carrie Stevens Walter, "The Preservation of Big Basin," regarding Andrew Hill. Kathy Bailey, "Headwaters Mark-up Scheduled for Wednesday," undated memo, papers of Kathy Bailey, Philo, CA; Kathy Bailey, memo to Chuck Powell, Cecelia Lanman, Paul Mason, and Kevin Bundy, Draft 1, August 19, 1997; Hamburg and Anderton interview; Kathy Bailey to Robert Redford, "Re: Headwaters Update," October 17, 1994, papers of Kathy Bailey, Ukiah, CA; Daily Schedule "Blue Sheet" for Congressman Dan Hamburg, August 9, 1994, papers of Dan Hamburg, Ukiah, CA; Pacific Lumber Company, press release, August 15, 1994, papers of Kathy Bailey, Philo, CA; Campbell interview; Jim Maddy, president of LCV, "Support H.R. 2866, the Headwaters Forest Act (Hamburg, D-CA)," letter to all members of the House of Representatives, August 15, 1994, papers of Kathy Bailey, Philo, CA; "For Fish, Forests and a Future: Support the Headwaters Forest Act," letter from Ancient Forest Alliance to all members of House of Representatives, August 15, 1994, papers of Kathy Bailey, Philo, CA.

55   Bailey interview; Cherney interview. Regarding the votes on the Hamburg bill see Thomas Database of Bills and Resolutions at the Library of Congress (http://www.thomas.gov/cgi-bin/bdquery/z?d103:HR02866:@@@S); (http://thomas.loc.gov/cgi-bin/bdquery/D?d103:4:./temp/~bdtuEM:@@@L&summ2=m&|/bss/103search.html).

56   50 CFR Part 17, Final Designation of Critical Habitat for the Marbled Murrelet; Final Rule, *Federal Register* 61, no. 102 (1996).

57   Alicia Littletree interview and map of Owl Creek hikes from Littletree's personal papers, Ukiah, CA (author has a copy of the map); *Sierra Club v. California State Board of Forestry*, 7 Cal. 4th 1215, 4.

58   *Sierra Club v. California State Board of Forestry*, 1, 12.

59   Marbled murrelet listing is 50 CFR Part 17; Rules and Regulations section RIN 1018-AB56, *Federal Register* 57, no. 191 (1993). See EPIC brief before CA appellate court, A059797, requesting a stay (1992), 4–8, EPIC unprocessed archives, Eureka, CA.

60   *Marbled Murrelet v. Pacific Lumber*, C-93–1400 (1997), 36, EPIC unprocessed archives, Eureka, CA; Department of Interior memo 1–1-92-TA-81, Wayne White, Field Supervisor, FWS, to EPIC attorney Mark Harris, November 29, 1992, EPIC unprocessed archives, Eureka, CA; CA *EPIC v. Board of Forestry*, Emergency Stay Order A059797 (1992); Supreme Court deny of writ of cert

So31969 (1993), Chief Justice Lucas and Justices Panellie and Baxter, EPIC unprocessed archives, Eureka, CA.

61 Duggan interview; *Marbled Murrelet v. Pacific Lumber*, C-93–1400-FMS slip op. at 12 (ND Cal., February 2, 1994), EPIC unprocessed archives, Eureka, CA.

5. THE TRANSFORMATION

1 Bailey interview.

2 Bailey interview.

3 Bailey interview; Bailey e-mail to the author, July 31, 2015.

4 Bailey interview.

5 Campbell interview.

6 See Yaffee, *Wisdom of the Spotted Owl*, 137, for a brief introduction to the "train wreck theory."

7 Lloyd Keefer, Region Chief, Department of Forestry to Ray Miller, The Pacific Lumber Company, November 29, 1994, papers of Kathy Bailey, Philo, CA

8 Brian Gaffney, "Litigation Synopsis—August 1994 for EPIC Board and Litigation Committee," memo, August 30, 1994, EPIC archives, Eureka, CA; "A Headwaters Forest Chronology," fact sheet/fund-raising appeal/action alert, EPIC archives, Eureka, CA; "Notice of Timber Operations That Are Exempt from Timber Harvesting Plan Requirements," 1–94EX-1357 HUM, from Pacific Lumber to CA Dept. of Forestry, December 9, 1994; Lloyd Kiefer, Department of Forestry Region Chief, to The Pacific Lumber Company, "re: 1–94EX-1357 HUM," December 21, 1994, EPIC archives, Eureka, CA.

9 Brian Gaffney to Kathy Bailey, January 19, 1995, papers of Kathy Bailey, Philo, CA; EPIC litigation strategy memo "re: systematic failures of Department of Forestry," 1995, EPIC archives, Eureka, CA.

10 Brock Evans, National Audubon Society, Douglass Inkley, National Wildlife Federation, Judy Norisake, Pacific Rivers Council, Marty Hayden, Sierra Club, John Fitzgerald, Western Ancient Forests Campaign, Paul Pritchard, National Parks and Conservation Association, Julia Levin, Natural Heritage Institute, Kevin Kirchner, Sierra Club Legal Defense Fund, Frances Hunt, Wilderness Society to Leon Panetta, White House Chief of Staff, "Re: Headwaters Forest, FDIC and OTS," February 14, 1995, papers of Kathy Bailey, Philo, CA.

11 Paul McHugh, "Warden Says State Hinders Protection," *San Francisco Chronicle*, February 16, 1995; Rob Taylor, "Alarming: Salmon Getting Smaller," *San Francisco Examiner*, February 12, 1995; Steve Hart, "Russian River's Steelhead at Risk," *Press Democrat* (Santa Rosa), March 7, 1995; Manny Frishberg, "Coho's Federal Listing Still Undecided," *Redwood Record* (Garberville), April 6, 1995; Steve Hart, "Wilson Accused of Trying to Downgrade Coho's

Status," *Press Democrat* (Santa Rosa), June 29, 1995; Scott Sonner, "Species Act Gets Review," *Eureka Times Standard*, February 24, 1995, A1. The EPIC archives in Redway, CA contain hard copies of all articles.

12 See Salzman and Thompson, *Environmental Law and Policy*, 267, for brief discussion of the precedent-setting nature of *Marbled Murrelet v. Pacific Lumber.* *Marbled Murrelet v. Pacific Lumber*, C-93–1400-LSB (N.D. Cal February 27, 1995), 83 f.3d 1060 (9th Circuit); 519 US 1108 (Supreme Court rejection of PL writ of cert); "PL to Log Headwaters!" *Mendocino Country Environmentalist*, March 1, 1995, EPIC archives, Redway, CA.

13 Jentri Anders, "Action on Headwaters Weighed," *Redwood Record* (Garberville), March 16, 1995, 1; David Anderson, "PL Seeks State OK to Harvest Headwaters Sections," *Eureka Times Standard*, March 26, 1995; Mike Geniella, "Plan to Log Headwaters," *Press Democrat* (Santa Rosa), March 3, 1995, A12; Greg Lucas, "Logging to Resume in Humboldt," *San Francisco Chronicle*, March 3, 1995; Christine Sackey, "Headwaters Forest to Be Logged: PALCO Announced Last Week," *Redwood Record* (Garberville), March 9, 1995, 1; Todd Woody, "Pacific Lumber Throws Down Gauntlet after Murrelet Defeat," *Recorder*, March 7, 1995, 1. The EPIC archives in Redway contain hard copies of all articles.

14 EPIC, press release, March 3, 1995, EPIC archives, Eureka, CA; "PL to Log Headwaters!" *Mendocino Country Environmentalist*, March 1, 1995, EPIC archives, Redway, CA; Kathy Bailey, Sierra Club California, "Illegal Logging Planned or Headwaters Forest [sic]," press release, March 3, 1995, papers of Kathy Bailey, Philo, CA; Pacific Lumber Company, "This Is Our Stand," *San Francisco Chronicle*, March 3, 1995, papers of Kathy Bailey, Philo, CA.

15 Kathy Bailey to Governor Wilson, "Re: Headwaters Forest," March 16, 1995, papers of Kathy Bailey, Philo, CA; Statement of Terry Gorton, Assistant Secretary for Resources, State of California, press release, March 16, 1995, papers of Kathy Bailey, Philo, CA; and Manny Frishberg, "Wilson's Species Act Reform Plan Unveiled," *Redwood Record* (Garberville), April 6, 1995, EPIC archives, Redway, CA.

16 Littletree interview; Earth First!, "Headwaters Forest Red Alert," flier, March 22, 1995, papers of Alicia Littletree Bales, Ukiah, CA; "Summary of EPIC Forestry Lawsuits, 1982 to 1996," EPIC archives, Eureka, CA. The state exemption suit was *Sierra Club and EPIC v. Keefer and California Department of Forestry.* The federal suit was *Marbled Murrelet, Northern Spotted Owl, and EPIC v. Bruce Babbitt, Secretary, Department of the Interior; Mollie Beattie, Director, USFWS; Michael Spear, Region 1 Director, USFWS; the U.S. Fish and Wildlife Service; Pacific Lumber Company; Scotia Pacific Holding Company; and the Salmon Creek Corporation.* David Anderson, "Judge Delays PL Salvage Bid," *Eureka Times Standard*, May 2, 1995, A1, EPIC archives, Redway, CA.

17 "Demonstration against Headwaters Logging Tuesday March 28th," public service announcement text for KMUD and CSAR, March 27, 1995; Coalition

to Defend Headwaters, "Headwaters Demo Set for Sept. 15: Logging Dead-
line Looms," flier, ca. August 20, 1995; "Headwaters Forest Threatened:
URGENT ACTION ALERT," flier, March 1995, EPIC archives, Eureka,
CA; Michael Corbett, "Protest over Logging in Headwaters," *Redwood
Record* (Garberville), March 30, 1995, page 1, EPIC archives, Redway, CA;
"Pacific Lumber Target of Demonstrations," *Press Democrat* (Santa Rosa),
March 29, 1995, EPIC archives, Redway, CA; David Anderson, "Earth First,
Others Decry Log Plans for Headwaters," *Eureka Times Standard*, March 29,
1995, A1, EPIC archives, Redway, CA; Littletree interview; Darryl Cherney,
"History of Headwaters Campaign—an Outline," 1998, 2007, papers of Dar-
ryl Cherney, Redway, CA; "Summary of EPIC Lawsuits 1982 to 1996," *Doug
Thron, EPIC, & Bald Eagle Restoration Project v. Pacific Lumber, Scotia Pacific
Holding Company, Department of Forestry, Tom Osipowich as Deputy Chief of
Department of Forestry Region 1, Lloyd Keefer as Chief of Region of Department
of Forestry, and Richard Wilson as Director of Department of Forestry* (Humboldt
Ct. #95DRO100), EPIC archives, Eureka, CA; David Anderson, "PL Layoffs Indefinite, Firm Says," *Eureka Times Standard*, April 18, 1995, A1, EPIC
archives, Redway, CA.

18   Dennis Pfaff, "Jurist Takes Himself out of Humboldt Logging Case," *San
Francisco Daily Journal*, April 21, 1995, A1, EPIC archives, Redway, CA; David
Anderson, "Judge Buffington Removes Himself from Logging Case," *Eureka
Times Standard*, April 20, 1995, A1, EPIC archives, Redway, CA; Todd Woody,
"Judge Recuses Himself from Timber Dispute," *Recorder*, April 21, 1995, EPIC
archives, Redway, CA.

19   Darryl Cherney, "History of Headwaters Campaign—an Outline"; Kathy
Bailey, memo to Chuck Powell, Cecelia Lanman, Paul Mason, and Kevin
Bundy, Draft 1, August 19, 1997; Bailey interview; Kathy Bailey, memo to
Katie Merrill, "Re: Headwaters Forest," May 5, 1995, papers of Kathy Bailey,
Philo, CA; Pacific Lumber Company, *1993 Annual Report*, SEC Form 10-K, 3.

20   *Sierra Club and EPIC v. Lloyd Keefer and the California Department of Forestry*,
HUM 95DR0072, May 18, 1995, EPIC archives, Eureka, CA; *Doug Thron and
EPIC v. Pacific Lumber, et al.*, HUM95DR100, June 14, 1995, EPIC archives,
Eureka, CA; "Pacific Lumber/Scotia Pacific THP Submittals—1995," papers
of Kathy Bailey, Philo, CA; Pacific Lumber Company, "Pacific Lumber Company Announces Restarting of Mill A Operation," *Life and Times* (Garberville), May 2, 1995, EPIC archives, Redway, CA; Pacific Lumber Company,
"Pacific Lumber Company Releases King Salmon," *Life and Times* (Garberville), June 6, 1995, EPIC archives, Redway, CA.

21   Mike Geniella, "Bay Area Politicians Seek to Halt Logging," *Press Democrat*
(Santa Rosa), June 24, 1995, EPIC archives, Redway, CA; Jane Kay, "Log-
ging Protesters Arrested in Humboldt," *San Francisco Examiner*, June 23, 1995,
A25, EPIC archives, Redway, CA; "Logging Ban Stays in Place against PL,"
Eureka Times Standard, June 29, 1995, EPIC archives, Eureka, CA; "Judge

Halts Logging at Yager Creek," *San Francisco Chronicle*, June 29, 1995, A19, EPIC archives, Eureka, CA; Littletree interview; Darryl Cherney, "History of Headwaters Campaign—An Outline."

22   Glen Martin, "34 Protesters Arrested," *San Francisco Chronicle*, July 6, 1995, EPIC archives, Redway, CA; Mary Lane, "Earth First Protesters Block Gates to PL Land: 8 arrested," *Eureka Times Standard*, July 6, 1995, EPIC archives, Redway, CA; Jentri Anders, "Use of Pepper Spray at Protest Questioned," *Redwood Record* (Garberville), July 20, 1995, EPIC archives, Redway, CA; Darryl Cherney, "History of Headwaters Campaign—an Outline"; Manny Frishberg, "Activist Group Calls for Redwood Boycott," *Redwood Record* (Garberville), July 27, 1995, EPIC archives, Redway, CA; "Judge Won't Halt PL Logging Plans," *Eureka Times Standard*, July 9, 1995, EPIC archives, Redway, CA.

23   "Agreement to Mediate," 1995, EPIC archives, Eureka, CA; Mike Geniella, "Timber Mediation Effort Fails," *Press Democrat* (Santa Rosa), July 21, 1995, EPIC archives, Redway, CA; Campbell interview.

24   Mike Geniella, "Timber Mediation Effort Fails," *Press Democrat* (Santa Rosa), July 21, 1995; Jentri Anders, "Logging to Resume on Yager Creek," *Redwood Record* (Garberville), July 27, 1995; "Court Says PL Can Log Yager Creek," *Eureka Times Standard*, July 22, 1995. The EPIC archives in Redway contain hard copies of all articles.

25   The author attended the 1995 demonstration while an undergrad at Humboldt State University. Mary Lane, "2,000 Rally against PL," *Eureka Times Standard*, September 16, 1995, A1; Glen Martin, "2,000 Rally to Protect Redwood Grove," *San Francisco Chronicle*, September 16, 1995, A1; May Callahan, "Senate Passes Legislation to Force Headwaters Deal," *Press Democrat* (Santa Rosa), September 16, 1995. The EPIC archives in Redway contain hard copies of all articles.

26   "Protests Spread to Area near Headwaters Tract," *Press Democrat* (Santa Rosa), October 11, 1995; Manny Frishberg, "Logging Protests Continue at 'Northern Headwaters,'" *Redwood Record* (Garberville), October 12, 1995, 1; Michael Corbett, "Timber Demonstrations Spur County Plea for Help," *Redwood Record* (Garberville), October 12, 1995; David Anderson, "Earth Firsters End Tree-sitting," *Eureka Times Standard*, October 15, 1995; Cherney, "History of Headwaters Campaign—an Outline"; "Tree-sitters Climb Down Monday Ending Six-Day Anti-logging Action," *Redwood Record* (Garberville), October 19, 1995; "Headwaters Protest," *Eureka Times Standard*, October 19, 1995. The EPIC archives in Redway contain hard copies of all articles.

27   Mike Geniella, "Payday in Pacific Lumber Suit," *Press Democrat*, December 16, 1995, EPIC archives, Redway, CA; letter from Lloyd Keefer, Department of Forestry Region Chief, to Thomas Herman, Salmon Creek Corporation/ The Pacific Lumber Company, December 20, 1995, papers of Kathy Bailey, Philo, CA; Jane Kay, "Ancient Redwood Trees Find Friends," *Globe and Mail*

(Canada), December 22, 1995, reprinted from the *San Francisco Examiner*; Nancy Vogel, "Measure Calls for Swap of Forests," *Sacramento Bee*, December 2, 1995; "Clinton Responds to Headwaters Fray," *Eureka Times Standard*, December 24, 1995; Quentin Hardy, "Regulators Charge Maxxam, Its Chief in Thrift's Failure," *Wall Street Journal*, December 27, 1995, A4; OTS Order No. AP 95–40, Notice of Charges and of Hearing for Cease-and-Desist Order, Order of Prohibition, Restitution, Civil Money Penalties, and Other Appropriate Relief, in the Matter of United Savings Association of Texas, United Financial Group, Inc., Maxxam, Inc., Federated Development Co., Charles E. Hurwitz, Barry A. Munitz, Jenard M. Gross, Arthur S. Berner, Ronald Huebsch, and Michael Crow, December 26, 1995, EPIC archives, Eureka, CA.

28 Turner, *Promise of Wilderness*, 340–47.

29 Letter from Jared G. Carter, legal representation for Pacific Lumber Company, to Lloyd Keefer, Department of Forestry, January 5, 1996, papers of Kathy Bailey, Philo, CA; Paul Rogers, "Forest Feud," *San Jose Mercury News*, September 11, 1996, 1A, EPIC archives, Redway, CA; Julia Levine to HFCC Members!, February 28, 1996, papers of Kathy Bailey, Philo, CA.

30 Richard Epstein, *Takings: Private Property and the Power of Eminent Domain* (Cambridge, MA: Harvard University Press, 1985); Helvarg, *War against the Greens*, 226–32; *Lucas v. South Carolina Coastal Commission*, 505 U.S. 1003 (1992); "Logging Violations Result in Fine for PL," *Eureka Times Standard*, April 30, 1996, EPIC archives, Redway, CA; Kathy Bailey, memo to Chuck Powell, Cecelia Lanman, Paul Mason, and Kevin Bundy, Draft 1, August 19, 1997, papers of Kathy Bailey, Philo, CA; Rex Bossert, "Eco-Bar Gets Win, Loss in Logging Ruling," *Ukiah Daily Journal*, May 8, 1996, EPIC archives, Redway, CA; Todd Woody, "Pacific Lumber Tries New Tack in Timber Wars," *Daily Recorder*, May 10, 1996, EPIC archives, Redway, CA; Associated Press, "State Supreme Court Clears Headwaters Salvage Logging," *Eureka Times Standard*, June 13, 1996, EPIC archives, Redway, CA.

31 *Federal Register* 60, no. 154 (1995): 40496, EPIC archives, Eureka, CA; Reynolds Holding, "Nest Areas Protected for Seabird," *San Francisco Chronicle*, May 17, 1996, EPIC archives, Redway, CA; "Feds: Headwaters Critical for Murrelet," *Press Democrat* (Santa Rosa), May 16, 1996; Carolyn Lochhead, "Democrats Block Bid to Log Murrelet Habitat," *San Francisco Chronicle*, June 20, 1996, EPIC archives, Redway, CA; Tom Lippe to Robert L. Baum, Associate Solicitor for Division of Conservation and Wildlife, Dept. of the Interior, June 4, 1996, EPIC archives, Eureka, CA; Tom Lippe to Honorable John Garamendi, Deputy Secretary of the Department of the Interior, July 3, 1996, EPIC archives, Eureka, CA; "HFCC Overall Budget 1996," personal papers of Kathy Bailey, Philo, CA; Darryl Cherney, "History of Headwaters Campaign—an Outline."

32 Tim Golden, "Talks on Saving Redwoods May Be near Decisive Point," *New York Times*, August 27, 1996, A9.

33 Kathy Bailey, "Headwaters Update," August 22, 1996, EPIC archives, Eureka, CA; Charles McCoy, "Maxxam's Hurwitz Nears Pact to Swap Redwood Grove for Thousands of Acres," *Wall Street Journal*, July 19, 1996, A4; David Brower, "Why I Won't Vote for Clinton," *Los Angeles Times*, July 22, 1996, papers of Kathy Bailey, Philo, CA; full-page *New York Times* advertisement placed by Dan Hamburg, "Clinton doling out corporate welfare to Hurwitz, Clinton must do debt-for-nature instead. Clinton protecting less than 20% of the Interior Dept.'s critical habitat area," *New York Times*, August 22, 1996, Hamburg papers, Ukiah, CA; Bailey interview; Hamburg interview; Cherney interview; and Bundy interview.

34 Campbell interview; Mike Geniella, "Lumber Firm: Cut Land Deal or Cut Trees," *Press Democrat* (Santa Rosa), August 6, 1996, EPIC archives, Redway, CA; Golden, "Talks on Saving Redwoods"; Mike Geniella, "Feinstein Credited as Headwaters Catalyst," *Press Democrat* (Santa Rosa), October 2, 1996, EPIC archives, Redway, CA; "D.C. Talks Intensify over Headwaters Land Swap," *Eureka Times Standard*, August 15, 1996, EPIC archives, Redway, CA; Mike Geniella, "Showdown over Headwaters," *Press Democrat* (Santa Rosa), September 8, 1996, A1, EPIC archives, Redway, CA; Jane Kay, "Headwaters Fight Comes to a Head," *San Francisco Examiner*, September 8, 1996, EPIC archives, Redway, CA.

35 Tracy Katelman to EPIC, Kathy Bailey, Ken Miller, Karen Pickett, Karin Rosman, Jill Ratner, "HFCC 8/29," EPIC archives, Eureka, CA; Doug Linney to HFCC, "Consulting for the Headwaters Forest Campaign," August 6, 1996, EPIC archives, Eureka, CA; letter from Kathy Bailey, Sierra Club California, to Assistant Secretary John Garamendi, "Headwaters Forest," August 21, 1996, EPIC archives, Eureka, CA; Campbell interview; full page advertisement in *New York Times*, September 3, 1996, "An ancient redwood can withstand centuries of drought, wind, fire, and flood. It's Charles Hurwitz it can't handle," EPIC archives, Redway, CA; Carl Pope to Environmental Leaders, circa September 5, 1996, papers of Kathy Bailey, Philo, CA; letter from Carl Pope to President Bill Clinton, circa September 5, 1996, papers of Kathy Bailey, Philo, CA; Carl Pope, Sierra Club, David Brower, Earth Island Institute, John Buettler, CA Sportfishing Protection Alliance, Deb Clallahan, League of Conservation Voters, Randy Hayes, Rainforest Action Network, Jay Watson, The Wilderness Society, John McCaul, National Audubon Society, Jim Jontz, Western Ancient Forests Campaign, Jim Eaton, California Ancient Forest Alliance, Jim Crenshaws, United Anglers of CA, Victor M. Sher, Sierra Club Legal Defense Fund, Rodger Schlickheisen, Defenders of Wildlife, Dominick Dellasala, World Wildlife Fund, David Edelson, Natural Resources Defense Council, Schaust, CA League of Conservation Voters, Julia Levin, Natural Heritage Institute, Steve Evans, Friends of the River to President Clinton, September 11, 1996, papers of Kathy Bailey, Philo, CA; David Brower, "Forest on the Verge," *New York Times*, September 15, 1996,

E15; Kathy Bailey, memo to Chuck Powell, Cecelia Lanman, Paul Mason, and Kevin Bundy, Draft 1, August 19, 1997; Kathy Bailey, copy of testimony to Chairman Kersteins and Members of the Board, September 9, 1996, papers of Kathy Bailey, Philo, CA; Felicia Marcus, Regional Administrator, Environmental Protection Agency to Robert Kersteins, Chairman, CA Board of Forestry, October 1, 1996, papers of Kathy Bailey, Philo, CA; Elliot Diringer, "Headwaters Deal Was a Close Call," *San Francisco Chronicle*, September 30, 1996, A1, EPIC archives, Redway, CA.

36 Paul Rogers, "Forest Feud," *San Jose Mercury News*, September 11, 1996, 1A, EPIC archives, Redway, CA; Mike Geniella, "Hurwitz, Feds Try to Cut Deal on Headwaters," *Press Democrat* (Santa Rosa), September 12, 1996, EPIC archives, Redway, CA; Mike Geniella, "Critical Talks on Headwaters Open Today," *Press Democrat* (Santa Rosa), September 11, 1996, EPIC archives, Redway, CA; Marla Cone, "Wilson Asks Firm to Delay Cutting Redwoods," *Los Angeles Times*, September 12, 1996, A3, EPIC archives, Redway, CA; Christopher Rosche, "No Headwaters Deal Soon, Official Says," *Eureka Times Standard*, September 13, 1996, EPIC archives, Redway, CA; Alex Barnum and Carolyn Lochhead, "Headwaters Logging Delayed," *San Francisco Chronicle*, September 14, 1996, EPIC archives, Redway, CA.

37 Stephen Levine, "Rally for Redwoods Attracts 5,000: Environmentalists Push to Save Old-Growth Forest in California," *Washington Post*, September 16, 1996, A11; Mike Geniella, "Forest Talks at 'Critical Stage,'" *Press Democrat* (Santa Rosa), September 20, 1996, EPIC archives, Redway, CA; Eric Brazil, "New Fight for Redwoods Radical," *San Francisco Examiner*, December 15, 1996, EPIC archives, Redway, CA; Barbara Henry, "Logging Protesters Persevere," *Eureka Times Standard*, September 17, 1996, EPIC archives, Redway, CA; Mike Geniella, "Forest Talks at 'Critical Stage,'" *Press Democrat* (Santa Rosa), September 20, 1996, EPIC archives, Redway, CA.

38 Geniella, "Forest Talks at 'Critical Stage'"; letter from Tom Lippe to Honorable John Garamendi, September 24, 1996, EPIC archives, Eureka, CA; Senator Barbara Boxer to The Honorable Pete Wilson, September 23, 1996, papers of Kathy Bailey, Philo, CA; "Tree-sitters in 10th Day of Vigil near Headwaters," *Eureka Times Standard*, September 24, 1996, EPIC archives, Redway, CA; Mark Heimann, "Woo-Woo and the Fight to Save Headwaters," *Anderson Valley Advertiser*, September 25, 1996, 7, EPIC archives, Redway, CA; Mike Geniella, "Today's Talks Key to Saving Redwoods," *Press Democrat* (Santa Rosa), September 24, 1996, B1, EPIC archives, Redway, CA; Mike Geniella, "Headwaters Negotiations Continue Today," *Press Democrat* (Santa Rosa), September 27, 1996, EPIC archives, Redway, CA; Elliot Diringer, "Headwaters Deal Was a Close Call," *San Francisco Chronicle*, September 30, 1996, A1, EPIC archives, Redway, CA; Mike Geniella, "Marathon Talks Lead to Headwaters Agreement," *Press Democrat* (Santa Rosa), September 28, 1996, EPIC archives, Redway, CA.

39   "Environmentalists Protest Forest Pact," *New York Times*, September 30, 1996, accessed January 4, 2016, http://www.nytimes.com/1996/09/30/us/environmentalists-protest-forest-pact.html; The Department of the Interior and Related Agencies Appropriation Act, 1998, subsec. (a), is Pub. L. 105–83, Nov. 14, 1997, 111 Stat. 1543, accessed January 4, 2016, http://uscode.house.gov/view.xhtml?req=granuleid:USC-prelim-title16-section471j&num=0&edition=prelim.

40   John H. Cushman Jr., "U.S. Using Swaps to Protect Land," *New York Times*, September 30, 1996, A1; "Wheeling, Dealing Surround Possible Land Swaps, Litigation," *Mine Regulation Reporter*, November 17, 1997.

41   Michael Satchell, "To Save the Sequoias," *U.S. News and World Report*, October 7, 1996, 42, EPIC archives, Redway, CA; Kathy Bailey, memo to Chuck Powell, Cecelia Lanman, Paul Mason, and Kevin Bundy, Draft 1, August 19, 1997; Paul Rogers, "Headwaters Pact Criticism Is Widespread," *San Jose Mercury News*, October 1, 1996, EPIC archives, Redway, CA; Mike Geniella, "Environmentalists Call Pact a 'Slap in the Face,'" *Press Democrat* (Santa Rosa), September 29, 1996, EPIC archives, Redway, CA.

42   Kathy Bailey to Darryl Cherney, October 4, 1996, papers of Kathy Bailey, Philo, CA; Darryl Cherney, "History of Headwaters Campaign—an Outline"; "California Protest Targets Redwoods Pact," *USA Today*, September 30, 1996, 3A, EPIC archives, Redway, CA; "Clear-Cutting Credibility," *San Francisco Chronicle*, October 2, 1996, EPIC archives, Redway, CA; "New Protests: Workers Wary of Losing Jobs," *Press Democrat* (Santa Rosa), October 1, 1996, EPIC archives, Redway, CA; Mikal Jakubal, "Preface to the Proposed Campaign Organization System: On the Importance of Solidarity and Morale," 1997, EPIC archives, Eureka, CA; Mike Geniella, "Feinstein Credited as Headwaters Catalyst," *Press Democrat* (Santa Rosa), October 2, 1996, EPIC archives, Redway, CA; Jane Kay, "Treetop Protesters Won't Go Away," *San Francisco Examiner*, October 6, 1996, EPIC archives, Redway, CA; "Confrontation over Redwoods," *New York Times*, October 2, 1996, EPIC archives, Redway, CA; Glen Martin and Alex Barnum, "Earth First Ready to Defy Loggers," *San Francisco Chronicle*, October 9, 1996, EPIC archives, Redway, CA; Jessie Faulkner, "Headwaters Rally Brings New Arrests," *Eureka Times Standard*, October 13, 1996, EPIC archives, Redway, CA; Associated Press, "Seven More Arrested at Headwaters Rally," *Press Democrat* (Santa Rosa), October 13, 1996, EPIC archives, Redway, CA; Associated Press, "Arrests Continue in Redwoods Protest," *San Francisco Examiner*, October 13, 1996, EPIC archives, Redway, CA; Jessie Faulkner, "Headwaters Rally Brings New Arrests," *Eureka Times Standard*, October 13, 1996, EPIC archives, Redway, CA; "Protesters Rally at State Forestry Office," *San Jose Mercury*, October 22, 1996, 3B, EPIC archives, Redway, CA; Associated Press, "Noisy Protest at State Forestry Office," *San Francisco Chronicle*, October 22, 1996, EPIC archives, Redway, CA; "Fighting for the Trees," *San Francisco Examiner*,

November 1, 1996, EPIC archives, Redway, CA; "Grandmas Join Up in Head-waters Rally," *Eureka Times Standard*, November 13, 1996, EPIC archives, Red-way, CA; "60 Arrested at Timber Protest," *Eureka Times Standard*, November 16, 1996, EPIC archives, Redway, CA; "25 Arrested in Headwaters Protest," *Press Democrat* (Santa Rosa), November 16, 1996, EPIC archives, Redway, CA; "Headwaters Stunt," *Press Democrat* (Santa Rosa), November 26, 1996, EPIC archives, Redway, CA; "Throw the Book at Them," *San Francisco Chronicle*, November 26, 1996, EPIC archives, Redway, CA.

43 Memo from Kathy Bailey to HFCC, "Where We Go from Here," October 22, 1996, EPIC archives, Eureka, CA; Tracy Katelman to HFCC, "Re: Ongoing HFCC, Finances, etc...," October 22, 1996, EPIC archives, Eureka, CA; Dar-ryl Cherney, "Official Statement to HFCC," October 22, 1996, EPIC archives, Eureka, CA; Kathy Bailey to EPIC and Whoever, "Re: What I have been saying and doing which may have caused some concerns to arise," November 21, 1996, EPIC archives, Eureka, CA; Michael Shellenberger to HFCC Media Committee, "Where We Are Now," October 24, 1996, EPIC archives, Eureka, CA.

44 Glen Martin and Alex Barnum, "Earth First Ready to Defy Loggers," *San Francisco Chronicle*, October 9, 1996, EPIC archives, Redway, CA; Jessie Faulkner, "Headwaters Rally Brings New Arrests," *Eureka Times Standard*, October 13, 1996, EPIC archives, Redway, CA; Felicia Marcus, Regional Administrator, Environmental Protection Agency, to Robert Kersteins, Chairman, CA Board of Forestry, October 1, 1996, papers of Kathy Bailey, Philo, CA; Department of Forestry, "Board Rejects Proposed Emergency Rule," news release, October 9, 1996, EPIC archives, Redway, CA; Senator Diane Feinstein to Governor Pete Wilson, October 18, 1996, papers of Kathy Bailey, Philo, CA; Kathy Bailey to Secretary Garamendi, "Re: Board of For-estry—Oct. 8," October 3, 1996, papers of Kathy Bailey, Philo, CA; Kathy Bailey, "Draft by KB 895–3716 October 11, 20:00 PDT: Environmental Groups Call for Cease Fire in Headwaters Forest," October 11, 1996, EPIC archives, Eureka, CA; Jessie Faulkner, "Headwaters Rally Brings New Arrests," *Eureka Times Standard*, October 13, 1996, EPIC archives, Redway, CA; Kathy Bailey to Elyssa Rosen, Josh Kaufman, Adam Werbach, Julia Bott, David Nesmith, Bill Craven, Joel Brecher, EPIC, "Subject: HW OF report," March 5, 1997, papers of Kathy Bailey, Philo, CA.

45 Bundy interview; Kevin Bundy, e-mail to the author, October 16, 2011.

46 Phone interview with Paul Mason by the author, October 27, 2011 (all notes in the possession of the author).

47 Trees Foundation, "Headwaters Forest Stewardship Plan." Regarding free market regulation and neoliberalism, see Richard B. Stewart, "A New Gener-ation of Environmental Regulation?" *Capital University Law Review* 29 (2001): 21–182; and Cass Sunstein, *Risk and Reason: Safety, Law, and the Environment* (Cambridge: University of Cambridge Press, 2002).

48 Trees Foundation, "Headwaters Forest Stewardship Plan," 10–13; Franklin, "Toward a New Forestry."

49 Trees Foundation, "Headwaters Forest Stewardship Plan," 1, 3, 11, 16–28, 30–57.

50 Regarding the community-based business approach, see Trees Foundation, "Headwaters Forest Stewardship Plan," 27, 30–57. Again, the ideas of the Headwaters Forest Stewardship Plan run counter to the general analysis of radical environmentalists as defined by Richard White, Ramachandra Guha, William Cronon, Robert Gottlieb, and even more recently by Darryl Fears, "Within Mainstream Environmental Groups, Diversity Is Lacking," *Washington Post*, March 25, 2013, C1. For Tom Power's work, see *Environmental Protection and Economic Well-Being: The Economic Pursuit of Quality* (New York: M. E. Sharpe, 1996); *Lost Landscapes and Failed Economies: The Search for a Value of Place* (Washington, DC: Island Press, 1996); "Economic Well-Being and Environmental Protection in the Pacific Northwest," *Illahee: Journal of the Northwest Environment* 12, no. 1 (Spring 1996); "The Economic Values of Wilderness," *International Journal of Wilderness* 2, no. 1 (April 1996); "Ecosystem Preservation and the Economy of the Greater Yellowstone Area," *Conservation Biology* 5, no. 3 (September 1991). The activists specifically stated that their plan was not one for "locking up" wilderness; see Trees Foundation, "Headwaters Forest Stewardship Plan," 1.

51 Memo from Josh Kaufman to HFCC, "Idea," October 3, 1996, EPIC archives, Eureka, CA; Mason interview.

52 Pastor David S. Kilmer, "Biblical Guides for Forest," *Eureka Times Standard*, June 21, 1997; "Tentative Workshop Schedule," 1997; fax from Darryl Cherney to Kevin Bundy, funder proposal for Jail Hurwitz Campaign and website, May 7, 1997, EPIC archives, Eureka, CA; Terri Langford, "Headwaters Proposal Thwarted," *Press Democrat* (Santa Rosa), May 23, 1997; David Ivanovich, "Protesters Confront Maxxam," *Houston Chronicle*, May 23, 1997, papers of Kathy Bailey, Philo, CA; Shaun Walker, "3 Arrested in Protest at PL Site," *Eureka Times Standard*, August 23, 1997; Barbara Henry, "Earth First Stages Headwaters 'Teach-in' on College Campuses," *Eureka Times Standard*, September 16, 1997; "Carlotta: Protesters Block Road near PL Land," *Eureka Times Standard*, September 19, 1997; "Protesters Halt Pacific Lumber Logging Operation," *Eureka Times Standard*, September 27, 1997; Mike Geniella, "Activists Tree-sit in Protest, but Old-Growth Logging Goes On," *Press Democrat* (Santa Rosa), October 2, 1997; "Riggs Office Closes Early after Death Threats Made," *Eureka Times Standard*, October 31, 1997; Associated Press, "9 Arrested in Sacramento," *Press Democrat* (Santa Rosa), November 4, 1997; David Anderson, "Mystery Flier Heats Forest Tiff," *Eureka Times Standard*, November 4, 1997; "Police Observe Another Protest," *Eureka Times Standard*, November 14, 1997; Andrew LaMar, "Humboldt Deputies Arrest 13 Protesters," *Press Democrat* (Santa Rosa), October 9, 1996; Suzanne Zalev, "Another

Man Out on a Limb," *Eureka Times Standard*, October 20, 1998; Jason Kennedy Steele, "Activists Vow PL action today," *Eureka Times Standard*, November 16, 1998; Jason Kennedy Steele, "Deputies Arrest 18 Activists," *Eureka Times Standard*, November 17, 1998; Jason Kennedy Steele, "Vandals Hit Car at Tree-sit," *Eureka Times Standard*, December 28, 1998. The EPIC archives in Redway contain hard copies of all articles.

53 "Carlotta: Protesters Block Road Near PL Land," *Eureka Times Standard*, September 19, 1997; "Protesters Halt Pacific Lumber Logging Operation," *Eureka Times Standard*, September 27, 1997; Mike Geniella, "Activists Treesit in Protest, but Old-Growth Logging Goes On," *Press Democrat* (Santa Rosa), October 2, 1997. Another example of counterproductive actions can be found in "Alleged Pie Hitter to Get Own Lawyer," *Eureka Times Standard*, September 28, 1997. The EPIC archives in Redway contain hard copies of all articles.

54 Kathy Bailey, "Summary and Update on the Pepper Spray Cases: June 24, 1998," papers of Kathy Bailey, Philo, CA; Jason Van Derbeken, George Snyder, and Sabin Russell, "FBI Probing Pepper Spray 'Swabbing,'" *San Francisco Chronicle*, November 1, 1997, EPIC archives, Redway, CA; letter from Tim McKay to Attorney General Janet Reno, "Earth First and Congressman Frank Riggs AND the distribution of false documents. . . ," November 6, 1997, EPIC archives, Eureka, CA; James W. Sweeney, "Protesters Heckle Riggs at Holiday Ceremony," *Press Democrat* (Santa Rosa), November 12, 1997; "Lungren on Pepper Spray," *Press Democrat* (Santa Rosa), November 20, 1997; James W. Sweeney, "Riggs Urges Law against Demonstrators' Devices," *Press Democrat* (Santa Rosa), November 21, 1997; Mikal Jakubal, "Saving the Forest for the Trees," proposal, March 20, 1998, EPIC archives, Eureka, CA; David Anderson, "Southern Humboldt Rancher Tries to Bar PL Logging," *Eureka Times Standard*, July 22, 1998, CA; Jonathan Jeisel, "Civil Suit to Follow on Death of Activist," *Humboldt Beacon*, December 24, 1998; James W. Sweeney, "Activist's Family Calls Report Biased," *Press Democrat* (Santa Rosa), December 19, 1998; Rhonda Parker, "Pepper Spray Suit Dismissed," *Eureka Times Standard*, October 27, 1998. The EPIC archives in Redway contain hard copies of all articles.

55 Regarding the technical challenges of the Dinosaur campaign and the politics of administration, see Harvey, *Symbol of Wilderness*, chapter 7; and Hays, *Beauty, Health, and Permanence*, chapter 14. Regarding the HFCC campaign, see "1997 EPIC and Sierra Club California Habitat Conservation Plan / Sustained Yield Plan Monitoring Project," papers of Kathy Bailey, Philo, CA; memo from Brian Gaffney to Kathy Bailey and Paul Mason, "Garamendi Hdwtrs Agreement," October 3, 1996, EPIC archives, Eureka, CA; Kathy Bailey, memo to Chuck Powell, Cecelia Lanman, Paul Mason, and Kevin Bundy, Draft 1, August 19, 1997, EPIC archives, Eureka, CA; Kathy Bailey letter to Friends, July 12, 1997, papers of Kathy Bailey, Philo, CA; Tara Mueller memo

to Josh Kaufman, Elyssa Rosen, and Paul Mason, "Headwaters Agreement," July 31, 1997, EPIC archives, Eureka, CA; Tara Mueller to Paul Mason and Josh Kaufman, "Re: Your HW Agreement Memo," August 2, 1997, EPIC archives, Eureka, CA; Josh Kaufman to Kathy Bailey, Brian Gaffney, Elyssa Rosen, Tom Lippe, Tara Mueller, EPIC, "Subject: Tom's Memo," August 11, 1997, EPIC archives, Eureka, CA; Kathy Bailey, memo to Cecelia, Paul, Kevin, Elyssa, and Josh, "Confidential: Common Interest in Litigation Privilege: Offer of Financial Assistance from Environment Now!" June 1, 1998, papers of Kathy Bailey, Philo, CA; Kathy Bailey to Dave Montgomery, Chris Frissell, Peter Moyle, and George Pess, "PL HCP Review," June 30, 1998, papers of Kathy Bailey, Philo, CA; Susan Reed Clark to Cecelia Lanman, "RE: Grant #99-38," October 15, 1998, papers of Kathy Bailey, Philo, CA.

56 Carolyn Lochheard, "Headwaters Deal Runs into More Trouble in House," *San Francisco Chronicle*, January 24, 1997; Mike Geniella, "Feinstein Urges All-Cash Deal for Headwaters," *Press Democrat* (Santa Rosa), January 24, 1997; David Anderson, "PL Spurns State Offer, Seeks Cash for Forest," *Eureka Times Standard*, February 5, 1997; Mike Geniella, "Forest Deal Delayed until '98," *Press Democrat* (Santa Rosa), March 13, 1997; John Howard, "Hurwitz to Get Cash Offer for Headwaters," *Press Democrat* (Santa Rosa), March 15, 1997; Associated Press, "U.S. Finds Cash for Forest," *Eureka Times Standard*, May 17, 1997; David Anderson, "Timber Deal May Hit Snag," *Eureka Times Standard*, May 20, 1997; Carolyn Lochhead, "Clinton OKs $250 Million to Buy Headwaters Forest," *San Francisco Chronicle*, November 15, 1997. The fight over how to address "the Deal" was ugly at times. See Karen Picket to Darryl Cherney, April 8, 1998, EPIC archives, Eureka, CA. The EPIC Archives in Redway contain hard copies of all articles.

57 Mike Geniella, "Headwaters Impasse Feared," *Press Democrat* (Santa Rosa), December 13, 1997; David Anderson, "Forest Rescue May Go to Vote," *Eureka Times Standard*, June 16, 1997; "Thompson Details Headwaters Bond, Vote Plan," *Eureka Times Standard*, September 24, 1997; "Joint Committee on Headwaters Forest and Ecosystem Management: Transcript; Habitat Conservation Plan Hearing," March 16, 1998, EPIC archives, Eureka, CA; Kathy Bailey, "Damned If We Do; Damned If We Don't—Draft," memo to undisclosed recipients, July 21, 1998, papers of Kathy Bailey, Philo, CA; Bailey interview.

58 Greg Lucas, "Redwoods Protection Plan in Jeopardy," *San Francisco Chronicle*, August 14, 1998, EPIC archives, Redway, CA; Seth Hettena, "Stars Protest Headwaters Buyout Plan," *Eureka Times Standard*, August 21, 1998, EPIC archives, Redway, CA; Greg Magnus, "Headwaters in Public Hands," *Eureka Times Standard*, September 20, 1998, EPIC archives, Redway, CA; Greg Lucas, "Burton Says Headwaters Deal Is Off," *San Francisco Chronicle*, August 22, 1998, EPIC archives, Redway, CA; letter from Carl Pope to Members of the California Legislature, "OPPOSE AB 1986 (Headwaters) as

amended today," August 31, 1998, papers of Kathy Bailey, Philo, CA; Greg
Lucas, "Wilson Sent New Deal on Redwoods," *San Francisco Chronicle*, Sep-
tember 2, 1998, EPIC archives, Redway, CA; David Anderson, "Headwaters
Hits Roadblock," *Eureka Times Standard*, September 1, 1998, EPIC archives,
Redway, CA; Greg Lucas, "A New Deal to Protect Headwaters," *San Francisco
Chronicle*, September 1, 1998, EPIC archives, Redway, CA; memo from Carl
Pope to Sierra Club Board of Directors, circa September 5, 1998, papers of
Kathy Bailey, Philo, CA; undated memo from Kathy Bailey to HFCC, SC,
G07, and other colleagues, "Brief Summary of AB 1986 (Migden) as Passed
August 31, 1998," papers of Kathy Bailey, Philo, CA; David Anderson, "The
Headwaters Deal," *Eureka Times Standard*, September 13, 1998, EPIC archives,
Redway, CA; Bailey interview.

59 Kathy Bailey, "Timeline of Last-Minute Events on Headwaters Deal," confi-
dential memo for attorneys and clients, March 17, 1999, Bailey papers, Philo,
CA; Bailey interview; Mason phone interview; Pacific Lumber Company,
"Pacific Lumber/Scotia Pacific File Information on Sustained Yield Plan
with California Department of Forestry and Fire Protection," news release,
February 17, 1999, papers of Kathy Bailey, Philo, CA; Agreement Relating to
Enforcement of AB 1986, contract signed by California Resources Agency,
California Department of Fish and Game, California Department of For-
estry, California Wildlife Conservation Board, Pacific Lumber Company,
Scotia Pacific Company LLC., and Salmon Creek Corporation, February 25,
1999, papers of Kathy Bailey, Philo, CA; Richard Wilson to John Campbell,
"Re: SYP No. 96–002 Determination," February 25, 1999, papers of Kathy
Bailey, Philo, CA.

60 Mike Spear and William T. Hogarth to Richard Wilson, "Re: SYP 96–002
Determination," February 27, 1999, papers of Kathy Bailey, Philo, CA; L.
Ryan Broddick to Richard Wilson, "Subject: SYP No. 96–002 Determina-
tion," February 27, 1999, papers of Kathy Bailey, Philo, CA; Richard Wilson
to John Campbell, March 1, 1999, papers of Kathy Bailey, Philo, CA; David
Hayes and Terry Garcia to John Campbell, "Re: The Pacific Lumber Com-
pany Habitat Conservation Plan," March 1, 1999, papers of Kathy Bailey,
Philo, CA; Jim Carlton, "After Maxxam Spurns Headwaters Deal, Govern-
ment Agencies Prepare for Battle," *Wall Street Journal*, March 1, 1999, A6;
Andrew Gumbel, "Ancient Californian Forests under Threat as Deal Col-
lapses," *Independent* (London), March 1, 1999, 10; David J. Hayes, "Saving the
Headwaters Forest: A Jewel That Nearly Slipped Away," *Environmental Law
Review* 30, no. 2 (February 2000), papers of Kathy Bailey, Philo, CA.

61 Bureau of Land Management, "Notice of Availability of the Headwaters Forest Reserve Draft Resource Management Plan," *Federal Register* 67, no. 77
(2002): 19585–86; "Headwaters Forest and Elk River Property Acquisition,"
Pub. L. No. 105–83, 111 Stat. 1543 (1997), http://uscode.house.gov/statviewer.
htm?volume=111&page=1543; Headwaters Forest, Owl Creek, and Grizzly

Creek Appropriation Bill, AB 1986, accessed January 4, 2016, http://leginfo. ca.gov/pub/97–98/bill/asm/ab_1951–2000/ab_1986_bill_19980901_enrolled. html; and Agreement Relating to Enforcement of AB 1986, contract signed by California Resources Agency, California Department of Fish and Game, California Department of Forestry, California Wildlife Conservation Board, Pacific Lumber Company, Scotia Pacific Company LLC., and Salmon Creek Corporation, February 25, 1999, papers of Kathy Bailey, Philo, CA.

62   Joseph L. Sax, "Environmental Law at the Turn of the Century: A Reportorial Fragment of Contemporary History," *California Law Review* 88, no. 6 (2000); US Fish and Wildlife Service, *Status of Habitat Conservation Plans* (Washington, DC: US Government Printing Office, 1997). Additionally, see Shi-Ling Hsu, "The Potential and Pitfalls of Habitat Conservation Planning under the Endangered Species Act," *Environmental Law Review* 29 (October 1999): 10592–601.

EPILOGUE

1   Mary Callahan, "Logging Blamed in Mudslide: Humboldt Town Fears Repeat," *Press Democrat* (Santa Rosa), January 10, 1997, B1; Glen Martin, "Clear-Cutting Blamed for Many Mudslides," *San Francisco Chronicle*, January 9, 1997, A17; Paul Rogers, "Mudslide on Land That Was Clear Cut Destroys Seven Homes," *Contra Costa Times*, January 9, 1997, D11; Hill, *The Legacy of Luna*.

2   Timothy Egan, "Bracing for Worst in West Coast Salmon Country," *New York Times*, April 5, 1992, A18; Linda Wertheimer, "Salmon Fishing to Be Cut in Half in North West," *All Things Considered*, National Public Radio, April 13, 1992; Marla Cone, "U.S. Protection of Coho Salmon Spawns Criticism," *Los Angeles Times*, October 26, 1996, 1; Julie Tamaki, "California and the West: Famers, Tribes Have State in River Ruling," *Los Angeles Times*, August 9, 2000, 3; Eric Bailey, "Administration May Cut Klamath's Flow Again," *Los Angeles Times*, October 11, 2002, B10; Eric Bailey, "U.S. Report Cites Low Levels in Klamath River for Fish Die-Off," *Los Angeles Times*, November 19, 2003, B6; Eric Bailey, "Salmon Fishing Ban Considered," *Los Angeles Times*, March 4, 2006, B1; Eric Bailey, "U.S. Acts to Help Wild Salmon in Klamath River," *Los Angeles Times*, March 30, 2006, B1; Tom Chandler, "A Brief History of the Contentious Klamath River Salmon Recovery/Dam Removal Issue," *Trout Underground*, November 13, 2011, accessed October 8, 2013, http://troutunderground.com/2008/11/a-brief-history-of-the-contentious-klamath-river-salmon-recoverydam-removal-issue/.

3   EPIC, "Summary of EPIC Forestry Lawsuits, 1997–Present," EPIC archives, Eureka, CA; Kathy Bailey, "Facts and History on Headwaters Forest Transaction," memo to Sierra Club, undated (after 2001), Bailey papers, Philo, CA; EPIC, "Summary of EPIC Forestry Lawsuits, 1997–Present," EPIC archives,

Eureka, CA; Kathy Bailey, "Why I Should Feel Good (Even If I Don't)," memo, March 4, 1999, Bailey papers, Philo, CA; "Maxxam Tries to Hide from Shareholders at Annual Meeting," *Investor Relations Business*, June 7, 1999; Mike Geniella, "Pacific Lumber to Keep Logging," *Press Democrat* (Santa Rosa), August 4, 1999, EPIC archives, Redway, CA; "Complaint for Declaratory and Injunctive Relief," *Environmental Protection Information Center and Sierra Club v. William D. Daley, Secretary of Commerce, Penelope D. Dalton, Director, National Marine Fisheries Service, Bruce Babbitt, Secretary of the Interior, Jamie R. Clark, Director United States Fish and Wildlife Service, The Pacific Lumber Company, Scotia Pacific Company, LLC, and Salmon Creek Corporation*, U.S. District Court for the Northern District of California, San Francisco Division (1999), EPIC archives, Eureka, CA; Luna Preservation Agreement, December 15, 1999, EPIC archives, Eureka, CA; Julia Butterfly Hill, "Out on a Limb," *Earth Island Institute* 15, no. 1 (Spring 2000): 48; "Woman Strikes Deal with Lumber Company to Leave Redwood Home," *New York Times*, December 19, 1999, 1, 39; Carl Pope to Senator Dianne Feinstein, "Re: Headwaters Debt for Nature Exchange," January 12, 2000, papers of Kathy Bailey, Philo, CA; John Howard, "Environmentalists Urge Immediate Halt to Logging Old-Growth Timber," *Associated Press State and Local Wire*, January 12, 2000; EPIC, "Summary of EPIC Forestry Lawsuits, 1997–Present."

4   Sara March, "Mattole Watershed under Attack, Resistance Continues," Mendocino Environmental Center website, October 22, 2002, accessed October 9, 2013, http://www.mecgrassroots.org/NEWSL/ISS43/43.08mattole.html; BBW Associates, "Mattole Forest Futures Project," California Department of Forestry and Fire Protection, May 17, 2011.

5   "The Pacific Lumber Company Statement on Posting Bond in THP 520 Litigation," *Business Wire*, July 20, 2000; John Howard, "Forestry Board Rejects Proposed Logging Rules," *Associated Press State and Local Wire*, October 4, 2000; Don Thompson, "California Board Takes First Step to Protect Old-Growth Trees," *Associated Press State and Local Wire*, September 10, 2001; "Come On Down, At Least for Now," *New York Times*, March 19, 2003, 23; "California: Injunction against Tree-Sitters," *New York Times*, March 12, 2003, 20; Don Thompson, "State Water Board Orders Monitoring of Palco's Headwaters Cuts," *Associated Press State and Local Wire*, October 18, 2001; Dean E. Murphy, "Scientists' Report Finds Grounds for Regulating Redwood Harvest," *New York Times*, January 14, 2004, A21; Kai Ryssdall and Craig Miller, "Pacific Lumber Threatens Bankruptcy Due to Lawsuits and Water Regulations," *Marketplace*, National Public Radio, June 22, 2005; S. C. Gwynne, "Tree Ring Circus," *Texas Monthly*, April 2006; Loren Steffy, "It Seems Like Charles Hurwitz Just Can't Catch a Break," *Houston Chronicle*, January 23, 2007; Paul Elias, "Supreme Court Orders New Headwaters Logging Plan," *Associated Press State and Local Wire*, July 17, 2008; John Blakeley, "Palco Emerges from Ch. 11," *Daily Deal/The Deal*, August 1, 2008; Terence

Chea, "Gap Family Takes Over Troubled Timber Firm," *San Francisco Chronicle*, July 30, 2008; Evelyn Nieves, "Last Tree-Sitters Come Down from Calif. Redwoods," *Associated Press State and Local Wire*, September 23, 2008.

6   Natalynne DeLapp, "Rare Redwood Tract Protected as Community Forest," EPIC website, June 25, 2012, accessed September 11, 2015, http://www.wildcalifornia.org/blog/mckay/.

7   Bonnano and Constance, *Stories of Globalization*, introduction and 180–88.

8   Sutter, *Driven Wild*.

SELECTED BIBLIOGRAPHY

Andrews, Thomas. *Killing for Coal: America's Deadliest Labor War*. Cambridge, MA: Harvard University Press, 2010.

Barbour, Michael, Sandy Lydon, Mark Borchert, Marjorie Popper, Valerie Whitworth, and John Evarts. *Coast Redwood: A Natural and Cultural History*. Los Olivos, CA: Cachuma Press, 2001.

Bari, Judi. *Timber Wars*. Monroe, ME: Common Courage Press, 1994.

Baumol, William. *Welfare Economics and the Theory of the State*. Cambridge, MA: Harvard University Press, 1967.

Bedford, Henry F. *Seabrook Station: Citizen Politics and Nuclear Power*. Amherst: University of Massachusetts Press, 1990.

Bevington, Douglas. *Rebirth of Environmentalism: Grassroots Activism from the Spotted Owl to the Polar Bear*. Washington, DC: Island Press, 2009.

Binkley, Cameron. "'No Better Heritage Than Living Trees': Women's Clubs and Early Conservation in Humboldt County." *Western Historical Quarterly* 33, no. 2 (Summer 2002).

Bonnano, Alessandro, and Douglas H. Constance. *Stories of Globalization: Transnational Corporations, Resistance, and the State*. University Park: Pennsylvania State University Press, 2008.

Brock, Emily K. *Money Trees: The Douglas Fir and American Forestry, 1900–1944*. Corvallis: Oregon State University Press, 2015.

Brooks, John, *The Takeover Game: The Men, the Moves, and the Wall Street Money behind Today's Nationwide Merger Wars*. New York: Truman Talley Books, 1987.

Brüggemeier, Franz-Josef, Marc Cioc, and Thomas Zeller, eds. *How Green Were the Nazis? Nature, Environment, and Nation in the Third Reich*. Athens: University of Ohio Press, 2005.

Bryner, Gary C. *Blue Skies, Green Politics: The Clean Air Act of 1990 and Its Implementation*. Washington, DC: Congressional Quarterly Press, 1995.

Callicott, J. Baird, and Michael P. Nelson, eds. *The Great New Wilderness Debate: An Expansive Collection of Writings Defining Wilderness from John Muir to Gary Snyder*. Athens: University of Georgia Press, 1998.

Carpenter, Daniel P. *The Forging of Bureaucratic Autonomy: Reputations, Networks,* and Policy Innovation in Executive Agencies, 1862–1928. Princeton, NJ: Princeton University Press, 2001.

Carranco, Lynwood, and John T. Labbe. *Logging the Redwoods*. Caldwell, ID: Caxton, 1975.

Chase, Alston. *In a Dark Wood: The Fights over Forests and the Myths of Nature*. New Brunswick, NJ: Transaction, 2001.

Chong, Dennis. *Collective Action and the Civil Rights Movement*. Chicago: University of Chicago Press, 1991.

Clar, C. Raymond. *California Government and Forestry from Spanish Days until the Creation of the Department of Natural Resources in 1927*. Sacramento: Division of Forestry, Department of Natural Resources, State of California, 1959.

———. *California Government and Forestry II: During the Young and Rolph Administrations*. Sacramento: Division of Forestry, Department of Conservation, State of California, 1969.

Cohen, Lizabeth. *A Consumer's Republic: The Politics of Mass Consumption in Postwar America*. New York: Vintage Books, 2003.

———. *Making a New Deal: Industrial Workers in Chicago, 1919–1939*. New York: Cambridge University Press, 1990.

Cohen, Michael P. *The History of the Sierra Club, 1892–1970*. San Francisco: Sierra Club Books, 1988.

Cronon, William. *Changes in the Land: Indians, Colonists, and the Ecology of New England*. New York: Hill and Wang, 1983.

———. *Nature's Metropolis: Chicago and the Great West*. New York: W. W. Norton, 1991.

Cronon, William, ed. *Uncommon Ground: Rethinking the Human Place in Nature*. New York: W. W. Norton, 1996.

Crosby, Alfred W. *Ecological Imperialism: The Biological Expansion of Europe, 900–1900*. Cambridge: Cambridge University Press, 1986.

Czech, Brian, and Paul R. Krausman. *The Endangered Species Act: History, Conservation Biology, and Public Policy*. Baltimore, MD: Johns Hopkins University Press, 2001.

Dana, Samuel Trask, and Myron Krueger. *California Lands: Ownership, Use, and Management*. Washington, DC: American Forestry Association, 1958.

Devall, Bill, and George Sessions. *Deep Ecology*. Salt Lake City, UT: G. M. Smith, 1985.

Dietrich, William. *The Final Forest: The Battle for the Last Great Trees of the Pacific Northwest*. New York: Penguin Books, 1993.

Duggan, Sharon. "Citizen Enforcement of California's Private Land Forest Practice Regulations." *Journal of Environmental Law and Litigation* 8 (Spring 1994): 291–315.

Duggan, Sharon, and Tara Mueller. *A Guide to the California Forest Practice Act and Related Laws*. Point Arena, CA: Solano Press Books, 2005.

Dunlop, Thomas R. *Faith in Nature: Environmentalism as Religious Quest.* Seattle: University of Washington Press, 2004.

Dunning, Joan. *From the Redwood Forest: Ancient Trees and the Bottom Line: A Headwaters Journey.* White River Junction, VT: Chelsea Green Publishing, 1998.

Durbin, Kathie. *Tree Huggers: Victory, Defeat and Renewal in the Northwest Ancient Forest Campaign.* Seattle, WA: Mountaineers, 1996.

Edsall, Thomas Byrne, and Mary D. Edsall. *Chain Reaction: The Impact of Race, Rights, and Taxes on American Politics.* New York: W. W. Norton, 1991.

Ellefson, Paul V., and Robert N. Stone. *U.S. Wood-Based Industry: Industrial Organization and Performance.* New York: Praeger, 1984.

Farmer, Jared. *Trees in Paradise: A California History.* New York: W. W. Norton, 2013.

Findley, Roger W., Daniel A. Farber, and Jody Freeman. *Cases and Materials on Environmental Law.* 6th ed. Saint Paul, MN: Thomson/West, 2003.

Flippen, J. Brooks. *Nixon and the Environment.* Albuquerque: University of New Mexico Press, 2000.

Foreman, Dave. *Confessions of an Eco-Warrior.* New York: Harmony Books, 1991.

Fox, Stephen. *The American Conservation Movement: John Muir and His Legacy.* Madison: University of Wisconsin Press, 1985.

Fraser, Steve, and Gary Gerstle, eds. *The Rise and Fall of the New Deal Order, 1930–1980.* Princeton, NJ: Princeton University Press, 1989.

Frohlich, Norman, and Joe A. Oppenheimer. "I Get By with a Little Help from My Friends." *World Politics* 23 (October): 104–21.

Galambos, Louis, and Joseph Pratt. *The Rise of the Corporate Commonwealth: United States Business and Public Policy in the 20th Century.* New York: Basic Books, 1988.

Gerstle, Gary. *American Crucible: Race and Nation in the Twentieth Century.* Princeton, NJ: Princeton University Press, 2001.

Gitlin, Todd. *The Sixties: Years of Hope, Days of Rage.* Toronto: Bantam Books, 1987.

Gottlieb, Robert. *Forcing the Spring: The Transformation of the American Environmental Movement.* Washington, DC: Island Press, 1993.

Guha, Ramachandra. "Radical American Environmentalism and Wilderness Preservation: A Third World Critique." In Callicott and Nelson, *The Great New Wilderness Debate,* 231–45.

Hardin, Russell. *Collective Action.* Baltimore, MD: Johns Hopkins University Press, 1982.

———. "Collective Action as an Agreeable N-Prisoners' Dilemma." *Behavioral Science* 16, no. 5 (1971): 472–79.

Harris, David. *The Last Stand: The War between Wall Street and Main Street over California's Ancient Redwoods.* New York: Times Books, 1995.

Harvey, Mark W. T. *A Symbol of Wilderness: Echo Park and the American Conservation Movement.* Seattle: University of Washington Press, 1994.

Hawley, Ellis W. *The New Deal and the Problem of Monopoly: A Study in Economic Ambivalence.* Princeton, NJ: Princeton University Press, 1966.

———. "The Discovery and Study of a 'Corporate Liberalism.'" *Business History Review* 52, no. 3 (Autumn 1978): 309–20.

Hays, Samuel P. *Beauty, Health, and Permanence: Environmental Politics in the United States, 1955–1985.* Cambridge: Cambridge University Press, 1987.

———. *Conservation and the Gospel of Efficiency: The Progressive Conservation Movement, 1890–1920.* Cambridge, MA: Harvard University Press, 1959.

———. *A History of Environmental Politics since 1945.* Pittsburgh, PA: University of Pittsburgh Press, 2000.

———. *Wars in the Woods: The Rise of Ecological Forestry.* Pittsburgh, PA: University of Pittsburgh Press, 2007.

Helvarg, David. *The War against the Greens: The "Wise-Use" Movement, the New Right, and the Browning of America.* Boulder, CO: Johnson Books, 2004.

Hidy, Ralph W., Frank Ernest Hill, and Allan Nevins. *Timber and Men: The Weyerhaeuser Story.* New York: MacMillan, 1963.

Hill, Julia Butterfly. *The Legacy of Luna: The Story of Tree, a Woman, and the Struggle to Save the Redwoods.* New York: HarperCollins, 2000.

Hirt, Paul. *A Conspiracy of Optimism: Management of the National Forests since World War Two.* Lincoln: University of Nebraska Press, 1994.

Hodgson, Godfrey. *The World Turned Right Side Up: A History of the Conservative Ascendancy in America.* Boston: Houghton Mifflin, 1996.

Houck, Oliver A. *The Clean Water Act TMDL Program: Law, Policy and Implementation.* Washington, DC: Environmental Law Institute, 2002.

Kelman, Ari. *A River and Its City: The Nature of Landscape in New Orleans.* Berkeley: University of California Press, 2003.

Kraft, Michael E. *Environmental Policy and Politics.* New York: Pearson Longman, 2007.

Langston, Nancy. *Forest Dreams, Forest Nightmares: The Paradox of Old Growth in the Inland West.* Seattle: University of Washington Press, 1995.

Lasch, Christopher. *The True and Only Heaven: Progress and Its Critics.* New York: W. W. Norton, 1991.

Lazarus, Richard J. *The Making of Environmental Policy.* Chicago: University of Chicago Press, 2004.

Lears, T. J. Jackson. *No Place of Grace: Antimodernism and the Transformation of American Culture, 1880–1920.* New York: Pantheon Books, 1981.

Lemaster, Dennis C. *Decade of Change: The Remaking of Forest Service Statutory Authority during the 1970s.* Westport, CT: Greenwood Press, 1984.

Leopold, Aldo. "Wilderness as a Form of Land Use." In Callicott and Nelson, *The Great New Wilderness Debate*, 75–84.

Leydet, Francois. *The Last Redwoods and the Parkland of Redwood Creek.* San Francisco: Sierra Club, 1960.

Lippe, Thomas N., and Kathy Bailey. "Regulation of Logging on Private Lands in California under Governor Gray Davis." *Golden Gate University Law Review* 31, no. 4 (2001): 351–431.

Loomis, Erik. *Out of Sight: The Long and Disturbing Story of Corporations Outsourcing Catastrophe.* New York: New Press, 2015.

Lowood, Henry E. "The Calculating Forester: Quantification, Cameral Science, and the Emergence of Scientific Forestry Management in Germany." In *The Quantifying Spirit in the Eighteenth Century,* edited by Tore Frangsmyr, J. L. Heilbron, and Robin E. Rider, 315–42. Berkeley: University of California Press, 1990.

Manes, Christopher. *Green Rage: Radical Environmentalism and the Unmaking of Civilization.* Boston: Little, Brown, 1990.

Marsh, Kevin R. *Drawing Lines in the Forest: Creating Wilderness Areas in the Pacific Northwest.* Seattle: University of Washington Press, 2007.

Marshall, Robert. "The Problem of Wilderness." In Callicott and Nelson, *The Great New Wilderness Debate,* 85–96.

McCloskey, J. Michael. *In the Thick of It: My Life in the Sierra Club.* Washington, DC: Island Press, 2005.

McGirr, Lisa. *Suburban Warriors: The Origins of the New American Right.* Princeton, NJ: Princeton University Press, 2001.

Merchant, Carolyn. *Columbia Guide to American Environmental History.* New York: Columbia University Press, 2002.

———. *Radical Ecology: The Search for a Livable World.* New York: Routledge, 2005.

Morris, Aldon D., and Carol McClurg Mueller. *Frontiers in Social Movement Theory.* New Haven, CT: Yale University Press, 1992.

Muncy, Robyn. *Creating a Female Dominion in American Reform, 1890–1935.* New York: Oxford University Press, 1991.

Naess, Arne. *Ecology, Community, and Lifestyle: Outline of an Ecosophy.* Translated by David Rothenberg. Cambridge: Cambridge University Press, 1989.

Namorato, Michael V. "Lumber and Wood Products, 24.0." In *Manufacturing: A Historiographical and Bibliographical Guide,* edited by David O. Whitten and Bessie E. Whitten, 117–31. Westport, CT: Greenwood Press, 2000.

Nash, Roderick. *The Rights of Nature: A History of Environmental Ethics.* Madison: University of Wisconsin Press, 1989.

———. *Wilderness and the American Mind,* New Haven, CT: Yale University Press, 1973.

Nelson, Robert H. "The Gospel According to Conservation Biology." *Philosophy and Public Policy Quarterly* 27, nos. 3–4 (Summer/Fall 2007): 10–16.

———. "Ineffective Laws and Unexpected Consequences: A Brief Review of Public Land History." In *Public Lands and Private Rights: The Failure of Scientific Management,* 5–35. Lanham, MD: Rowman and Littlefield, 1995.

———. *The Making of Federal Coal Policy.* Durham, NC: Duke University Press, 1983.

Noss, Reed F., ed. *The Redwood Forest: History, Ecology, and Conservation of the Coast Redwoods*. Washington, DC: Island Press, 2000.

Olson, Sigurd. "Why Wilderness." In Callicott and Nelson, *The Great New Wilderness Debate*, 97–102.

Orren, Karen, and Stephen Skowronek. *The Search for American Political Development*. Cambridge: Cambridge University Press, 2004.

Payne, Charles M. *I've Got the Light of Freedom: The Organizing Tradition and the Mississippi Freedom Struggle*. Berkeley: University of California Press, 1995.

Pincetl, Stephanie S. *Transforming California: A Political History of Land Use and Development*. Baltimore, MD: Johns Hopkins University Press, 1999.

Piven, Frances Fox, and Richard A. Cloward. *Poor People's Movements: Why They Succeed, Why They Fail*. New York: Vintage, 1977.

Preston, Richard. *The Wild Trees: A Story of Passion and Daring*. New York: Random House, 2008.

Riley, Glenda. *Women and Nature: Saving the "Wild" West*. Lincoln: University of Nebraska Press, 1999.

Rome, Adam. *The Bulldozer in the Countryside: Suburban Sprawl and the Rise of American Environmentalism*. Cambridge: Cambridge University Press, 2001.

———. "'Give Earth a Chance': The Environmental Movement and the Sixties." *Journal of American History* 90, no. 2 (September 2003): 525–54.

Runte, Alfred. *National Parks: The American Experience*. Lincoln: University of Nebraska Press, 1997.

Sagoff, Mark. "The View from Quincy Library or Civic Engagement in Environmental Problem Solving." In *Price, Principle, and the Environment*, 201–31. New York: Cambridge University Press, 2004.

Salzman, James, and Barton H. Thompson. *Environmental Law and Policy*. New York: Foundation Press, 2003.

Sax, Joseph. *Mountains without Handrails: Reflections on the National Parks*. Ann Arbor: University of Michigan Press, 1980.

Scarce, Rik. *Eco-Warriors: Understanding the Radical Environmental Movement*. Walnut Creek, CA: Left Coast Press, 2006.

Schrepfer, Susan R. *The Fight to Save the Redwoods: A History of Environmental Reform, 1917–1978*. Madison: University of Wisconsin Press, 1983.

———. *Nature's Altars: Mountains, Gender, and American Environmentalism*. Lawrence: University of Kansas Press, 2005.

Sellers, Christopher C. *Crabgrass Crucible: Suburban Nature and the Rise of Environmentalism in Twentieth-Century America*. Chapel Hill: University of North Carolina Press, 2012.

Sheldon, Karin P. "Habitat Conservation Planning: Addressing the Achilles Heel of the Endangered Species Act." *New York University Environmental Law Journal* 6 (1998): 279–340.

Sher, Victor M. "Travels with Strix: The Spotted Owl's Journey through the Federal Courts." *Public Land Law Review* 14 (Spring 1993).

Sicilia, David B. "The Corporation under Siege: Social Movements, Regulation, Public Relations, and Tort Law since the Second World War." In *Constructing Corporate America: History, Politics, Culture*, edited by Kenneth Lipartito and David B. Sicilia. Oxford: Oxford University Press, 2004.

Sklar, Martin J. *The Corporate Reconstruction of American Capitalism, 1890–1916: The Market, the Law, and Politics*. Cambridge: Cambridge University Press, 1988.

Skocpol, Theda. *Diminished Democracy: From Membership to Management in American Civic Life*. Norman: University of Oklahoma Press, 2003.

Stanford Law Society. *The Endangered Species Act*. Palo Alto, CA: Stanford University Press, 2001.

Steinberg, Theodore. *Nature Incorporated: Industrialization and the Waters of New England*. Amherst: University of Massachusetts, 1991.

Stewart, Richard B. "A New Generation of Environmental Regulation?" *Capital University Law Review* 29 (2001): 21–182.

Sutter, Paul S. *Driven Wild: How the Fight against Automobiles Launched the Modern Wilderness Movement*. Seattle: University of Washington Press, 2002.

Swedlow, Brendon. "Scientists, Judges, and Spotted Owls: Policymakers in the Pacific Northwest." *Duke Environmental Law & Policy Forum* 13 (2003): 187–278.

Turner, James Morton. *The Promise of Wilderness: A History of American Environmental Politics since 1964*. Seattle: University of Washington Press, 2012.

Unger, Nancy C. *Beyond Nature's Housekeepers: American Women in Environmental History*. New York: Oxford University Press, 2012.

Vaughn, Jacqueline. *Green Backlash: The History and Politics of the Environmental Opposition in the U.S.* Boulder, CO: Lynne Rienner, 1997.

Wakild, Emily. "Border Chasm: International Boundary Parks and Mexican Conservation, 1935–1945." *Environmental History* 14 (July 2009): 453–75.

———. *Revolutionary Parks: Conservation, Social Justice, and Mexico's National Parks, 1910–1940*. Tucson: University of Arizona Press, 2011.

Wayburn, Edgar. *Your Land and Mine: Evolution of a Conservationist*. San Francisco: Sierra Club Books, 2004.

Webb, W. Prescott. *The Great Plains*. Boston: Ginn, 1931.

Wellock, Thomas R. *Preserving the Nation: The Conservation and Environmental Movements, 1870–2000*. Wheeling, WV: Harlan Davidson, 2007.

Weston, John Lowe. "The Endangered Species Committee and the Northern Spotted Owl: Did the 'God Squad' Play God?" *Administrative Law Journal of the American University* 7 (Fall 1993/Winter 1994).

White, Richard. "Are You an Environmentalist or Do You Work for a Living?" In *Uncommon Ground: Rethinking the Human Place in Nature*, edited by William Cronon, 171–85. New York: W. W. Norton, 1996.

———. *The Organic Machine*. New York: Hill and Wang, 1995.

Widdick, Richard. *Trouble in the Forest: California's Redwood Timber Wars*. Minneapolis: University of Minnesota Press, 2009.

Wiebe, Robert H. *The Search for Order, 1877–1920.* New York: Hill and Wang, 1967.

Winks, Robin W. *Laurance S. Rockefeller: Catalyst for Conservation.* Washington, DC: Island Press, 1997.

Williams, Michael. *Americans and Their Forests: A Historical Geography.* Cambridge: Cambridge University Press, 1989.

Worster, Donald. "John Muir and the Roots of American Environmentalism." In *The Wealth of Nature.* Oxford University Press, 1993.

———. *Rivers of Empire: Water, Aridity, and the Growth of the American West.* New York: Oxford University Press, 1985.

Yaffee, Steven Lewis. *The Wisdom of the Spotted Owl: Policy Lessons for a New Century.* Washington, DC: Island Press, 1994.

Zakin, Susan. *Coyotes and Town Dogs: Earth First! and the Environmental Movement.* Tuscon: University of Arizona Press, 1993.

Zaremba, Joseph. *Economics of the American Lumber Industry.* New York: Robert Speller & Sons, 1963.

INDEX

appropriations (*cont.*)
248; Headwaters appropriations bill,
246–47; highway appropriations bill,
51; for Sinkyone, 96
Arbit, Hal, 180–81, 182, 183, 184
Arcata, CA, xximap2, 32; activists
base in, 195; Arcata Earth First!,
191; Harris, Mark, 227; North Coast
Environmental Center, 146; rallies,
148, 149, 189, 236; tree-sits, 161
Arcata case, 80–83, 97, 281n13
Arcata National Corporation, 80–81, 83
Arctic National Wildlife Refuge,
283n37
arrests: Bari-Cherney bombing,
172, 188; Blanton Creek blockade,
225–26; Foreman, Dave, 191; Fort
Bragg rally, 190; images of, 240;
Littletree, Alicia, 193, 195; of North
Coast activists, 54, 85, 94, 226, 228,
237; September 15 rally, 234, 237, 239;
tree-sitting, 119, 151; trespassing,
94–95, 106fig.6, 189, 226, 228; and
Wise Use activists, 191
associationalism, 260
Atomic Energy Commission, US,
79–80
Avenue of the Giants, 62, 72, 101fig.1

B

Babbitt, Bruce, 211, 250–51
back-to-the-land lifestyles, 86, 196
backwoods actions: Earth First!,
196, 229, 232, 235, 236; Earth First!
splinter groups, 227, 245, 256; and
Littletree, 193, 226, 228
Bailey, Kathy, xv, 22, 176–78, 180, 267;
and EPIC, 219; and Forest Forever
initiative, 179, 180, 181, 182, 183, 184;
and Headwaters appropriation bill,
247, 248; and Headwaters Forest,
204, 205, 213, 215–17; land swap deals,

225; and legislative proposals, 197,
198; as North Coast activist, 238; and
Redwood Wars, 178
bald eagle protections, 223, 249
Bald Mountain direct action, 93
Bales, Alicia Littletree. *See* Littletree,
Alicia
Ball, Betty, 22, 147, 171, 179, 189
Ball, Gary, 22, 147, 171, 179
ballot initiatives: against Agent
Orange, 197; Big Green initiative,
180–82, 183; Grapevine Station
meeting, 179. *See also* Forests Forever
ballot initiative
Bar Harbor Ranch, 86
Bari, Judi: arrest of, 171–72, 188; attacks
on, 3–4, 5, 8, 162, 171, 174; death of,
245; and Earth First!, 160–61, 186–87,
193; and FBI lawsuit, 172, 192, 194;
FBI lawsuit settlement award, 5; as
female leader, 178; and Forest For-
ever initiative, 182; and HLAP, 200;
labor union activism, 159; and legis-
lative proposals, 198; as North Coast
activist, 238; North Coast Earth
First!, xi, 20, 22; photo of, 108fig.8.
See also Bari-Cherney bombing
Bari-Cherney bombing, 3–4, 5, 108fig.8,
171–72, 174, 188–89, 245
"Battle for Seattle", 264
Bayside case, 75–77, 80, 82, 223, 291n62
Bayside Timber Company, 75
Bechtle, Louis, 218, 220, 224
Beck, Ed, 136
Bedford, Henry F., 272n14
Bell, Sally, 92
Berkeley, CA, 44
Bevington, Douglass, 270n4
Biebe, Dave, 194
Big Basin conflict, 63, 143, 259
Big Basin Lumber Company, 46
Big Basin State Park, xxmap1, 13, 44,
45, 46, 64

Butcher, Marilyn, 188
Bytheriver, Marylee, 88

C

Cahto Peak, 162
California, State of, 23, 88; acquired
from Mexico, 37; first state park,
46; Humboldt Community Forest,
257; and industrial corporatism,
41–42; map, xxmap1; and redwood
forest acquisition, 46; regulatory
boards, 15; and Save the Redwoods
League, 56; and timber industry's
self-regulation, 6; timber operations
management, 77; and timber regulation system, 57, 60; transformation
of, 75–79
California Department of Fish and
Game (DFG), 156, 210, 278n52
California Department of Forestry
(CDF): and Board of Forestry, 82–83;
CEQA violations, 96; clearcutting
strategies, 90; cumulative impacts,
167; and EPIC, 94; and Forest
Practice Act, 97; and forest practice
rules creation, 77; former leaders of,
179; intransigence of, 84; and Little
Jackass Creek, 92; Mattole River
watershed, 256; Maxxam II case, 158;
and Pacific Lumber Company, 157;
plans monitoring, 98; reforms of,
99; resistance to responsibilities,
196; and Sally Bell harvest plan, 98;
and salvage logging permits, 218–19;
under scrutiny, 168; and THP, 183;
and Timber Harvest Plans, 155–56,
165, 167; and WCB contract, 248; and
wildlife surveys, 208
California Department of Health, 82
California Desert Lands Act, 206
California Endangered Species Act
(CESA), 16, 84

California Environmental Quality
Act (CEQA): and Board of Forestry duties, 82, 196; and CDF, 99;
citizen suit provision, 88; cumulative impacts evaluation, 99; Duggan
article on, 282n23; Gallegos case,
82–83; impacts, 80, 81, 83; litigation
strategies, 99; requirements, 97, 167,
209; Sally Bell Grove case, 96–97;
and Timber Harvest Plans, 80–81,
155; and timber industry, 99
California Fish and Game, 156, 210
California Forest Practice Act (FPA).
See Forest Practice Act (FPA),
California
California gold rush, 37
California Highway Commission, 71
California Licensed Foresters Associa-
tion, 158
Californians for Native Salmon and
Steelhead Association, 168
California Parks and Recreation Com-
mission, 94
California Public Interest Research
Group, 180
California Redwood Association, 130
California Resources Agency, 179, 230
California State Park and Recreation
Commission, 56, 87
California Water Quality Control
Board, 254
Calpella, CA, 161
Calvert Cliffs, 79–80
Campbell, John: and activist confron-
tations, 151–52, 233; and Carpenter,
129; Death Road plan, 230; early life,
128; and Feinstein, 227; and Forest
Forever initiative, 181; on Hamburg,
201; and Headwaters Deal, 217; and
Headwaters Forest Act, 203, 205; on
Hurwitz, 134; on industry norms,
285n10; legal challenge patterns,
156; at Pacific Lumber, 129–132, 137,

clearcutting strategies (*cont.*)
285n10; challenges to, 79; citizen
groups complaints about, 61; effects
of on redwoods, 81, 253; expansion
of, 95; Georgia-Pacific Lumber Mill,
90; Headwaters Grove, 105fig.5, 155;
and liquidation logging, 4; Mill
Creek site, 74; and National Forest
Management Act, 152; in national
forests, 82; of old-growth forests,
98; of Pacific Lumber Company, 40,
105fig.5, 131–32, 142; public awareness of, 47, 101fig.1; second-growth
forests, 131; and watershed issues, 87
Clinton, William, 114fig.15, 115fig.16,
250–51, 254; and endangered species
policy, 230, 261–62; and Hamburg,
197; and Headwaters Deal, 17, 230,
232–33, 246, 247; land deals, 6, 10, 17;
Owl Creek cases, 167; and Redwood
Wars, 211
Clinton administration: attacks on, 214;
and Elk River Timber, 228; and EPIC,
256; and HCPs, 250–51; and initiative
work, 215; interventions, 24, 220, 250,
262; land deals, 6; and negotiations,
235, 237; Northwest Forest Plan,
199; and Pacific Lumber Company,
114fig.15, 115fig.16, 212, 231, 234, 261;
Redwood Wars intervention, 7
Cloverdale, CA, xximap2, 187, 191
Cloverdale tragedy, 150, 187
Coast Range, 29–30, 32, 58
coast redwoods: Coast Range, 29; distribution map, xxmap1; range of, 29;
and Sierra Club, 44; terminology, 28
Code of Civil Procedure, 78
Cohelan, Jeffery, 73
Cohen, Michael, 272n11, 276n24
collaborative negotiations, 7, 263
collective bargaining, 54
conflict/negotiation patterns, 51, 62, 98
confrontation traditions, 69, 84, 254

conservationism, 17, 19, 145, 235, 257,
260, 265, 272n11, 275n19; Alaskan
public land protection, 157; con-
servation/preservation split, 168,
264–65; conservation-to-environment narrative, 265–66; naming the
forest tradition, 151
Constance, Douglas H., 270n4
consumerism, 19, 20, 21, 144, 145, 168
Coope, John F., 45
corporate capitalism, and North Coast
activists, 115fig.16
Corporate Fallers, 191
corporate power: activists against, 7,
14, 108fig.9; and citizen environmentalism, 8; and Redwood Wars, 5–6;
rise of modern, 8
corporatism: attacks on, 65; and Board
of Forestry, 60, 65, 83–84; corporatist
tradition, 80; corporatist traditions,
85; defined, 270n7; de jure/de facto,
169, 241; and early preservation
movement, 260; end of, 76, 100, 157;
litigation strategies, 99; and self-
regulation, 41–42, 67; undercut by
activist groups, 62, 122
Corte, Mary, 194
cost-benefit analysis, 165
countercultural values, 87, 88, 147, 178
court cases, 7, 84, 90, 121, 152, 229,
281n11, 282n16. *See also specific cases*
court rulings, 6, 123, 165, 180
court system, 23, 24, 79, 81
Cowles, Macon, 210
Crespí, Juan, 28
Cronon, William, 308n50
cumulative impacts: CDF evaluation
requirements, 99; CEQA requirements about, 97, 167–68; and
Department of Forestry, 157, 167;
Sally Bell Grove case, 96; in SYP for
Pacific Lumber, 255; of THP, 97, 99

Environmental Protection Information Center (*cont.*)

skepticism of, 21, 152; responsibilities of regarding endangered species, 5; and state government collaboration, 74; wilderness protection politics, 93

Federated Development Company, 133

Feinstein, Dianne, 180, 206, 227, 229, 233, 234, 236, 237, 248

feller bunchers, 187

Felton, CA, 45

female leadership, 178

Fern Canyon, 62, 71

Ferndale, CA, 32

ferns, 29, 121

field-trip tactics, 91, 131

Fifth Amendment issues, 6, 174, 231

fire prevention, 60, 75

Fish and Wildlife Service (FWS), US, 15, 186, 198–99, 201, 208, 223, 231

fishermen/fisheries, 33, 78, 160, 255

Fisher Road, xximap2, 151, 158

fish species, 31, 61–62, 223, 253. *See also* salmon

floods, 62, 63, 64, 65, 71, 102fig.2

flora, 88

Ford Foundation, 71

Foreman, Dave: arrest of, 191; and direct action activism, 123; Earth First! creation, 20, 93; and ecotage, 149; goals of, 145, 200; and North Coast Earth First!, 188; and Sally Bell Grove, 94; and tree spiking, 150, 187

foresters, 31, 158, 224

Forest Practice Act (FPA), California: *Bayside* case and, 281n13; and Board of Forestry, 82, 84, 209; and CDF, 97; and CEQA requirements, 83, 97; citizen suit provision, 16, 78, 89, 282n17; and corporatism, 60; cumulative impact regulations, 289n48; enforcement of, 120; litigation strategies, 99; and private land management, 77; and private

property rights, 16; repeal of, 75–76; restrictions of, 204

Forest Practice Rules, 61, 76–77, 97, 99

forestry regulations, 5, 67, 77

Forest Service, US, 15, 49, 57, 63, 123, 152, 250

Forests Forever ballot initiative, 4, 225, 267; and Big Green initiative, 180–81; campaign efforts, 182–83; early obstacles, 181; failure of, 184; initial planning, 175–79; and New Forestry, 179; and Redwood Summer, 181–82, 184–191

"The Forest through the Trees" (documentary), 183

Forestville, CA, 39, 40

Forest Watch, 169

Fort Bragg, CA, xximap2, 33

Fort Bragg rally, 189–190

Fortuna, CA, xximap2, 32

FPA (California Forest Practices Act). *See* Forest Practice Act (FPA), California

Frampton, George, Jr., 220

Franklin, Jerry, 179, 199, 241

Freshwater Creek, xximap2

fundraisers, 123

FWS (United States Fish and Wildlife Service). *See* Fish and Wildlife Service (FWS), US

G

Gaffney, Brian, 219

gahsay, 28

Galanty, Sidney, 183

Galitz, Dave, 161, 164

Gallegos, Francine, 82

Gallegos case, 82, 83, 97, 291n62

Garamendi, John, 230

Garberville, CA, xximap2, 32, 89, 144, 145, 191, 239

Garden Clubs of America, 178

Headwaters Forest (*cont.*)
organizations, 5; *Outside* article, 119; and private property rights, 23; and Redwood Summer, 4; and Redwood Wars, 8, 9; residual forest areas, 118fig.19; riparian reserve, 118fig.19; Salmon Creek, 167; salvage operations, 236; and shareholder activism, 283n37; Shaw Creek Grove, 116fig.17; THPs, 154–55; upstream conservation easement, recommended, 118fig.19; and Wall Street financing, 9; watercourses, 118fig.19. *See also* Headwaters Forest Stewardship Plan; Headwaters Grove; Owl Creek Grove; tree-sitting

Headwaters Forest Act, 201–6, 218

Headwaters Forest Complex, 107fig.7, 114fig.15, 118fig.19

Headwaters Forest Coordinating Committee (HFCC): forming of, 204–5; and Headwaters acquisition, 232; and Headwaters Deal, 236, 237; joint campaign of, 224; and land management plans, 116fig.17; proposal for Headwaters acquisition, 116fig.17, 228; public advocacy, 246

Headwaters Forest Reserve, xxmap1, xximap2; appropriations bill for, 213; comparison with Complex, 118fig.19; effects on North Coast activists, 254; naming of, 250; proposed boundaries comparison, 118fig.19

Headwaters Forest Stewardship Plan, 116fig.17, 117fig.18, 240–41, 242, 308n50

Headwaters Grove: acquisition of, 228; and Board of Forestry, 180; Death Road plan, 186, 229, 230; description of, 121; and Forest Forever initiative, 181; and Headwaters Deal, 215, 235; map of, 116fig.17; naming of, 93, 121, 151; purchase of, 183, 228; and salvage

exemptions, 221–22, 224

Headwaters Legislative Action Plan (HLAP), 199, 200, 201

heartwood, 30

helicopter logging, 258

herbicide issues, 88, 177–78

Hetch Hetchy Valley, 63, 70, 73, 279n54

HFCC (Headwaters Forest Coordinating Committee). *See* Headwaters Forest Coordinating Committee (HFCC)

Highway 101, 32, 33, 47, 71, 86, 158, 246, 253

Highway Commission, California, 71

Hill, Andrew P., 45–46, 143, 206, 257

Hill, Julia "Butterfly", 8, 245, 253, 254, 256

Hill, Mem, 95, 162, 185

"hit the donkey" strategy, 94, 154–58, 165, 219

HLAP (Headwaters Legislative Action Plan). *See* Headwaters Legislative Action Plan (HLAP)

"Hole in Headwaters", 257–58

Holmes Eureka Lumber Company, 54, 58

homesteaders, 87, 160

hostility, 81, 84, 152

housing boom, 55, 57, 60

"How to Sue CDF" (EPIC manual), 158

HRZ (habitat recovery zones), 242

humanity: benefits to, 19, 43, 45; and biodiversity, 173; consumerism/capitalism effects on, 154; and deep ecology, 144; history of, 10; impacts on planet, 61, 121, 144, 196; integration of, 20–21

Humboldt Bay, 32, 37, 39

Humboldt County, CA: ancient redwoods in, 47; back-to-the-land lifestyles in, 15; coastal region of, 74; dominant features of, 32; and EPIC, 22; features of, 33; Humboldt

rulings, 6; environmental protection laws, 6, 18; logging laws, 6; minimum-diameter law, 60; Nejedly bill, 77; pollution control laws, 20; proposals, 6; public participation provisions, 6; reform efforts, 6; reports/studies on forestry practice rules, 61; timber operations, 75. *See also* Forest Practice Act (FPA), California

Leone, William, 134, 135, 138

Leopold, Aldo, 265

leverage strategies, 17, 124

Lewallen, John, 179, 181

Lewis, Dennis, 228

lichen, 29

LightHawk group, 227

Lippe, Tom, 205

liquidation logging practices, 4, 7, 13, 90

litigation strategies: as activists' tool, 6, 53; and corporatism, 99; and de facto corporatist regime, 209; and direct action activism, 94; and EPIC, 89; of Georgia-Pacific Lumber Mill, 96; and logging practices, 5; patterns of, 16; and Redwood Wars, 113fig.14

Little Jackass Creek, 91, 92. *See also* Sally Bell Grove

Littletree, Alicia: backwoods action campaign, 228, 234; car bomb litigation, 245; and Earth First!, 193–95; Environmental Protection Information Center (EPIC), 22; nightly hikes, 113fig.14, 208; as North Coast activist, 238; Week of Outrage, 202

lobbying, 21, 46, 64, 123, 197

local communities: local activists, 88, 89, 95; local courts, 7, 229; local developments, 254; local economy, 89, 243; local governance, 75–76, 124; local groups, 52; local interests, 272n11; local knowledge, 291n64; local radicalism, 53; local residents,

87; local stories, 17; local support, 7, 226

"locking up" wilderness, 308n50

lodgepole pine, 12

loggers: confrontations with activists, 22; and forest, 160; labor issues, 47; as North Coast residents, 33; and Redwood Wars, 5; white, European descent, 12

logging industry: development of, 33–36; direct action activism against, 3; intransigence of, 84; logging bans, 96; logging controls, 84; logging laws, 6; logging plans, 87; logging politics, 85; mechanization of, 38; post-WW II, 103fig.3; and Redwood Wars, 5

logging practices: and ancient redwood trees, 6; and citizen activists, 84; and court ruling applications, 6; defining of, 8; and EPIC, 89; Headwaters Deal, 253; Headwaters Forest Stewardship Plan, 117fig.18; historical, 37; increase of, 8; and liquidation logging, 4; and litigation strategies, 5; logging regulations, 89; logging tools, 37; logging towns, 32; log transport, 37–38; monitoring of, 106fig.6, 113fig.14; reforms of, 107fig.7, 215, 254, 265; selective harvesting, 61; timber families' opposition to, 111fig.12

long-range management plans, 13, 82, 117fig.18, 118fig.19, 242

loomeen, 28

Lorimar-Telepictures, 140

Lost Coast: backwoods actions on, 15; Bell, Sally, 92; clearcutting strategies, 90, 103fig.3, 155; and EPIC, 90; homesteaders on, 86; Lancaster Logging blockade, 161–62; local activists, 94; map of, xxmap1; Sinkyone region of, 88; state park creation along, 87. *See also* Sally Bell Grove case

Louisiana-Pacific: Albion Uprising, 194; "Boskeenhauser" deal, 181, 185, 187, 203, 211; in Calpella, 161; in Carlotta, 138; clearcutting strategies, 146, 176; departure of, 267; and Forest Forever initiative, 181; hostility of, 190; land sales, 130; local timber companies acquisition, 95, 103fig.3; Mexican mill, 160; Osprey Grove, 189; production levels, 127; protests against, 112fig.13; purchase from, 151; reputation of, 124; retreat of, 39; workers protests, 188

LTMA (long-term management area), 242–43

Lucas, Gail, 177

Lucas v. South Carolina Coastal Commission, 231

lumber workers. *See* workers, timber

Luna (giant redwood), 253, 254

lungless salamander, 31

M

MacKaye, Benton, 265

Mad River, 32

madrone, 30

Mahan, Laura Perrott, 50, 51, 52, 53, 65, 85, 178, 260

Malarkey, Tom, 138

Mannix, Bill, 179, 181

Mantell, Michael, 230

The Man Who Walks in the Woods, Woods. *See* Woods (Sutherland, Robert)

mapping projects, 106fig.6, 149–150, 227, 241

Marbled Murrelet Conservation Area, 246, 247, 248

marbled murrelet habitat, 211, 231

marbled murrelet regulations, 289n48

marbled murrelets: and Bailey, 216–17; breeding grounds, 156, 213, 219, 222, 255; cumulative impacts, 165, 167, 219; and Department of Forestry, 156, 157; as endangered species, 209, 221; habitat, 167, 218, 248; and HCP, 249; and Headwaters complex, 204; listed as threatened, 199; Murrelet Grove, 93, 189, 190; in Owl Creek, 211; protection efforts, 21, 31, 207–8, 248; recovery, 250

Marbled Murrelet v. Pacific Lumber, 218–222, 224, 227, 229, 244, 246

marijuana trade, 33, 124

Marin, CA, 44

market relationships, 56, 57, 130

Marshall, Robert, 265

Mason, Paul, 238–240, 244

Massini, Susan, 185

Mather, Stephen, 48

Mattole River, 32, 87, 256

Mattole River watershed, 86, 87, 155, 256

Maurer, John, 160, 163

Maxxam Corporation: acquisition, 105fig.5; acquisition of Headwaters Forest, xi, 117fig.18; "Battle for Seattle", 264; Earth First! focus on, 147–48, 151; EPIC focus on, 151; and Headwaters Forest Complex, 118fig.19; and Headwaters Grove, 213; lawsuit settlement, 228–29; MCO transformation into, 134–35; naming of, 135; opposition to, ix; Pacific Lumber Company acquisition, xi, 9, 120, 121, 124, 132, 135–141; post-Deal, 258; shareholder activism, 283n37; and United Financial Group, 202; *Washington Post* on, 287n22. *See also* Hurwitz, Charles

Maxxam I case, 154–56, 168

Maxxam II case, 156–58

McCloskey, Michael, 73

McCoy, Charles, 201, 210

Muir, John: anthropocentrism, 272n11; and Big Basin, 64; field-trip tactics, 91; on forest management, 276n24; Hetch Hetchy conflict, 279n54; ideals of, 19, 257, 265; ideology of, viii; influence of, 265; public relations campaigns, 65; and Sierra Club, 44–45

Muir Woods National Monument, xxmap1, 48

Mullens, Mark, 145

multinational corporations, 103fig.3, 159, 169, 180, 213, 263

Munitz, Barry, 135

Murphy, Albert Stanwood, 55, 58, 59

Murphy, Simon Jones, 39–40

Murphy family: and board, 141; business decisions, 58, 59; company holdings, 126, 128; early history of, 40; lawsuits, 163, 228; and merger, 136

Murrelet case. *See Marbled Murrelet v. Pacific Lumber*

Murrelet Grove, 93, 189, 190

Music for Little People, 191, 239

N

Nader, Ralph, 233

Naess, Arne, 145

naming/name changes: conservationism, 151; of Headwaters Forest, 121, 151, 250; of Headwaters Grove, 93, 121, 151; of Maxxam Corporation, 135; Murrelet Grove, 93; naming the forest, 11; of Sally Bell Grove, 92–93, 98; terminology, 11, 12

Nash, Roderick, 265, 271n10

National Association of State Foresters, 158

National Consumers League, 50

National Environmental Policy Act (NEPA), 18, 68, 70, 77, 78, 80, 122, 169; and environmental impact statements, 148, 256; federal court cases, 79–80; impacts, 272n14; North Coast activists use of, 255

National Forest Management Act, 18, 78, 82, 152, 169

national forest reserves, 15, 17, 56, 152, 215

National Industrial Recovery Act, 54

National Marine Fisheries Service (NMFS), 255

national monument declaration

national monument declarations, 262, 263

National Origins Act, 48

national parks, 65, 70, 71, 272n11

National Park Service, 48, 50, 71, 73, 174

National Tribute Grove, 62

National Wilderness Preservation System, 202

Native Americans, 86; archeological sites/legacy of, 92; displacement of, 42; impact on forests, 12; inclusion of, 243; InterTribal Sinkyone Wilderness, 98; Native American Heritage Commission, 97; Sinkyone tribe, 86, 91, 92, 94, 98

Native Salmon case, 168

natural resource issues, 8, 44, 70

Natural Resources Defense Council, 80, 180

Navarro, CA, 162

Nearing, Mary Beth, 119, 121, 151

Needle Rock, 90, 92

Nejedly, John A., 77

Nelson, Kim, 204

NEPA (National Environmental Policy Act). *See* National Environmental Policy Act (NEPA)

New Forestry strategy, 179–180, 199, 241, 242

new growth forests, defined, 12

Newman, Kurt, 149, 195, 198

Princetl, Stephanie S., 275n19
private land management, 56; and
    Clinton administration, 235–36,
    250–51; debates/battles over, 23; fed-
    eral confiscation, 100; and forestry
    regulations, 77; private landholder
    negotiations, 6, 8, 53, 62, 65; pri-
    vate timberland regulation, 41–42;
    property rights, 123; Redwood Wars,
    23, 100, 261; regulations, 23; timber
    cutting regulation, 56
private ownership: Earth First!'s irrev-
    erence towards, 112fig.13; and land
    management plans, 6; of redwood
    groves, 3; trespassing and, 106fig.6
private property rights, 123, 158, 241,
    272n11; conflicts over, 176; direct
    action activism against, 4; and envi-
    ronmental politics, 23; and Headwa-
    ters Deal, 235–36; and Headwaters
    Forest, 23; laws effecting, 16; legal
    issues, 24; tensions over, 267
product grading systems, 130
production levels, 127, 143, 285n14
professionalization narrative, 20,
    271n10
Progressive Era: industrial self-regu-
    lation, 41; and land use, 275n19; and
    ownership patterns, 275n19; tradi-
    tions, 68, 69
progressivism, 43, 44, 49, 275n19
protests, 85, 104fig.4, 110fig.11, 113fig.14,
    120
public acquisition strategy, 45, 170, 230
public awareness, 47, 101fig.1, 150–51, 173
public interest, 44, 46, 72
Public Interest Environmental Law
    Conference, 186
publicity campaigns, 8, 46
public land development, 79; activist
    groups against, 3–4; in Alaska, 82;
    Sagebrush Rebellion, 122
public land management: conflicts

over, 23; nature of, 142; protection
    efforts, 122, 157; reclamations, 93, 199;
    regulation of, 15, 123
public relations, 53, 65; North Coast
    activists use of, 21; Sierra Club, CA,
    63–64
Public Resource Code, 282n17
public support, 6, 12, 173, 226, 260

R

radical environmentalists, 4, 9, 10, 20,
    121, 308n50
radicalization, 119–170; 1989 reckoning,
    158–168; Campbell, John, 128–132;
    conclusions, 168–170; Earth First!
    returns, 142–153; "hit the donkey"
    strategy, 154–58; Humboldt move-
    ment, 49; Hurwitz, Charles, 132–142;
    overview, 119–124; Pacific Lumber
    Company, 124–28
railroads, 37–40, 42, 49, 50, 54
Rainforest Action Network, 148
rainforest activists, 69, 173
Raker-Kent federal park bill, 50
rallies, 4, 148, 264; anti-logging ral-
    lies, 10, 149, 264; Fort Bragg rally,
    189–190; and public awareness, 6,
    120, 161; Samoa docks rally, 189; Sep-
    tember 15 rally, 223, 227–28, 234
Ratner, Jill, 205
raw log exports ban, 180
Reagan, Ronald, 57, 77, 89, 173
Reagan administration, 122
recreation, outdoor, 49, 61, 243; and
    Forest Practice Act of 1973, 78; post-
    WWI, 70; as Sierra Club goal, 44
red-bellied newt, 31
redwood, terminology, 28
Redwood Action Team, 288n31
Redwood Chapter, Sierra Club, 64
Redwood Country: development of,
    23; environmental campaigns, 46;

residual old-growth redwoods, 118fig.19, 219, 237, 242, 244
resource conservation, 19, 77, 275n19
restoration, 117fig.18, 199–200, 241, 242, 243
Riggs, Frank, 207
ring-tailed cats, 31
Rio Dell, CA, 32, 95
riparian reserve zones, 118fig.19, 180, 242
roadblocks, 185; Blanton Creek, 225–26; Earth First!, 3, 93; and logging prevention, 6; North Coast activists, 106fig.6; North Coast Earth First!, 161–62, 194
Rockefeller, John D., Jr., 53, 260
Rockefeller, Laurance, 73
Rockefeller Forest, 53, 56, 62, 130
Rome, Adam, 271n10
Roosevelt, Theodore, 49, 64, 91
Roosevelt elk, 27, 31
Rose Foundation, 202, 205
Roselle, Mike, 93, 94, 148–49
Rosen, Robert, 138
Round River Rendezvous, 147, 161
rubber-stamping harvest plans, 155, 157
Runte, Alfred, 70
rural culture, 15, 272n11
Russian American Company, 37
Ryan Creek, 257

S

Safe Harbor Agreements, 251, 262
Sagebrush Rebellion, 122
salamanders, 21, 27
Sally Bell Grove: blocking of logging in, 94; naming of, 92–93, 98; protest against logging of, 104fig.4; Timber Harvest Plan (THP), 96; Trust for Public Land purchase, 98
Sally Bell Grove case, 90–99, 154, 223; on-the-ground resistance, 93, 94–95; litigation, 95–96, 103fig.3; Native American Heritage Commission, 97; Sally Bell model, 124; and Save the Redwoods League, 98. *See also EPIC v. Johnson*
Salmon Creek, xximap2, 155
Salmon Creek Corporation, 225
Salmon Creek plan, 155
Salmon Creek watershed, 167
salmon habitat protection: activists' strategies, 225, 248; and Bailey, 217; buffer zones creation, 242; and ESA, 254; and foresters, 221; and Habitat Conservation Plans, 213; in Headwaters complex, 204, 244; and Headwaters Deal, 250, 253; and HFCC, 246; *Native Salmon* case, 168; and New Forestry goals, 180; plight of salmon runs, 220, 223, 246, 247, 258, 267; and Salmon Wars, 255–56
salmon species: cumulative impacts on, 219; declines, 61–62, 253; and Headwaters Forest, 232; king salmon release, 225; population declines, 223; relative value of, 240; salmon breeding grounds, 228, 255; salmon spawning grounds, 228, 257; salmon streams, 256
Salmon Wars, 255–56
salvage logging permits, 91, 218–19, 221–22, 225, 231, 233, 244
Samoa docks rally, 189
San Bruno Mountain area, 251
Sanctuary Forest, 162
San Francisco Bay Area: activists from, 22, 166–67, 177; expansion of, 37; media campaigns, 183, 222, 232; mission blue butterfly protection, 251; and railroads, 40, 49; rallies in, 236; recruitment in, 4; redwood lumber demand, 39; redwood preservation movement, 13, 43–44; Sutherland in, 87

Summit Group, 133
support, activist, 7, 52
sustainability, 107fig.7, 169, 176, 254, 264; and Bari, 159; and EPIC, 89; Headwaters Forest Stewardship Plan, 117fig.18, 204, 241; legal campaign strategies for, 84; and North Coast activists, 19, 85, 100, 114fig.15, 264; post-Deal issues, 237, 257; self-defined levels, 128; sustainable forestry, 45; and SYP, 242, 258
Sustained Yield Plans (SYPs): Forest Forever initiative, 180, 183; and Headwaters Deal, 235, 249, 250; and Headwaters Forest Stewartship Plan, 242; post-Deal litigation over, 255, 256, 257, 258
Sutherland, Robert, 22, 85, 87–88, 104fig.4. See also Woods (Sutherland, Robert)
Sutter, Paul S., vii–xiii, 271n10
Swanson, Eric, 179
Sweeney, Mike, 159
SYP (Sustained Yield Plan). See Sustained Yield Plan (SYP)

T

tailed frog, 31
takings suit, 231, 234, 235
tanbark oak, 30
tax code incentives, 55–56
Taxodium sempervires classification, 28
technological innovations, 38, 278n47
Telico River dam project, 153
Tennessee Valley Authority v. Hill, 282n16
Thanksgiving Massacre of 1992, 210
"The Predator's Maul" (periodical article), 119
"The Tragedy of Bull Creek" (Wayburn & Drury), 64
This Is Dinosaur (Sierra Club), 63

Thomas, Jack Ward, 199
THP (Timber Harvest Plan). See Timber Harvest Plans (THP)
Thron, Douglas, 206, 223, 226, 227
timber companies: before 1964, 8; and Bari-Cherney bombing, 5; and EPIC, 94; giant redwood trees value to, 11; profits, support for, 13; and renewability of ancient redwood trees, 13; resistance to laws/court orders, 81; revisions/resubmissions, 99; support for, 13; timber cutting regulation, 56; timber families, 111fig.12
Timber Harvest Plans (THPs), 78, 85, 103fig.3, 281n13, 282n23, 285n10; *Arcata* case, 80–81; and CEQA requirements, 97, 155, 167; citizen challenges of, 83, 158; cumulative impacts, 97, 99, 165; Death Road plan, 230; and Department of Forestry, 183; and Elk River Timber, 228; environmental impacts, 83, 97; Georgia-Pacific Lumber Mill, 90, 92; and Headwaters Forest, 237; held up in court, 121, 198; Lost Coast property, 90; Pacific Lumber Company, 223–24, 237, 258; refiling of rejected, 99, 221; for Sally Bell Grove, 96, 97; and salvage logging permits, 218; and timber industry, 84
timber industry: approach to land management, 23; and Board of Forestry, 78, 157; development trajectory, 38; families' resentment of environmentalists, 111fig.12; and federal government actions, 75; and Forest Practice Act, 76; goodwill image, 53; land management reform, 84; mechanization, 38; Mill Creek site clear-cutting, 74; nonrenewable/renewable conflict, 13; opposition of activism, 7, 69; post-WW II, 103fig.3; and private citizens relationships,

US Atomic Energy Commission, 79–80
US Department of Agriculture, 60, 61
US Department of the Interior, 219, 232, 248–49
US Fish and Wildlife Service, 201
US Fish and Wildlife Service (FWS), 15, 186, 198–99, 208, 223, 231
US Forest Service, 15, 49, 57, 63, 152, 250

V

values: anti-corporate values, 88, 266; countercultural values, 88, 147, 178; ecological values, 11, 86; environmental values, 11, 19; of industrial society, 144; middle-class values, 18, 19, 87, 266, 291n64; of North Coast activists, 107fig.7, 115fig.16, 291n64
Van Duzen River, 58
Victor Equipment Company, 126
violence: against activists, 161–62, 188, 228; of cutting old-growth forests, 12; and environmental protest, 5; Headwaters conflict, 169; labor/industrialist conflicts, 47; North Coast Earth First! activists, 110fig.11, 158, 162; and Redwood Wars, 8, 54, 84, 120, 121; Wise Use movement, 122, 174, 182, 224
virgin forest term, 12

W

Wagner, Naomi, 189, 194
Walker, Carrie Stevens, 45, 53
Walking Rainbow, 171
Wallop, Malcolm, 206
Wall Street issues: corruption, 139–140; and Headwaters Forest, 9, 67, 119; insider trading scandal, 119, 139; and Maxxam, 163; and Pacific Lumber Company, 125, 128, 163; and redwoods assets, 128

Wall Street Journal article, 210
Washington, DC, Headwaters Bill, 196–207
Watershed Gathering, 90
watersheds: cumulative impacts on, 154, 168; damage to, 75, 95; Eel River watershed, 87; and Forest Practice Act of 1973, 78; and herbicide issues, 88; Lawrence Creek watersheds, 58, 225; Little Jackass Creek, 92; Mattole River watershed, 86–87, 155, 256; Pacific Watershed Associates, 199; protection efforts, 14, 16, 61, 70, 73, 77, 221; Redwood Creek, 71, 80, 81; repairs of, 86–87; reports on, 61; Sally Bell Grove watershed, 92; Salmon Creek watershed, 167; and Sierra Club, 73; Sinkyone watershed, 91; stewardship plans and, 243; Watershed Gathering, 90; Yager Creek, 58, 223
Watson, Paul, 186
Wawona, Meca, 178–79
Wayburn, Edgar, 70–71
Wayburn, Peggy, 64, 71
WCB (Wildlife Conservation Board), 248–250
Weaverville, CA, 197
Week of Outrage, 202, 203
Welch's Big Trees Grove Park, 45
Wellock, Thomas R., 271n10
Wells, Frank, 182
Weott, CA, xximap2, 34
western hemlock, 27, 30
Western Timber Services, 88
Wetherbee, Henry, 39
Weyerhaeuser Company, 56, 125
Whale Gulch, CA, xximap2, 86, 193
White, Richard, 291n64, 308n50
white oak, 12
Whitethorn, CA, xximap2, 86, 161, 185
Whitman, Walt, 43, 46
Widdick, Richard, 270n4

Wilderness Act, 78; activism and, 18, 265; enforcement of, 169; as landmark environmental law, viii; and national environmental politics, 61, 64, 93; passage of, 68; and public hearings, 78; and Sierra Club, 64; and timber industry, 122; and wilderness designation, 20

wilderness areas: creation of, 69, 157; expansion of, 93, 157; and national monument designation, 262; and Native American legacies, 92; and parks creation, 70; reclamation of, 93; and Wilderness Act, 68; wilderness movement, 72; wilderness parks, 200

Wilderness Society, 61, 80, 93, 220, 265

Wildlife Conservation Board (WCB), 248–250

Wildlife Protection and Reforestation Act, 183

wildlife species: activists interest in, 70, 156, 183, 208, 221; clearcuts and roads effects on, 204; concessions to, 238; and cumulative impacts, 154, 165–66, 168; and Forest Practice Act of 1973, 77–78; in modern redwood forest, 31; and surveys, 183, 208–9; sustainability, 89; and WCB, 248

Willamette National Forest, 148

Willits, CA, xximap2, 179

Wilson, Pete, 222, 228, 234, 235, 248

Wilson, Richard, 248–49

Wise Use movement, 122, 174, 175–76, 182, 191, 224

Wolf Creek Timber Company, 86

women: as advocates, 53; leadership roles, 178, 259; Women's Federation, 178; women's groups, 49–52, 190; Women's League, 51, 52, 53

Woods (Sutherland, Robert): and EPIC, 88–89, 91, 158, 167; field-trip tactics, 91, 95; and Forest Forever initiative, 175, 179, 180, 181–83, 267; "hit the donkey" strategy, 94, 154, 219; as Man Who Walks in the Woods, 87–88, 104fig.4, 196, 238; and Sally Grove case, 95, 98; as Sutherland, Robert, 22, 85, 87–88, 104fig.4

Wooster, Donald, 290n58

workers, timber: and Bari, 159–160; against company practices, 163; and Earth First!, 148–49; and employment issues, 13, 81, 82, 163; environmentalists disdain for, 20; inclusion of, 243; initiatives gains to, 59; in interwar era, 54–56; management of, 38; tactics of, 65; values of, 291n64; welfare capitalist movement, 55, 57; worker provisions, 22

Y

Yager Creek watersheds, xximap2, 58, 223, 224, 225, 226

Yard, Robert Sterling, 265

Yellow Ribbon Coalition, 110fig.11, 189, 190

Yellowstone National Park, 70, 174

Yosemite National Park, 63, 70, 91

Young, McGee, 279n54

young-growth forest, 149

young-growth trees, 285n14

Yurok tribe, 31

Z

Z'berg, Edwin L., 77

WEYERHAEUSER ENVIRONMENTAL BOOKS

Toxic Archipelago: A History of Industrial Disease in Japan, by Brett L. Walker

Dreaming of Sheep in Navajo Country, by Marsha L. Weisiger

Shaping the Shoreline: Fisheries and Tourism on the Monterey Coast, by Connie Y. Chiang

The Fishermen's Frontier: People and Salmon in Southeast Alaska, by David F. Arnold

Making Mountains: New York City and the Catskills, by David Stradling

Plowed Under: Agriculture and Environment in the Palouse, by Andrew P. Duffin

The Country in the City: The Greening of the San Francisco Bay Area, by Richard A. Walker

Native Seattle: Histories from the Cross-Over Place, by Coll Thrush

Drawing Lines in the Forest: Creating Wilderness Areas in the Pacific Northwest, by Kevin R. Marsh

Public Power, Private Dams: The Hells Canyon High Dam Controversy, by Karl Boyd Brooks

Windshield Wilderness: Cars, Roads, and Nature in Washington's National Parks, by David Louter

On the Road Again: Montana's Changing Landscape, by William Wyckoff

Wilderness Forever: Howard Zahniser and the Path to the Wilderness Act, by Mark Harvey

The Lost Wolves of Japan, by Brett L. Walker

Landscapes of Conflict: The Oregon Story, 1940–2000, by William G. Robbins

Faith in Nature: Environmentalism as Religious Quest, by Thomas R. Dunlap

The Nature of Gold: An Environmental History of the Klondike Gold Rush, by Kathryn Morse

Where Land and Water Meet: A Western Landscape Transformed, by Nancy Langston

The Rhine: An Eco-Biography, 1815–2000, by Mark Cioc

Driven Wild: How the Fight against Automobiles Launched the Modern Wilderness Movement, by Paul S. Sutter

George Perkins Marsh: Prophet of Conservation, by David Lowenthal

Making Salmon: An Environmental History of the Northwest Fisheries Crisis, by Joseph E. Taylor III

Irrigated Eden: The Making of an Agricultural Landscape in the American West, by Mark Fiege

The Dawn of Conservation Diplomacy: U.S.-Canadian Wildlife Protection Treaties in the Progressive Era, by Kirkpatrick Dorsey

Landscapes of Promise: The Oregon Story, 1800–1940, by William G. Robbins

Forest Dreams, Forest Nightmares: The Paradox of Old Growth in the Inland West, by Nancy Langston

The Natural History of Puget Sound Country, by Arthur R. Kruckeberg